LABOURS OF ATTENTION:
WORK, CLASS AND SOCIETY IN FRENCH AND FRANCOPHONE
LITERATURE AND CULTURE

ESSAYS FOR EDWARD J. HUGHES

LEGENDA

LEGENDA is the Modern Humanities Research Association's book imprint for new research in the Humanities. Founded in 1995 by Malcolm Bowie and others within the University of Oxford, Legenda has always been a collaborative publishing enterprise, directly governed by scholars. The Modern Humanities Research Association (MHRA) joined this collaboration in 1998, became half-owner in 2004, in partnership with Maney Publishing and then Routledge, and has since 2016 been sole owner. Titles range from medieval texts to contemporary cinema and form a widely comparative view of the modern humanities, including works on Arabic, Catalan, English, French, German, Greek, Italian, Portuguese, Russian, Spanish, and Yiddish literature. Editorial boards and committees of more than 60 leading academic specialists work in collaboration with bodies such as the Society for French Studies, the British Comparative Literature Association and the Association of Hispanists of Great Britain & Ireland.

The MHRA encourages and promotes advanced study and research in the field of the modern humanities, especially modern European languages and literature, including English, and also cinema. It aims to break down the barriers between scholars working in different disciplines and to maintain the unity of humanistic scholarship. The Association fulfils this purpose through the publication of journals, bibliographies, monographs, critical editions, and the MHRA Style Guide, and by making grants in support of research. Membership is open to all who work in the Humanities, whether independent or in a University post, and the participation of younger colleagues entering the field is especially welcomed.

ALSO PUBLISHED BY THE ASSOCIATION

Critical Texts
Tudor and Stuart Translations • *New Translations* • *European Translations*
MHRA Library of Medieval Welsh Literature

MHRA Bibliographies
Publications of the Modern Humanities Research Association

The Annual Bibliography of English Language & Literature
Austrian Studies
Modern Language Review
Portuguese Studies
The Slavonic and East European Review
Working Papers in the Humanities
The Yearbook of English Studies

www.mhra.org.uk
www.legendabooks.com

EDITORIAL BOARD

Chair: Professor Jonathan Long (University of Durham)
For *Germanic Literatures*: Ritchie Robertson (University of Oxford)
For *Italian Perspectives*: Simon Gilson (University of Warwick)
For *Moving Image*: Emma Wilson (University of Cambridge)
For *Research Monographs in French Studies*:
Diana Knight (University of Nottingham)
For *Selected Essays*: Susan Harrow (University of Bristol)
For *Studies in Comparative Literature*:
Dr Emily Finer, University of St Andrews, and
Professor Wen-chin Ouyang, SOAS, London
For *Studies in Hispanic and Lusophone Cultures*:
Catherine Davies (Institute of Modern Languages Research)
For *Studies in Yiddish*: Gennady Estraikh (New York University)
For *Transcript*: Matthew Reynolds (University of Oxford)
For *Visual Culture*: Carolin Duttlinger (University of Oxford)

Managing Editor
Dr Graham Nelson
41 Wellington Square, Oxford OX1 2JF, UK

www.legendabooks.com

Labours of Attention

*Work, Class and Society in
French and Francophone Literature and Culture*

Essays for Edward J. Hughes

Edited by Adam Watt

Modern Humanities Research Association
2022

Published by Legenda
an imprint of the Modern Humanities Research Association
Salisbury House, Station Road, Cambridge CB1 2LA

ISBN 978-1-83954-055-4 (HB)
ISBN 978-1-83954-056-1 (PB)

First published 2022

All rights reserved. No part of this publication may be reproduced or disseminated or transmitted in any form or by any means, electronic, mechanical, photocopying, recording or otherwise, or stored in any retrieval system, or otherwise used in any manner whatsoever without written permission of the copyright owner, except in accordance with the provisions of the Copyright, Designs and Patents Act 1988, or under the terms of a licence permitting restricted copying issued in the UK by the Copyright Licensing Agency Ltd, Saffron House, 6–10 Kirby Street, London EC1N 8TS, England, or in the USA by the Copyright Clearance Center, 222 Rosewood Drive, Danvers MA 01923. Application for the written permission of the copyright owner to reproduce any part of this publication must be made by email to legenda@mhra.org.uk.

Disclaimer: Statements of fact and opinion contained in this book are those of the author and not of the editors or the Modern Humanities Research Association. The publisher makes no representation, express or implied, in respect of the accuracy of the material in this book and cannot accept any legal responsibility or liability for any errors or omissions that may be made.

Trademark notice: Product or corporate names may be trademarks or registered trademarks, and are used only for identification and explanation without intent to infringe.

© Modern Humanities Research Association 2022

Copy-Editor: Charlotte Wathey

CONTENTS

Acknowledgements		ix
Notes on Contributors		x
Beau présent: 'Edward Joseph Hughes, Emeritus' ANNA KEMP		xv
Introduction ADAM WATT		1

PART I: REVISITING CAMUS

1. Albert Camus and the Place of the Literary — 15
   DAVID R. ELLISON

2. Camus's Travel Writing, or the Road to Pamina — 25
   PETER DUNWOODIE

3. Camus, *La Peste* et le coronavirus: 'une histoire collective' — 36
   JEANYVES GUÉRIN

4. Oran's Endogenous Evil: A Rereading of Albert Camus's *La Peste* — 48
   IEME VAN DER POEL

PART II: ALGERIA AND THE FRENCH COLONIAL PROJECT

5. *Ces hommes qu'on raie de l'humanité*: Transcolonial Connections in the French Penal Colony — 63
   CHARLES FORSDICK

6. Empire, Memory and Language in Pierre Michon's 'Vie d'André Dufourneau' — 77
   PATRICK CROWLEY

7. Resnais's Kaleidoscope — 89
   ANNA MAGDALENA ELSNER

8. Feeling the French-Algerian War: Male Vulnerability, Shame and the Wounds of Brotherhood in Yacine Balah's *Frères ennemis* (2013) — 101
   JAMES S. WILLIAMS

PART III: WORKS AND DAYS: LABOUR, CLASS, SOCIETY

9. 'Tu renonces à toi pour devenir tout le monde': Visions of Labour and Society in Blaise Cendrars and Fernand Léger — 117
   ERIC ROBERTSON

10	'Le naufrage de l'homme profane': Genet and the Anecdotal RICHARD MASON	132
11	Late-life Care and the Labours of Attention in Contemporary Women's Writing SHIRLEY JORDAN	144
12	Proustian Afterlives: Paolo Sorrentino's *La grande bellezza* (2013) MARION SCHMID	156

PART IV: MARCEL PROUST: LABOURS OF LANGUAGE

13	Along the rue Jean de La Fontaine: The *Fables* in *A la recherche du temps perdu* MICHAEL MORIARTY	171
14	Proust's Prosopopoeias JOHN O'BRIEN	181
15	Proust's House of Fiction PATRICK O'DONOVAN	192
16	Des 'parasites précieux': impureté et antinationalisme dans le roman proustien MARISA VERNA	204
17	Proust, an Inevitable *engagé*? CYNTHIA GAMBLE	213

PART V: MARCEL PROUST: LABOURS OF LOVE

18	Community in Solitude: Inter-art Epistolarity through Late-modern Critical Thought SUSAN HARROW	229
19	'Les noms magiques': Names, Places and Persian-ness in Noailles, Bibesco and Proust JULIA CATERINA HARTLEY	243
20	L'Érotique d'*A la recherche du temps perdu* JACQUES DUBOIS	256
21	Echoes of Sodom in Gomorrah: The Chastisement of Albertine in Proust's *La Prisonnière* MARGARET E. GRAY	266
22	Edward Hughes and the Quality of Awareness ALISON FINCH	276
	Edward J. Hughes: A Select Bibliography 1983–2021	280
	Index	283

ACKNOWLEDGEMENTS

Thanks must go, first and foremost, to Graham Nelson for his support of this project from idea to completion, and for his patience during the somewhat extended final stages. I would like to record my warmest thanks to my contributors, whose work it has been an honour to edit and prepare for publication. Charlotte Wathey was a model of clearsighted-ness and efficiency as copy-editor. I would like to acknowledge here the great regret of Danielle Marx-Scouras, Will McMorran and Martin Crowley, who would have been part of the volume but were obliged to withdraw on account of the circumstances imposed by the pandemic. Alison Finch, Tim Chesters and Stacey Hynd gave support and assistance of various sorts at just the right moments. The goodwill and thoughtfulness of all involved in this undertaking have made it a most pleasurable and rewarding labour at a time of considerable turmoil. The final vote of thanks, of course, must go to Eddie Hughes for all that he has done for our community through his teaching, research, leadership and advocacy. French Studies is all the richer for his contributions and through the pages that follow we record our gratitude and admiration.

A.W., Exeter, January-June 2022

NOTES ON CONTRIBUTORS

Patrick Crowley teaches French at University College Cork. The primary focus of his research is on literary form: its construction, its destabilization and its relationship to the contexts of history. His published work includes *Pierre Michon: The Afterlife of Names* (2007), a scholarly edition of *L'Exotisme: la littérature coloniale* by Louis Cario and Charles Régismanset (1911), was published in 2016 and he has edited or co-edited a number of volumes including *Postcolonial Poetics: Genre and Form* (2011), *Algeria: Nation, Culture and Transnationalism 1988–2015* (2017), and *What Forms Can Do: The Work of Form in 20th- and 21st-Century French Literature and Thought* (2020).

Jacques Dubois est professeur émérite de l'Université de Liège. La sociologie de la littérature et celle de la communication furent et sont encore ses spécialités. Il a publié dans la Bibliothèque de la Pléiade (Gallimard) trois volumes consacrés à l'œuvre de Georges Simenon. Il a également collaboré au récent *Romans et nouvelles* de Joris-Karl Huysmans dans la même collection. Il est l'auteur de deux ouvrages sur Proust parus aux éditions du Seuil: *Pour Albertine: Proust et le sens du social* (1994); *Le Roman de Gilberte Swann: Proust sociologue paradoxal* (2018), ce dernier étant couronné en 2019 par le 'Prix de la Madeleine d'or' (Cabourg).

Peter Dunwoodie is Emeritus Professor at Goldsmiths, University of London. His fields of expertise are comparative and francophone literatures: the Caribbean novel, French and francophone Algerian fiction; authors including Camus, Céline, Louis Bertrand. His publications include *Camus: L'Envers et l'endroit* and *L'Exil et le royaume* (1985); *Une Histoire ambivalente: Le dialogue Camus-Dostoïevski* (1996); with E. J. Hughes, *Constructing Memories: Camus, Algeria and 'Le Premier Homme'* (1998); *Writing French Algeria* (1998); *Francophone Writing in Transition. Algeria 1900–1945* (2005). Chapters include 'From *Noces* to *L'Étranger*', in *The Cambridge Companion to Camus* (2007); 'Negotiation or Confrontation? Camus, Memory and the Colonial Chronotope', in *Camus in the 21st Century* (2008); and '"Ma vraie patrie": Camus and Algeria', in *Camus Among the Philosophers* (2019).

David R. Ellison is Distinguished Professor in the Humanities Emeritus (University of Miami, Florida). He is the author of *The Reading of Proust* (1984), *Understanding Albert Camus* (1990), *Of Words and the World: Referential Anxiety in Contemporary French Fiction* (1993), *Ethics and Aesthetics in European Modernist Literature: From the Sublime to the Uncanny* (2001 hardback, 2006 paperback), *A Reader's Guide to Proust's 'In Search of Lost Time'* (2010) and *Proust et la tradition littéraire européenne* (2013). Ellison taught at Mount Holyoke College (1976–92) and at the University of Miami

(1992–2013), where he was Chairperson of the Department of Modern Languages and Literatures.

Anna Magdalena Elsner is Assistant Professor of French Literature and Culture at the University of St. Gallen, Switzerland. Her doctorate, from the University of Cambridge, was examined by Eddie Hughes. She is the author of *Mourning and Creativity in Proust* (2017) and has published on Proust, French cinema and the connection between medicine, literature and philosophy in modern and contemporary French writing.

Alison Finch is Professor Emerita of French Literature, University of Cambridge, and a Fellow of Churchill College Cambridge. Her books and articles have focused mainly on the nineteenth and twentieth centuries, but she has written on wider-ranging aspects of French literature. Among her books are *Women's Writing in Nineteenth-Century France* (2000) and *French Literature: A Cultural History* (2010).

Charles Forsdick is James Barrow Professor of French at the University of Liverpool. He has published widely on exoticism, travel writing, colonial history, postcolonial literature, comics, penal culture and the afterlives of slavery. He is also a specialist on Haiti and the Haitian Revolution, and has written in particular about representations of Toussaint Louverture. He contributed an essay on Jean-Paul Sartre and Albert Camus to *The Cambridge Companion to Camus* (2007).

Cynthia Gamble is Honorary Research Fellow, University of Exeter and a member of the Académie des Sciences, Belles-Lettres et Arts de Rouen. Her interdisciplinary work focuses on Marcel Proust, John Ruskin, the belle époque and related areas. She is the author of several books including *Proust as Interpreter of Ruskin: The Seven Lamps of Translation* (2002), *John Ruskin, Henry James and the Shropshire Lads* (2008), *Voix entrelacées de Proust et de Ruskin* (2021), and co-author of *Ruskin-Turner: dessins et voyages en Picardie romantique* (2003) and *L'Œil de Ruskin: l'exemple de la Bourgogne* (2011). She has also contributed chapters to the *Cambridge Companion to Proust* (2001) and to the *Cambridge Companion to John Ruskin* (2015), and fourteen entries to the *Dictionnaire Marcel Proust* (2004, second edition 2014).

Margaret Gray is an Associate Professor in the French and Italian Department at Indiana University, Bloomington, USA, where she teaches courses in French and Francophone literature, particularly concerning the twentieth-century novel. She has published on Proust (*Postmodern Proust*, 1992, as well as additional articles and book chapters) and authors such as George Sand, Colette, Camus, Simone de Beauvoir, Beckett, Jean-Philippe Toussaint, Calixthe Beyala and Noémi LeFebvre. Her current manuscript, "Stolen Limelight: Gender, Display, and Displacement in Twentieth-Century French and Francophone Narrative", under contract, explores narrative dynamics of display across a range of novels — from canonical works of the Hexagon, to African colonial narratives, to detective fictions — and the ways in which they work toward politicized purposes of struggle, resistance or repression.

Jeanyves Guérin est professeur émérite à l'Université Sorbonne nouvelle. Il a consacré trois livres à Camus: *Camus: portrait de l'artiste en citoyen* (1993), *Albert Camus: littérature et politique* (2013), *Voies et voix de la révolte chez Albert Camus* (2020). Il a été le maître d'œuvre du *Dictionnaire des pièces françaises du vingtième siècle* (2005), du *Dictionnaire Albert Camus* (2009) et du *Dictionnaire Eugène Ionesco* (2012). Il a également publié *Art nouveau ou homme nouveau* (2002), *Le Théâtre en France de 1914 à 1950* (2019), *Les Listes noires de 1944* (2016), *Cyrano de Bergerac* (2018).

Susan Harrow is Ashley Watkins Professor of French at the University of Bristol. Her research specialisms lie in the later nineteenth and twentieth centuries, with a particular focus on the interrelation of literary modernism and visual culture. She is the author of *Colourworks: Chromatic Innovation in Modern French Poetry and Art-Writing* (2020); *Zola, the Body Modern: Pressures and Prospects of Representation* (2010); and *The Material, the Real and the Fractured Self: Subjectivity and Representation from Rimbaud to Réda* (2004). Her current work on epistolarity has been supported by a Leverhulme Trust Research Fellowship. She served as President of the *Society for French Studies* (2010–12) and is the curator of Legenda's *Selected Essays* series. In 2011 she was awarded the rank of Officier dans l'Ordre des Palmes Académiques for services to French culture.

Julia Caterina Hartley is Lecturer in Comparative Literature at King's College London. She completed her doctorate, examined by Edward Hughes, at the University of Oxford in 2016. She is the author of *Reading Dante and Proust by Analogy* (Legenda, 2019), as well as articles on Dante, Proust, Baudelaire and French receptions of Persian literature. Her second book, on Iran in nineteenth-century French literature, is forthcoming with I. B. Tauris. Julia is also a BBC New Generation Thinker and regularly discusses her research interests on Radio 3.

Shirley Jordan is Professor of French Studies at Newcastle University and Co-Director of the Centre for the Study of Contemporary Women's Writing (IMLR). She has published widely on twentieth- and twenty-first-century women's writing in French, on art and art criticism, on photography and on experimental self-narrative across media. Her latest book, *Marie NDiaye: Inhospitable Fictions* was published with Legenda in 2017. Her subsequent research has focused on ageing, ageism and care as explored in a range of narratives, visual representations and feminist theory. Current projects include a book on the contribution made by Belgian-born photographer Martine Franck to visual gerontology, and a special issue of *French Studies* entitled *Ageism, Ageing and Old Age in Contemporary French Culture*.

Anna Kemp is a writer and former colleague of Eddie Hughes. Anna worked with Eddie from 2012 to 2019 at Queen Mary University of London where she was a Senior Lecturer in French specialising in twentieth- and twenty-first-century writing with a particular interest in the work of Georges Perec and the Oulipo. She fondly remembers satsumas and chats in Eddie's office.

Richard Mason is Lecturer in French at Queen Mary University of London. His doctoral thesis, entitled 'Writing Intimacy in Proust and Genet' (KCL), was examined by Edward Hughes. Situated at the intersection of literary studies and education studies, his present research explores the consonant ways in which educators and writers in modern and contemporary France have conceived of the relationship between language and selfhood, with a focus on the (trans)formative effects of learning to read and write.

Michael Moriarty is Drapers Professor of French at the University of Cambridge, and a Fellow of Peterhouse. His publications include *Taste and Ideology in Seventeenth Century France* (1988), *Roland Barthes* (1991), *Early Modern French Thought: The Age of Suspicion* (2003), *Fallen Nature, Fallen Selves: Early Modern French Thought II* (2006), *Disguised Vices: Theories of Virtue in Early Modern French Thought* (2011) and *Pascal: Reasoning and Belief* (2020). He is joint editor of *The Cambridge History of French Thought* (2019). He is a Fellow of the British Academy and a Chevalier dans l'Ordre des Palmes Académiques.

John O'Brien is Professor of French Emeritus at the University of Durham. A specialist of the Renaissance, his research focuses on the Wars of Religion, and notably on the writings of Montaigne and La Boétie. His collaborative volume setting out, transcribing and discussing new manuscript discoveries of La Boétie's *Discours de la servitude volontaire* was published in 2019 and a further volume, on seditious literature in France c. 1550–1610 is forthcoming. He will shortly be editing a special number of the journal *Early Modern French Studies* on the theme 'Freedom, Servitude and Politics in Renaissance France', and is concurrently at work on a monograph entitled *Essays in Licence: Civil War, Disorder, and Free Speech in Montaigne*.

Patrick O'Donovan is Professor of French at University College Cork. He has published widely on nineteenth- and twentieth-century literature and thought, most recently on the French personal novel, Vigny and Certeau, and has co-edited volumes on literature and linguistics and on cosmopolitanism. He is writing a book on Benjamin Constant. He is a former editor of *French Studies* and a Chevalier dans l'Ordre des Palmes Académiques.

Eric Robertson is Professor of Modern French Literary and Visual Cultures at Royal Holloway, University of London. He is the author of *Writing Between the Lines: René Schickele, citoyen français, deutscher Dichter* (1995), *Arp: Painter, Poet, Sculptor* (2006; winner of the 2007 R. H. Gapper Book Prize), *Arp: The Poetry of Forms* (2017) and *Blaise Cendrars: The Invention of Life* (2022), and has co-edited books on Yvan and Claire Goll (1997), Robert Desnos (2006) and Dada (2011, 2012). He has written extensively for art museums and galleries, and with Frances Guy he co-curated the international touring exhibition *Arp: The Poetry of Forms* (Kröller-Müller Museum and Turner Contemporary, 2017–18).

Marion Schmid is Professor of French Literature and Film at the University of Edinburgh. She has published extensively on the interactions between literature, film and the visual arts and on modern French literature. Her books include *Intermedial Dialogues: The French New Wave and the Other Arts* (2019), *Chantal Akerman* (2010), *Proust dans la décadence* (2008), *Proust at the Movies* (2005, co-authored with Martine Beugnet) and *Processes of Literary Creation: Flaubert and Proust* (1998). She co-edits the Peter Lang series *European Connections: Studies in Comparative Literature, Intermediality and Aesthetics* with Hugues Azérad.

Ieme van der Poel is Professor Emeritus of French Literature at the University of Amsterdam. She has published widely on Francophone, Maghrebin literature, including Sephardic Literature, and is currently working on the annotation of the new Dutch translation of Marcel Proust's *A la recherche du temps perdu*. In 2004 she was appointed Chevalier dans les Arts et les Lettres by the French government for her work in the field of Francophone literature. Her most recent works include *De Tijdmachine van Marcel Proust* (2022) and *New Literary Voices of the Moroccan Diaspora: Republic of Cousins* (2022).

Marisa Verna est professeur de littérature française à l'Université Catholique de Milan, où elle dirige le Département de Sciences Linguistiques et Littératures Étrangères. Elle est spécialiste de Marcel Proust et du théâtre symboliste français. Elle a publié aussi une traduction commentée de la *Dame aux Camélias* de Dumas fils et diverses études sur la poésie et le théâtre français du dix-neuvième siècle.

Adam Watt is Professor of French & Comparative Literature at the University of Exeter where he Deputy Pro-Vice-Chancellor for the Faculty of Humanities, Arts & Social Sciences. His publications on Proust including *Reading in Proust's 'A la recherche': le délire de la lecture* (2009) and, as editor, *Marcel Proust in Context* (2013). He has published comparative work on Proust and a range of writers from Valéry, Beckett and Barthes to Kosofsky-Sedgwick and Anne Carson. He is the editor of *The Cambridge History of the Novel in French* (2021) and co-editor, with Brian Nelson (Monash) of the forthcoming Oxford World Classics translation of *A la recherche du temps perdu*.

James S. Williams is Professor of Modern French Literature and Film at Royal Holloway, University of London. His books include work on Duras, a *Critical Guide to Camus's La Peste* (2000), *The Cinema of Jean Cocteau* (2006), *Space and Being in Contemporary French Cinema* (2013), *Encounters with Godard: Ethics, Aesthetics, Politics* (2016) and *Ethics and Aesthetics in Contemporary African Cinema: The Politics of Beauty* (2019). He is also (co-)editor of numerous works, including *Jean-Luc Godard: documents* (2006) (catalogue of the Godard exhibition held at the Centre Pompidou), *May 68: Rethinking France's Last Revolution* (2011) and *Queering the Migrant in Contemporary European Cinema* (2020). His critical biography of Frantz Fanon is forthcoming with Reaktion.

This poem is a
Beau présent.

Invented by Georges Perec, the *Beau présent* is a poem written in honour of a person, and it respects a specific constraint: it may only include the letters found in the dedicatee's name. Not being Georges Perec, I've cheated a bit and added 'Emeritus'.

Anna Kemp

Edward Joseph Hughes, Emeritus

He sees, gathers, weighs,
A metaphor, a phrase.
Teatime with Proust,
Is tastier with Eddie.
Admired tutor too,
Studious groups tap heads,
'Aujourd'hui [...] est morte'
How to put it? Mother? Dead?
Just retired. We miss him.
A star, a map, a guide.
Satsumas, gratis, sometimes grapes.
Our thoughts dug deep, dug wide.
Reader, writer, tutor... egghead?
A good, GOOD egg,
The eggiest.
So raise a rouge to Eddie Hughes,
Our *Premier homme* — the Eddie-est.

INTRODUCTION

Adam Watt

Walter Benjamin famously argues that 'Proust's pointing finger is unequalled'. James Wood cites Anton Chekov as the prime example of the writer as 'serious noticer'. George Steiner's remarkable late work on the poetry of thought amounts to what he calls 'an attempt to listen more closely'; and in his recent memoir, Pierre Nora has written of 'le "regardeur"', the figure of the watcher, with whom he associates himself, who is 'par définition un esprit critique, porté à débusquer les postures sociales ou intellectuelles, à faire des portraits et à raconter des histoires' [by definition a critical thinker, given to flushing out social or intellectual posturing, creating portraits and telling stories].[1] What these observations have in common is a prizing of the faculty of critical *attention* that is so characteristic of the work of Edward Hughes that we celebrate in the present volume.

From his first, immensely insightful and still important monograph on the 'quality of awareness' in Marcel Proust, his explorations of marginality in literary works from Loti to Genet, to his prize-winning biography of Albert Camus and his most recent ground-breaking book on class disturbance and levelling in modern and contemporary writing in French, Eddie, as he is known to friends and colleagues, has produced scholarship that is socio-politically engaged, intellectually acute and elegantly crafted. For over three decades, through sparkling critical readings of literary and philosophical texts both canonical and less well known Eddie has pursued and illuminated questions of class, community and nation; the role of work and the evolution of society and social bonds; he has interrogated the relations between France and Algeria and France's wider colonial project; and weighed up the respective endeavours of writer and labourer, artist and artisan.

Our title, *Labours of Attention*, was chosen for the apt way in which it offers a shorthand both for Eddie's scholarly achievements throughout his career and for our collective homage to him. It is borrowed from James Swenson's translation of *Courts voyages au pays du peuple* by Jacques Rancière, a thinker who has developed an important place in Eddie's writing in recent years.[2] Eddie quotes the phrase in 'By way of Rancière', the introduction to his most recent book, where he sets out his goal of exploring how in literary texts writers 'might draw into contiguity antagonistic social identities in such a way as to lead to the attenuation or interrogation of such antagonisms'.[3] Throughout his career Eddie's writing has attended to issues of class and identity, inclusion and exclusion and the ways in which different groups navigate, mark out and inhabit social spaces. Two vitally important figures, Marcel

Proust and Albert Camus, stand at the heart of his labours of attention, his critical explorations of how literary texts provide us with lenses through which we can appraise and interrogate history, nationalism and class-based politics. But Eddie's interests and readings range far beyond these two canonical authors. Over the years he has written illuminatingly on Assia Djebar, Marguerite Duras, Mohammed Dib and Pierre Michon (*entre autres*), and proposed new constellations of literary production through his juxtaposed and imbricated readings of writers as diverse as Pierre Loti, Henry de Montherlant and Jean Genet, Claude Simon, François Bon and Charles Péguy. Always astute and nuanced in his thinking, Eddie enriches his arguments with a deft handling of the best suited critical writing on his authors as well as richly detailed dialogues with key thinkers and theorists, among them Rancière, of course, but also Michel Foucault, Pierre Bourdieu and Gilles Deleuze, together with contemporaries such as Antoine Compagnon and Jacques Dubois. What is especially noteworthy when one reads through the list of Eddie's published work (see the List of Publications at the end of this volume) is that though there is an ongoing criss-crossing between authors or 'primary texts' (his first five published articles and chapters focused on four separate writers), there is at the same time a remarkable consistency to his critical preoccupations. Hierarchies, for instance, the performance of gender identities, and the ways in which literary writing engages with politics and sociality are so many *fils conducteurs* running through Eddie's work from the 1980s to the present. Read retrospectively, with an awareness of his later research, it is striking, for instance, how much foreshadowing of later preoccupations one finds in Eddie's early article on 'Parisian Pastoral' in *A la recherche du temps perdu*.[4] Here, a consideration of the representation of the French capital in Proust's novel, enriched by references to Robert Delaunay and Umberto Boccioni, brings into focus the question of social hierarchies and parallelisms between contrasting realms of activity: chaotic urban modernity in all its technological manifestations on the one hand and rarefied, idealised pastoral on the other, tethered to Proust's present via the enchanting cries of street-traders.

There is no 'Proust period' or 'Camus moment' for Eddie. Both writers have always cohabited his shelves and fuelled the critical writings that he has published: chapters on both are included in Eddie's first multi-author study, *Writing Marginality in Modern French Literature: From Loti to Genet*, but in general they move in and out of focus across his research trajectory, a little like the bell-towers of the Martinville and Vieuxvicq churches as perceived by Proust's young protagonist in *Du côté de chez Swann*.[5] The nimbleness of mind (and intellectual bandwidth) required to sustain this extended dialogue with such different and challenging authors is testament to Eddie's qualities as a scholar and a thinker.

'The bond between a man and his profession,' writes Primo Levi, 'is similar to that which ties him to his country', and it was at secondary school in Belfast that Eddie began to develop his own early qualities of awareness.[6] He was greatly influenced by an outstanding teacher of French, James Frazer, who spent two months every year in France and brought the living language and culture of the country back into the Northern Irish classroom, inspiring for Eddie what would become a life-long devotion to language and literature and, in time, to teaching.[7] In a characteristically self-effacing manner, upon his election to the Fellowship of the British Academy in 2019 Eddie remarked that receiving this recognition allowed him to reflect on the great teachers he had had. Many hundreds of undergraduate students have in turn benefited from Eddie's wisdom and warmth in the classroom and his energy and insight in the lecture theatre. His attention to detail and his unstinting compassion are traits that have made him an exacting, understanding and supportive examiner to many doctoral candidates over several decades.

He thrived during his BA in French and Spanish at Queen's University Belfast (1971–76), where new inspiration came from Professor Henri Godin, the chair in the French department at the time. Godin was a popular lecturer and tutor; amongst his publications is *Les Ressources stylistiques du français contemporain*, a guidebook to the core tenets of writing in French, published in 1948, with a focus on rhetoric and close study of key texts illustrating the stylistic evolution of literary expression, from Jules Michelet to Paul Morand and Pierre Loti, writers who would in due course enter Eddie's orbit in various ways. 'French literary works,' argues Godin, 'have [...] a double appeal: their beauty is aesthetic as well as factual. The subtle fusion of style and content is the great artistic achievement of French prose.'[8] This precious alloy of linguistic finesse and intellectual appeal captured and sustained Eddie's attention as an undergraduate, though his accomplishment was by no means limited only to French. He graduated with first-class honours in French and Spanish in 1976, winning the French Government medal for the best graduate in French as well as the Xavier Giralt Prize for the best graduate in Spanish. To this day Eddie speaks excellent Spanish (as well as good Italian, as recent collaborators can attest).[9] It was the pull of French, however, that was strongest, and so, in 1976, Eddie embarked on his doctoral research on Proust under the supervision of another inspirational and immensely accomplished scholar in the department at Queen's, Richard Bales. The originality and impact of Eddie's doctoral work are outlined in Alison Finch's chapter in the present volume, which revisits the monograph, *Marcel Proust: A Study in the Quality of Awareness*, that was based on his thesis.[10] Through the attention it pays to hitherto largely ignored characters and aspects of Proust's novel, this research injected new energy and insights into the critical field. Indeed, as Finch puts it, 'Hughes's revolutionary concentration on relatively uneducated, even inarticulate, characters predated the surge of French cultural studies but can retrospectively be read through that lens'. *A Study in the Quality of Awareness* built on substantive labours of attention in the Cabinet des Manuscrits at the Bibliothèque Nationale in Paris, where Eddie spent many formative hours and established lasting connections with the international community of scholars who were exploring and interpreting the extraordinary manuscript materials that are the foundation of Proust's novel and had been acquired by the Bibliothèque nationale in 1962. Richard Bales was a key figure, alongside other luminaries such as Kazuyoshi Yoshikawa, Jean Milly and Bernard Brun, in establishing genetic criticism in the field of Proust studies, and Eddie learned a great deal working in Paris alongside them, and others, in the early years of his career.

After a temporary lectureship at Saint Mary's College of Education, Belfast (1979–80), Eddie took up a permanent appointment as Lecturer in French at Birkbeck, University of London in 1980. There he received the Ronald Tress Prize for Best Early Career Researcher in 1984 (the year after the publication of his first book). Eddie remained at Birkbeck until 1991 when he moved to Royal Holloway, University of London, where he was promoted to Senior Lecturer the following year. His readable and informative introduction to Camus's *Le Premier homme* and *La Peste* appeared in the valuable Glasgow Introductory Guides series in 1995, closely followed by a collection of essays, co-edited with Peter Dunwoodie, also on *Le Premier homme*, in 1998.[11] The same year he became Reader and was promoted to Professor of French in 2002, the year after the publication of his *Writing Marginality in Modern French Literature*, mentioned above, and Richard Bales' landmark edited volume, *The Cambridge Companion to Proust*, to which Eddie contributed a sparklingly insightful account of Proustian sociality, pointing the way to his later work on class and nation in Proust's writings.[12] *Writing Marginality in Modern French Literature* is a bold and intellectually ambitious work, bringing together a fascinating constellation of writers, and one painter, as case studies facilitating an exploration of cultural accounts of marginality. Via chapters focused on Loti and Paul Gauguin, Proust, Henry de Montherlant, Camus and Jean Genet, the book 'addresses contexts in which modern French writers, through contact with what a metropolitan consensus deems to be marginal, reflect on how cultural value and ethical authority are constructed, defended and called into question'.[13] Eddie's readings of his chosen figures are lucid and balanced, sensitive at once to textual nuance and historical context, and they are supported by an extraordinarily rich cast of supporting voices, from Jean-Paul Sartre, Edouard Glissant and Albert Memmi, to Michel Leiris and Victor Segalen, R.D. Laing, Roland Barthes, Jacques Derrida and Jonathan Dollimore. *Writing Marginality in French Literature* embraces head-on the challenges, tensions and contradictions of metropolitan attitudes to and constructions of marginality, historicizes their production and problematizes their reception. To give just a brief flavour of how Eddie's far-sighted intellectual engagement translates to the page in this work, let us cite the following example, from his discussion of Camus's *Le Minotaure* and *Noces*:

> Sartre and Laing [...] enable us to politicize Camus's reverie as a form of radical social isolationism. Moreover, seen in the light of Barthes's observations on myth as depoliticized speech, Camus's stone-like self stands as an attempt to inject into reality an essence that would prevent, in Barthes's words, 'its flight towards other forms of existence'.[14]

Once again, read retrospectively, we can see Eddie's thinking here preparing the ground for questions that will be broached again and reframed in later work. At the conclusion of *Writing Marginality*, referring to his chosen corpus of writers, he indicates that 'the crucial question is the extent to which their iconoclasm and gesturing towards otherness ever become relationality', a question that evolves into or perhaps subtends, in an evolved form, the later inquiry into class disturbance and levelling.[15]

Alongside the late Michael Sheringham (who would become Marshal Foch Professor of French at Oxford, 2004–2015), Sonya Stephens (now President of Mount Holyoke College) and others, some of whom are contributors to the present volume, Eddie played a key part in the high-flying French department at Royal Holloway that would achieve outstanding results in the UK's 2001 Research Assessment Exercise. At this time he made a substantive contribution of seven main articles, twenty short articles and twelve notes to the *Dictionnaire Marcel Proust*, published in 2004. This major publication, which quickly became an invaluable point of reference in the field, was co-ordinated by Annick Bouillaguet and Brian Rogers, and was awarded the Académie française's Emile Faguet prize for literary criticism in 2005.[16] Meanwhile, Eddie chaired Royal Holloway's Modern Languages Committee from 2003 to 2005, before moving to a professorial appointment at Queen Mary, University of London, where he remained until his retirement at the end of 2019.

Eddie's years at Queen Mary were greatly productive. A steady stream of articles continued (work on Mohammed Dib, Proust, Assia Djebar, Camus and Genet appeared between 2005 and 2009), even while major book-length projects were brought to fruition.[17] Like his mentor Richard Bales before him, Eddie prepared an extremely fine addition to the Cambridge Companions series, on Camus, which was published in 2007.[18] As well as assembling and marshalling a balanced and illuminating set of essays from contributors in Europe, the UK and the US, Eddie provides a lucid introduction, a chapter on autobiographical elements in *L'Envers et l'endroit* that provides wide-ranging reflections on, amongst other things, mother-figures in Camus ('a source of enduring preoccupation and enigma in his writing') and a 'Postface' which is a model of sensitive synthesis and critical reflection, that weighs up the cumulative achievements of the voices he has gathered together in the *Companion*.[19] In 2011, with a pendulum swing back towards the belle époque and the politics of culture and nationalism, Eddie published his second monograph on Proust: *Proust, Class, and Nation*, which was runner-up for the Franco-British Society's Literary Prize for that year.[20] The book offers, as one reviewer put it, 'an original and powerful thesis', reading *A la recherche*, Proust's letters, his other writings and those of his contemporaries in the historical context of societal upheavals relating to class, state and nationalism around the turn of the century and beyond.[21] Though often associated with social conservatism, Proust emerges from this reading as at once politically engaged and playful, iconoclastic, always resistant to categorisation, as Hughes writes:

> The unavailability of tidy labels for the author of *A la recherche du temps perdu* derives substantially from Proust's capacity both to identify with and assume the tribal mindset and to demonstrate a countervailing will to transcend and often disown group identities.[22]

Eddie's own capacity to mine contemporary sources in the service of arguments that cast new light on Proust's long-familiar novel is strongly in evidence here, as the writings of Maurice Barrès, Paul Bourget, Daniel Halévy and Julien Benda are sounded out individually and in counterpoint to Proust's own. Eddie uses the insights of genetic criticism to show how Proust worked actively to give increased prominence to material relating to class and social stratification as he developed the base text of 1913–14 during the war and thereafter. A major contribution to Proust scholarship, the book is also studded with insights relating to the complex interplay of language and human agency in the establishment of (and resistance to) hierarchies, taxonomies, social roles and class distinctions; the roles played by servants within the novel's narrative economy; the importance of Balbec as a space of new, and newly juxtaposed, forms of sociality; and Proust's capacity, noted above, to toy with, yet nevertheless voice 'independent-minded wariness about stridently formulated group identities and attitudes'.[23]

Alongside this uninterrupted production of first-rate research, Eddie was concurrently channelling his energies (and considerable acumen) into the leadership of our community. A long-serving member of the Executive Committee of the Society for French Studies, he was a popular and immensely efficient president in 2009 and 2010, and vice-president during the two years either side of his tenure as president. Eddie brought his warm and compassionate character to this role (as evinced by his exemplary chairing of meetings and thoughtful, inclusive handling of all items of business, large and small) as well as his strong resolve and steely powers of persuasion and diplomacy (as evinced by the efficacy of his tireless efforts in renegotiating the terms of the Society's journal contract with Oxford University Press: no small accomplishment).

Following these years of collaborative endeavour and generosity (and uninterrupted teaching and administration at Queen Mary), Eddie secured a one-year research fellowship from the Leverhulme Trust in 2013–14 that granted him the time needed to complete a project the seeds of which had been sown in his chapter on the autobiographical in Camus's writings in his *Cambridge Companion*. The new undertaking was a biography of Camus for Reaktion Books' well respected Critical Lives series and the book appeared in 2015.[24] With great economy of means, in just under two hundred pages of text, Eddie crafts a clear-eyed, unsentimental account of the engaged thinker and writer-activist who was viscerally opposed to injustice and who, familiar with the experience of poverty and hardship, was unequivocally committed to the cause of those whose voices tend not to be heard. The book draws shrewdly on Camus's rich correspondence, spliced with readings of his equally rich literary and journalistic output and helpful accounts of the volatile local, national and international political climates during Camus's short life. Eddie writes with admirable clarity about Camus's challenging insights: for instance the metaphor of 'l'envers et l'endroit' [the two sides of a piece of fabric, respectively that which is typically unseen and that which faces outward] is used, as Eddie puts it, 'to draw attention to what [Camus] saw as the regular blinkering of human perception: how the love of life goes hand in hand with, and yet often conceals, a despair at living'.[25] Camus the journalist is characterized as a 'a wielder of words': not a factory hand or a manual worker, but someone whose labours might serve those performing such roles and many others besides.[26]

In the spring of 2021, Liverpool University Press published Eddie's most recent book, mentioned above, *Egalitarian Strangeness: On Class Disturbance and Levelling in Modern and Contemporary French Narrative*. Like *Writing Marginality*, this is an intellectually ambitious multi-author study, and one which gains additional dynamism from a structure that is not a linear chronological one. Rather, the chapters (on well-known figures such as Proust, Marie Ndiaye and François Bon, on less studied and less familiar figures such as Charles Péguy and Louis-Gabriel Gauny; and spanning a range of genres, by authors including Paul Nizan, Simone Weil and Pierre Michon) are arranged in three sections: 'The Refrain of Class', 'Disturbance and *Dressage*' and 'Audible Voices', across which Hughes interrogates the manifold ways in which modern literary writing in French encounters, problematizes and explores questions of class, social hierarchy and physical and mental labour. Rancière's thought, in particular his 'advocacy of radical equality,' is a guiding thread, and repeatedly connections (links that the Proustian narrator would call 'transversals') are made between writers and texts quite distant from each other in time.[27] It is an invigorating read from start to finish. Primo Levi suggests that:

> The bond between a man and his profession is similar to that which ties him to his country; it is just as complex, often ambivalent, and in general it is understood completely only when it is broken: by exile or emigration in the case of one's country, by retirement in the case of a trade or profession.[28]

Egalitarian Strangeness was written prior to Eddie's retirement but completed and published after: given its many accomplishments, the promise of what might come next, once its author (by Levi's account) has fully understood his calling, is a tantalising prospect.

Eddie's decision to retire from Queen Mary became a reality at the end of the 2019 calendar year. No doubt had he remained in post he would have dealt calmly, creatively and with characteristic patience and good humour with the advent of 'blended learning', virtual lectures and online meetings and the various other challenges that the coronavirus pandemic brought to our campuses. Instead, however, Eddie stepped away, with characteristic modesty, self-effacement and without fanfare. This volume is our way of collectively sounding the trumpets and celebrating his career and the immense contributions he has made to French Studies over many years.

It begins with a poetic homage, an Oulipian *beau présent* by Anna Kemp which, using only the letters of the phrase 'Edward Joseph Hughes, Emeritus' captures many of the traits of a long-admired and much esteemed colleague. The body of the book is arranged in five parts reflecting the key axes of Eddie's research outlined above. The first, 'Revisiting Camus', opens with David Ellison's chapter on the place of Camus's writings, between the political and the literary, a place, he suggests, we might fruitfully think of as that of *hospitality*. Peter Dunwoodie's chapter then focuses on the texts we might consider as Camus's travel writings, opening up a range of questions concerning genre, ethnography and perspective in relation to these little-studied texts. The next two chapters focus in different ways on one of Camus's best-known works, *La Peste*. Jeanyves Guérin revisits the novel through the lens of our contemporary experience of the coronavirus pandemic, reading its preoccupations against the geopolitical (and local) concerns of 2020 and 2021. Finally Ieme Van der Poel interrogates the relationship between *La Peste* and its colonial locus — Oran around the time of the Second World War — not from a postcolonial perspective, but with the goal of better appreciating the relational dynamics between the story, its location and moment, and the lack of Algerian characters in it.

Part II consists of four chapters engaging with a range of topics germane to Eddie's interest in (and publications relating to) 'Algeria and the French Colonial Project'. Charles Forsdick's chapter opens this section, drawing on a range of sources to consider the presence of Algerian convicts in New Caledonia and French Guiana. Building in part on Eddie's 2011 article on Pierre Michon's *Vies minuscules*, Patrick Crowley's chapter examines the memory of empire that persists in the social imaginary of peasant France as depicted in Michon's 'Vie d'André Dufourneau', read alongside, amongst others, statements made in the opening volume of Pierre Nora's *Les Lieux de mémoire*, which was published in the same year as *Vies minuscules* (1984).[29] The two chapters that close Part II respond to filmic engagements with the legacies of the French-Algerian war, both continuing this part of the volume's interest in marginality and memory. Anna Elsner examines personal and social identities in Alain Resnais's *Muriel ou le temps d'un retour* (1963), teasing out Proustian resonances via the figure of the kaleidoscope. James Williams explores subjectivity, embodiment, violence and memory in the powerful but little acknowledged short film *Frères ennemis* (2013) by Yacine Balah.

Part III, 'Works and Days: Labour, Class, Society', extends the exploration of artistic engagements with the lived experience of work in the modern era via a series of chapters, each of which grapples with aspects of labour, class and society from a different standpoint. Eric Robertson assesses the vision of work and society that emerges from the creative endeavours in writing and painting of Blaise Cendrars and Fernand Léger, whose aesthetics embrace artisanship yet maintain a fraught relation to class struggle. In his chapter, through a consideration of the anecdotal in Jean Genet's writings, Richard Mason seeks to reframe prominent tensions within Genet's work, especially his writing on art: between the particular and the universal, between centre and margin, and between lived experience and literary expression. Shirley Jordan looks to literary accounts of late-life care in modern and contemporary women's writing, principally in Simone de Beauvoir's *Une mort très douce* [A Very Easy Death] (1964) and Chantal Akerman's *Ma mère rit* [My Mother Laughs] (2013), as well as texts by other authors including Annie Ernaux, to suggest how such acts of attentiveness may offer an important route into re-valorising the difficult, often marginalised labour of care. From the care for others we move, with Marion Schmid's chapter on Paolo Sorrentino's *La grande bellezza*, to the self-absorption of the socialite. Schmid's chapter reads Sorrentino's 2013 film in dialogue with both Fellini and Proust, unravelling questions of *mondanité*, class, art and creation that are central to all three artists and are threads throughout each of the chapters in Part III.

Part IV, 'Marcel Proust: Labours of Language', offers a series of critical engagements with Proust's novel that intersect with Eddie's interests in literary language and aesthetics and their connections with class, politics and sociality. Michael Moriarty, John O'Brien and Patrick O'Donovan offer new insights into Proust's 'house of fiction' via scrutiny of intertextual borrowings (Moriarty tracks the role of La Fontaine in *A la recherche*); rhetorical figures (O'Brien assesses the place of prosopopoeia in Proust's emergent modernist aesthetics); and the figure of the house itself (O'Donovan explores the combinatory political and aesthetic implications of the figurations of space in Proust's novel). These chapters, all attentive as much to discrete, fine details and what Ali Smith has called the 'handshake between sources' as to the grander architectonics of the Proustian world, connect us with the 'multiplicity of moods, the interplay of emotional and intellectual states' to which Eddie's first monograph so adroitly drew critical attention.[30] The chapters that close Part IV, by Marisa Verna and Cynthia Gamble, switch attention to Proust's political engagement and its means of articulation. Verna scrutinises questions of (im-)purity in relation to nationalism, language and *étrangeté* in *A la recherche*, whilst Gamble offers a cultural historical reading of Proust's various acts of writerly 'engagement' with the socio-political issues of his time, a dimension of his work highlighted in *Proust, Class, and Nation*, but all too often ignored or occluded.

The final section of the book, Part V, 'Marcel Proust: Labours of Love', continues the exploration of Proust's work via chapters that appraise the interpersonal and the intimate in the author's writing, relating these variously to the themes of class, community and appearance. Susan Harrow, drawing on Rancière and Agamben amongst others, asks how letter-writing by Proust and other key modernist writers and artists (Cézanne, Mallarmé, Van Gogh) might be seen to shape creative communities, articulating everyday experience as a dimension of sociability and creativity. Julia Hartley interrogates the intertextual relations between *A la recherche* and the writings of two of Proust's dearest acquaintances, Anna de Noailles and Marthe Bibesco, focusing on the associative, poetic interplay of names and places and the construction(s) of 'Persian-ness' in their work. Jacques Dubois offers a survey of the Proustian erotic, which is manifest throughout *A la recherche* in multifarious ways. He proposes that snobbery and class-based attitudes become freighted with eroticism within a narrative economy that holds indecency and elegance in a delicate balance. In her chapter, complementary to and illustrative of Dubois's observations, Margaret Gray turns attention away from the much analysed same-sex, inter-class courtship scene between Charlus and Jupien early in *Sodome et Gomorrhe* to examine Albertine's little-studied encounter with a working-class *pâtissière* in *La Prisonnière*, shedding new light on Proust's presentation of desire and attraction within and across class boundaries, as well as revealing previously unacknowledged structural parallels within the novel. Finally, the volume closes with a capstone chapter by Alison Finch that gives a lucid critical (re-)appraisal of *Marcel Proust: A Study in the Quality of Awareness* (1983), revisiting its insights into attentiveness, identity, desire and self-other relations (amongst other things), to acknowledge the prescience and enduring value of this landmark critical work.

* * * * *

Together, then, the following chapters combine to celebrate and to honour Edward Hughes's contributions to our field. What is harder to convey in the form of scholarly essays is our appreciation of his qualities as a person — his kindness, his generosity, his wit and *joie de vivre*. Eddie's research has always grappled with the human and the social as they are explored and constructed in cultural production. His critical readings are not ancillary to the works in question but represent what Pierre Bourdieu calls 'un moment de la production de l'œuvre, de son sens et de sa valeur' [a moment in the production of the work, of its meaning and its value].[31] For this, and all of Eddie's many labours of attention, with what follows we express our gratitude and admiration.

Notes to the Introduction

1. Walter Benjamin, 'The Image of Proust' [1929], in *Illuminations*, ed. by Hannah Arendt, trans. by Harry Zohn (London: Pimlico, 1999), pp. 197–210 (p. 207); James Wood, 'Serious Noticing', in *Serious Noticing: Selected Essays* (London: Vintage, 2019), pp. 49–73; George Steiner, *The Poetry of Thought: From Helenism to Celan* (New York: New Directions, 2011), p. 13; Pierre Nora, *Jeunesse* (Paris: Gallimard, 2021), pp. 232–33.
2. Jacques Rancière, *Courts voyages au pays du peuple* (Paris: Seuil, 1990), p. 159; *Short Voyages to the Land of the People*, trans. by James B. Swenson (Stanford, CA: Stanford University Press, 2003), p. 123.
3. Edward J. Hughes, *Egalitarian Strangeness: On Class Disturbance and Levelling in Modern and Contemporary French Narrative* (Liverpool: Liverpool University Press, 2021), p. 3. The phrase 'labour of attention' appears on p. 12, quoted in the context of accounting for the book's title, itself (*étrangeté égalitaire*) borrowed from the same text by Rancière.
4. Edward J. Hughes, 'Parisian Pastoral in *A la recherche du temps perdu*', *Romance Studies*, 22 (1993), 17–25.
5. Edward J. Hughes, *Writing Marginality in Modern French Literature: From Loti to Genet* (Cambridge: Cambridge University Press, 2001), Chapters 2, 'Exemplary Inclusions, Indecent Exclusions in Proust's *Recherche*', and 4, 'Camus and the Resistance to History'.
6. Primo Levi, 'Ex-Chemist', in *Other People's Trades*, trans. by Raymond Rosenthal (London: Abacus, 1989), pp. 174–76 (p. 174).
7. See the interview with Eddie for the Franco-British Connections website in 2017 <https://www.fb-connections.org/mr-edward-hughes/> [accessed December 2021].
8. Henri Godin, 'Introduction' [English in original], in *Les Ressources stylistiques du français contemporain* (Oxford: Basil Blackwell, 1948), pp. vii–viii (p. vii).
9. Eddie gave the invited opening talk at the conference 'Proust politique: de l'Europe du Goncourt 1919 à l'Europe de 2019' at the Catholic University of Milan in May 2019. His paper, 'Le Commun et le quelconque: Proust en 1919', is published in *Proust politique: de l'Europe du Goncourt 1919 à l'Europe de 2019*, ed. by Anne Simon and others (= special issue of *Quaderni proustiani*, 14 (2020)), 63–72 <https://quadernipoustiani.padovauniversitypress.it/2020/1/6> [accessed December 2021].
10. Edward J. Hughes, *Marcel Proust: A Study in the Quality of Awareness* (Cambridge: Cambridge University Press, 1983). The original PhD thesis was entitled 'Modes of Existence and Consciousness in the Works of Marcel Proust: A Study in the Quality of Awareness' (Queen's University Belfast, 1979).
11. Edward J. Hughes, *Albert Camus, 'Le Premier Homme'/ 'La Peste'*, Glasgow Introductory Guides to French Literature, 33 (Glasgow: University of Glasgow French and German Publications, 1995); *Constructing Memories: Camus, Algeria and 'Le Premier Homme'*, ed. by Peter Dunwoodie and Edward J. Hughes (= special issue of *Stirling French Publications*, 6 (1998)).

12. See Edward J. Hughes, 'Proust and Social Spaces', in *The Cambridge Companion to Proust*, ed. by Richard Bales (Cambridge: Cambridge University Press, 2001), pp. 151–67.
13. Hughes, *Writing Marginality*, p. 3.
14. Ibid., p. 109.
15. Ibid., p. 168.
16. Eddie's contributions range from entries for the 'Drame du coucher' [Bedtime drama] and 'Doncières' to the 'Affaire Dreyfus' and 'Xénophobie', as well as biographical portraits of figures including Edouard Drumont and Albert Le Cuziat. See *Dictionnaire Marcel Proust*, ed. by Annick Bouillaguet and Brian G. Rogers (Paris: Honoré Champion, 2004).
17. For details of the articles, see the List of Publications at the end of this volume.
18. *The Cambridge Companion to Camus*, ed. by Edward J. Hughes (Cambridge: Cambridge University Press, 2007). One uncredited review indicates the work is 'likely to be the essential introductory text for many a French studies scholar and interested reader for some time to come' (*Forum for Modern Language Studies*, 45.2 (2009), 217).
19. See Edward J. Hughes, 'Autobiographical Soundings in *L'Envers et l'Endroit*', in *The Cambridge Companion to Camus*, ed. by Hughes, pp. 39–49 (p. 43).
20. Edward J. Hughes, *Proust, Class, and Nation* (Oxford: Oxford University Press, 2011). The prize was won by Eddie's then Queen Mary colleague Jeremy Jennings for his book *Revolution and the Republic: A History of Political Thought in France since the Eighteenth Century* (Oxford: Oxford University Press, 2011).
21. André Benhaïm, review in *French Studies*, 67.2 (2013), 271.
22. Hughes, *Proust, Class, and Nation*, p. 4. Proust's extraordinary capacity to hold 'countervailing' positions is further explored by Christopher Prendergast in his bracing study *Mirages and Mad Beliefs: Proust the Skeptic* (Princeton, NJ, & Oxford: Princeton University Press, 2013).
23. Hughes, *Proust, Class, and Nation*, p. 268.
24. Edward J. Hughes, *Albert Camus*, Critical Lives (London: Reaktion, 2015). It was joint winner of the Franco-British Society Literary Prize for 2015. The co-laureate was David Loosley for his book *Edith Piaf: A Cultural History* (Liverpool: Liverpool University Press, 2015).
25. Ibid., pp. 32–33.
26. Ibid., p. 89. The image of wielding or handling words like an artisan or labourer manipulating his or her tools is aptly chosen and redolent of Primo Levi's observation, reflecting on his move from chemistry to writing, that 'now my trade is a different one, it is the trade of words, chosen, weighed, fitted into a pattern with patience and caution'. See Primo Levi, 'The Language of Chemists (II)', in *Other People's Trades*, pp. 106–10 (p. 106). One also recalls Camus's fellow Nobel laureate and Eddie's countryman Seamus Heaney, who 'had no spade to follow men like them' [his father and grandfather] but instead chose the pen. See Seamus Heaney, 'Digging', in *Death of a Naturalist* [1966] (London: Faber, 1999), pp. 3–4.
27. Hughes, *Egalitarian Strangeness*, p. 9.
28. Levi, 'Ex-Chemist', p. 174.
29. Edward J. Hughes, 'Pierre Michon, "Small Lives", and the Terrain of Art', *Romance Studies*, 29.2 (2011), 67–79.
30. Hughes, *Marcel Proust*, p. 189; and see Ali Smith, *Artful* (London: Hamish Hamilton, 2012), p. 201.
31. Pierre Bourdieu, *Les Règles de l'art: genèse et structure du champ littéraire* [1992] (Paris: Seuil, rev. ed. 1998), p. 285.

PART I

Revisiting Camus

CHAPTER 1

Albert Camus and the Place of the Literary

David R. Ellison

Like Émile Zola before him, or Jean-Paul Sartre his contemporary, or Bernard-Henri Lévy today, Albert Camus was a public intellectual. What he said or wrote about Algeria, in particular, was part of the news of the day and generated considerable controversy. Algeria was a major stumbling-block for Camus, who desperately sought for a third way between two radicalisms: that of the Front de libération nationale (FLN) and that of an increasingly repressive French colonial regime.[1] But what of Albert Camus as literary creator, as author of literary texts? In his Nobel Prize acceptance speech of 14 December 1957 on the topic 'L'Art est-il un luxe mensonger?' [Is Art a deceitful luxury?] it is clear that Camus viewed himself as an artist, and that, as he puts it, art resides between 'le refus et le consentement' [refusal and acquiescence], that it is 'un déchirement perpétuellement renouvelé' [a continually renewed tearing-apart].[2] Can one situate Camus's art inside or outside the political domain? Is there a place for literary art, a specific place? And especially, can one go beyond Camus's love for balancing figures, such as 'le refus et le consentement' or *L'Envers et l'endroit*, or *L'Exil et le royaume*, or 'Ni victimes ni bourreaux' etc., which he used throughout his work, both literary and journalistic, as a structuring principle? The question is whether another space exists, which is neither within nor without, where Camus wished to go, where he sometimes went. This space, I shall suggest in the pages that follow, is that of hospitality — which occurs within a narrative pause, and which exists within a realm of mutual understanding, admiration, pity and respect.

Before beginning my development, properly speaking, I would like to quote from a curious collaborative work called *La Postérité du soleil*, in which René Char, the contemporary poet whom Camus knew and admired the most, states of his new-found friend:

> Je m'aperçus que ce qui m'avait prévenu favorablement [...] prenait tout son sens: une simplicité tantôt ironique et grave, le geste délié sans excès, une mesure non recherchée, une discrétion subite dans les échanges, au seuil d'une confiance prématurée, faisaient que cet homme [Albert Camus] *n'était jamais un étranger parmi les autres, un importun à peine dessiné. Etranger, celui qui se présente, sans parler*

le premier, à des êtres qui ignorent tout de lui et désirent apprendre, et qui saura tout sans souhaiter trop savoir. (OC, IV, 734; my emphasis)

[I recognised that what had predisposed me towards him [...] became meaningful: a sometimes ironical and grave simplicity, a subtle, not excessive, gesture, a non-refined sense of measure, a sudden discretion in verbal exchanges, at the threshold of a premature confidence, meant that this man [Albert Camus] was never *a stranger among others, a troublesome, barely-drawn figure. A stranger, that person who presents himself, without speaking at first, to beings who know nothing of him yet desire to learn, and who will know everything without wishing to know too much.*]

Aside from being an excellent portrait of Camus the person, this passage says a great deal about the writing efforts of Camus the artist. Char understands the fundamental position of the stranger, or foreigner (*l'étranger*) in Camus's writings. Camus the person is not to be considered a stranger, or at least, a 'stranger among others', but the figure of the Stranger as such is an important one, in that he is silent, or mostly silent to others (who desire to know him); but in the end, he will know everything without wishing to know too much. The Stranger, or Foreigner, comes from outside to a certain inside. He is not to be confused with those who occupy the inside, but they depend upon him; there is reciprocity here, and a mutual desire for understanding. My point is that, from *L'Étranger* (written starting in 1939, but first published by Gallimard in 1942) onward, until his death on 4 January 1960, Camus was obsessed with the figure of the Stranger, whom he depicted metamorphosing from an individual outsider to social norms, to a Plague insinuating itself into the life and regular rhythms of a city, to a 'judge-penitent' living on the fringes of a place in which he is a perpetual foreigner, to several fictional representatives (in his final published short stories) who represent, in various ways, intruders into spaces not their own. What was it about this figure that fascinated Camus so much that its multiple forms inflected his writings to this degree? It is to this question that I now turn.

The scholar to whom the chapters in this volume are dedicated, Edward J. Hughes, writes quite perceptively about the figure of the Stranger, and about the 'shared space' he inhabits. After Meursault has been apprehended, toward the beginning of Part II of *L'Étranger*, he explains to the others inhabiting the same place what he has done and why he has been incarcerated. Although his explanation is greeted with silence, he is told by the other prisoners how to arrange the matting provided him into a semblance of a bed. Hughes writes:

> The cell, and the shared misery it represents for its inhabitants, thus becomes a culturally plural space which North African and European prisoners occupy. [...] It delivers a sharing of space, albeit parenthetically, in the regimented, punitive surroundings of the prison regime.[3]

In his analysis, Hughes alludes not only to Meursault, but also to Daru, the protagonist of the ambiguously titled 'L'Hôte', who is both host and guest in the unforgiving environment of the mountains above the North African coast. In this short story, included in the volume *L'Exil et le royaume* (1957), as a teacher Daru represents France and French culture, but does not want to get involved in surrounding events, which are political and violent. In the same way that Meursault shares space with other prisoners, some of them North African (i.e. not European), Daru shares his modest dwelling with an 'Arab' man who is accused of murdering his cousin. The evening in which they sleep in the same room together is described in these terms by the narrator of 'L'Hôte':

> Dans la chambre où, depuis un an, il dormait seul, cette présence [celle de l'Arabe] le gênait. Mais elle le gênait aussi parce qu'elle lui imposait une sorte de fraternité qu'il refusait dans les circonstances présentes et qu'il connaissait bien: les hommes, qui partagent les mêmes chambres, soldats ou prisonniers, contractent un lien étranger comme si, leurs armures quittées avec les vêtements, ils se rejoignaient chaque soir, par-dessus leurs différences, dans la vieille communauté du songe et de la fatigue. (*OC*, IV, 55)

> [In the room where, since last year, he slept alone, this presence [that of the Arab] bothered him. But it bothered him also because it imposed on him a kind of fraternity which he refused in the present circumstances and which he knew well: men who share the same rooms, soldiers or prisoners, share a strange link as if, having shed their armour with their clothes, they came together each evening, above and beyond their differences, in the ancient community of dreams and of fatigue.]

What Hughes has understood is that such a moment of respite from the evils of the world can only be 'parenthetical'. Camus emphasises this throughout his mature work. Moments such as the one his narrator describes in 'L'Hôte' occur infrequently, and are, so to speak, outside of events and outside of Time itself. But this does not make them less significant, and, in alluding to 'la vieille communauté du songe et de la fatigue' [the ancient community of dreams and of fatigue], Camus in fact points back to the very beginnings of Western literature, which is born in violence but which contains, hidden within its earliest stories, the desire for a world without enemies, or, at least, a world in which the violence of human against human, is attenuated by mutual admiration and respect.[4]

First Digression: By Way of Homer

The scene to which Camus alludes, in 'L'Hôte', whether consciously or unconsciously, is taken from the final book of Homer's *The Iliad*, XXIV.508–812 in Robert Fagles's translation.[5] The narrative set-up is important here, so I shall be as precise as possible. The god Hermes accompanies the Trojan king Priam to reclaim the body of his son Hector, whom the Greek hero Achilles has killed. It can be said that the battle between Hector and Achilles, which takes place in Book XXII, is the climax of the epic poem. The funeral games for Patroclus, which occupy the entirety of Book XXIII, are an interlude which simply puts off the conclusion of the epic in Book XXIV: Priam's traversing of the camp of Achilles (helped by Hermes); his entreaty, via ransom, to Achilles, to regain the dead body of his son; the ritual meal and sleep (in which Achilles, who has Priam within his power, does nothing to harm him); and Priam's departure, the next morning, accompanied (in fact, made invisible) by Hermes, through the Greek camp and then through the walls of Troy. In the scene I am examining, Priam asks Achilles for ten days in which to mourn Hector after the return to Troy; after that moment, war can begin again. The poem concludes with the line 'And so the Trojans buried Hector breaker of horses' (v. 944). This means that the moments in which Priam and Achilles meet each other in the latter's tent are surrounded by the violence of war, but that war itself does not intrude into the tent. Priam's moments with Achilles are therefore quite literally 'parenthetical', in that they constitute an episode of quiet and retreat within a bloody universe.

In what is probably the first instance recorded in the Western literary tradition of the theme of hospitality, we can see elements that will be repeated throughout the tradition, but with some variations. The presence of the god who accompanies and makes possible the voyage to the host will be discarded as one God replaces plural gods and as nation-states replace tribes as primal units of the social order (Troy is really a Greek outpost, not to be confused with a nation unto itself). But the order of events within the isolated tent will be often repeated: the movement from a threatening outside to an inside haven; the consuming of a meal and the sleeping of enemies under the same, now-safe roof; the exchange of gifts (in this case, Priam brings a ransom, Achilles hands over Hector's body); and the departure from the comforts of the inside world back to the threatening world of the outside. As the reader of Camus can see, the short story 'L'Hôte' is structured along these same lines. Balducci, like Hermes, but representing France as a secular state, brings the 'Arab' to Daru; Daru receives the accused man, prepares a meal for him and sleeps under the same roof with him (here, there is no exchange of gifts per se, both men being too poor to engage in this kind of activity); then, the following morning, a departure from the frugal comforts of the inside world to the outside, where the 'Arab' must decide which road to take — to his freedom, or to his imprisonment. Although throughout the story Daru is depicted as a person who prefers to refuse the violence of the outside world, he returns to his home and discovers that the blackboard on which he has drawn the rivers of France is now overlaid with the statement 'Tu as livré notre frère. Tu paieras' [You have handed over our brother. You will pay] (*OC*, IV, 58). In other words, the 'parenthetical' episode of hospitality exists only as momentary relief from the pressure exerted by the outside on the inside. This pressure, which is that of violence itself, in this story at least, cannot be resisted.

Throughout his life and literary career, Camus was interested not only in what words can do, but also in what precedes words, in the silence that sometimes 'says' as much as words.[6] In this, he is repeating Homer, who in the scene to which I refer has Priam and Achilles, before and after they have addressed each other in words, look at each other silently, in wonder. To my mind, this is the crux of the scene. When Achilles has laid out the meal they are about to consume, we read:

> They reached out for the good things that lay at hand
> and when they had put aside desire for food and drink,
> Priam the son of Dardanus gazed at Achilles, marveling
> now at the man's beauty, his magnificent build —
> face-to-face he seemed a deathless god ...
> and Achilles gazed and marveled at Dardan Priam,
> beholding his noble looks. (*Iliad*, XXIV.738–44)

The original Greek, here translated as 'marveling' and 'marveled', uses the verb *thaúmazein*.[7] The verb is related to the noun *thaúma*, meaning 'wonder, marvel, wondrous thing'.[8] We are here in the realm of the magical, before rationality, before speech itself. It is in this intermediate, parenthetical space that hospitality as such lives.

Second Digression: Theories of Hospitality

Before I turn, in a final section, to Camus's own development of the theme of hospitality, I would like to define more carefully what I mean by 'hospitality as such'. The term 'hospitality' has a long tradition, in literature, but also in anthropology, linguistics and philosophy — ranging from Homer, via Kant to Marcel Mauss and Émile Benveniste, to Anne Dufourmantelle and Jacques Derrida.[9] In a nutshell: hospitality is a mutual act of exchange (gifts are fundamental to its earliest appearance in the Western tradition) whereby the host invites a guest into his abode and offers him or her tokens of the abundance contained in his *chez-soi*.

In his seminar of 1995–97 entitled 'Hostipitalité', Jacques Derrida focuses on the issue of hospitality in a particular way, which has a bearing on Camus's treatment of the subject. Beginning with the fact that the Latin word *hostis* can mean either 'host' or 'guest' (which Camus exploits to maximum effect in his story 'L'Hôte'), Derrida shows that the domain of contemporary technique (the internet, the fax machine, the telephone and television etc.) has extended the notion of private space, to such a degree that it has become difficult to define it in contradistinction to public space. This fact is important when one looks at texts which prioritise what Derrida calls 'absolute' or 'unconditional' hospitality (texts which I am foregrounding in my essay), in which a person is welcomed into a private space without being named, or being asked to name him- or herself. This is quite different from what Derrida calls 'conditional' hospitality, in which names, identity and laws come to the fore (one thinks here of the immigrants languishing at the border of the United States, subject to an array of legal factors which can prohibit them from entering the country), in which public space has blotted out private space.

For Derrida, the system of hospitality cannot be separated from the problems of violence and of sovereignty. In this respect he is close to Pierre Klossowski who, in a volume from *Les Lois de l'hospitalité* entitled *Roberte, ce soir*, tells the story of a stranger who penetrates the interior of a house run by 'an eminent professor of scholastics' married to a woman named Roberte, who is the aunt of the narrator.[10] In a bizarre mixture of abstract philosophy and pornography, the narrator describes the encounter between the stranger and Roberte. Most important to the narrative itself, however (and most important to Derrida's argument), is the fact that the host is described as a sovereign figure who has inscribed on the wall of the room destined for strangers a paragraph in which he defines what he means by hospitality, and which begins with the following sentence:

> Le maître de céans n'ayant de souci plus urgent que celui de faire rayonner
> sa joie sur n'importe qui, au soir, viendra manger à sa table et se reposer sous

son toit des fatigues de la route, attend avec anxiété sur le seuil de sa maison l'étranger qu'il verra poindre à l'horizon comme un libérateur.[11]

[The master of the house having no more urgent care than that of casting his joy over anyone who, in the evening, comes to eat at his table and rest under his roof from the weariness of the road, waits with anxiety at the threshold of his home for the stranger he sees appearing on the horizon like a liberator.]

The fact that Camus probably read Klossowski (*Roberte, ce soir* was originally published in 1954) is borne out, first, by the curious use of the term 'le maître de céans', an old French expression meaning 'the master of the house' or 'the master of the interior' (*céans* comes from the combination of *çà* and *enz*, Old French for 'inside') both in Klossowski and in Camus's *La Chute* (1956), where the owner of the Mexico City bar is described as both 'our host' and as 'le maître de céans' in the third paragraph of that convoluted tale (*OC*, III, 698). The proprietor of the establishment has hung a picture above the bar (just as the professor of scholastics has hung his definition of hospitality above the bed in his *chambre d'ami*, in *Roberte, ce soir*), but, as we learn in the final chapter of the narrative, the picture, now absent, is the stolen panel *The Just Judges* from Van Eyck's *Adoration of the Lamb*, now residing in Clamence's room. Camus brings together, in *La Chute*, the themes of mastery/sovereignty and of hospitality, in a variation on the theme proposed by Klossowski. And, of course, Klossowski's image of the stranger who appears on the horizon will be taken up and varied by Camus in 'L'Hôte', where Daru initially sees Balducci and his prisoner appearing on the horizon below him.

For Klossowski and for Derrida following in his footsteps, hospitality is therefore inseparable from questions of power and of violence. In his seminar of 17 January 1996 entitled 'Pas d'hospitalité', in examining the right to hospitality of the stranger penetrating his host's abode, Derrida writes:

Il s'agit d'un modèle conjugal, paternel et phallogocentrique. C'est le despote familial, le père, l'époux et le patron, le maître de céans qui fait les lois de l'hospitalité. Il les représente et s'y plie pour y plier les autres dans cette violence du pouvoir d'hospitalité, dans cette puissance de l'ipséité [...] le problème de l'hospitalité [est] coextensif au problème éthique. Il s'agit toujours de répondre d'une demeure, de son identité, de son espace, de ses limites, de l'*ethos* en tant que séjour, habitation, maison, foyer, famille, chez-soi.[12]

[At stake is the conjugal, paternal and phallogocentric model. It is the familial despot, the father, the spouse and the boss, the master of the house [*le maître de céans*] who establishes the laws of hospitality. He represents them and bows to them in order to make others bow as well, in this violence of the power of hospitality, in this power of selfhood [...] the problem of hospitality [is] coextensive with the ethical problem. One must always answer for one's dwelling, identity, space, limits, for one's *ethos* understood as a sojourn, place of living, house, hearth, family, *chez-soi*.]

The question that follows from Derrida's analysis and from Klossowski's narrative presentation is this: what if the space into which the host invites the guest is not his own home (*ethos* in the Heideggerian sense), but rather a neutral space, an in-between place where hospitality can function without violence and without the power of selfhood? Camus, who has probably read Klossowski and who is himself preoccupied with the question of hospitality — is it possible *without violence*, where is it possible? — answers this question in his own way, by going back to it several times, in narratives from *La Peste* to the stories of *L'Exil et le royaume*. It is to these narrative presentations that I turn now briefly, with excursions into the world of the plague, then, into the strange universe of the Growing Stone.

Camus and the Question of Hospitality

In a chapter located some sixty pages before the end of *La Peste*, the narrator (who, we later find out, is also the hero of the narrative, Dr Rieux), depicts a scene in which Rieux joins Tarrou after a visit to the often-visited old asthmatic gentleman, on the rooftops overlooking Oran (*OC*, II, 202–13). It is important to note that we are neither in the dwelling of Rieux nor that of Tarrou, but in a neutral space, in which the two men temporarily shed their workaday identities. Once again, we are in a 'parenthetical' place which is surrounded on both sides by the travails of these men fighting the plague (the final phrase of the chapter states, quite simply: 'il fallait maintenant recommencer' [it was necessary now to begin again], *OC*, II, 213).

During the scene properly speaking, Tarrou tells the story of his childhood, emphasising his father's work as a judge (one thinks here of Clamence before the central moment of *La Chute*, when he does not save a drowning woman and becomes *juge-pénitent*) and his own negative reaction to his father's righteousness and sense of abstraction. According to Tarrou, one cannot participate in death and one must see the concrete everywhere — i.e. actual people, not those categorised as *des condamnés à mort* (those who are condemned to death). The crucial point Tarrou makes as he tells his story is that the plague (cholera then, the COVID-19 pandemic in 2020–22) is 'natural' (*OC*, II, 209), whereas what we consider to be normal, a plague-free world (a world in which killing does not exist) is, in fact, an exception to the rule. Interestingly, once this conversation comes to an end, Tarrou and Rieux, making use of a *laissez-passer*, swim in the sea together, their subjectivities merging in an act of friendship.[13] The climax of the scene, therefore, is not so much the philosophically-dense conversation as the moment outside Time in which the two men join in an act that has nothing to do with the plague surrounding them. Here, Camus seems to be saying that absolute hospitality (what Derrida calls 'hospitalité inconditionnelle') is only possible in a very narrow space, and that it is abolished by the return of the fight against the plague that consumes the protagonists from the start to the finish of the narrative. In *La Peste*, as will be the case later in *La Chute*, hospitality exists in an in-between space (here, on the *terrasses* overlooking Oran, there in the Mexico City bar), but the power of the outside world to impinge upon the inside cannot be overlooked (here, the relentless work to tame the plague will continue, there the panel of *The Just Judges* is in Clamence's apartment only temporarily — the protagonist's hold on the work of art is tenuous at best).

As I conclude, I would like to turn to the sixth and final story of *L'Exil et le royaume*, entitled 'La Pierre qui pousse' (*OC*, IV, 84–111), which, in my view, encapsulates and furthers Camus's examination of the theme of hospitality. This story is not typical of the volume as a whole. First, it takes place neither in North Africa nor in a large European city, but in a Brazilian town called Iguape, a bit up the coast from the Amazon, in the Ribeira valley near São Paulo. Important in the nineteenth century, its influence declined in the twentieth when an ill-conceived effort was made to widen its estuary, but which came to naught. Second, the protagonist, D'Arrast, comes to this remote place in Brazil as representative of colonial France, ostensibly to construct a small dyke whose purpose is to divert the river's waters from the dwelling places of the town's poor. But as the story progresses, the reader finds that, increasingly, the ostensible purpose of D'Arrast's visit fades into the background as he opens himself to this particular new world and to the possibilities it holds for him. The official reason that he is in Brazil (the role he plays as agent of France's *mission civilisatrice*) becomes occluded by the theme of hospitality, which eventually takes over the text. Hospitality, as it is presented here, is unconditional. It occurs in a precise context, but it punctures that context and, like the waters of the river D'Arrast he is here to tame, it flows over its bounds and drowns the text in its message of communal respect.

The narrative set-up for the story of hospitality involves several steps. First, D'Arrast must rid himself of the trappings of the European 'saviour' (like Daru, in 'L'Hôte', he refuses to engage in local politics, in his case he refuses to punish the town's police chief for his rude behaviour); then, he must seek to understand the local people, who speak a different language from his (he communicates in Spanish because he knows no Brazilian Portuguese) and who worship God in a syncretic religion that is different from mainstream Catholicism; and finally, he must meld with them in such a way that, at the end of the *récit*, he carries a large stone in the annual procession and becomes, through his actions, one of them. What is important in this well-delineated narrative (it is longer than the other stories; it needs time to develop the change taking place within the mind of the protagonist) is that D'Arrast develops from self-absorbed engineer to a person whose subjectivity, in flux, changes by the end of the tale.

At the centre of the story is a legend, that of the Growing Stone. One day in the past, a statue of Jesus came from the ocean and went up the river. Fishermen found it, washed it and placed it in a grotto. There, a stone is said to have grown, from which the townspeople cut off fragments each year. The cook of a small vessel running off the coast which went up in flames was able to escape, orienting himself by the dome of the Church of Jesus in Iguape. He made a promise to Jesus that he would carry a stone weighing fifty kilos at the next procession devoted to St George killing the dragon. D'Arrast has arrived in Iguape at the time of this annual procession, and, having met the leading citizens of the town as well as the simple people living in huts below, begins his stay as an outsider, both to local politics and to the ceremonies surrounding the procession, then becomes an insider. He moves from the outer world of the political and of the attempts to master the environment to the inner world of openness to others and to thoughts beyond his own.

'La Pierre qui pousse' is not only a suitable conclusion to *L'Exil et le royaume* because it opens outwards, but it is also a recapitulation. In staging a story based on the overcoming and overflowing of subjective desire by what the narrator calls 'waters' and by the protagonist's ultimate finding of himself within a larger group, it makes one think of Janine in 'La Femme adultère' (who opens herself to 'the water of the night', *OC*, IV, 18) and of Daru in 'L'Hôte'. Indeed, in answering the 'Arab' whom he hosts and who asks him, 'Tu viens avec nous?' [Are you coming with us?], Daru can only respond: 'Je ne sais pas. Pourquoi?' [I don't know. Why?] (*OC*, IV, 54). By contrast, D'Arrast, once he has carried the Growing Stone away from the church to a hut located far below the lodgings of the town's principal citizens, having taken up the stone initially carried by the cook,[14] encounters a small group of people, seated in the middle of their dwelling, who ask him to join their group:

> D'Arrast, debout dans l'ombre, écoutait, sans rien voir, et le bruit des eaux l'emplissait d'un bonheur tumultueux. Les yeux fermés, il saluait joyeusement sa propre force, il saluait, une fois de plus, la vie qui recommençait. [...] Le frère s'écarta un peu du coq et se tournant à demi vers d'Arrast, sans le regarder, lui montra la place vide: 'Assieds-toi avec nous'. (*OC*, IV, 111)

> [D'Arrast, standing in the shadows, listened, without seeing anything, and the noise of the waters filled him with a tumultuous happiness. His eyes shut, he joyfully hailed his own strength, he hailed, once again, life which started over. [...] The brother moved slightly away from the cook and, turning partially towards d'Arrast, without looking at him, showed him the empty place: 'Sit down with us'.]

It may be that absolute hospitality is a tenuous phenomenon at best, it may be that the only way to affirm one's subjectivity is through violence; but if one has shed one's subjectivity, if one has sacrificed oneself for the well-being of others, one might be able to find, in a narrow, constricted space, a sense of non-violent community. This is the place of Hospitality for Camus, the place in which the literary, momentarily, is detached from violence and from the political — in which the literary, briefly, exists, in solitude.

Notes to Chapter 1

1. On this point, see David Carroll's useful and important volume entitled *Albert Camus the Algerian: Colonialism, Terrorism, Justice* (New York: Columbia University Press, 2007). Camus's eliding and non-depiction of Arabs and the Arab world is treated, fictionally, by Kamel Daoud in *Meursault, contre-enquête* (Arles: Actes Sud, 2014), which won the Prix Goncourt du premier roman in 2015. In 2016, Joseph Andras published *De nos frères blessés* (Arles: Actes Sud), which also won the Prix Goncourt du premier roman, that same year, though Andras refused it. In his portrayal of the life and death of Fernand Iveton, *pied-noir* worker and independentist who was guillotined on 11 February 1957, Andras referred liberally to the references contained in *Pour l'exemple, l'affaire Fernand Iveton* (Paris: L'Harmattan, 1986) by Jean-Luc Einaudi.
2. See Albert Camus, *Œuvres complètes*, ed. by Jacqueline Levi-Valensi, Raymond Gay-Crosier and others, 4 vols, Bibliothèque de la Pléiade (Paris: Gallimard, 2006–08), IV, 258. Hereafter referenced as *OC* in the main text. All translations from the French in this essay are mine.
3. Edward J. Hughes, 'Postface', in *The Cambridge Companion to Camus*, ed. by Edward J. Hughes (Cambridge: Cambridge University Press, 2007), pp. 203–09 (p. 208).
4. One of the most eloquently stated formulas of what Camus faced as a writer is to be found in Colin Davis's essay, 'Violence and Ethics in Camus' (in *The Cambridge Companion to Camus*, ed. by Hughes, pp. 106–17). Davis writes: 'Camus's refusal to give legitimacy to violence may be the foundation of the moral stature he has acquired amongst his admirers; but it is also, as his texts constantly remind us both through their depictions of murder and through their suspension

of interpretive certainty, an irrelevance in face of the conviction that violence against the threatening Other is the subject's most fundamental form of self-assertion' (p. 116). The central point I shall be making in the present chapter is that, although the moments of suspended Time, or hospitality, might be considered 'an irrelevance' for a subject who can only affirm himself through violence, they need to be read for what they contain concerning a narrating voice's wish, or desire, to create a space in which one lives without enemies.

5. See Homer, *The Iliad*, trans. by Robert Fagles, ed. by Bernard Knox (London: Penguin, 1990) (all translations of the *Iliad* in this chapter are those of Fagles), pp. 602-11. The original Greek is XXIV.410–691, to be found in *Homeri Opera. Tomus II*, ed. by David B. Munro and Thomas W. Allen, 3rd edn (Oxford: Oxford University Press, 1966). *Homeri Opera* is unpaginated, giving only verse numbers.

6. On this point, see especially Camus's relation to his mother, who was deaf and whose silence he evokes, fictionally, in his earliest published fictional work, *L'Envers et l'endroit* (1937). In the story entitled 'Entre oui et non', he writes: 'Il a pitié de sa mère, est-ce l'aimer? Elle ne l'a jamais caressé puisqu'elle ne saurait pas. [...] Elle ne l'entend pas, car elle est sourde. Tout à l'heure, la vieille [la grand'mère] rentrera, la vie renaîtra: la lumière ronde de la lampe à pétrole, la toile cirée, les cris, les gros mots. Mais maintenant, ce silence marque *un temps d'arrêt*, un instant démesuré' [He pities his mother, is that to love her? She has never caressed him because she wouldn't know how. [...] She doesn't hear him, because she is deaf. A bit later, the old woman [the grandmother] will come back, and life will be reborn: the round light of the gas lamp, the oil-cloth, the cries, the swear-words. But now, this silence acts *as a pause*, a moment of excess] (*OC*, I, 49–50; my emphasis). One can see, even in this early work, that Camus was fascinated with the notion of the *temps d'arrêt*, that moment in which Time itself is abolished, that moment of excess caught in an in-between which he will develop, with greater mastery, in 'L'Hôte'.

7. See *Homeri Opera*, II (XXIV.629 and 631).

8. See *A Lexicon, Abridged from Liddell and Scott's Greek-English Lexicon* (Oxford: Oxford University Press, 1966), p. 312.

9. The best way for the novice to examine this question is to look at the dossier called 'Hospitalité: choix de textes pour les enseignants' <www.histoire-immigration.fr/sites/default/files/musee-numerique/documents/ext_media_fichier_790_fiche3-textes-profs.pdf> [accessed November 2021]. This thirty-six-page digital document, group-edited by the Centre national de l'histoire de l'immigration, contains a good overview of the ways in which the theme of hospitality has been treated in the West since Homer (though, curiously, it does not contain an allusion to the scene from the *Iliad* that I analysed briefly). Most important to my argument will be the distinction made by Jacques Derrida between 'hospitalité conditionnelle' and 'hospitalité inconditionnelle'.

10. Pierre Klossowski, *Les Lois de l'hospitalité* (Paris: Gallimard, 2009), pp. 105–73 (p. 107).

11. Ibid., p. 110.

12. See Jacques Derrida and Anne Dufourmantelle, *Anne Dufourmantelle invite Jacques Derrida à répondre: de l'hospitalité* (Paris: Calmann-Lévy, 1997), pp. 131, 133.

13. The theme of friendship is a major one in Camus's writings. The degree to which he read and engaged with Maurice Blanchot remains a matter for debate. But Blanchot read Camus, and Blanchot is the author of some of the more beautiful statements on the reciprocity of friendship that exists in French literature since Montaigne. See for example, *L'Amitié* (Paris: Gallimard, 1971), which is a testimony to his friendship for Georges Bataille and which contains, as an exergue, the following quoted passage from Bataille: 'amis jusqu'à cet état d'amitié profonde où un homme abandonné, abandonné de tous ses amis, rencontre dans la vie celui qui l'accompagnera au-delà de la vie, lui-même sans vie, capable de l'amitié libre, détachée de tous liens' [friends up to this state of profound friendship where an abandoned man, abandoned by all his friends, meets in life that one person who will accompany him beyond life, himself without life, capable of free friendship, a friendship unmoored of all relations] (p. 7).

14. The procession of the Growing Stone recalls the Stations of the Cross, with the cook standing for Jesus and D'Arrast for Simon of Cyrene, who assists Jesus in the carrying of the cross. As in *La Chute*, Camus uses Christian imagery to buttress his humanistic ideas.

CHAPTER 2

Camus's Travel Writing, or The Road to Pamina

Peter Dunwoodie

'Voyager,' wrote Céline, 'c'est bien utile, ça fait travailler l'imagination. Tout le reste n'est que déceptions et fatigues' [Travelling is really useful, it gets the imagination working. The rest is just disappointment and dreariness].[1] Camus would probably have disagreed. He travelled relatively little: Algeria and one or two countries in central Europe in the 1930s; sponsored trips to New York (and Canada) in 1946, Latin America in 1949; Holland, Italy, Greece in the 1950s. Few readers would associate him with the category 'travel writer', even though the genre — and its neighbours, journalism and cultural history — is notoriously open-ended and resistant to definition.[2] Even 'Amérique du Sud', the longest text immediately classifiable as travel writing, was archived separately according to his editor Roger Quilliot who felt that Camus had clearly wondered about what use to make of it. Were the two texts finally brought together in the 1970s as *Journaux de voyage*, 'New York' and 'Amérique du Sud', intended for publication? Were they, indeed, unfinished, as Quilliot suggested? And if so, were they to retain the 'journal de bord' or diary format in which they were left? These remain unanswerable questions, of course.

Yet when one revisits Camus's journalistic reporting of a trip to Kabylia in 1939 (for the newspaper *Alger Républicain*), the seminal role of specific sites and the reflexions on travel in autobiographical literary pieces brought together in *L'Envers et l'endroit* (1937), *Noces* (1939) or *L'Été* (1954), the day-to-day immersion recorded at times in his *Carnets*, the transposition of travel material into fiction in *L'Exil et le royaume* (1957) or *La Mort heureuse* (1971), it is clear that travel is neither an adjunct nor a marginal topic to be treated as merely context or catalyst for more central tropes. Hence, in reassessing some of these texts, the aim is not simply to review what Camus saw or felt when travelling, but to examine, across the range of genres involved (essay, diary, notebooks, correspondence) some of the features of his practice. How does he mix the experiential with the intertextual or ethnographic? What is targeted when he admits that he is 'fatigué de noter des riens' [tired of recording insignificant things]: outer reality, subjective experience?[3] In the New York pages of *Journaux de voyage* his initial, brutally negative reaction is immediately qualified by 'mais je sais qu'on change d'avis' [but I realise one's opinion can change] (*OC*, II, 1052): (how) do the texts handle such a shift of perspective? In short, the analysis will focus on his approach to the selection and narrativisation of travel material, as developed between the two poles identified in the *Carnets* as inherent in all travel, *ascèse* and *plaisir* [asceticism, pleasure].

The travel genre will be understood as the first-hand non-fictional account of the (always mediated) exposure of the author to places previously unfamiliar, recording the transformation of experience into text. While far from covering all the features of such a Protean genre (epistemological for example), the approach will help us appreciate both his deployment of some of the salient characteristics of travel writing and its function in Camus's *œuvre*, and encourage future connections and comparisons. It will become clear from the outset that travel (and writing thereon) was for Camus not an end in itself, not, to use Dennis Porter's terms, a 'protracted act of understanding' designed to better apprehend the Other.[4] It always has a highly personal dimension, on the contrary, and its primary function can be summarised as one of defamiliarisation. This is at the heart of Camus's reflections in parts of his pre-war essays, while in the post-war texts the autobiographical character of the diary form foregrounds the immediacy of personal, destabilising experiences triggered by travel. While, as Carl Thompson for instance shows, normally 'all journeys are [...] a confrontation with, or more optimistically a negotiation of, what is sometimes termed alterity',[5] this scarcely fits Camus's experience where the other is actually closer to what Julia Kristeva terms 'l'étranger [qui] nous habite, il est la face cachée de notre identité' [the stranger [who] lives within us, he is the hidden face of our identity].[6] And crossing paths with this self-as-other, as *Le Mythe de Sisyphe* demonstrates, can be simultaneously the end and the beginning of a journey: 'l'étranger qui, à certaines secondes, vient à notre rencontre dans une glace, le frère familier et pourtant inquiétant que nous retrouvons dans nos propres photographies, c'est encore l'absurde' [the stranger who, at a given moment, comes to meet us in a mirror, the familiar and yet disturbing brother that we rediscover in photographs of ourselves, that too is the absurd] (*OC*, I, 229).

Camus's essays — *L'Envers et l'endroit*, *Noces*, *L'Été* — develop an extended retrospective reflexion on the use and effects of travel as one of the triggers for that destabilising experience. These early autobiographical texts cover multiple locations/destinations, ranging from Camus's *quartier* in Algiers to trips to the Balearic Islands and central Europe; and they link the time of writing to multiple timeframes, from 'this evening' or 'now', to 'not long ago' or 'two years ago'. Camus had actually travelled relatively little at this stage, yet the narrator strikes a pose with aphoristic pronouncements ('tout pays où je ne m'ennuie pas est un pays qui ne m'apprend rien' [a country where I am not bored is a country that teaches me nothing], *OC*, I, 42), or blasé, world-weary ones à la Oscar Wilde ('sans les cafés et les journaux, il serait difficile de voyager' [were it not for cafes and newspapers, travel would be tedious], *OC*, I, 57). Similarly, he adopts a stance of ironic distance from the conventional traveller, implicitly seen as docile consumer of the circuit of churches, palaces and museums that are the staple of any guidebook. He claims instead (in pieces that record visits to Prague and Palma) that such activities not only fail to open onto something new — especially when packaged in that way — but fail to keep at bay the existential experience said to be inherent in travel itself, namely an unsettling cohabitation, then confrontation, not with the world outside but with the self. The initial experience of the unease generated by this enforced self-awareness is recorded firstly in 'La Mort dans l'âme' where he also stresses that it is taken from a text written *in situ* (hence supposedly spontaneous, unguarded) and now copied word for word: 'quel autre profit vouloir tirer du voyage? Me voici sans parure' [what other benefit is there in travel? I am now unadorned] (*OC*, I, 57). Then again, in 'Amour de vivre' [Love of Life]: 'Ce qui fait le prix du voyage, c'est la peur. Il brise en nous une sorte de décor intérieur' [What makes travel worthwhile is fear. It shatters within us a sort of inner stage-set] (*OC*, I, 65).[7] Stripped of both a familiar, protective support network and engrossing *divertissements*, the traveller is 'face à face avec lui-même. Je le défie d'être heureux... Et c'est pourtant par là que le voyage l'illumine' [face to face with himself. I challenge him to feel happy... And yet that is how travel enlightens him] (*OC*, I, 57). Instead of absorption in what is outside, Camus's autobiographical story is that of a traveller embroiled in introspection. What is 'revealed' is a mind in turmoil, for whom the outside world is merely an echo-chamber for the self, amplifying the 'panique', 'inquiétude', 'torpeur', 'peur', 'âme malade' [panic, anxiety, lethargy, fear, soul-sickness] that permeate the text and record the traveller's collapse and blank withdrawal into the protective shell of a banal hotel room.

While the diary format chosen for the Latin American travelogue in 1949 (and published in *Journaux de voyage* in 1978) could obviously not accommodate such lengthy musings, it does chart a similarly deeply personal journey of physical and psychological collapse in the midst of the sponsored public *tournée*. To achieve this, it weaves a double temporality: on the surface, marked by dates and times of day, necessarily incomplete and fragmentary, the collage of people, places, movement, light and noise, the slow motion of time suspended during the crossing, followed by the accelerated, demented rhythm of the cities, and then suspended again in the lengthy descriptions of exoticised practices like the *macumba, bomba-menboi, candomblé* or Iguape festivities — practices that no tourist guide would ignore and clearly the sort of 'events' that the diary was intended to record.[8] But now, shadowing surface time, there is also a private continuum, starkly noted through dates and times, but one which is only tangentially related to external events, tracking instead an inexorable descent through insomnia, fatigue, flu and fever into depression and, in Camus's terms, a 'débâcle psychologique' (*OC*, IV, 1048).[9] Whereas 'La Mort dans l'âme' retraced the collapse retrospectively (and thus implied the traveller-narrator's recovery), the Latin-American diary mapped the day-to-day stages of a mental and emotional *descente aux enfers* which is graphically summarised in the sentence that brutally shuts it down: 'Le voyage se termine dans un cercueil métallique entre un médecin fou et un diplomate, vers Paris' [The trip is ending in a metal coffin between a deranged doctor and a diplomat, destination Paris] (*OC*, IV, 1056).[10]

Camus clearly found the diary or *journal de bord* format both convenient and constraining when travelling, and in both the *Journaux de voyage* and his *Carnets* there are recurrent references to dates, to the moments of writing and working (in cabin, hotel room or aeroplane), to entries used to catch up on 'forgotten' events, to revising text, to moments when an entry could have been extended or has been abandoned and, occasionally, to lassitude at the inanity of such jottings. Thanks to the diary form the reader is exposed to a mix of immediacy and discontinuity, a fragmented narrative that is at best a collage of impressions — of both people and places — jotted down on the spur of the moment, hence one that eschews elaboration or the overtly ethnographic. The 1940s trips to North and South America are both recorded using this technique of brief, seemingly truncated notes, and the position of uninvolved spectator that the narrator calls on will be illustrated by a brief contrastive reading of the first few pages of a contemporary first-person travel text by Camus's friend Simone de Beauvoir, also recording a visit to the USA in 1947.[11]

By the 1940s the USA was not unknown to Camus's generation, and its direct impact was perhaps best summarised by Sartre in a piece for *The Atlantic Monthly* in August 1946:

> The greatest literary development in France between 1929 and 1939 was the discovery of Faulkner, Dos Passos, Hemingway, Caldwell, and Steinbeck. [...] At once, for thousands of young intellectuals the American novel took its place together with jazz and the movies, among the best of the importations from the United States.[12]

Or, put more flippantly in *Les Mots*, his willingness to drop Wittgenstein in favour of the American crime fiction in Gallimard's 'Série Noire' (directed by Marcel Duhamel)! By 1945/46, when the Direction générale des affaires culturelles at the Quai d'Orsay offered to finance Camus's trip it was the high-profile journalist of the Resistance newspaper *Combat* rather than the author of *L'Étranger* that they had in mind, as part of a programme which saw Sartre, Beauvoir, Caillois and others visit the States as a new generation at the forefront of a French revival — visits recorded in Sartre's long series of articles for *Le Figaro* between January and March 1945, or Beauvoir's *L'Amérique au jour le jour*, published in 1948. In financing such trips the Quai d'Orsay and the State Department were already embarked on a post-war cultural battle between the US and Europe, all the more effective perhaps because when publishers like Alfred A. Knopf introduced the contemporary French novel to cultured circles in post-war America, they were promoting writers who had themselves enthusiastically embraced American techniques when revolutionising French fiction: Beauvoir's use of interior monologue and disrupted temporalities in *Le Sang des autres* is well documented, along with the discontinuities and objective or impersonal style in Camus's *L'Étranger*, Sartre's radical use of simultaneity in *Le Sursis*, or the simple, direct and unanalytical prose of Robert Merle's *Week-end à Zuydcoote*.[13] It is clear that American writers, frequently translated in the 1930s — even those, as Beauvoir records, who were usually met with disdain by her American interlocutors — brought to the French cultural world not just a vision of social and metaphysical alienation but innovations in style and technique with which to articulate it.[14] Culturally, then, this could be seen as familiar territory, shaping the 'textual attitude' of the day for these immediate post-war travellers; and the conventional log-book format that Camus adopted helps us to appreciate how his account of the encounter on-the-ground made dispassionate but personal use of that complex set of contemporary commonplaces and cultural presuppositions.[15]

Beauvoir's *L'Amérique au jour le jour*, published after a four-month trip in 1947, can thus provide an interesting comparison. The 'gigantesques dominos de pierre et de lumière' [gigantic domino pieces of stone and light], traffic 'sur une chaussée feutrée' [on a muffled road surface], unfamiliar coins, a public telephone that she cannot operate... numerous details like these are recounted throughout as encounters that Beauvoir is forced to deal with; and she is conscious of both the resistance and the banal self-sufficiency of such material, seen as 'autre', 'autonome', 'séparé' [other, autonomous, separate]. She recounts such everyday contact as unsettling yet exhilarating, because even the images of the USA mediated through film in the comfort of a Paris cinema (a major leitmotif), through novels or illustrated magazines, prove to be disconcerting because what was previously deemed clichéd is turning out to be demonstrably 'true': 'Ce n'était pas un mirage. New York est là, tout est vrai. [...] Tout m'émerveille, aussi bien les visions imprévues et celles que je prévoyais' [It wasn't a mirage. New York is there, it's all true. [...] I'm astonished by it all, the unexpected sights just as much as the ones I'd foreseen] (*L'Amérique*, pp. 19, 25).[16] Beauvoir consciously embraced that mix of novelty and mediated familiarity, aware that on the contrary 'voyager [d'ordinaire] c'est tenter d'annexer à [son] univers un objet neuf' [to travel [normally] is to seek to annex the new for one's own world] (*L'Amérique*, p. 14) via a more or less defensive and reductive comparison with (the comfort of) the already-known. In the *Journaux de voyage*, on the contrary, Camus shows little sign of acknowledgement either of an encounter with novelty or of vicarious knowledge that might then be confirmed or corrected. Instead, the dominant tone colouring his evocations of people, places or events is more *désabusé* (and, frequently, indifferent) than amused, bemused or excited. Significantly, on the rare occasions when his texts do establish a juxtaposition unknown-known, the process refers back not, as could be expected, to France (apart from the weather in Seine et Oise, the rue Sainte Honoré and the Porte d'Orléans, or the mimosas of Menton) but to Algeria, Palma de Mallorca, the Casbah, Oran or *maisons mauresques* [Moorish dwellings].[17] These function perhaps as comforting emotional havens that avoid reference to Paris and the part it was playing in the personal collapse that, as we shall see, infuses, then submerges, the 1940s texts. Far from the well-established discourse of discovery or adventure (or the playful/ironic querying thereof common in twentieth-century accounts), the traveller-narrator of the New York section of *Journaux de voyage*, for instance, strikes the reader as markedly unenthusiastic, recording a 'spectacle qui ne [le] touche pas' [a spectacle that leaves [him] unmoved] (*OC*, II, 1052). What Camus terms 'curiosity' does not even last the trip (*OC*, II, 1059), his account fading at times into a feeling that some entries could be developed, 'mais à quoi bon?' [but why bother], and ending somewhat bathetically in a 'bizarre sentiment d'éloignement' [an odd feeling of detachment] (*OC*, II, 1061, 1062). The 'légère angoisse' [slight anxiety] (*OC*, II, 1046) that the incipit claims is part of every departure permeates the text,[18] and a horizon always 'lourd', 'monotone', 'sale', 'cafardeux' [heavy, monotonous, grimy, depressing] positions Camus as reluctant anti-traveller, emerging at the end from a 'désert de fer et de ciment' [a desert of iron and cement] (*OC*, II, 1062) — far removed, in short, from the 'ville debout [...] bien raide [...] raide à faire peur' [vertical city [...] rigid [...] frighteningly rigid] of Céline's Bardamu, the 'ville légère, éphémère' [light, ephemeral city] that Sartre described in *Situations III* or Beauvoir's 'New York qui est partout et nulle part' [New York which is everywhere and nowhere] (*L'Amérique*, p. 37).[19]

Most travel writing is made up of a variable mix of personal reportage and socio-cultural enquiry, increasingly intertwined in the twentieth century with reflexions on seer-seen relations and the changes wrought by the experience. This was a model reproduced in Beauvoir's text, allowing her to map the evolution of her view of the USA, recording and commenting on the stages in a process of discovery and (re-)assessment. Camus's travelogues, on the other hand, are obviously too short and monologic (and the Latin American one too disruptive) to allow such a mix. Camus's declared intention was to keep a diary 'sans rien dire d'intime, mais en n'oubliant rien des événements de la journée' [revealing nothing personal, but forgetting none of the day's events] (*OC*, IV, 1008). This focus, while resolutely turned to the contingencies of the outside world, is not that of a would-be chronicler or ethnographer, nevertheless, since it is actually interspersed with the subjective, as implemented in his account of the New York trip for instance. Whereas his pages on the crossing centred on his fellow travellers, via portraits and anecdotes, the role of viewer-assessor is announced on arrival, and it will dominate throughout the trip: 'spectacle formidable [...] admirable inhumanité [...] Au premier regard, hideuse ville inhumaine' [incredible spectacle [...] admirably inhuman [...] At first sight, awful inhuman city] (*OC*, II, 1052). In short, immediate confrontation with a display of a modernity deemed alienating — summarised as order, power, economic strength — and registered through an account that rarely gets beyond brief observation, impressions, at best lukewarm acknowledgment of an occasional 'good time' (*OC*, II, 1055) or 'surprising night' (*OC*, II, 1057). Refusing to be taken in by New York as spectacle, Camus deprives urban icons like the Empire State Building or Times Square of their metonymical function, as condensations of the 'new world' and the dominant American 'success story'. Instead, 'cafardeux', 'emmerdant', 'ennui', 'éloignement' [depressing, annoying, boredom, distance] are the terms most frequently appended to the jaundiced record of most visits or encounters, in a diary that is still anchored mentally in the Europe left behind, as revealed by the way it registers the shock of the contrast between the 'five years of darkness' or ruined buildings of war-torn Europe and the 'orgy of bright lights' and skyscrapers of Manhattan (*OC*, II, 1052). Clearly it registers not immersion, which could have encouraged exchange, but dispassionate assessment, filtered through the ideological lens via which Camus judged the American capitalist juggernaut. This explains, perhaps, why a significant number of the sites visited and anecdotes recounted prove to be not clichéd components in a New York tourist tour (or a supposedly racier 'New York by night') but selected glimpses of America's underbelly, concrete sites of extreme poverty, inequality and racism.[20]

While it is hard to conclude that Camus's view evolved — despite his opening admission 'mais je sais qu'on change d'avis' [but I realise one's opinion can change] (*OC*, II, 1052) — shifts of perspective do occasionally intervene where positive personal experiences are singled out amidst the urban cacophony, social chatter and frenetic schedules. But they are no doubt recorded precisely because they are welcomed as radical alternatives that allow the traveller, however briefly, to enter spaces that either have a concrete human dimension (beyond the social façade or protocol that Camus abhorred) or facilitate a salutary withdrawal or stillness: China Town, 'la vraie vie pullulante et mesurée que j'aime' [the real life I like, teeming and measured]; the poverty of the Bowery, 'enfin le concret' [the real at last]; 'la vie, la passion et la nostalgie' [the energy, passion and nostalgia] of African-Americans; or Cape Diamond in Quebec (*OC*, II, 1056, 1057, 1059).[21] The Latin American trip in 1949 would also provide a few episodes in which the impersonal onrush of events and places gives way, momentarily, to fraternity and intimacy: an encounter in Rio with a Spanish Republican exile; Recife; or a little garden in Iguape. Other moments, less explicit but no less positive, are recorded via what is in effect a staple of travel writing, the elevated position from which the traveller can stand back and survey the unfamiliar vista. In New York, for instance, when momentarily extracted from the towering built environment and the urban/social noise, temporal suspension and spatial distance take over: 'Above Harlem', 'from the roof of the Plaza', 'from the top of the Empire States [*sic*]', 'the Bowery. And the *elevated* [*sic*]', 'from way above Riverside'.[22] On the Latin American trip: the mountains around Rio or Térésopolis, 'la tendresse, la nostalgie à peine farouche' [the tenderness, the barely timid nostalgia] of an evening sky, the bay of Bahia from a hotel window, 'ronde et pure, pleine d'un étrange silence' [curved and pure, filled with a strange silence] (*OC*, IV, 1022, 1033). These are similar moments of withdrawal, but now explicitly infused with harmony and wellbeing, in what is otherwise largely an experience of discomfort (tracks, forest, heat, dust etc.) where 'la nature suffoque l'homme' [man is smothered by nature] (*OC*, IV, 1027). The experiences were later reworked as fiction for *L'Exil et le royaume*, in the Brazil of 'La Pierre qui pousse' and an oasis town of the Algerian interior in 'La Femme adultère', when the local reality (bush and desert) that has been experienced by the traveller as harsh and forbidding gives way to fantasy, of entry into a family community for the former, of an exoticised nomadic way of life for the latter.[23]

★ ★ ★ ★ ★

Travel also supplied the antidote, however, but it did so in a way that exemplifies the systematic inversion of the traditional narrative, in which the traveller normally reaches, glimpses or falters on the threshold of fantasy lands like Arcadia.

If the land- and seascapes that populate Camus's writings — and that he terms in *Noces* 'lieux privilégiés' [privileged sites] (*OC*, I, 117) — can be approached as a (compensatory) cartography of desire, it is because the selected locations have little to do with orthodox maps and 'elsewhere' (*l'ailleurs*). They form instead a psycho-geographical construct, a utopian and intensely life-enhancing, 'Mediterranean' (made up primarily of Greece, Italy, Algeria) at the centre of Camus's *œuvre*.[24] In this highly personal mapping, travel 'out' is expulsion or exile, as we have seen; while travel 'in' is always lived as a return, a homecoming, whether to his birthplace, Algeria, or to the unbounded 'Mediterranean', as many of his texts reiterate. The incipit of 'Entre oui et non' provides the earliest formulation of this key trope: 'S'il est vrai que les seuls paradis sont ceux qu'on a perdus, je sais nommer ce quelque chose [...] qui m'habite aujourd'hui. Un émigrant revient dans sa patrie' [If it is true that our only paradises are those we have lost, I know how to describe the feeling [...] that fills me today. An emigrant returning to his *patrie*] (*OC*, I, 47). The essay then returns to it twice when the narrator is back in Algiers, via the repetition of 'et me voici rapatrié' [and I'm in my *patrie* once again] (*OC*, I, 47, 48). In 'La Mort dans l'âme' he notes: 'J'entre en Italie. Terre faite à mon âme' [I enter Italy. Land close to my soul] (*OC*, I, 160).[25] And in his *Carnets* of 1955, when waking in Athens on the first morning of an extended trip to Greece: 'Sentiment étrange pendant toute la matinée d'être ici depuis des années, chez moi d'ailleurs. [...] En montant à l'Acropole [...] je constate que j'y vais "en voisin", sans une émotion' [Odd feeling the whole morning of being here for years, at home really. [...] On the way up to the Acropolis [...] I realise that I am going 'as a neighbour', without any emotion] (*OC*, IV, 1221). All notion of an elsewhere yet to be 'discovered' is excluded in favour of a daily account of a simple and joyous immersion (*jouissance*) in a natural world condensed into light, sea and colour in which the primacy of the Mediterranean world is repeatedly proclaimed. The museums, galleries or ruins dismissed as tourist fodder and *divertissement* in the pre-war essay now metamorphose into auratic sites of maximum intensity where, for example, the 'prodigieuse audace' of the architects of the Acropolis is said to meet the 'prodigieuse extravagance' of nature: 'Ce n'est pas le Parthénon qu'ils ont construit mais l'espace lui-même et dans des perspectives délirantes' [It is not the Parthenon they built but space itself, and on a fabulous scale] (*OC*, IV, 1224). The concentration of superlatives in these travel notes is unique in Camus's *œuvre* and the 'espace et vastitude' [space and vastness] (*OC*, IV, 1223) viewed from promontories or cliffs, from the fortress at Mycenae or the theatre of Epidaurus dwarf the escapist fantasy destinations at the heart of much European travel writing, like Java, Cipango or Sumatra (*OC*, IV, 1195, 1196, 1231). They allow instead total immersion in a place and time that the returnee experiences as a 'second revelation, a rebirth' (*OC*, IV, 1231).[26] Insofar as each site has to be left behind, at this point in space/time, for the journey to continue, the text also registers the traveller's awareness of being uprooted: 'Difficile de m'arracher à ces lieux, les premiers depuis Tipasa où j'ai connu un abandon de tout l'être' [Hard to tear myself away from these sites, the first since Tipasa where my whole being was able to surrender] (*OC*, IV, 1211).[27] That experience, recorded in the youthfully lyrical 'Noces à Tipasa', recurs in 'Retour à Tipasa' (1953), which links it to both a visit amidst the barbed wire of the immediate post-war and the current trip. This explicit 'return' proclaims the privileged status of this *locus amœnus* at the joyful centre of the traveller's imaginary, untouched by time or temporary vicissitudes: 'Il me semblait que j'étais enfin revenu au port, pour un instant au moins, et que cet instant désormais n'en finirait plus' [It seemed to me that I had returned to port at last, for a moment at least, and that henceforth the moment would never end] (*OC*, III, 612).

It is typical of Camus's humour that one of the most succinct formulations of the tension between routes and roots, of the path back to moments of salutary and expansive fusion and belonging like those among the ruins of Tipasa, is appended to an ironic pastiche of the tourist guide (for Algiers, Oran and Constantine). In *L'Été* (1947), a 'Petit guide pour des villes sans passé' exhorts a motley collection of travellers (from the aesthete to newly-weds) to opt for safer destinations, but has playful advice for others (if 'still young' or 'sensitive'). Like a depository of *Guide Bleu* commonplaces, it lightly twins picturesque ('ville arabe', 'village nègre', 'quartier juif') and practical (where to eat, drink or hear local music) before dismissing them in favour of a message of life at its simplest (hence most meaningful) in a 'desert' said to resemble Spain stripped of its past and all *divertissement*: 'Etant né dans ce désert, je ne puis songer [...] à en parler comme un visiteur' [Having been born in this desert, I cannot imagine [...] talking about it like a visitor'] (*OC*, III, 194). Unable to stand 'outside', his perspective is necessarily that of the insider for whom, as he claims in 'L'Exil d'Hélène', 'elsewhere' is synonymous with separation, hence loss, in an unequal contest between the lived vitality and 'tragique solaire' [solar tragedy] (*OC*, III, 197) of the Mediterranean and the baneful mists beyond.[28] This spatio-cultural division (the much-discussed 'exile and kingdom') remains firmly anchored in a binary model, opposing a valorised here (light, sensual and fraternal) and a devalued elsewhere (dark, rationalist and history-bound). But such antimonies actually fade once the traveller is back home in the 'Mediterranean', lived as process rather than place, a permanent, joyous immersion fed by the 'goût triomphant de la vie' [triumphant taste for life].[29]

Spontaneous diary entries in the *Carnets* of autumn 1958 reveal Camus's final Mediterranean haven: Provence and, more particularly, the Luberon 'où [il se sent] soudain abrité et pacifié' [where he feels suddenly sheltered and at peace] (*OC*, IV, 1289). Here the pull of fixity and permanence dissipates the *arrachement* [uprooting] that coloured the inevitable end of the joyous experiences triggered or intensified by travel, whether within Algeria, Italy or, more especially, Greece. The record of a simple shared moment with a close friend effectively links all these auratic sites via immersion in light and space: 'grande promenade avec R[ené] C[har] sur la route des crêtes du Luberon. La violente lumière, l'espace infini me transportent. À nouveau je voudrais vivre ici, trouver la maison qui me convient, me fixer un peu enfin' [long walk with RC on the path along the top of the Luberon. Carried away by the harsh light, the boundless space. Yet again I would like to live here, find a suitable house, settle down a bit finally] (*OC*, IV, 1289–90). And letters to Maria Casarès in 1959, equally spontaneous, express the stark, undemanding simplicity of that need to feel at home envisaged at the end of the road — and that he was seeking at the time to record in the (unfinished) novel *Le Premier homme*:

> Pamina (c'est la bourrique de Catherine) [...] se prélasse à Lourmarin. Elle se prélasse même sur les pétunias que j'avais fait repiquer en juin. Je ne sais pourquoi, la pensée que j'ai un âne en toute propriété me réjouit le cœur.[30]

[Pamina (Catherine's donkey) [...] is stretched out here in Lourmarin. She's even stretched out among the petunias I had transplanted in June. I don't know why, but I'm delighted at the idea that I'm the proud owner of a donkey.]

Camus, clearly, had never really wished to be 'elsewhere'.

Notes to Chapter 2

1. Louis-Ferdinand Céline, *Voyage au bout de la nuit* (Paris: Gallimard, 1952), p. 12. All translations from the French in this essay are mine.
2. See for instance Sara Mills, *Discourses of Difference: An Analysis of Women's Travel Writing and Colonialism* (London & New York: Routledge, 1991); Mary Louise Pratt, *Imperial Eyes: Travel Writing and Transculturation* (London: Routledge, 1992); James Buzard, *The Beaten Track: European Tourism, Literature, and the Ways to 'Culture', 1800–1918* (Oxford: Clarendon Press, 1993); Charles Forsdick, Feroza Basu and Siobhán Shilton, *New Approaches to Twentieth-Century Travel Literature in French: Genre, History, Theory* (Bern & Oxford: Peter Lang, 2006); *Travel Writing, Form, and Empire: The Poetics and Politics of Mobility*, ed. by Julia Kuehn and Paul Smethurst (New York: Routledge, 2008).
3. Albert Camus, *Œuvres complètes*, ed. by Jacqueline Lévi-Valensi, Raymond Gay-Crosier and others, 4 vols, Bibliothèque de la Pléiade (Paris: Gallimard, 2006–08), IV, 1039. Hereafter referenced as *OC* in the main text.
4. Dennis Porter, *Haunted Journeys: Desire and Transgression in European Travel Writing* (Princeton, NJ: Princeton University Press, 1991), p. 3.
5. Carl Thompson, *Travel Writing* (London: Routledge, 2011), p. 9.
6. Julia Kristeva, 'Réflexions sur l'étranger', Collège des Bernardins, 1 October 2014 <http://kristeva.fr/reflexions-sur-l-etranger.html> [accessed November 2021].
7. The trip to the Balearic Islands (Palma) took place in 1935; to Prague and central Europe in 1936, when his first marriage was breaking down.
8. Camus's ambivalence is simply put in a letter to Maria Casarès: 'J'en suis sorti plein d'horreur et d'attrait' [I emerged both horrified and attracted]. Albert Camus and Maria Casarès, *Correspondance 1944–1959*, ed. by Béatrice Vaillant (Paris: Gallimard, 2017), p. 130.
9. His letters to Maria Casarès reveal the extent to which the trip had become unwelcome, an unbearable 'separation' (Camus and Casarès, *Correspondance*, p. 109), and one which impacts the entire travelogue: 'Jusqu'aujourd'hui je n'ai écrit que dans mon journal — mais je l'ai fait fidèlement chaque soir [...]. Je n'y ai rien mis que le détail de chaque jour d'une vie monotone, mais je n'ai rien écrit que pour toi, dirigé vers toi, coloré par toi' ['Til now I've written only in my diary — but I have done so faithfully each evening [...]. I have noted only the daily details of a monotonous existence, but I have written everything for you, with you in mind, filtered through you] (p. 115).
10. The sepulchral metaphor already has a central role in the reworked material of 'Pluies de New York' (1947) where, 'dans la brume grise, les gratte-ciel devenus blanchâtres se dressent comme les gigantesques sépulcres d'une ville de morts' [in the grey mist, the skyscrapers, now whitish, rear up like the gigantic sepulchres of a city of the dead] (*OC*, II, 1062).
11. Simone de Beauvoir, *L'Amérique au jour le jour* [1948] (Paris: Gallimard, 1997). Hereafter referenced as *L'Amérique* in the main text.
12. Jean-Paul Sartre, 'American Novelists in French Eyes', *The Atlantic Monthly* (August 1946), 114–17.
13. See Jean-Paul Sartre, *Situations I* (Paris: Gallimard, 1943): essays on Faulkner, Dos Passos and Camus. 1940s' studies include Jean Bruneau, 'Existentialism and the American Novel', *Yale French Studies*, 1 (1948), 66–72; Sartre, 'American Novelists in French Eyes'; Claude-Edmonde Magny, *L'Age du roman américain* (Paris: Seuil, 1948). Critical analyses of the impact on French artists and intellectuals have included Philip Thody, 'A Note on Camus and the American Novel', *Comparative Literature*, 9.3 (1957), 243–49; John Cruickshank, 'The Novel in France since 1945', *Critical Survey*, 1.2 (1963), 65–69; Claire Gorrara, 'Cultural Intersections: The American

Hard-boiled Detective Novel and Early French *roman noir*', *Modern Language Review*, 98.3 (2003), 590–601.
14. French translations of US authors in the 1930s were often published with prefaces by prominent French writers including André Malraux, Jean Prévost, André Maurois, Raymond Queneau and Marcel Duhamel, among others.
15. Edward Said, *Orientalism* [1978] (London: Penguin, 2003), p. 92.
16. Beauvoir's text is enthusiastically intertextual and, in referencing Chateaubriand in response to her first disappointment (the Niagara Falls) for instance, she draws attention to the interplay of cultural baggage and present perception (*L'Amérique*, pp. 117–20).
17. Palma de Mallorca was central to 'Amour de vivre' in *L'Envers et l'endroit*.
18. Camus's anxiety is confirmed in a letter to Maria Casarès prior to his departure. See Camus and Casarès, *Correspondance 1944–1959*, p. 109.
19. Céline, *Voyage au bout de la nuit*, pp. 236–37. Jean-Paul Sartre, *Situations III* (Paris: Gallimard, 1949), p. 121.
20. Beauvoir's pleasure at the 'American dream' was repeatedly tempered by evidence of gross inequality, poverty and prejudice. The Bowery in New York and the slaughterhouses of Chicago are key examples.
21. In an informative article on 'Le Québec et Camus', Vincent Grégoire explains the political issues affecting Camus's visit and the 'effet de miroir' [mirror effect] which linked settlement in Quebec and Algeria (*French Review*, 84.6 (May 2011), 1214–29).
22. One elevated position instils unease, that of Camus as upper-deck passenger en route for Rio, looking down on the passengers 'logés dans l'entrepont dans des couchettes superposées, style concentrationnaire' [housed in steerage in tiered bunks, concentration-camp style] (*OC*, IV, 1008). The simile evokes brutal recent images, but reflexions in the two texts show that his sensitivity to journeys of settler emigration to Latin America or Canada (and, by implication, Algeria) loom large too.
23. The exoticism in both remains a display of alterity, showing that travel does little to reduce estrangement (*dépaysement*). See Jean Andreu, 'Un rendez-vous manqué: le voyage d'Albert Camus en Amérique du Sud (1949)', *Caravelle*, 58 (1992), 79–97.
24. Spain too, but Camus refused to travel there as long as Franco remained in power.
25. The *Carnets* of 1954 make the north-south, exile-kingdom contrast explicit: 'Il y a des villes comme Florence, les petites villes toscanes ou espagnoles, qui portent le voyageur, le soutiennent à chaque pas et rendent sa démarche plus légère. D'autres qui pèsent tout de suite sur ses épaules et l'écrasent, comme New York' [There are towns like Florence, little towns of Tuscany or Spain, where the traveller is borne along, where they support each step and lighten his movements. Others that weigh immediately on his shoulders and crush him, like New York] (*OC*, IV, 1203–04).
26. The multiple references to swimming during the 1958 trip in Greece recall its central role in the pre-war essays (and *La Peste*), as a moment of withdrawal into harmonious fusion with nature.
27. Tipasa, which in the *Guide Bleu* of the 1920s and 30s, is granted merely a lukewarm 'visite [...] fort intéressante' [a most interesting visit].
28. This radical division is summarised, just as humorously, in his claim in 'New York' that one way to understand a foreign country is to 'find out how people die there' (*OC*, II, 1054): at one extreme, denial via the business-like 'You die and we do the rest' of US funeral homes; at the other, the numerous *pompes funèbres* of Oran, needed because they make more fuss about it. In between, the pathos of solitary death in a Prague hotel room; the indifference following two fatal road accidents in Rio, reduced to *faits divers*; and the jocular 'Tu montes, chérie?' of hearse drivers when passing a pretty girl in Oran's streets.
29. Albert Camus, 'La Culture indigène: la nouvelle culture méditerranéenne' [1937], in *OC*, I, 565–66.
30. Camus and Casarès, *Correspondance 1944–1959*, p. 1229; and again pp. 1238 and 1240.

CHAPTER 3

Camus, *La Peste* et le coronavirus: 'une histoire collective'

Jeanyves Guérin

Camus est de loin l'écrivain français du vingtième siècle le plus lu dans le monde. Aucun autre n'a connu une telle fortune sur tous les continents. *L'Étranger* a été traduit en soixante-quatorze langues, *La Peste* en cinquante-neuf. La *Camusmania* n'est pas un phénomène européen ni même occidental. Après le Japon, elle touche aujourd'hui la Corée, la Chine, l'Iran. Les années passent. Les modes changent. Les générations se succèdent. Camus demeure.

Enfant du peuple pour ne pas dire de prolétaires, Camus est un intrus dans la république des lettres. Il vient de l'Algérie qui n'est pas la France. Le public accueille mieux ses romans et essais que la critique qui se montre souvent réservée. Comme Corneille et Molière, il l'a avec lui quand les doctes le chicanent. Le plébiscite des lecteurs lui a épargné le purgatoire des écrivains. Quant au citoyen, que cette idée plaise ou non, l'Histoire a tranché et lui a donné raison à Moscou, à Prague et aussi, d'une certaine façon, à Alger. La conséquence est que, comme Voltaire jadis, comme Orwell aujourd'hui, il risque d'être embaumé, totémisé, ses idées déformées et ses valeurs bafouées. Il est devenu une 'icône' que même les personnalités les plus éloignées de ses convictions s'efforcent de récupérer. Les camusiens de la dernière heure ne sont pas les moins diserts. Citer Camus, écrivait Daniel Cohn-Bendit, 'c'est un peu un passage obligé'. Mais il faut 'lire, enfin et vraiment, l'œuvre et toute l'œuvre'.[1] Le test des œuvres complètes fait apparaître parfois des banalités, jamais des propos qui vont contre les valeurs de la démocratie, des éloges de dictateurs, des célébrations de la torture, du système concentrationnaire ou des apologies de crimes contre les peuples. Jamais Camus n'a tenu le discours de la haine ni attisé la guerre civile.

Toute réception, on le sait, est datée. Une nouvelle situation historique suscite de nouvelles lectures. On ne reçoit pas *L'Étranger*, *La Peste*, *L'Homme révolté* de la même façon dans les années 1950, dans les années 1990 et en l'année 2021. La guerre froide, la décolonisation et les Trente Glorieuses appartiennent au passé. Le mur de Berlin est tombé. À la révolution de velours a succédé le printemps arabe. Le *trend* progressiste s'est achevé. Une rupture d'horizon s'est produite. L'orthodoxie néo-libérale a supplanté l'orthodoxie marxiste. L'économie est mondialisée. Le défi terroriste est devenu un phénomène global. L'idée européenne, l'idée de solidarité, référent collectif historique, et l'idée même d'avenir sont en crise. Le *trend* néo-libéral à son tour touche déjà à sa fin et se prépare un nouveau *trend*. De nouvelles peurs se font jour et nourrissent un tournant réactionnaire. Les boutiques du populisme prospèrent. La haine répand ses poisons. Après une vingtaine d'années fastes, les démocraties et les démocrates sont sur la défensive et en proie au doute. Jamais Camus n'a été aussi nécessaire. Quels textes peuvent nous aider à penser la lutte contre la pandémie?[2]

D'abord, *Ni Victimes ni bourreaux*. Cet ensemble d'articles que l'on peut lire comme un essai politique est publié dans le journal *Combat* en novembre 1946. Sa traduction américaine paraît l'année suivante dans *Politics*. Il est repris dans *Actuelles*. Premier texte: 'Le siècle de la peur' (*OC*, II, 436–38). Peur de la guerre et des idéologies meurtrières. Nous y sommes en plein depuis un certain 11 septembre 2001. Camus évoque aussi 'le monde de l'abstraction, des bureaux et des machines, des idées absolues et des messianismes sans nuances'. Il ajoute, pour le regretter, que 'la terreur n'est pas un élément favorable à la réflexion'. Que celle-ci est alors nécessaire est une idée qui sera reprise dans *La Peste* (*OC*, II, 49). Deuxième texte: 'Sauver les corps' (*OC*, II, 438–40). C'est un des thèmes de *La Peste*. Troisième texte: 'Démocratie et dictature internationales' (*OC*, II, 446–48). Arrêtons-nous sur lui. Camus y affirme que le monde est un. Il est la maison commune de l'humanité. D'autres ont parlé de l'œcumène, de la terre-patrie, du village planétaire. Tout événement produit une chaîne de répercussions. Une décision prise par un État a des effets sur ses voisins. 'Nous savons aujourd'hui qu'il n'y a plus d'îles et que les frontières sont vaines [...] que dans un monde en accélération constante, où l'Atlantique se traverse en moins d'une journée, nous sommes forcés à la solidarité ou à la complicité' (*OC*, II, 446).

Les virus et la pollution ne connaissent pas de frontières. La question bioclimatique concerne l'humanité tout entière. 'Aujourd'hui,' écrit Camus, 'la tragédie est collective'. Elle appelle 'la solidarité des nations' (*OC*, II, 446). Le local, dirions-nous, est inséparable du global. Le vivre ensemble se pense désormais à l'échelle de la planète. 'Aucun problème ne peut se régler sans la solidarité des nations' (446). L'autarcie est impossible. 'Beaucoup d'Américains voudraient continuer à vivre dans leur société qu'ils trouvent bonne. [...] Ils ne le peuvent et ne le pourront plus jamais' (446). En proposant de relativiser l'idée même de souveraineté, Camus touche à un tabou et à un dogme. Il va plus loin. Il risque l'utopie d'une démocratie mondiale et d'un 'nouvel ordre international' qui devra être universel ou ne sera pas. Cet ordre serait appuyé non pas sur les gouvernements mais sur les peuples devenus acteurs à part entière et solidaires. On ne peut pas faire confiance aux seuls États pour défendre les peuples. Il faut qu'existe une société civile mondiale.

Quatrième texte: 'Le monde va vite' (*OC*, II, 448–50). Camus propose que les ressources naturelles, le pétrole, l'uranium, on ajouterait aujourd'hui les vaccins, l'air que nous respirons, la biodiversité, la forêt amazonienne sont *biens communs* de l'humanité. Il évoque leur 'collectivisation' (450). Ils n'appartiennent à personne et surtout pas aux maîtres du marché. Cette idée chemine lentement.[3] Cinquième texte: 'Un nouveau contrat social' (451–53). Camus y revient sur la nécessité d'une coopération. 'On ne guérit pas la peste avec les moyens qui s'appliquent aux rhumes de cerveau. Une crise qui déchire le monde entier doit se régler à l'échelle universelle' (452).

Camus, en 1946, pose l'interdépendance des peuples et l'idée d'un intérêt général mondial. Il plaide pour le multilatéralisme. Celui-ci a pris la forme d'institutions transnationales qui ont fonctionné tant bien que mal et plutôt mal que bien. L'urgence d'un monde solidaire appelle leur réforme et leur refondation. La coopération doit s'imposer face aux fléaux que sont le coronavirus et la catastrophe écologique. Alors que l'un et l'autre frappent une société mondiale, l'heure semble être aujourd'hui à l'unilatéralisme et aux bilatéralismes. *America first*. Des traités longuement négociés peuvent être rayés d'un coup de plume. Citant Camus, le ministre (social-démocrate) allemand des affaires étrangères écrit que 'le coronavirus est bien notre affaire à tous, et ce, à l'échelle mondiale'. Il ajoute:

> Les manifestations d'égoïsme, que ce soit dans la concurrence pour les masques de protection ou l'approvisionnement en médicaments, aggravent la crise pour tout le monde. [...] L'un des meilleurs investissements dans la lutte contre la pandémie consiste à renforcer les Nations Unies, et en premier lieu l'Organisation mondiale de la santé sous-financée, notamment pour mettre au point et distribuer des tests et des vaccins.[4]

La Commission européenne et les vingt-sept semblent avoir fait le choix d'une coopération renforcée pour affronter la méga-crise produite par le coronavirus.

Le Roman de la révolte

Avant de passer à *La Peste*, je voudrais dire un mot de la révolte. En 1944, Camus écrit dans le journal *Combat*: 'Ce qui a porté la Résistance pendant quatre ans, c'est la révolte. C'est-à-dire le refus entier, obstiné, presque aveugle au début d'un ordre qui voulait mettre les hommes à genoux' (OC, II, 530). Camus la définit d'emblée par un refus. 'Qu'est-ce qu'un homme révolté? Un homme qui dit non' (OC, III, 71). Le spectacle, le scandale de l'injustice, de l'oppression ou du malheur l'indignent. Un scandale doit cesser. Une injustice dont il est la victime ou le témoin appelle une réparation. Le révolté affirme des valeurs, la liberté et la solidarité. 'Je me révolte, donc nous sommes' (OC, III, 73). C'est ce que font les personnages de *La Peste*.

Les ventes de *La Peste* ont explosé en France, en Italie, au Japon, en Chine, au Brésil et sans doute un peu partout dès que la pandémie a fait les gros titres des journaux. De nombreux articles parus dans ces pays et en Allemagne (*Die Welt, Berliner Morgenpost*), en Belgique (*Le Soir, L'Écho...*), en Suisse (*Le Temps*), en Grande Bretagne (*The New Statesman, The Guardian...*), aux États-Unis (*The New York Times, The Washington Post, Foreign Affairs...*), au Canada (*Journal de Montréal, Le Devoir, The Globe and Mail...*), en Inde (*Outlook, The Week*), en Afrique du Sud (*Mail & Guardian*) ont proposé leur relecture d'un roman publié en 1947 pour affirmer son extraordinaire actualité.[5] *La Peste* est 'le grand livre du coronavirus'.[6] 'Il est saisissant de voir à quel point ce roman déroule, étape par étape, le scénario catastrophe que nous vivons aujourd'hui', peut-on lire dans *L'Obs*. 'Des réactions des autorités au courage des soignants en passant par le confinement, tous les épisodes du terrifiant feuilleton médical actuel sont passés au scanner camusien'.[7] La réalité rejoignant la fiction, le lecteur retrouve tout un lexique devenu familier, immunité, épidémie, etc. Mais le narrateur se fait essayiste. Il propose des analyses socio-politiques. C'est pourquoi l'écrivain et journaliste Kamel Daoud, citoyen oranais, ajoute: 'Relire *La Peste*, c'est un peu lire un manuel de survie de l'esprit'.[8]

Camus a fait le choix d'un récit allégorique. Il y a distillé et éparpillé des remarques qui, mises bout à bout, constituent un essai philosophique et politique. La pandémie qui frappe Oran représente d'abord le totalitarisme nazi, puis tous les totalitarismes, donc le communisme soviétique.[9] À un Roland Barthes mal inspiré qui lui avait asséné une leçon de marxisme-léninisme, il réplique calmement, en 1955, qu'il a voulu que *La Peste* puisse 'servir à toutes les résistances contre toutes les tyrannies'. 'La terreur' ayant plusieurs visages, il n'en nomme aucun pour 'les frapper tous' (*OC*, II, 287). De nouveaux fléaux lui ont donné raison. Aux États-Unis, la peste a fait penser au SIDA; en Chine, au SRAS; en Iran, à l'islam politique.[10] La force de l'allégorie réside dans sa polysémie, dans sa disponibilité à de nouvelles lectures. C'est une lecture au premier degré que je propose ici. Je prends *La Peste* pour le récit — 'la chronique,' dit le narrateur (243) — de l'épidémie qui frappe une société. Si celui-ci a tant impressionné ses lecteurs et relecteurs récents, c'est que Camus s'est documenté sur le sujet.[11]

Pour combattre le mal, il faut le désigner, donc le connaître. Ceux que le narrateur appelle 'nos concitoyens' sont d'abord insouciants comme si la peste ne les concernait pas. Le fléau est pour eux 'irréel' (*OC*, II, 59). Quand les portes de la ville sont fermées, leurs attitudes changent. Leur psychologie est celle de prisonniers et d'exilés (82). La peste dérange des habitudes et atteint des intérêts (86). Puis vient le moment de l'abattement, du 'consentement provisoire') et de la 'résignation' (160, 162). La peste et la 'peur' qu'elle a suscitée renvoient les gens à leur solitude et à leur présent (102, 160). 'L'angoisse de la contagion' (116) distend voire brise les liens sociaux. 'Personne ne pouvait espérer l'aide du voisin et chacun restait seul avec sa préoccupation' (84). Tarrou l'écrit: 'On sait trop bien qu'on ne peut pas avoir confiance en son voisin, qu'il est capable de vous donner la peste à votre insu' (170). Camus raconte la fatigue et la désocialisation de la population. À cela Rieux oppose que la peste est 'l'affaire de tous' (78, 124). Rambert, reprenant une formule du médecin (92), finit par en convenir: 'Cette histoire nous concerne tous' (178). Le narrateur, comme en écho avec le mot cité plus haut de *Ni victimes ni bourreaux*, évoque une 'histoire collective' (149).

De nombreux chiffres et statistiques sont lancés dans les deux premières parties du roman. Il est question aussi de graphiques (*OC*, II, 197). Le narrateur enregistre la progression de l'infection, sa virulence, sa 'contagiosité' (197) et sa létalité, et même, métaphores aujourd'hui familières, son 'sommet' (129, 149), son 'plateau' (197), son 'palier' (156, 197), son 'recul' (218, 222). Chroniqueur et témoin de la peste, Rieux ne met pas en doute l'exactitude de ces données anxiogènes. Une chose a marqué récemment l'opinion. Chaque soir, les autorités et des sites dont celui de l'université Johns Hopkins, fournissaient les derniers chiffres (contaminations, hospitalisations, décès). Pour certains pays (Chine, Russie, Iran, Brésil, Nicaragua) elles étaient soupçonnées d'être largement sous-évaluées. De toute façon, les statistiques, si frappantes soient-elles, sont des abstractions, avertit Camus. Elles ne disent pas les souffrances des personnes, les vies fracassées et le malheur.

Rieux est un lanceur d'alerte comme le docteur Li Wenliang de Wuhan. Il se heurte à l'inertie et à l'impéritie des autorités. L'ordre des médecins, dans un premier temps, réagit comme l'Organisation mondiale de la santé. Le docteur Richard nie qu'il y ait épidémie. Il use d'euphémismes et de circonlocutions. 'Il faut appeler les choses par leur nom' (*OC*, II, 62), déclare Grand qui figure l'homme simple selon Orwell. Le parler vrai, on le sait, est un grand paradigme camusien. C'est ce qui s'oppose aux mensonges de la propagande totalitaire comme aux arguties technocratiques. On y voit un préalable à l'action démocratique. On ne cesse de citer sa phrase: 'Mal nommer un objet, c'est ajouter au malheur de ce monde' (*OC*, I, 908).

'La première réaction' de la population est 'd'incriminer l'administration' (*OC*, II, 86). Elle est 'débordée' (119), estime Tarrou. Camus n'en dit guère plus. C'est une différence avec l'événement récent. Du Royaume Uni à l'Italie, de la France à l'Espagne, les gouvernements ont été mis sur la sellette, accusés d'imprévoyance et d'incurie. La critique des autorités, dans le roman, est le fait de quelques personnages, non de partis ou de syndicats. Le préfet dont le narrateur dit qu'il apparaît 'désorienté' (118) est un grand commis de Vichy qui attend les ordres. Son principal souci qu'il partage avec la municipalité est de ne pas 'inquiéter l'opinion publique' (69). 'L'opinion publique, c'est sacré', disait le vieux docteur Castel (58). Camus écrivait cela avant que les techniques de la communication aient imposé leurs modes opératoires et que soient apparus les *spin doctors*. La communication des autorités oranaises passe par des affiches et des communiqués confiés aux journaux. On en reste à du bricolage. On n'en est pas encore aux éléments de langage ressassés par les officiels et aux vérités alternatives que véhiculent aujourd'hui les réseaux sociaux.

La réunion de la commission sanitaire que le préfet a convoquée est un dialogue de sourds. D'un côté, Castel et Rieux; de l'autre, le préfet et le docteur Richard. À lire le passage, on retrouve des arguments entendus en 2020. Écoutons le dernier minimisant la dangerosité du fléau: 'les bavardages exagèrent tout'; 'Il ne fallait rien pousser au noir'; 'la vérité est que notre confrère croit à la peste' (66, 67, 68). L'incertitude justifie l'inaction. Ce n'est qu'une 'fièvre' (66, 69). On se souvient que, face au coronavirus, des institutions (l'OMS) et des politiciens ont finassé, pratiqué le déni. On pense à ce président répétant entre deux parties de golf que le virus était moins dangereux que celui de la grippe. C'était aussi l'avis de son complice et ami brésilien. Ce n'était, pour un autre bravache, qu'une 'grippe saisonnière'.[12] Des mois plus tard, on compte des centaines de milliers de morts ici et autant là. Trump et Bolsonaro ont ignoré les avertissements des épidémiologistes et plus largement méprisé les avis des experts. Dans le roman, parce que les autorités oranaises n'ont pas pris la mesure des menaces et des ravages que va exercer la peste, elles ne prennent pas les 'mesures' — mot-clé du roman — qui s'imposent. Elles en restent trop longtemps aux phrases (76) et aux vœux pieux. Des politiques,

Rieux dit à Tarrou: 'Ce qui leur manque, c'est l'imagination. Ils ne sont jamais à l'échelle des fléaux. Et les remèdes qu'ils imaginent sont à peine à la hauteur d'un rhume de cerveau' (119). Quant à la municipalité, elle ressemble à ces monstres froids dont parle Nietzsche. Son conseil aurait pu être un lieu de délibération. Il n'en est pas question. Les maires et les conseils avaient perdu toute autonomie sous l'Occupation. Là est une différence avec l'événement récent. Plus proches des populations, les municipalités ont souvent joué leur rôle et, grâce à une chaîne de décisions plus rapide, pris des initiatives concrètes tandis que l'État en restait à des mesures administratives et apparaissait dépassé.

Camus pointe la responsabilité des journaux. Ils ont reçu une 'consigne d'optimisme' (OC, II, 198). Surtout pas de nouvelles anxiogènes. Occultation des faits perturbants. Le lecteur de 1947 pense à la presse des années noires qui fut aux ordres de l'Etat français et/ou des nazis. La presse oranaise n'informe pas ses lecteurs. Elle transmet les communiqués des autorités et leur ajoute des publicités intéressées. En 2020, la presse écrite et audio-visuelle, là où elle est pluraliste, a joué son rôle d'information dans les démocraties. Ailleurs non. Il n'y a pas que les journaux. Le narrateur signale, sans insister, les 'rumeurs' qui circulent, les 'légendes' qu'on appelle aujourd'hui urbaines (242, 153).[13] On sait que les *fake news* ont récemment pullulé sur les réseaux sociaux: le gouvernement français a autorisé l'euthanasie des personnes âgées; les réseaux de téléphonie 5G propagent l'épidémie; ce sont les Américains (variante: les Chinois) qui ont fabriqué le virus; boire de l'alcool protège contre le coronavirus, etc. Cette dernière allégation figurait dans *La Peste*: 'Le vin probe tue les microbes' (88). Manque dans le roman la prolifération des obsessions complotistes.

'Nous manquons de matériel' (OC, II, 137). Face au coronavirus, les stocks de masques, les tests de dépistage, le gel hydroalcoolique, les respirateurs ont cruellement fait défaut en France et un peu partout alors que flambait la pandémie.[14] 'L'organisation du système sanitaire est mauvaise' (119): ce constat de Tarrou a pu être fait en 2020. Les hôpitaux publics ont été vite saturés car ils étaient mal préparés à la déferlante d'un virus pathogène après des années et des années de purge néo-libérale. On a accusé les pouvoirs d'imprévoyance. Dans le roman, manquent aussi les sérums. Le docteur Castel est le seul à en fabriquer un avec les moyens du bord. C'est un savant à l'ancienne. La recherche est aujourd'hui l'affaire d'équipes nombreuses et pluridisciplinaires. Encore faut-il que l'épidémiologie bénéficie d'une priorité budgétaire. Ce fut rarement le cas.

Vu la faillite de l'État techno-bureaucratique, vu les carences des services publics, ne reste que la société civile. Rieux organise les 'formations sanitaires' (OC, II, 124 et passim). Il met sur pied une ONG. Le principe d'humanité appelle la solidarité, des interactions sociales inédites. Tarrou, Grand, Rambert se portent volontaires et le juge Othon lui aussi, une fois déconfiné.[15] 'Limiter les dégâts', '[se] mettre du côté des victimes', dit Tarrou (210). Ce propos faisait rire jadis. Un Francis Jeanson moquait une 'morale de Croix-Rouge'.[16] Il prend toute sa force aujourd'hui. Camus souligne '[l'] effort épuisant', le 'travail surhumain' des médecins et de leurs aides (197). 'Ce travail peut être mortel,' (119) dit Rieux à Tarrou. On sait le lourd tribut que les soignants et plus encore les soignantes, d'Italie en Iran en passant par la

Russie, ont payé à la pandémie. À longueur d'articles, la presse les présente comme les héros de la lutte contre le coronavirus. Eux-mêmes, comme le narrateur de *La Peste* (124) se dénient cette qualité. Ils veulent seulement plus de moyens.[17] Dans le roman, il est question de médailles (151).

Joseph Grand que Camus décrit comme 'insignifiant et effacé' est le seul personnage qu'il qualifie de 'héros' (*OC*, II, 128). Il lui prête ce mot: 'Il faut bien s'entraider' (47). L'employé possède le sens inné de la solidarité qui est, pour George Orwell, la vertu des gens qu'on appellera simples ou ordinaires. Le docteur Rieux, lui, veut simplement 'bien faire son métier' (147). Il est de 'sauver les corps'. La 'santé' de ses semblables est son seul souci, il abandonne leur 'salut' aux prêtres … ou aux politiques (185). Nous retrouvons la formule de *Ni victimes ni bourreaux*. Il est sensible à la douleur et peu porté aux abstractions. L'urgence fait passer les personnes concrètes avant les principes. C'est, pour lui, une question d''honnêteté' (147). Le traducteur britannique du roman utilise le mot-valeur *decency* dont on sait qu'il est essentiel chez Orwell mais que son champ sémantique est plus large.[18] À l'époque, on ne parle pas du *care*. Mais en 1946, vient d'être fondée aux États-Unis une association dont c'est l'acronyme (*Cooperative for American Remittances to Europe* devenue *Cooperative for Assistance and Relief Everywhere*). Rien dans ses *Carnets* et sa correspondance n'indique que Camus en ait eu connaissance lors de son séjour outre-Atlantique.

De la peste, le narrateur dit seulement qu'elle est venue 'de l'extérieur' (*OC*, II, 84). Il évoque aussi une 'invasion brutale' (78). Camus pense ici à l'idéologie portée par les organisations inféodées à des États totalitaires et là à l'occupation du territoire métropolitain, par les forces du Reich. Ainsi, fut lue, métaphoriquement, *La Peste* en 1947. L'épidémie est localisée à Oran. Jamais il n'est précisé qu'elle frappe d'autres villes ou pays. Le reste du monde est hors champ. Il n'existe pas. Les deux référents du roman, la France occupée et une épidémie, sont en tension. Rieux et le père Paneloux mentionnent des pestes historiques (61 et 101). Ce sont également des épidémies localisées, en l'occurrence à Athènes, Constantinople, Marseille, Jaffa, Londres, Milan, pas des pandémies. Or toute l'Europe fut affectée. On sait que, de la peste noire à la grippe espagnole, les grandes pandémies de l'histoire ont suivi les routes commerciales. La dernière en date frappe plus de 200 pays selon le *Johns Hopkins Coronavirus Map*.[19] Elle est le produit d'une économie mondialisée. Ce sont les vols internationaux qui ont transporté le virus aux quatre coins de la planète.

On a entendu en 2020 des propos xénophobes. Pour un président, le coronavirus est un 'virus étranger'.[20] Le même désigne des boucs émissaires, la Chine puis l'Union européenne. De nombreux pays ont fermé leurs frontières et confiné les gens chez eux pour enrayer la progression du coronavirus. Le confinement, écrit Camus, c'est 'l'exil chez soi' (*OC*, II, 83). Cette formule est extrêmement juste. L'auteur utilise aussi le mot de 'claustration' (102). En 2020, il y a le téléphone et Internet. La ville d'Oran est coupée du monde comme l'a été la région de Hubei le 20 janvier 2020. Les trains et les bateaux n'y arrivent et n'en partent plus. Camus, insistant sur les gardes armés (79, 85 et *passim*), en fait la métaphore de la France occupée de 1940 à 1944. Le dédoublement du référent pose un problème de cohérence. À plusieurs reprises, le narrateur évoque la fermeture des portes (78, 90 et *passim*). La topographie de la ville référentielle ici est malmenée. Car si la France fut cadenassée et, pendant deux ans, séparée en plusieurs zones, l'Oran des années 1940 n'est pas une ville fortifiée comportant des portes. L'auteur en a eu conscience quand il situe l'action de *L'État de siège* à Cadix.

Selon que vous serez puissant ou misérable...

Oran était la ville la plus francophone, la plus hispanophone et la plus juive de l'Algérie coloniale. Au recensement de 1948, elle compte 249 000 habitants dont 82 000 'musulmans'. La part de ces derniers augmente rapidement par l'afflux de ruraux. Les quartiers appelés par Camus 'd'affaires' et 'de plaisance' (*OC*, II, 150) constituent le cœur de la ville. C'est là que vivent les Européens et les Juifs indigènes. La petite bourgeoisie indigène vit dans le quartier nègre appelé ultérieurement 'la ville nouvelle'. Camus ne reprend pas l'expression de 'villages indigènes'.[21] C'est là, en marge, que vivent les Arabes et, comme à Alger, quelques Européens déshérités, espagnols ou maltais. Une frontière invisible sépare le centre des 'faubourgs' (110, 116, 123, 240, 241, 242). Le mot utilisé au pluriel désigne des quartiers populaires dans la littérature du dix-neuvième siècle. Il a pris une connotation dépréciative. Sa récurrence dans le texte fait sens. Ces quartiers sont une entité distincte. Ils sont pauvres et/ou mal famés. Ils appartiennent à la ville sans y appartenir pleinement. Leurs habitants sont topographiquement proches, sociologiquement lointains car différents. Deux sociétés se tournent le dos.

Le coronavirus a fait mourir des personnalités de la culture et de la politique mais aussi, en grand nombre, des petits, des sans grade. Ce que l'on sait aujourd'hui des décès conforte le propos du roman. D'un côté, le père Paneloux, le juge Othon, Tarrou; de l'autre, le concierge et beaucoup d'anonymes, des hommes et des femmes. Les quartiers extérieurs (*OC*, II, 43, 150, 157) de la ville coloniale sont lourdement frappés. Le fléau révèle un territoire ségrégué et accroît les inégalités socio-économiques:

> Les familles pauvres se trouvaient dans une situation très pénible, tandis que les familles riches ne manquaient à peu près de rien. Alors que la peste, par l'impartialité efficace qu'elle apportait dans son ministère, aurait dû renforcer l'égalité chez nos concitoyens, par le jeu normal des égoïsmes, au contraire, elle rendait plus aigu dans le cœur des hommes le sentiment de l'injustice. (*OC*, II, 198)

Il en est de même du coronavirus. C'est que l'état sanitaire de ces quartiers populeux est mauvais, Rieux l'avait dit à Rambert (41). L'événement corrobore la remarque du narrateur. La cohésion d'une société repose sur des institutions mais aussi sur certains métiers, les *dirty jobs* qui ont été les plus exposés et vulnérables au virus. Le récit de Camus mentionne les fossoyeurs et les infirmiers (156). On ajoute aujourd'hui les chauffeurs-livreurs, les éboueurs, les caissier(e)s. Les métiers socialement dévalorisés ne sont pas féminisés dans le roman comme ils le sont aujourd'hui. Le problème n'est pas seulement socio-économique. Quand Camus parle de quartiers pauvres, on pense en 2020 aux ghettos suburbains et aussi aux *favelas* et aux communautés indigènes du Brésil. On a constaté la surmortalité des minorités ethniques dans plusieurs pays. Ce sont elles qui fournissent un gros contingent de *key* ou de *frontline workers*.[22] Les sociétés industrielles ont découvert une évidence refoulée: elles ont plus besoin de ces hommes et femmes oubliés, invisibles que des *traders*, *startuppers* et autres premiers de cordée.

D'autres font des affaires. Camus évoque la 'spéculation' (*OC*, II, 198) et incarne les profiteurs en la personne de Cottard. Il pense en 1947 aux trafics liés aux pénuries et, pour le dire net, au marché noir qui avait fleuri sous l'Occupation. Le coronavirus, comme la peste, a eu ses agioteurs, ses arnaqueurs, ses vendeurs de remèdes miracles. Des fortunes indécentes se sont faites dans la commercialisation des masques. Les sociétés de vente en ligne ont vu leur chiffre d'affaires exploser. Déjà des fonds spéculatifs se préparent à fondre, tels des vautours, sur les entreprises promises à la faillite.

Camus évoque rapidement des faits qui font la une des journaux en 2020: 'le commerce mort de la peste' (*OC*, II, 86), la désorganisation de la vie économique (156) et le chômage qui en résulte, fait sur lequel on reviendra, les problèmes de ravitaillement, qui étaient cruciaux dans la France libérée et aussi les plages interdites, les hôtels vides, 'la ruine du tourisme' (113). Ajoutons cette phrase qu'on croirait écrite à propos de Paris, de Madrid ou de Rome: 'C'est ainsi qu'on vit la circulation diminuer progressivement jusqu'à devenir à peu près nulle, des magasins de luxe fermer du jour au lendemain' (87). Les journaux, relayant des intérêts privés, esquissent une campagne comme on en a connu récemment, notamment mais pas seulement aux États-Unis. 'Ne pourrait-on pas envisager un assouplissement des mesures?' (86).[23] La priorité est désormais à la relance de l'économie, c'est-à-dire, entre autres choses, à la sauvegarde des dividendes et tant pis s'il faut pour cela sacrifier des vieux et des pauvres. Cela dit, de nouvelles différences se font jour. Les tramways sont bondés à Oran. Les cinémas, les cafés et les restaurants affichent complet. Les autorités n'ont pas ordonné leur fermeture non plus que celle des églises, comme elles l'ont fait un peu partout en 2020. C'est la ville qui est confinée, les habitants ne le sont pas chez eux. Il n'est pas question de distanciation physique non plus ni de gestes ou mesures barrières. Mais on n'en est pas loin puisque Camus écrit: 'Chose curieuse, cependant, tous les occupants [des tramways], dans la mesure du possible, se tournent le dos pour éviter une contagion mutuelle' (116).

La tentation autoritaire et la régression de la démocratie

Camus mentionne non seulement la quarantaine mais aussi l'instauration d'un 'couvre-feu' (*OC*, II, 137, 153), des 'patrouilles' (110, 157), des 'équipes spéciales' (110), des 'camps' (180–98).[24] Surveiller et punir. Les autorités craignent plus que tout que le mécontentement de la population (et d'abord des faubourgs) se transforme en révolte (110, cf. 152: 'un souffle de révolution'). Les forces de l'ordre tirent sur les réfractaires.[25] Il s'agit plus que de violences policières. Il est question aussi de 'suspects'. Le sont non seulement les protestataires mais le premier venu. 'Tout le monde était suspect,' dit Tarrou (113). Le mot a ici sa connotation politique.[26] C'est qu'il y a péril en la demeure. Il ne faut pas que la crise sanitaire devienne une crise sociale et politique. 'L'état de peste' (77) se transforme en 'état de siège' (151, 152). 'Un nouvel ordre' (158) a été instauré. Le lecteur de 1947 pense au régime dictatorial de Vichy, celui d'aujourd'hui aux atteintes portées çà et là aux libertés fondamentales. Le coronavirus, on l'a vu, a permis l'étouffement de révoltes démocratiques à Hong Kong comme en Algérie. En Hongrie, le premier ministre national-conservateur a obtenu du parlement l'autorisation de légiférer par ordonnances dans le cadre d'un état d'urgence à durée indéterminée. La lutte contre l'épidémie a été le prétexte pour suspendre l'application de lois et brider la presse encore libre.

Dans *L'État de siège*, la Peste effectue un coup d'État. Le dictateur prend 'les mesures qui conviennent' (*OC*, II, 314), celles que le ci-devant gouverneur n'a pas su ou osé prendre. Il ferme les portes de la ville. On passe immédiatement à l'application d'un programme. Il s'agit de construire un ordre nouveau. L'État remodèle la société. 'Vous devez vous adapter, déclare le personnage. Vous avez tout à apprendre' 322). D'où l'importance de la propagande. Il faut endoctriner et manipuler les masses. 'Nous sommes seuls,' dit le chœur (318, 321). Le résultat est une société enfermée dans des frontières étanches, écrasée, réduite au silence. La parole est contrainte, contrôlée, car elle permet l'échange, la communication des idées. C'est un 'véhicule de l'infection' (321). Le peuple est embrigadé, mis en 'rangs'. La discipline, la conformisation idéologique modèlent des 'bons citoyens'.[27]

La protection de la santé publique a appelé l'état d'urgence sanitaire, à savoir des mesures exceptionnelles dont la nécessité a été généralement acceptée, comme elles le sont en temps de guerre, même les entraves à la liberté de circulation et de réunion. Le droit à la vie n'est-il pas la première des libertés? Il est tentant, pour l'exécutif, de banaliser, de prolonger indéfiniment les restrictions et dérogations et de les faire entrer dans le droit commun. 'La peur de la contamination, très sensible dans la société, ne saurait être compensée par un excès de mesures autoritaires'.[28] L'équilibre entre libertés et sécurité est, on le sait, délicat à maintenir. La circonstance épidémique permet de rogner les libertés publiques, de détricoter le code du travail et de saper les modestes réglementations environnementales. Une vigilance citoyenne s'impose donc, lorsque, la crise sanitaire ayant été contenue, la méga-crise économique frappe durement l'emploi et que les parlements ont à légiférer. La lecture de Camus ici aussi sera utile.

Tarrou pense que 'la peste changerait et ne changerait rien dans la ville, et que tout recommencerait comme auparavant, c'est-à-dire comme si rien ne s'était passé' (*OC*, II, 227). Au final, Rieux ne partage pas la liesse de la foule oranaise qui est celle des villes libérées à l'été 1944. Il craint que l'épreuve soit considérée comme une parenthèse qu'on veut oublier et que tout reprenne comme avant. Que l'on fasse des discours et qu'on n'effectue pas les réformes indispensables. Que l'on ne fournisse pas les moyens financiers et humains aux services publics. Que l'on abandonne la recherche virologique aux intérêts privés. La dernière page du roman est, à cet égard, capitale. Elle est un appel à la vigilance. 'Le bacille de la peste ne meurt ni ne disparaît jamais' et aucune 'cité heureuse' n'est à l'abri de son atteinte (248). Pour le médecin humaniste, les lendemains de la peste ne chanteront pas si les leçons économiques, sociales et politiques n'en ont pas été tirées. Le pire peut toujours revenir. Une nouvelle catastrophe risque d'advenir. La pandémie peut rebondir là où la croyait jugulée: 'On ne pouvait rien prévoir, l'histoire des épidémies comportant des rebondissements imprévus' (197). Les sociétés, la planète ont besoin d'hommes révoltés. La lutte contre les fléaux est à recommencer sans cesse. 'Recommencer' est un mot-clé du roman (seize occurrences). 'Vos victoires sont toujours provisoires, voilà tout,' dit Tarrou à Rieux. Celui-ci lui répond: 'Toujours, je le sais. Ce n'est pas une raison pour cesser de lutter' (122).

L'épidémie est un paradigme herméneutique pour Camus. Un article publié juste avant la sortie de *La Peste* le 10 mai 1947 s'intitule 'La contagion' (*OC*, II, 429–31).[29] L'éditorialiste de *Combat* y pose la question du racisme en système colonial. Le racisme tue aussi et partout. Il est d'autres virus que ceux que véhiculent les bacilles. On les qualifiera de socio-idéologiques. Comme la peste qui peut être bubonique puis pulmonaire, ils mutent selon les situations. Qui sème la haine récolte la barbarie.

Il demeure une différence entre la peste relatée par Camus et le coronavirus. Elle réside dans la situation historique. On peut penser en 1947 (et plus encore en 1989) que l'avenir est aux institutions et aux valeurs de la démocratie. Il est à craindre en 2020–22 que le coronavirus amène ou maintienne au pouvoir des despotes et des démagogues populistes hystérisant le débat public, mobilisant les peurs, les phobies et les rancœurs et activant les mécanismes identitaires. La coagulation mortifère du complotisme, du souverainisme, du populisme et de l'illibéralisme, bref une nouvelle peste brune, menace les démocraties. 'La dictature n'est pas un vaccin,' a écrit l'auteur de *Meursault contre-enquête*.[30] Le nouveau monde risque de ressembler à l'ancien, mais en pire.

Notes to Chapter 3

1. Daniel Cohn-Bendit, '(Re)lire Camus', *Le Nouvel Observateur*, 16–22 mai 2013.
2. Edition de référence: *Œuvres complètes*, 4 volumes, sous la direction de Jacqueline Lévi-Valensi (t. 1 et t. 2) et de Raymond Gay-Crosier (t. 3 et t. 4) (Paris: Gallimard, 2006–08). Désormais *OC*, I, II, III.
3. Le secrétaire de l'ONU, António Gutteres, a déclaré: 'Un vaccin contre le Covid-19 doit être vu comme un bien public mondial, un vaccin pour les peuples' (*Le Monde*, 5 juin 2020).
4. Heiko Maas, '*Was Europa aus der korona-crise lernen kann*', *Die Welt am Sonntag*, 12 avril 2020.
5. Une adaptation scénique de *La Peste*, créée un peu plus tôt au Théâtre des Galeries à Bruxelles, était à l'affiche du Théâtre Jean Vilar de Louvain-La-Neuve en février 2020.
6. Jean-Claude Raspiengeas, '*La Peste*, le grand livre du coronavirus', *La Croix*, 19 mai 2020.
7. Élisabeth Philippe, 'Coronavirus: Camus avait vraiment tout prédit, étape par étape', *Bibliobs*, 26 mars 2020.
8. Kamel Daoud, '*La Peste*, un manuel de dignité', *Le Point*, 10 mars 2020. Voir aussi Tahar Ben Jelloun, 'De la peste au coronavirus', *Le Point*, 10 mars 2020.
9. Je me permets de renvoyer à deux de mes études sur ce sujet: *Albert Camus: portrait de l'artiste en citoyen* (Paris: François Bourin, 1993), pp. 63–82; *Albert Camus: littérature et politique* (Paris: Honoré Champion, 2013), pp. 159–80.
10. Trois articles parmi d'autres: Charles E. Rosenberg, 'What is an Epidemic? AIDS in Historical Perspective', *Daedalus*, 118.2 (1989), 1–17; Sheryl L. Geisler, 'Albert Camus' *The Plague*: Corollaries to the AIDS Epidemic', *Journal of Physician Assistant Education*, 18.1 (2007), 64–66; Larry Zaroff, 'Always a Plague: Camus' Dr Rieux and the AIDS Pandemic', *Literature and the Arts in Medical Education*, 42.7 (2010), 479–80.

11. Pour un état de ses lectures, voir *OC*, II, 1134–35.
12. Philippe Boulet-Gercourt, 'Trump, Bolsonaro, Johnson: radiographie de l'aveuglement des populistes face au coronavirus', *L'Obs*, 17 avril 2020.
13. Voir Jean-Bruno Renard, *Rumeurs et légendes urbaines* (Paris: Presses universitaires de France, 1999).
14. Dans le roman, il est d'ailleurs question des masques (*OC*, II, 176, 177, 197).
15. En mai 2020, l'Assurance maladie a mis en place des 'brigades sanitaires'. Ses membres, des soignants, des médecins, des travailleurs sociaux sont des bénévoles. Ils sillonnent les rues des villes, contactant les relations des personnes contaminées afin de casser les chaînes de transmission.
16. Francis Jeanson, 'Albert Camus ou l'âme révoltée', *Les Temps modernes*, 79 (1952), 2070–90 (p. 2072).
17. Collectif Confinés mobilisés, 'Nous ne voulons pas de héros', *Libération*, 31 mars 2020.
18. La notion de *common decency* apparaît dans *The Road to the Wigan Pier* (London: Gollanz, 1937). Orwell ne l'a pas définie précisément. Sur ce sujet, voir Bruce Bégout, *De la décence ordinaire* (Paris: Allia, 2017).
19. <https://coronavirus.jhu.edu/map.html> [consulté novembre 2021].
20. Allocution du 11 mars 2020 depuis la Maison-Blanche.
21. Voir René Emsalem, 'Les villages indigènes d'Oran', *Revue de géographie de Lyon*, 25 (1950), 289–99, et surtout René Lespès, *Oran: étude de géographie et d'histoire urbaine* (Paris: Alcan, 1938) (ouvrage réédité à Oran en 2003).
22. Dominique Méda, 'Les plus forts taux de surmortalité concernent les travailleurs essentiels', *Le Monde*, 23 mai 2020. L'auteur, sociologue, s'appuie sur des études britanniques.
23. La formule 'assouplir l'état d'urgence sanitaire' revient en boucle dans la presse française en juin 2020.
24. De nombreux pays, dont l'Égypte, le Sénégal, la Côte d'Ivoire, le Kenya, l'Arabie saoudite, la Géorgie, ont instauré un couvre-feu dans les grandes villes. Ce fut le cas aussi en France à la fin de 2020.
25. Comme aux États-Unis en juin 2020.
26. Nous faisons référence aux lois prises par les Jacobins en 1793 et sous le second Empire en 1858.
27. Pour une analyse de *L'État de siège*, voir Guérin, *Albert Camus: littérature et politique*, pp. 181–202.
28. Éditorial du *Monde*, 4 mai 2020.
29. Voir Dany Laferrière, 'Le racisme est un virus', *Bibliobs*, 10 juin 2020.
30. Kamel Daoud, 'La dictature n'est pas un vaccin', *Le Point*, 16 avril 2020.

CHAPTER 4

Oran's Endogenous Evil: A Rereading of Albert Camus's *La Peste*

Ieme van der Poel

Introduction

Albert Camus's story *La Peste* [*The Plague*], which he wrote and reworked from 1942 to 1946 and which was published in June 1947, is set in the city of Oran.¹ While it is generally accepted that this is a fable about European resistance to Nazism, the choice of location has not really been questioned in the criticism to date. Taking their cue from the Camusian narrator, critics have been content to emphasise the *banal* rather than the *colonial* aspect of the urban space presented in the story. This point of view is illustrated, for example, by the following quotation:

> Pourquoi donc déchaîner la peste à Oran? [...] Parce que Camus venait d'y vivre quelque temps et en connaissait bien la topographie, parce que la ville aussi lui semblait, d'une certaine façon, la moins algérienne des cités d'Algérie, la plus européenne, donc la plus propre dans sa banalité au mythe de portée universelle.²
>
> [Why unleash the plague in Oran? [...] Because Camus had just lived there for a short while and knew its topography quite well, and also because of all Algeria's cities, the city in a certain way seemed the least Algerian to him, the most European, and therefore, in all its mundaneness, most appropriate for a myth of universal understanding.]

The author of this passage, Roger Quilliot, by focusing on the topography of Oran, disregards the uniqueness of its history. This is similarly the case in the annotated edition of *La Peste* in the 'Foliothèque' collection, even though its author, Jacqueline Lévi-Valensi, seems to be claiming the opposite: 'La période d'élaboration de *La Peste* correspond à une époque historique particulièrement riche, à laquelle Camus a participé activement, et au cours de laquelle les événements n'ont pu manquer infléchir sa conception du roman' [The period during which *La Peste* reached its completion coincides with a moment in time that was particularly challenging, filled with events in which Camus was actively involved, and which over the years cannot fail to have shaped his ideas about the novel].³

But rather than trying to re-situate Camus's text within its colonial context, that is, within the history of Oranie, the French overseas department, Lévi-Valensi turns to the history of metropolitan France to justify her thesis: Camus is assumed to have transposed the experience of the Liberation of Paris into the description of Oran liberated from the plague. In a more general fashion, by focusing its attention on the characters resisting the plague, particularly Tarrou and Rieux, the criticism has skirted the question of the essence of this scourge with respect to the Oranian context. And so, the experience of the colony under the Vichy regime and its possible echo in the text are deliberately ignored.

I have chosen to read *La Peste* as a colonial novel, written by an author who spent the greater part of his life in colonial Algeria and who set some of his most important works there: *L'Étranger*, *Le Premier homme* and *La Peste*. Starting from the idea that *La Peste* was born within the context of colonisation, of the city of Oran specifically, I propose to examine more thoroughly its historical and colonial foundation. This is because, contrary to Alfred Salinas, author of one of the rare studies on the history of Oran in the years 1940–42, I do not believe that Camus the writer was insensitive to the political situation of the city in which he lived from January 1941 until the summer of 1942.[4]

In order to find traces of a troubled past that have may have slipped into the folds of fiction, it is necessary to avoid an overly global 'postcolonial' approach. By reinserting the Camusian text into the context (as unusual as it is unknown) of the city of Oran at the time of the World War II, I hope to reconstruct the relationship between *La Peste* and the colonial city wherein lie its roots. With this approach, I shall also attempt to explain the absence of Algerian characters ('Arabs' as Camus and his 'European' contemporaries in Algeria would have said) in a story unfolding nonetheless in the Maghreb. For, while it has become good form to mention in passing this curious absence — obligatory postcolonial awareness — the criticism has not yet been able to explain it.

Camus in Oran

Camus the Algerian goes to Oran for the first time in 1937 with the troupe from Radio-Alger to play the role of young leading man in a play by Molière. Soon thereafter he falls in love with an Oranian woman, Francine Faure. In 1940, the young couple are married in Lyon and, on their return to Algeria, settle in Oran in the Faures' apartment on rue d'Arzew, in the centre of the European part of the city.[5] There, in the month of April 1941, Camus begins working on *La Peste*, although his first notes about this new project date back to 1939.[6] Since his health was deteriorating considerably during this period, Camus was obliged to take a cure in France, in the Massif Central.

Between the months of August 1942 and September 1943, he was busy writing a first version of his novel, followed by a second version that he would finish, though only provisionally, in 1946. Meanwhile, the landing of the Allies on the Oranian coast in November 1942, and the German invasion of southern France that followed, had prevented him from returning to Oran as he had wished. So for two years, until September 1944, Camus was separated from his native country and from his young wife, who had remained in Oran.[7] We find this same personal drama, though inverted, in the story of the protagonist in *La Peste*, Dr Rieux, whose wife, also ill, leaves Oran shortly before the start of the plague epidemic. The closing of the city for sanitary reasons separates the spouses forever. For, unlike Camus himself, Rieux's wife succumbs to her illness, never having been able to return to Oran.

While the connection between Camus's personal experience and the significance of the theme of exile in the novel is obvious, that does not, however, explain the explicit choice of Oran as the setting for the action. Even the excellent introduction to *La Peste* in the most recent Pléiade edition (2006), while characterising the story as '*fortement ancré dans son époque et dans l'existence de son auteur*' [*strongly anchored in its time* and in its author's existence], elaborates only the latter aspect.[8] It sheds no light whatsoever on the novel's relationship to the local, hence colonial, history.

There are multiple reasons, nevertheless, for us to wonder why this fable about the war is situated in Oran and not, for example, in Nevers.[9] First, the city is omnipresent in the novel and the topographical references, while not very numerous, are quite precise. Like Oran in the 1930s, the fictional city of the same name has 200,000 inhabitants and is endowed with a port, a waterfront boulevard and ramparts. The names of streets, of locales and of monuments that are mentioned correspond to those of the real city during the colonial era: place d'Armes; rue Faidherbe; the bronze lions in front of city hall; the Café de la Bourse; the Navy quarters; the *village nègre*.

Furthermore, the fact that the narrator of the account has a habit of expressing himself in the name of the Oranian community, of hiding behind it in a certain sense, reinforces the idea that the city is more than a simple backdrop. Witness the recurrent use of expressions emphasising this sense of belonging: 'in our little city', 'our city', 'our townsfolk'.[10] Granted this manner of speaking is ironic at times (I shall return to this at the end of the chapter), at other times in the text the narrator is careful precisely not to differentiate himself from what he considers the general opinion of the inhabitants of Oran:

> Ainsi, la première chose que la peste apportait à nos concitoyens fut l'exil. Et le narrateur est persuadé qu'il peut écrire ici, au nom de tous, ce que lui-même a éprouvé alors, puisqu'il l'a éprouvé en même temps que beaucoup de nos concitoyens. (*OC*, II, 81)
>
> [Thus the first thing that the plague brought to our town was exile. And the narrator is convinced that he can set down here, as holding good for all, the feeling he personally had and to which many of his friends confessed.][11]

This leads me to observe that the city in *La Peste*, or rather its social fabric, is the novel's true protagonist. Then, taking into account *both* current political affairs at the time Camus lived in Oran and began gathering information about the plague and Oran, on the eve of World War II, *and* the political engagement the author demonstrated all his life, we can assume that he was particularly sensitive to the political climate reigning there and that he sought to integrate it, in one fashion or another, into the text he was in the process of writing. Even if, over the course of the work's long gestation, current events in France under the Occupation had perhaps taken precedence in Camus's thoughts over those in Oran on the eve of the war, it is perfectly reasonable to believe that the history of this city, where his wife spent the war years, continues to resonate in the text.[12]

Oran and Francoist Spain

Let us begin with a little incursion into the history of Oran between the wars, in an attempt to determine the true nature of the epidemic evoked in the story, its 'Oranness' if you like. At the time of the French conquest on 17 August 1831, Oran had only 3000 inhabitants, the majority of them Jews. The latter had settled here when the city, for centuries a Spanish *presidio* on the Algerian coast, was conquered by the Ottomans (1791–1831). A century later, in 1936, the number of inhabitants had risen to more than 200,000. According to the demographic study carried out there by René Lespès in 1938, 67 per cent of the population were Europeans, a significant majority being of Spanish (65 per cent), Italian or Maltese origin. Metropolitan France, on the other hand, was not particularly well represented (19 per cent of the total population). The Jewish community constituted 11 per cent of the population, while Muslims (who used to represent a much smaller fraction, according to statistics from the beginning of the twentieth century) had attained a level of 24 per cent. Lespès characterises this recent growth of the Oranian Arab community as a veritable rush to the colonial city. Among their numbers were peasants from the surrounding countryside and from southern Algeria, workers re-emigrating from France because of the worldwide economic crisis, and a good number of Arab and Jewish immigrants of Moroccan origin.[13]

Lespès also presents very interesting information about the distribution of these different groups of inhabitants across the urban site. *La ville nouvelle*, consisting of the old Spanish city and a colonial expansion eastward, is inhabited by the Europeans and Jews. The latter, enjoying the same rights as the French colonist since 1870 (following the Crémieux decree that accorded them French citizenship), have succeeded in escaping the old Jewish quarter; in contrast, the bulk of the Algerian population find themselves relegated to the southern suburbs *extra muros* (like Lyautey and Lamur), which had over time been added onto the so-called *village nègre*. Located at the foot of the old ramparts, this area was created by General de Lamoricière in 1845 to rid the site of the future European city 'de tentes et de gourbis qui l'encombraient' [of encumbering tents and shacks].[14] And, lastly, living in the suburbs to the northeast and east of Oran are the Europeans of modest means, most often of Spanish origin. According to Lespès, nowhere in Algeria was the segregation of Europeans and Muslim Arabs as radical as in Oran:

> Un étranger pourrait parcourir la ville de l'Ouest à l'Est, selon sa plus grande dimension, sans soupçonner autrement que par la vue de deux ou trois minarets et par la rencontre de quelques indigènes musulmans, qu'elle en abrite un certain contingent. Il y chercherait en vain, même dans les quartiers où cette population domine, quelque chose de comparable à la Casbah d'Alger ou au quartier indigène de Constantine. En revanche, il lui suffirait d'un peu d'attention pour que son oreille perçût souvent sur son chemin le parler espagnol.[15]

[A stranger could cross the full expanse of the city from west to east, and apart from seeing, say, two or three minarets, and encountering a few Muslim natives, would never have guessed that this place was home to a considerable number of Muslims. Even in those parts of the city where these natives constituted the majority, he would have been hard put to find anything resembling the casbah of Algiers or the native quarter of Constantine. At the same time, though, it was fairly easy to hear Spanish spoken around him.]

One would have thought that the most Spanish city in colonial Algeria would please Camus, who made a veritable cult of his mother's country of origin.[16] But no, Camus did not much like Oran and the question arises whether his aversion was due solely to its lack of architectural charm, evoked in the opening of *La Peste* and in the brief essay that serves as introduction: 'Le Minotaure ou halte à Oran' (1939). For we can imagine equally well that Camus was repulsed more by the ethnic segregation reigning in Oran, along with the pronounced political conservatism of its population.[17]

As Caroline Bégaud explains very well in her thesis on the political life of Oran between the wars, the anti-Semitism inherited from the Dreyfus Affair, instead of fading away gradually as was the case in metropolitan France, became even keener in this colonial city in the early decades of the twentieth century.[18] Moreover, two successive mayors of Oran, Dr Molle (1923–31) and the very charismatic Abbot Lambert (1934–41) displayed a great sympathy for the pro-fascist Latin Unions. A sympathy that was shared, furthermore, by a large segment of the European community in Oran. In the years preceding World War II, this extreme-right faction grew increasingly influential.[19]

On this point, recall that the idea of a common Mediterranean culture held by Camus and his friends in Algiers was the antithesis of that of *Mare Nostrum* advocated by Mussolini and his Spanish counterparts. Witness the text of the inaugural speech that Camus delivered at the Maison de la Culture in Algiers on 8 February 1937, the year of his first visit to Oran. In it he reproaches the Italian Fascists for confounding Mediterranean and Latin and makes a plea for an inclusive Mediterranean culture, taking into account specifically the Oriental, meaning Arab, component of the Mediterranean melting pot.[20]

Obviously, there is a disparity between the political convictions of Camus on one side, and those of the good bourgeoisie of Oran on the other. In Oranie, tensions mount again in 1936 when the Front Populaire wins the elections in France and the new leftist government proposes a partial, limited assimilation measure in favour of the Algerian Muslims (the Blum-Violette project of 1936). Whereas Camus and his Algiers friends had fought for support of this reform, it was rejected out of hand by the colonists in Algeria. Note furthermore that, in Oran, resistance to this proposed law was even stronger than elsewhere in the colony. On 31 December 1937, the *Oran-Matin* (a fascist newspaper with a circulation of more than 50,000) publishes the following commentary: 'C'est qu'on muselle les Français qui ont fait de l'Algérie ce qu'elle est, et dont le travail et l'intelligence sont seuls capables de continuer et de mener à bien l'œuvre de civilisation entreprise' [This is how the

French are muzzled who have made Algeria into what it is today, and who, by their work and intelligence, are the only ones capable of turning the French colonial enterprise into an incontestable success].[21] On the eve of war, the widening gulf between the different political factions in Algeria, and particularly in Oran, proves to be insurmountable: whereas the Muslim Congress in Algiers calls for abrogation of Algeria's incorporation into France, the mayor of Oran, Lambert, pleads the case for the incorporation of the city of Oran into pro-Franco Spain. We can thus imagine that Camus (who, as a journalist for *Alger républicain*, a leftist paper, had naturally always supported Republican Spain) must have felt ill at ease in this murky atmosphere that deteriorated even more when metropolitan France was invaded by German troops.[22]

So it will be no surprise that, in 1940, the municipality of Oran allies itself immediately with the Vichy government. As for Pétain, he supports the German plan to give the region of Oran to pro-Franco Spain — a plan that will never be realised — and decides to annul the Crémieux decree, thus revoking the French citizenship of the Algerian Jews. These events also demonstrate the extent of the influence exercised by the colony over Metropolitan France at certain points in its history.[23]

The abolition of the Crémieux decree directly affected Camus's Oranian teacher friends. They found themselves expelled from the French schools overnight; Camus and his wife helped them as much as they could and it is clear that Camus, when he joined the French Resistance several years later, remembered this first experience of the social exclusion of Jews. In the context of Oran, however, Vichyism had revived a colonial, *fin-de-siècle* anti-Semitism that had never fully disappeared.[24]

This state of affairs seems to confirm the theory advanced by Paul Gilroy in *Against Race* that the racial politics associated with National Socialism grew out of, to some extent at least, colonial imperialism.[25] Camus, too, emphasised the link between colonial racism and fascism. Witness an article, published in *Combat* just after the war, that was no doubt inspired by the Sétif massacre of 8 May 1945:

> Il ne faut pas oublier que la politique de Vichy a trouvé en Algérie ses plus chauds partisans et qu'elle y a laissé des traces. À l'exception d'*Alger républicain* (et, dans une moindre mesure, d'*Oran républicain*), tous les quotidiens algériens ont collaboré.[26]

> [We should not forget that Vichy had its most devoted allies in Algeria and that this situation has left its mark on the country and its inhabitants. With the exception of *Alger républicain* (and, to a lesser extent, *Oran républicain*), all Algerian newspapers collaborated.]

Hence it is clear that for Camus the journalist there existed an undeniable link between colonial violence, such as was manifested at Sétif, and the dark political past of the colony, of which the recent history of Oran was the most obvious example.

The Plague: An Endogenous Illness

In order to situate *La Peste* as a literary text with respect to its colonial context, let us pass now from the history of events to the political discourse surrounding them. In the twentieth-century history of Oranian town planning, concerns about water and public health play a dominant role. The situation becomes even more urgent in the 1920s and 1930s, when the population density in Oran increases suddenly. As indicated above, this growth occurs primarily in the 'indigenous' suburbs.[27] In light of the real risk of a shortage of potable water, fear of a possible epidemic also heightens.

As Bégaud has pointed out, this fear (coloured no doubt by a feeling of being 'invaded,' even 'crushed', by a Jewish population in full social ascent and an ever-increasing mass of Algerians) will be exploited marvellously by the anti-Semitic and racist extreme-right, incarnated by the two successive mayors, Molle and Lambert: '[Pour Molle] l'association de la campagne de désinfection et du discours de la pureté de la race sont expressément concomitants. En 1934, l'abbé Gabriel Lambert s'inscrit dans un même cheminement populiste' [For Molle it went without saying that the disinfection campaign and the discourse on racial purity were very much of a kind. In 1934, the ideas of Father Gabriel Lambert showed a similar populist development].[28] We can imagine that the propagandist discourse linking urban hygiene to ethnic purging became more acrimonious during the era of the Front Populaire who wanted to grant citizenship to a greater number of the colonised in Algeria.

In one of the early drafts of *La Peste*, there is in fact a passage in which the narrator refers explicitly to the racism of the Oranians. The character Tarrou gives an account of a society soiree he had attended the evening before:

> En ce qui concerne la fièvre et les bruits qui se répandaient en ville, ce petit milieu avait été catégorique. *Tout venait de la saleté et la saleté venait des Juifs, des arabes et des étrangers qui étaient nombreux dans notre ville.*[29]

> [As for the fever and the rumours which spread across the town, this small circle had been adamant. *Everything was caused by filth and that filth came from the Jews, Arabs, and strangers who were numerous in our town.*]

In revising his text, Camus suppressed this passage. That did not prevent him, however, from appropriating, albeit in allegorical mode, the two constituent elements of the xenophobic discourse propounded by Oranian leaders (and taken up by the local press): the water problem and the fear of an epidemic. The first can be seen in a series of adjectives relating to the drought. From the opening description of Oran, the reader retains the arid and dusty nature of that city, the absence of water translating into an equal absence of greenery.

The risk of an epidemic is captured, of course, in the motif of the plague. But curiously (because it contradicts the idea of *La Peste* as an allegory of occupied France), the plague is not described as an exterior threat, but as an *endogenous* illness:

> Nos concitoyens stupéfaits découvraient les rats aux endroits les plus fréquentés de la ville. La place d'Armes, les boulevards, la promenade du Front-de-Mer,

> de loin en loin, étaient souillés. [...] On eût dit que la terre même où étaient plantées nos maisons se purgeait de son chargement d'humeurs, qu'elle laissait monter à la surface des furoncles et des sanies qui, jusqu'ici, *la travaillaient intérieurement*. (OC, II, 44; my emphasis)

> [Our townsfolk were amazed to find such busy centres as the Place d'Armes, the boulevards, the Strand, dotted with repulsive little corpses. [...] It was as if the earth on which our houses stood were being purged of its secreted humours — thrusting up to the surface the abscesses and pus-clots that had been forming in its entrails.] (*The Plague*, p. 13)

The image of the plague as a latent evil, ready to flare up again at any instant, is reprised in the last chapter of the novel:

> Car Rieux savait ce que cette foule en joie ignorait, et qu'on peut lire dans les livres, que le bacille de la peste ne meurt ni ne disparaît jamais, qu'il peut rester pendant des dizaines d'années endormi dans les meubles et le linge. (OC, II, 248)[30]

> [Rieux knew what those jubilant crowds did not know but could have learned from books: that the plague bacillus never dies or disappears for good; that it can lie dormant for years in furniture and linen-chests.] (*The Plague*, p. 297)

While the narrator seems to be referring here to potential future relapses of the illness, this passage, taken in a figurative sense, could also allude to the long history of racism in Oran evoked above. We can glean from it, in any case, that the city and the evil 'in its entrails' form an indivisible whole. Because, taking a stand against the prevailing racist discourse, this passage clearly indicates that the abject is inseparable from the town itself. The latter, as protagonist of the chronicle, does everything possible to project the abject outside of itself, by attributing it to 'others', specifically the non-Europeans.[31] On this point, we note that *La Peste* treats a theme very popular in Nazi propaganda of the same era, but inverts it. Under Camus's pen, the invasion of the rodents represents not 'the undesirable element' of society but the xenophobia that, in the case of Oran, is inherent to that society. In a certain sense, it is hatred of the other that seems to constitute the colonial city evoked in *La Peste*.[32]

This hypothesis would seem to be confirmed by the fact that the plague rages within the perimeter of the 'white' (protected) city rather than in the overpopulated 'indigenous' suburbs (which would have been much more realistic, from a purely medical point of view).[33] Moreover, the suburbs evoked in the novel are themselves of a decidedly European, indeed Christian, nature. Thus are mentioned, twice, 'the church bells of the city ringing'; and twice also, 'the cafés' and 'liquor' ('anise-flavored' or not); 'loving couples who fondled each other without a thought for appearances'; and again, 'churches' where 'thanksgiving services were being held' (OC, II, 239–41; *The Plague*, pp. 285–86). This leads me to observe, somewhat cautiously nonetheless, that the text is referring to the suburbs lying to the northeast and east of Oran, those inhabited, as was noted above, by 'Spaniards' of modest means.

Conclusion

In amputating the city of Oran from its unique Algerian aspect, namely, its overpopulated and increasingly populous southern suburbs, Camus has chosen to present the city to us as even more 'European' than it was at the time he knew it. But that does not in any way change my hypothesis that, in writing *La Peste*, Camus wished to confront his readers *additionally* with the specificity of a colonial reality with which he was preoccupied.

At the textual level, this is illustrated in various ways. First is the frequent use of irony by which the narrator, while taking refuge behind a 'we' representing the Oranian community, also distances himself from it at the same time. Second, and equally revealing, is the fact that the characters who resist the 'scourge' and who accordingly might be considered the real heroes of *La Peste* are not, for the most part, native to Oran. Tarrou is characterised as a 'foreigner' who lives at the hotel. Lambert, the Parisian journalist, is passing through. And Grand, finally, is originally from Montélimar. Rieux himself is also part of this tight intellectual circle within a city that, on the whole, is interested only in 'commerce and sports'.[34] Rieux will reveal himself, in the end, to be the somewhat aloof narrator of the story.

Third and last are two passages in the text that seem significant regarding this colonial reality. First, there is the passage in which Rieux and Tarrou go up to the rooftop terrace, and which is a foreshadowing of the scene in Camus's short story 'La Femme adultère' [*The Adulterous Woman*], in *L'Exil et le royaume* [*Exile and the Kingdom*] (1957), where the character Janine contemplates the landscape of southern Algeria from the upper terrace of an old fort.[35] In her analysis of this episode, Marie-Louise Pratt compares it to one of the recurrent figures in colonial discourse: the coloniser gazing out at the conquered land. By contrast, in 'La Femme adultère', written during the period when French domination of Algeria was coming to an end, the inverse takes place. The woman looking out is no longer able to 'decipher' the space stretching before her eyes. Like the French army, she apparently no longer has any hold on the colonised country.[36]

The nocturnal episode on the terrace in *La Peste* should be interpreted differently. It is not about the opposition between colonisers and colonised, but about the rift within the French community in Algeria: between a minority, represented by the two men on the terrace, promoting equal rights for various ethnic groups in the colony, and an opposing majority, symbolised by the city of Oran. In the passage under consideration, this opposition is conveyed by the panorama stretching before the eyes of the protagonists: the space of the Mediterranean is represented here as a world where one can breathe, whereas the urban space, observed from the rooftop terrace, offers a Dantesque sight. When the characters descend back into the city, 'il en venait un souffle chaud et malade *qui les poussait vers la mer*' [from it came warm, fetid breaths of air that urged them towards the sea] (*OC*, II, 212, my emphasis; *The Plague*, p. 245).

The contrast between the city and the Algerian countryside is reprised at the end of the story where the Mediterranean landscape is designated by the narrator as the 'true homeland' of the Oranians which:

> Se trouvait au-delà des murs de cette ville étouffée. Elle était dans ces broussailles odorantes sur les collines, dans la mer, les pays libres et le poids de l'amour. Et c'était vers elle, c'était vers le bonheur, que la foule des Oranais voulait revenir, se détournant du reste avec dégoût. (*OC*, II, 242)
>
> [Lay outside the walls of the stifled, strangled town, in the fragrant brushwood of the hills, in the waves of the sea, under free skies, and in the custody of love. And it was to this, their lost home, towards happiness, they longed to return, turning their backs disgustedly on all else.] (*The Plague*, p. 288)

We find here already the germ of the theme that the Algerian landscape, or rather the sentiment to which it gives birth, could serve as the cement between different ethnic groups of Algeria. A theme already present in Camus's earliest writings and to which he will return in 'L'Hôte' [*The Guest*], another of the short stories collected in *L'Exil et le royaume*.

This brings us back to the question I posed at the beginning: where must we search to find the great Absents of *La Peste*: the Algerians of Oran? I have no doubt that Camus meant for them to be included in the 'true homeland' of which the narrator of *La Peste* dreams. Their absence cannot be explained by an author's feeling of helplessness on finding himself confronted by a colonial policy caught in the gears of time and moving backward (the Blum-Violette project having failed and the Crémieux decree having been annulled some time earlier). The political disenchantment that had led to his Oranian sojourn indicated that Camus, as a novelist, was clinging once more to the hope that a celebration of a shared, native soil could succeed where politics had failed.

On this point, the following passage, taken from a letter from Camus to Roland Barthes, dated 11 January 1955, is quite revealing. Disagreeing keenly with the idea put forth by Barthes that the moral of *La Peste* was 'antihistorical', Camus replied to him: '*La Peste*, dans un sens, est *plus* qu'une chronique de la résistance. Mais assurément, elle n'est pas moins' [*The Plague*, in a sense, is *more* than a chronicle of the resistance. But it certainly is not less].[37] It is this '*more* historical' concealed in the text that I wanted to sound more deeply here. For it is not difficult to imagine that Camus, shortly after the Algerian resistance movement had declared war on the motherland on 1 November 1954, might have preferred to keep silent about the colonial 'truth' of his novel. It does, after all, concern the suppressed history of Oran as 'une ville sans soupçons' [a town without intimations], as it says in the opening of *La Peste* (*OC*, II, 36), where racism and fascism intersect.

Notes to Chapter 4

1. I wish to thank my two friends from Oran: Mohamed Daoud of the Centre de recherche en anthropologie sociale et culturelle (CRASC) for providing works crucial to this research; and Mohamed Sehaba for suggesting the key idea of a close study of the particular colonial history of his hometown.
2. Roger Quilliot in Albert Camus, *La Peste*, in *Œuvres complètes: théâtre, récits, nouvelles*, ed. by Roger Quilliot, Bibliothèque de la Pléiade (Paris: Gallimard, 1962), p. 1976, n. 2. It was not included in the second Pléiade edition, Albert Camus, *La Peste*, in *Œuvres complètes*, ed. by Jacqueline Lévi-Valensi, Raymond Gay-Crosier and others, 4 vols, Bibliothèque de la Pléiade

(Paris: Gallimard, 2006–08), II (hereafter referenced as *OC* in the main text). All translations in this chapter are mine unless stated otherwise.
3. Jacqueline Lévi-Valensi, *La Peste d'Albert Camus* (Paris: Gallimard, 1991), p. 35.
4. Cf. Alfred Salinas, *Quand Franco réclamait Oran: l'opération Cisneros* (Paris: Harmattan, 2008), pp. 179–80.
5. Camus's Oranian period is well documented by Olivier Todd in his biography of Camus, *Albert Camus: une vie* (Paris: Gallimard, 1996). Abdelkader Djemaï, *Camus à Oran* (Paris: Michalon, 1995), contains a wealth of information on Camus's Oran and also gives some detailed information on the reigning political climate at that time. For a less critical approach to the history of this city, see Mehdi Benchora, *Oran: sagesse et noblesse* (Es-Senia, Oran: Dar El Adib, 2007).
6. For the genesis of *La Peste*, I rely on the introductory bio-biographical note by Marie-Thérèse Blondeau in *OC*, II, 1133–69.
7. These biographical facts are taken from my chapter 'Albert Camus: A Life Lived in Critical Times', in *The Cambridge Companion to Camus*, ed. by Edward J. Hughes (Cambridge: Cambridge University Press, 2007), pp. 13–26.
8. Blondeau, *OC*, II, 1134 (my emphasis).
9. The provincial town of Nevers served as the setting for another war story that has become a classic: *Hiroshima, mon amour* (1959), the film directed by Alain Resnais, with screenplay by Marguerite Duras.
10. The concept of the city as a character in the novel is based on Hélène Yèche's excellent analysis of the *œuvre* of Berlin author Christoph Hein. Cf. Hélène Yèche, 'La Ville, acteur de l'histoire', in *Les Imaginaires de la ville*, ed. by Hélène and Gilles Menegaldo (Rennes: Presses universitaires de Rennes, 2007), pp. 453–61.
11. Albert Camus, *The Plague*, trans. by Stuart Gilbert [1948] (London: Penguin, 1960), p. 67 (hereafter referenced as *The Plague* in the main text).
12. This could also explain his wish, mentioned by Blondeau, to give a new orientation to his novel. Cf. *OC*, II, 1142, 1150, 1152. The quotation borrowed from Daniel Defoe that serves as the epigraph of *La Peste* seems to point in the same direction: 'Il est aussi raisonnable de représenter une espèce d'emprisonnement par une autre, que de représenter n'importe quelle chose qui existe réellement par quelque chose qui n'existe pas' [It is as reasonable to represent one kind of imprisonment by another as it is to represent anything which really exists by that which exists not]. The line is taken from Defoe's *Robinson Crusoe*.
13. René Lespès, *Oran: étude de géographie et d'histoire urbaines* [1938] (Oran: Bel Horizon, 2003), pp. 92–111.
14. Ibid., p. 115.
15. Ibid., p. 122.
16. On Camus the Hispanophile, see Frédéric Jacques Temple and others, *Albert Camus et l'Espagne* (Aix-en-Provence: Edisud, 2005), and Edward J. Hughes, 'Autobiographical Soundings in *L'Envers et l'Endroit*', in *The Cambridge Companion to Camus*, ed. by Hughes, pp. 39–49 (p. 46).
17. I do not address here the personal physical aspect that must have also played a role, but which, as indicated above, is largely documented by Blondeau in *OC*, II.
18. See Caroline Bégaud, 'La Troisième République française coloniale en Algérie: pour une histoire politique d'Oran de 1930 à 1939' (doctoral thesis, Université de Lille III, 1999). As the legibility of the microfiche copy I consulted left something to be desired, it is not always possible to indicate a page number.
19. Ibid.
20. Cf. Ieme van der Poel, '"La Méditerranée" d'Albert Camus', in *Albert Camus et les lettres algériennes*, ed. by Afifa Bererhi, 2 vols (Algiers: University of Algiers, 2007), II, 377–89. Camus does not mention the Jewish minority in Algeria in the text of this speech, but there is no doubt that he refuted all forms of racism without exception.
21. Cited by Bégaud in 'La Troisième République française coloniale en Algérie'. The information on *Oran-Matin* is borrowed from Pascal Blanchard who gives a detailed overview of the Algerian press in the 1930s. See Pascal Blanchard, 'La Vocation fasciste de l'Algérie coloniale dans les

années 1930', in *De l'Indochine à l'Algérie*, ed. by Nicolas Bancel, Daniel Denis and Youssef Fates (Paris: La Découverte, 2003), pp. 178–80.
22. This state of affairs renders less probable the interpretation of Javier Figuero who draws a comparison between the inhabitants of Oran ('Spanish city in Algerian France'), such as they are represented in *La Peste*, and the suffering of the Spanish Republicans. See Javier Figuero, *Albert Camus ou l'Espagne exaltée*, trans. by Marie-Hélène Carbonel (Gémenos: Autre Temps, 2008), pp. 160–61.
23. Cf. Marie-Louise Pratt, *Imperial Eyes: Travel Writing and Transculturation*, 2nd edn (London & New York: Routledge, 2008), p. 4.
24. Olivier Todd, *Albert Camus: A Life*, trans. by Benjamin Ivry (New York: Carroll & Graf, 2000), pp. 120–27.
25. Cf. Paul Gilroy, *Against Race: Imagining Political Culture Beyond the Color Line* (Cambridge, MA: Belknap Press of Harvard University Press, 2000), esp. Chapter 4, 'Hitler Wore Khakis'.
26. Albert Camus, 'C'est la justice qui sauvera l'Algérie de la haine', in *OC*, II, 617.
27. Whereas in 1901 the inhabitants of the suburbs represented only 13.2 per cent of the population of Oran, in 1936 they constituted 44.7 per cent (see Lespès, *Oran*, p. 114).
28. Bégaud, 'La Troisième République française coloniale en Algérie'; Blanchard, 'La Vocation fasciste de l'Algérie coloniale dans les années 1930', pp. 177–95. To this we shall also add personal testimonies about prevailing anti-Semitism, especially those of Hélène Cixous who grew up in the city of Oran in a Jewish family. Hélène Cixous, 'L'Affrance', in *C'était leur France: en Algérie, avant l'Indépendance*, ed. by Leïla Sebbar (Paris: Gallimard, 2007), pp. 89–105.
29. *OC*, II, 1176 (my emphasis).
30. On the plague and fabrics, see Frédéric Audoin-Rouzeau, *Les Chemins de la peste* (Rennes: Presses universitaires de Rennes, 2003), pp. 317–32.
31. For the notion of the abject, see Julia Kristeva, *Pouvoirs de l'horreur: essai sur l'abjection* (Paris: Seuil, 1980).
32. Cf. Andreas Huyssen, *Present Pasts: Urban Palimpsests and the Politics of Memory* (Stanford, CA: Stanford University Press, 2003), pp. 122–38.
33. On this point, a letter from one of Camus' friends, Lucette Maeurer, is quite revealing. Referring to a typhus epidemic that hit the region at that time, Maeurer mentions 'certains douars et villages [...] consignés' [certain locked-down settlements and villages], as well as a vaccination campaign, likewise targeted at the native, and not the European, population of the colony (cf. *OC*, II, 272–75).
34. This is confirmed by Bégaud, according to whom, Oran differed from Algiers in that it lacked an intellectual class predisposed to a more enlightened concept of colonialism ('La Troisième République française coloniale en Algérie').
35. Albert Camus, 'La Femme adultère', in *L'Exil et le royaume* [1957] (Paris: Gallimard Folio, 2001), pp. 25–28.
36. See Pratt, *Imperial Eyes*, pp. 218–20.
37. For the critical essay by Roland Barthes and the full text of Camus's response, see Roland Barthes, *Œuvres complètes*, ed. by Eric Marty, 5 vols (Paris: Seuil, 2002), I, 540–47.

PART II

Algeria and the French Colonial Project

CHAPTER 5

Ces hommes qu'on raie de l'humanité: Transcolonial Connections in the French Penal Colony

Charles Forsdick

In December 1938, Albert Camus witnessed (and immediately reported in *Alger républicain*, the paper for which he was working as a journalist at the time) the final convict voyage from Algiers to French Guiana of *La Martinière*, a vessel known as the 'bagne flottant' [floating prison].[1] Although the ship had undertaken other journeys (including with a cargo of Vietnamese political prisoners from the penal colony of Poulo Condore in 1931), its main role in the interwar period was to link the Île de Ré with Saint-Laurent-du-Maroni, transporting prisoners condemned to forced labour in French Guiana, which then served as France's principal penal colony.[2] In total, there were twenty-four transatlantic crossings, with the first leaving France in June 1921, and this the final one (observed by Camus) in November 1938. The ship had been built in Hartlepool and launched under the name of *Armanistan* in 1912. Sold the following year to the German company Hamburg-Amerika Linie, the vessel was renamed *Duala* and serviced West African routes until, in 1919, it was acquired by France in the aftermath of the First World War and entered service with the Compagnie nantaise de navigation à vapeur. Two years later, *La Martinière* began its transatlantic voyages, undertaking what was often a twice-yearly journey with up to 670 convicts held onboard in its eight cages below deck. The initial loading of prisoners from Saint-Martin-de-Ré is a topos in representations of the *bagne*, notably in the two cinematic versions of Henri Charrière's *Papillon* and also in the increasing number of *bandes dessinées* devoted to the penal colonies; but what is less known is *La Martinière*'s regular detour via the Algerian capital to collect the *bagnards* sentenced in the colony.[3] This chapter explores these rarely studied reflections by Camus on the *bagne* and then integrates them into broader debates about the place of the penitentiary of French Guiana in a broader transcolonial frame.

Mouloud Akkouche's *Cayenne, mon tombeau* (2001) (of which more below) is one of very few novels to explore the experience of Algerian convicts in the French penal system.[4] It interweaves the account of its late twentieth-century narrator, Rachid Benoucif (known under the name of Richard Lemaire), for whom integration into French society is a way to escape from his migrant roots, with that of his father, Mohamed, whose own nine-decade itinerary took him from rural Algeria in the 1920s via the penal colony of French Guiana to the postwar France of the *trente glorieuses* where he eventually settles and starts a family in Montreuil. Akkouche's text is a striking reminder that the *bagne* often operates in contemporary French culture as a *lieu d'oubli*, present often in a sensationalist form in the perennially popular autobiographical and cinematic narratives of celebrity convicts such as Henri Charrière (aka Papillon), but largely absent otherwise from the practices of memory in late twentieth- and early twenty-first-century France.[5] The penal colony was designed with a dual purpose in mind, to expunge from France those considered politically or socially undesirable while providing a workforce to exploit resources from parts of the colonial empire considered less desirable as settler destinations than, for instance, North Africa. In a postcolonial context, such a strategy seems doubly outmoded, meaning that those seeking to understand France's century-long policy of penal transportation must seek out what Patrick Chamoiseau, in a photo-essay on the French Guianese *bagne*, dubs 'traces-mémoires', i.e. fragmentary traces of memory evident in the ephemera of the past or via the imaginaries of the present.[6]

In his novel, Akkouche points to this ambivalent persistence of a carceral memory: Mohamed, having been freed from the forced labour of the *bagne* following the final abolition of the institution in 1945, rapidly abandons his family farm in Algeria to seek work in early 1950s France as a carpenter. His existence is a precarious one as he sleeps on the benches in a bar in return for helping its *patron* Amar with light tasks around the business. As they agree this arrangement, Amar notes: 'T'es mieux ici qu'à Cayenne, quand même' [still, you're better off here that in Cayenne] (*Cayenne*, 319), in response to which Mohamed merely shrugs his shoulders. As far as we know, Amar has no knowledge of Mohamed's past and views him as one of the thousands of North African workers who migrated to France in the wake of the Second World War. The reference to the *bagne* seems to be purely figurative, an example of integration of a reference to the penal colony's harsh conditions into everyday French language. Léon-Gontran Damas provides a similar example in *Retour de Guyane*: 'Toi, dira une mère qui souffre de trouver en son fils l'âme d'un dévoyé, tu finiras tes jours à Cayenne' [You, as a mother will say, seeing in her son the soul of one who has lost his way, you'll end your days in Cayenne], creating an allusion to a carceral everyday deployed as casual reference or threat but strangely removed from the context of its original signification.[7] As such, in metropolitan France itself, we see that the penal colony persists as a form of *trace-mémoire*, largely eclipsed despite its relative historical proximity when compared to its British equivalent in Australia, but nevertheless hidden (not least linguistically) in plain sight.

This chapter explores the dynamics of this absent presence, drawing initially on references to the *bagne* in the work of Albert Camus before considering more broadly — in particular via a closer reading of Akkouche's largely unstudied novel

— the hidden histories of the French penal colony as they begin to surface in the present. As the twentieth-century French author most committed to exploring the theme of justice, theoretical as well as practical, Camus inevitably includes the *bagne* in his field of reference. The most sustained focus on the institution appeared in the article cited above in *Alger républicain* in 1937, the year proceeding the abolition of the penal colony, when Camus the journalist observed the embarkation onto the convict ship *La Martinière* of the last Algerian *bagnards* condemned to serve their sentences in French Guiana. The *bagne* nevertheless features more broadly in his writings, most notably in the play *Les Justes*, Camus's 1949 reflection on the moral dimensions of murder and terrorism through the story of the group of Russian socialist revolutionaries who assassinated the Grand Duke Sergei Alexandrovich in 1905.[8] The fictional revolutionary Stepan Fedorov refers to the *bagne* in his aphorisms, but his nihilism is also explained by references to his own escape from a penal colony three years before the play's action, an experience of incarceration that leaves him with physical scars. The penal colony thus functions as one of a series of mechanisms of oppression, leading to the enslavement of the people, against which the revolutionaries seek their 'just revolt'.[9] Camus's other play dealing with state terror, *L'État de siège*, also includes a passing reference to penal colonies when the protagonist Diego says to the allegorical figure 'La Peste' [The Plague]: 'Dans tes bagnes et dans tes charniers. Les esclaves sont sur les trônes' [In your prisons and in your grave-pits. Slaves sit on thrones],[10] and in the first volume of *Carnets*, in the notes for *L'Étranger*, the *bagne* serves, like capital punishment, as a point of reference through which Camus reflects on the absurdity of the human condition.[11]

Allusions to penal colonies are relatively common elsewhere in Camus's *œuvre* too, with several references for instance in *L'Homme révolté*, where again they are not only figurative but also literal, often referring to the Soviet Union whose gulags provided a case study for reflections on the effects of witnessing the systematic brutalisation of others. In an editorial published in *Combat* on 30 August 1945 (reprinted in *Actuelles I*) Camus critiques the *Épuration* by claiming that the forced labour of 'le bagne' is a disproportionate punishment for the pacifist René Gérin.[12] There are also a number of more figurative references to the *bagne*, with for instance in *Les Justes* the aphoristic claim that 'la liberté est un bagne aussi longtemps qu'un seul homme est asservi sur la terre' [Freedom is a prison so long as even one single man on earth is enslaved], or with the penal colony being deployed in *L'Homme révolté* as a reflection of the human condition: 'Nous portons tous en nous nos bagnes, nos crimes et nos ravages. Mais notre tâche n'est pas de les déchaîner à travers le monde; elle est de les combattre en nous-mêmes et dans les autres' [We all carry within us our prisons, our crimes and what tears us apart. But our task is not to let them loose upon the world; it is to combat them within ourselves and in others].[13] While some of these allusions are rooted, as I have noted, in a reflection on the Soviet gulags, most of them remain primarily abstract, although it is possible that there are links between Camus's arguments for a Bill of Human Rights in the context of *le monde concentrationnaire* in the 1946 series of articles 'Ni victimes ni bourreaux' and the conditions in the French Guianese penitentiary under Vichy.[14]

As has been noted above, possibly the only direct engagement with the *bagne* in French Guiana occurs in his article in *Alger républicain* in December 1938, an account of a *fait divers* — the departure of the convict ship *La Martinière* for the last time from Algiers — that is transformed into a reflection on humanity and the implications of its systematic denial through the institutions of incarceration. The tensions between these two functions of the article, journalistic and philosophical, so common in Camus's work, are evident in the juxtaposition between the dramatic title ('Ces hommes qu'on raie de l'humanité' [These men who are erased from humanity]) and the matter-of-fact subtitle ('57 relégués ont quitté avant-hier Alger pour le bagne' [57 convicts left Algiers two days ago, bound for the penal colony]). The timing was significant, for two years previously, following notable interventions by the Salvation Army Captain Charles Péan and French Guianese *député* Gaston Monnerville, the French had decided to discontinue the use of the overseas penal colony. However, the relevant *décret-loi* was only signed in 1938, and this abolished only *transportation* to French Guiana (i.e. of those sent to South America, often for serious crimes, for a sentence of hard labour), and not yet *relégation* (i.e. the deportation of recidivists whom the penal colony distanced as far away as possible from France and Algeria).[15] It would only be in March 1945, following the Second World War, and following the deaths of hundreds of *relégués* under the Vichy regime, that the *bagne* was finally closed and the repatriation of convicts began. The irony would not have been lost on Camus who observed prisoners, often guilty of a series of minor crimes, being transported to serve their sentences in a barbaric institution with roots in the nineteenth century whose obsolescence, by December 1938, had already been acknowledged by the state.

Camus's account of the vessel is written sparingly. The ship is 'long et spacieux' [long and spacious], with its 'singulière marchandise' [singular merchandise] (the 609 recidivists who had embarked at Saint-Martin-de-Ré) already occupying the limited space allocated in the hold (*OC*, 1, 585). The article — with its reference to a storm in the Atlantic through which the ship has travelled — alludes to the harsh conditions onboard, but the curiosity of members of the public who had assembled to witness the arrival of *La Martinière* is left strangely dissatisfied by the spectacle of an empty deck and a boat left alone by all other users of the port. Camus speculates:

> Peut-être à cause de cette odeur de solitude et de désespoir qu'on rencontre dans les coursives où pas un homme ne vit ni ne plaisante. Mais peut-être à cause de cette vie sinistre et sans avenir qu'on devine sous les planches que le pied martèle. (*OC*, 1, 585)
>
> [Perhaps because of that smell of solitude and despair that one encounters in the gangways where no man lives or breathes. But perhaps because of that sinister and issueless future that can be sensed beneath the planks hammered by walking feet.]

The journalist embarks to view more closely the conditions onboard, and it is the soundscape of the convict ship — 'le bruit sourd et rauque qui monte par intermittences des profondeurs de la cale' [the muffled, hoarse sound that rises intermittently from the depths of the hold] (*OC*, 1, 586) — that strikes him initially.

Descending below deck, his eyes slowly grow accustomed to the dark as he describes the conditions (90–100 men in cages, measuring 10 × 5 metres, largely devoid of any natural light) in which the prisoners are detained during the voyage.[16] The author then takes in further details such as the two tiny punishment cells used for solitary confinement, or the vent above each cage used to spray scalding steam on the prisoners in cases of unrest, before the rolling motion of the ship, as it casts light from one side of the hold to the other, allows him at last to observe the human cargo: 'il me faut du temps pour voir et discerner des hommes dans cette masse sans visages qui respire et chuchote' [my eyes need time to adjust and discern men amidst this faceless mass that breathes and whispers] (OC, I, 586).

Camus's immediate reaction is to attempt to rehumanise what he witnesses, to discern in the faceless, shapeless, shadowy anonymous mass of men 'les signes de leur resemblance avec le monde qui m'entoure tous les jours' [signs of their resemblance to the world that surrounds me every day] (OC, I, 586). Moving to the rear of the hold, he finds a better lit space with smaller cages, one of which is empty as it is prepared to receive the Algerian prisoners about to embark. This second scene allows an exchange of gazes, although the article observes the inscrutability of faces described. The exception is a group of 'trois Arabes' who, huddled around a porthole, look towards Algiers. Camus detects in this scene a moment of acute dehumanisation. Whereas, for the French convicts, the view — despite its inherent exoticism — was a source of indifference in a context of imposed reclusion from the outside world ('une terre étrangère dans un monde désormais étranger' [a foreign land in a world from now on foreign]), for these Arab men it provided a trace of hope and of connection to their life before incarceration ('un peu d'eux-mêmes qu'ils cherchent à travers la pluie' [a bit of themselves that they are looking for through the rain]) (OC, I, 587). Camus's response veers between discomfort at his passive complicity in the scene he views ('Je ne suis pas très fier d'être là' [I am not very proud to be here]) and a sense that his presence more actively accentuates the alienation that the men experience: just his damp raincoat freights 'l'odeur d'un monde où les hommes courent et peuvent sentir le vent' [the smell of a world where men run and can feel the wind] (587). His role as what Michael Rothberg has dubbed an 'implicated subject' is palpable in a final detail: 'un des hommes me demande en arabe une cigarette' [one of the men asks me for a cigarette in Arabic] (587).[17] Camus's instinctive reaction is to state that the ship's rules prevent this (prisoners were forbidden from smoking or carrying knives onboard), but he remains silent: 'quelle dérisoire réponse pour qui demande seulement une marque de complicité et un geste d'homme' [what a derisory response for someone who only asks for an indication of complicity and a gesture of humanity] (587).

It is this dehumanised context, rendering impossible any act of reciprocity, that creates a more general sense of repugnance that Camus now associates with the actual embarkation of the Algerian prisoners. The miserable weather, wet and windy, sets the scene for the arrival, at 14h55 (the precision reflects the denial of individual agency, the imposition of institutionalised time), of the three buses transporting the *relégués*. Camus notes with irony that the means of transport is provided by the local Chemins de Fer sur routes d'Algérie, meaning that the prisoners might previously have used these vehicles in their everyday lives before their arrest ('Mais alors,' he notes, 'il y avait des arrêts. Et à ces arrêts, on descendait' [But then there were stops. And at these stops, you could get off] (*OC*, I, 587), playing undoubtedly on the polysemy of the term *arrêts*, meaning 'bus stops' but also, in military terminology, 'arrests'). The journey on that day has only one destination: 'ils descendent à l'extrémité de cette terre qui est la leur, à quelques pas de l'eau' [they get off at the extremity of this land that is their own, a few steps from the waterside'] (587). The final stage of the journey out of Algeria is on a barge, and the rainbow that temporarily interrupts the rain does nothing to distract the human cargo: 'Des cinquante-sept relégués accroupis au milieu du chaland pas un seul n'a relevé la tête' [Of the fifty-seven convicts crouched in the middle of the barge not one of them looked up] (588). Camus follows the embarkation of the men, noting their constant surveillance, the efficiency of their immediate incarceration in the cages he has recently observed.

In a matter of hours after its arrival, *La Martinière* departs with its 'honteuse et pitoyable cargaison' [shameful and pitiable cargo], and as Camus processes what he has seen and described, he turns to the one moment of (unrealised) human contact, the (non-)exchange with the man who addressed him in Arabic and requested a cigarette (*OC*, I, 588). His aim is not to romanticise those subject to French colonial justice: he acknowledges that these recidivists are the 'rebut de la société' [the dregs of society], while critiquing the social privilege of those willing to deploy such charged vocabulary of fellow human beings; but he makes it clear that his response is not that of pity but one rooted in a reflection on the extreme dehumanisation inherent in the penal system: 'Il n'y a pas de spectacle plus abject que de voir des hommes ramenés au-dessous de la condition de l'homme' [There is no more abject spectacle than to see men brought down beneath the condition of man] (588). Camus's attention is finally drawn away from the vessel to people beside him on the quay, notably 'les dames élégantes que la curiosité avait amenées là' [elegant ladies drawn there by curiosity] (588). Here, he describes a form of penal exoticism that, for centuries and culminating in forms of so-called dark tourism common in the twenty-first century, has turned punishment into spectacle.[18] He foregrounds an ethics of carceral spectatorship, seeking to generate among these women 'un sentiment qu'on est gêné d'avoir à leur rappeler et qui s'appelle la pudeur' [a feeling that one is troubled by having to remind them of and which is called modesty] (588). Camus concludes that judgement is no longer necessary, that pity would be a puerile response, but that there is a need to focus nevertheless (in terms anticipated already in his title) on 'ce destin singulier et définitif par lequel des hommes sont rayés de l'humanité' [this singular and definitive destiny by which men are erased from humanity] (588), a condition whose horror is exacerbated by its irrevocability. It is clear that the dehumanisation he recorded during the embarkation would continue throughout the voyage when accounts by crew members record the brutality including sexual assault inflicted on Algerian prisoners.[19]

The article in *Alger républicain* is not only a concrete illustration of the more metaphorical reflections on the *bagne* evident in Camus's other work discussed above, but also integrates the reality of French penal colony into an existing penal archipelago, stretching from the Nazi concentration camps to the Soviet gulags, of whose role in 'le fait concentrationnaire' the author remained a tireless student and critic. Camus could not have foreseen the convergence of the practices underpinning France's remaining penal colony in French Guiana and the genocide of which Nazi concentration camps served as a vehicle. It is likely that a number of the 666 *relégués* whose embarkation he describes were among the victims of the Vichy regime in French Guiana. Fear of convict escape (and in particular of their rallying to the Free French, as was the case of around seventy *bagnards* in February 1941) led to a hardening of conditions and regulations that had been notoriously harsh since the establishment of the penal colony in 1852.[20] The working day was lengthened, rations reduced and the punishment regime greatly enhanced, meaning that the death rate by 1942 reached nearly 50% (513 of 1,068 remaining *relégués* died during that year), a level of mortality close to that in Nazi concentration camps. In a 2017 'tribune' in *Le Monde*, Robert Badinter — an activist, like Camus himself, against the death penalty in France — called for recognition of the treatment of these men as a crime against humanity, but in this context it is important to underline the ways in which Camus's article serves an additional purpose, that of projecting a more inclusive view of the victims of the oppression it describes.[21] It fulfils, therefore, several functions in addition to chronicling an historic, final transatlantic crossing of *bagnards* to French Guiana. By emphasising the dehumanisation inherent in the penal system, he seeks to restore the humanity of the convicts undergoing transportation; but at the same time, as he foregrounds the presence of Algerian prisoners onboard *La Martinière*, he underlines the multi-ethnic and actively transcolonial dimensions of the penal colony and challenges metropolitan myths of its whiteness.

The *Alger républicain* article notes, not without irony, the fact that the ship was commonly known as the 'bateau blanc' [white boat], and it is true that *La Martinière* was associated primarily with journeys linking metropolitan France with Saint-Laurent-du-Maroni, the point of arrival of convicts in French Guiana. As has been suggested already, the fascination with penal exoticism led to a proliferation of iconography associated with the embarkation point on the Île de Ré, with numerous postcards or black-and-white illustrations in true crime magazines catering for this public appetite. What emerges from these popular cultural representations is a myth of the whiteness of the *bagne*, seen primarily as a destination for the French convicts who previously, until the mid-nineteenth century, would have been condemned to hard labour in the *bagnes métropolitains* of Toulon, Rochefort and Brest. The colour-blindness relating to the institution, reminiscent of that in other areas of French history such as popular accounts of the Liberation in 1944, is reflected also in the focus on celebrity prisoners who were both white and French: including Alfred Dreyfus, Henri Charrière and René Belbenoît in French Guiana, Louise Michel and Henri Rochefort in New Caledonia.

This is a tendency associated with the dark tourism increasingly evident at these sites of penal heritage. Ethnologist Bernard Cherubini sees evidence of the self-perpetuation of such views of whiteness in the various memorial practices associated with the *bagne*, all of which are to be understood in relation to the representations that often underpin them: 'tourists also come to Guiana to walk in the footsteps of the convicts they heard about in their youth through literature and cinema and through the stories, testimonials and biographical accounts of former political prisoners or transported convicts'.[22] Patrick Chamoiseau, in the photo-essay *Guyane* produced with the photographer Rodolphe Hammadi, has been instrumental in challenging such one-dimensional and homogenised views. Published in the wake of the *Éloge de la créolité*, this work seeks to decolonise and, in the process, diversify understandings of the *bagne*.[23] A direct response to the limitation of Pierre Nora's *Lieux de mémoire* project to the boundaries of metropolitan France, Chamoiseau's intervention challenges the dominance of the memorial landscape in French Guiana by monuments honouring Europeans ('Les statues et les plaques de marbres célèbrent découvreurs et conquistadores, gouverneurs et grands adminstrateurs' [statues and marble plaques celebrate discoverers and conquistadors, governors and senior administrators]) and seeks instead to commemorate the other groups who predated colonisation or were central to the establishment of empire: 'des autres populations (Amérindiens, esclaves africains, immigrants hindous, syro-libanais, chinois...) qui, précipitées sur ces terres coloniales, ont dû trouver moyen, d'abord de survivre, puis de vivre ensemble, jusqu'à produire une entité culturelle et identitaire originale' [other populations (Amerindians, African slaves, Hindu immigrants, Syrio-Lebanese, Chinese...) who, precipitated into these colonial lands, had to find a means first of all to survive, then to live together, to the point of producing an original cultural and identitarian entity] (*Guyane*, 13–14).

The fragmentation from which the *créoliste* potential for unity emerges is in part a function of the brutality that is detected in the remnants of the penal colony, evidence of the contagious dehumanisation associated with the institution that Camus himself had already described that affected the incarcerated as much as those who observe them. Chamoiseau claims: 'L'horreur emmêlait tout. Une telle inhumanité comme objet d'une administration infectait la fonction même de surveiller' [The horror contaminated everything. Inhumanity of this sort as the object of an administration infected the very function of surveillance] (*Guyane*, 29). He does not explicitly refer to prisoners of North African origin, but they inevitably must feature prominently, alongside *bagnards* from the colonies of Indochina, in any efforts to understand sites such as French Guiana in their transcolonial complexity. *Guyane* results from direct contact with the material ruins of the penal colony as its author, inspired by Hammadi's photographs, seeks an alternative form of memory practice that challenges dominant narratives and allows room for subaltern voices. Chamoiseau insists on the role of artists, stating that 'le conservateur sera l'engeance des poètes' [the curator will be the same breed as the poets] (*Guyane*, 45). Creative intervention thus plays a role in reanimating these memories once they have been recovered: 'il faudrait faire vivre ces Traces-mémoires après avoir immobilisé les procès de leur usure' [it would be necessary to invigorate these memory-traces after having immobilised the processes that wear them out] (*Guyane*, 44), with the result that traditional penal historiography is eschewed for reference to other sources: 'Il vaut mieux résister à l'écriture historique sur le bagne et tenter d'en percevoir ce que les Traces-mémoires nous murmurent' [It's better to resist historical writing on the penal colony and to try to ascertain from them what these memory-traces murmur to us] (*Guyane*, 23–24). The work that Chamoiseau proposes here has been conducted in another penal context, that of New Caledonia, by the Algerian film maker Mehdi Lallaoui who deployed his own creative practice to uncover the stories of Kabyle political prisoners banished to Melanesia following the 1871 Mokrani Revolt, the most significant local uprising against the French in Algeria since the conquest in 1830. It is customarily the Paris Communards, exiled to the Île des Pins around the same time as the Algerian rebels, who have attracted more attention, but in a book and film, both entitled *Kabyles du Pacifique*, Lallaoui explores the geographical and historical displacements of those evoked in his title and draws together the pieces of 'un puzzle dont les morceaux sont disséminés dans le monde entier' [a puzzle whose pieces are spread across the whole world].[24]

The place of Algerian *bagnards* in French Guiana has been the subject of increasing and parallel attention in recent years, not least because of the ways in which this field of inquiry illuminates broader understandings of colonial control. As Linda Amiri notes, 'ce territoire français en Amérique a été l'une des clefs de voûte du maintien de la domination coloniale, d'Alger à Yên Bái' [this French territory in America has been one of the keystones in maintaining colonial domination from Algiers to Yên Bái].[25] As the example of the 1871 Mokrani Revolt makes clear, deportation and transportation were key elements of the French response to anti-colonial resistance, with dissidents incarcerated in France itself and also on Corsica. With the development of overseas penal colonies for civil prisoners in the second half of the nineteenth century, a limited number of Algerians were sent to the *bagne* in Djibouti, newly inaugurated in 1886. More were transported to New Caledonia, where over 1800 convicts were sent between 1867 and 1897, and over one hundred and sixty recidivists between 1889 and 1897.[26] The majority, however, served their sentences in French Guiana, with Mustapha Hadj Ali estimating that over twenty thousand Algerian prisoners were sent there between 1852 and 1946, constituting almost 30 per cent of the total number of *bagnards* held there over this period.[27] The term *forçat arabe* [Arab convict] was first used in official statistics in 1866, a year before the French authorities suspended the transportation of metropolitan French prisoners to Guiana, as a result of which, for two decades, the percentage of Algerians in the total prison population rose significantly.[28] The annual numbers fluctuate according to external factors (such as the suspension of transportation during the First World War) as well as institutional considerations (such as the use of New Caledonia as an alternative destination). For the early decades of the twentieth century, there were two departures a year from Algiers, with an average of two hundred Algerian prisoners crossing the Atlantic each year. The interruption of the war led to overcrowding of Algerian gaols, meaning that there were four sailings from Algiers transporting over 1,000 *bagnards* in 1921.

Historian of the *bagne* Michel Pierre tracks the fluctuating numbers of Algerian prisoners sent to French Guiana, noting the steady increase as a percentage of the total number of those serving civil sentences in the colony: 'Très faible au début du bagne, il a été majoritaire au début des années 1880, autour de 20 à 30% de l'effectif sous la Troisième République, pour atteindre 40% dans les années 1930' [Very low at the beginning of the penal colony, the number of Algerian *bagnards* was the majority proportion by the early 1880s, around 20–30 per cent of the total number during the Third Republic, and reached 40 per cent in the 1930s].[29] Pierre also notes the lack of knowledge of the nature of the crimes being punished, although there is evidence in court records of a significant number of domestic incidents often linked to local vendettas, and it is clear that levels of criminality were increased by the pauperisation associated with enforced rural exodus under empire.[30] In French Guiana itself, it seems that the Algerian prisoners, many of whom came from rural communities and had limited literacy skills, lived as 'une communauté séparée par la langue, la religion, les coutumes et les modes de vie, des condamnés européens' [a community separated by language, religion, customs and ways of life, from European convicts].[31] The crimes for which they were committed were different from those for which French convicts had been found guilty, and the penal cultures they developed — notably in the limited adoption of tattooing — also diverged from French metropolitan practices. At the same time, Algerian prisoners often took on the role of *porte-clé* [key holder], reflecting a degree of trust among the penal authorities but also generating tensions with metropolitan prisoners upon ethnic grounds.[32]

With the *bagne* abolished following the Second World War, the repatriation of Algerian prisoners began in 1946, under the auspices of the Salvation Army. A large group of eight hundred returned in 1948, but a small community remained in French Guiana, with *lieux de mémoire* associated with them remaining limited. Having completed a similar project in New Caledonia entitled *Les Témoins de la mémoire*, the Algerian filmmaker Saïd Oulmi has sought to gather memorial traces of Algerian *bagnards* in French Guiana. Outside the work of a small group of historians, including Linda Amiri and Marine Coquet, the histories of this group, the embarkation of whose final members was witnessed by Camus in Algiers, have been rarely and only partially told. In this sense, the erasure to which Camus refers in the title of 'Ces homme qu'on raie de l'humanité' is two-fold, the dehumanisation of the *bagnards* in their contemporary interwar context compounded with their silencing in subsequent history. As is often the case with lacunae in French colonial historiography, the task of collecting and re-imagining these narratives has fallen to creative writers. It seems fitting, therefore, that the memory-traces in the article in *Alger républicain* should find contemporary echoes in *Cayenne, mon tombeau*, the novel by Algerian author Mouloud Akkouche cited above. It is with some reflections on this text that the chapter concludes.

The novel opens in Béjaïa in July 1927, at the trial of Mohamed Benoucif, aged twenty-four, accused of murdering two Frenchmen (one of whom was a soldier) when coming to the aid of a friend in a bar fight (Mohamed is at the time in the French army himself, on leave from service suppressing the Rif rebellion). Engaging with great difficulty in a trial conducted in a colonial language with which he is not well acquainted (his *tutoiement* of the judge is misconstrued as a further act of subordination), Benoucif (dismissed as an 'indigène analphabète' [illiterate native]) is sentenced to 'quinze ans de travaux forcés' (*Cayenne*, 12, 16). Akkouche describes his embarkation on *La Martinière* (a decade before Camus would witness its final voyage), evoking similar details to Camus but in his account from the perspective of the incarcerated and their families: 'Les pleurs des femmes se mêlèrent au clapotis des vagues contre les flancs du bateau' [the sound of the women's sobs mixed with the lapping of the waves against the sides of the boat] (93). The emphasis is again on the dehumanising context, evident in the environment on the ship: 'des cages où une odeur de crasse, de vomi et de moisi empuantissait l'air' [cages where the air stank of filth, vomit and dampness] (94), but the novelist adds details of the racial tensions on board, not least as the metropolitan prisoners combine anti-Arab prejudice with resentment at having their space reduced. The observation of the *bagne* itself suggests an oppressive environment whose elements — 'les postes de surveillance, les cases et les blockhaus' [the watch-towers, the huts and the bunkers] (120) — link the penal world to the *monde concentrationnaire*. Akkouche pays close attention to the carceral everyday, including details of the *plan* used by convicts to secrete valuables in their anus, the frequent appointment of North African prisoners as *porte-clés* and the culture of tattooing (Mohamed exchanges a canoe for the inking of 'Alger, mon berceau, Cayenne, mon tombeau' [Algiers my cradle, Cayenne my grave] (179) onto his skin, a marker that gradually fades after he leaves the penal colony). Freed in 1943 but condemned to the *doublage* that condemned prisoners to remaining in the *bagne* following the end of their sentence, Benoucif *père* avoided the extreme conditions associated with the penal colony under Vichy but nevertheless spent the war years there before being returned to Algeria.

The account of Benoucif's historic journey to and experiences of the penal colony of French Guiana is juxtaposed in the novel with a second journey, that of his son Richard's quest seventy years later to understand his family's past (and by extension his own present) and to face his estrangement from his father. The two narratives are told in alternate chapters, with that of the son distinguished typographically by the use of italics. Richard's story is one of active self-distancing from his Algerian roots as he avoids the cultures of social and literal incarceration in France to which many of migrant origin are subject: 'USINE, PRISON, CAME' [FACTORY, PRISON, DRUGS] (*Cayenne*, 111). His own contemporary journey begins with his accompanying his father's coffin to Algeria in October 1998 but develops into the detour of his visit to French Guiana where he unpicks the narrative of Mohammed's time as a *bagnard*, including uncovering unexpected aspects such as the existence of a half-sister Josiane. Richard's father's life story is characterised by labour: on the family farm in Algeria; in the penal colony itself; and as a carpenter in post-war Paris following his release and rehabilitation. Richard's engagement with the hidden story of his father's life in the *bagne* encounters indifference from most locals with whom he speaks, with a common reaction being impatience with any reduction of French Guiana to the penitentiary or scepticism regarding the role of the history of the penal colony in the country's future. Drawing on his father's file, presumably from the colonial archives in Aix-en-Provence, the protagonist nevertheless persists in seeking to uncover aspects of his own personal story that had been obscured. He eschews further engagement with the archives and seeks an embodied memory that is reminiscent of Chamoiseau's *trace-mémoire*.

This search for traces of his father's past occurs in the frame of dark tourism as Richard visits the key carceral sites of French Guiana, including the Camp de la Transportation at Saint-Laurent-du-Maroni. Showing little interest, however, in the physical ruins of the *bagne*, he seeks instead to recover the story of his father from the anonymity of the almost seventy thousand convicts sent to the penal colony during the century of its operation. This narrative, including the account of Mohamed's relationship with the half-English, half-Surinamese Elisabeth, mother of Richard's half-sister Josiane ('Qui aurait parié sur un couple composé d'une Blanche d'origine anglaise et d'un ancien forçat d'Afrique du Nord?' [Who would have bet on a couple composed of a white woman of English origin and an ex-convict from North Africa?], *Cayenne*, 274), serves not only to restore the individual humanity of the *bagnard*, but also to assert the heterogeneity of this category of men. As Mohamed lies on his deathbed, the narrator notes: 'Mêlées à la rivière de son enfance, les eaux boueuses du Maroni coulaient dans ses veines' [Mixed with the river of his childhood, the muddy waters of the Maroni ran in his veins] (*Cayenne*, 339). Bill Marshall reads the novel as one of 'the rigid separation of the two narratives', with closure for Richard consisting of a return to 'the nuclear family and the middle-class world summed up by the Parisian media' in which he works.[33] Reading the novel, however, in a frame of transcolonial memory practices, it is clear that Akkouche's achievement is to inscribe the *bagne* of French Guiana into a geographical network that, like the itineraries of *La Martinière* itself, links metropolitan France, North Africa and South America, disrupting in the process monolithic accounts of colonial history and replacing them with versions that are both transnational and transcolonial. At the same time, instead of isolating the penal colony as a peripheral aspect of French metropolitan history, he writes it back into a broader set of narratives that encompass not only the Second World War and the Algerian War of Independence (on his return from French Guiana, Mohamed learns for instance of the 1945 Sétif massacre), but also processes of migration in post-war France and their afterlives in the contemporary country.

Camus's 1938 article in *Alger républicain* forms part of a broader pattern evident in his work that associates the *bagne* in its various manifestations with the absurdity of the human condition, especially when this condition is further exacerbated by the mechanisms of state control. At the same time, there is a specificity to Camus's reflections as these operate as *traces-mémoires* in the largely forgotten and even actively silenced narrative of the transcolonial deportation of thousands of Algerian prisoners to France's overseas penal colonies. From the starting-point of Camus's article, and by reading it contrapuntally with one of the few novels to address these histories, this chapter has sought to challenge the widely perpetuated myth of the whiteness of the French *bagne* while reflecting on the role of penal transportation in the complex flows of people and practices between colonised spaces within the French colonial empire. The Algerian *bagnards* whom Camus observes and that

Akkouche then rehumanises by imagining the biography of one of them, Richard Benoucif, are to be understood as victims of intersectional erasure. They are 'ray[és] de l'humanité' for multiple reasons as a result of their ethnicity, of their status as colonial subjects, of their incarceration. The recovery of their stories is part of a reparative process, as much to do with colonial and penal history as with Franco-Algerian history more broadly. In challenging narratives of the *bagne* that reduce the institution to an extension of the penal histories of France, Chamoiseau proposed an ethics of remembering the past that attends to 'des histoires dominées, des mémoires écrasées' [dominated (hi-)stories, crushed memories] (*Guyane*, 16). As this chapter has sought to demonstrate, such an approach requires detection, recovery and re-assemblage of *memory-traces* that are 'brisées, diffuses, éparpillées' [broken, diffuse, scattered] (*Guyane*, 21).[34]

Notes to Chapter 5

1. Albert Camus, 'Ces hommes qu'on raie de l'humanité', in *Œuvres complètes*, ed. by Jacqueline Lévi-Valensi Raymond Gay-Crosier and others, 4 vols, Bibliothèque de la Pléiade (Paris: Gallimard, 2006–08), I, 585–88 (hereafter referenced as OC in the main text). See 'Le Bagne flottant (mémoires du commandant Rosier)', in Franck Sénateur, Bernard Cognaud and Paul Mauro, *Martinière: le transport des forçats (1910–1955)* (Rennes: Marine éditions, 2008), pp. 22–40.
2. On French Guiana as a penal colony, see Michel Pierre, *La Terre de la grande punition: histoire des bagnes de Guyane* (Paris: Ramsay, 1982), and Jean-Louis Sanchez, *À perpétuité: relégués au bagne de Guyane* (Paris: Vendémiaire, 2013).
3. On *bandes dessinées* and the penal colony, see Charles Forsdick, 'Bande dessinée and the Penal Imaginary: Graphic Constructions of the Carceral Archipelago', *European Comic Art*, 12.2 (2019), 1–16.
4. Mouloud Akkouche, *Cayenne, mon tombeau* (Paris: Flammarion, 2001) (hereafter referenced as *Cayenne* in the main text).
5. On the penal colony and postcolonial memory in modern and contemporary France, see Charles Forsdick, 'Le Bagne', in *Postcolonial Realms of Memory: Sites and Symbols in Modern France*, ed. by Etienne Achille, Charles Forsdick, and Lydie Moudileno (Liverpool: Liverpool University Press, 2020), pp. 227–36.
6. Patrick Chamoiseau and Rodolphe Hammadi, *Guyane: traces-mémoires du bagne* (Paris: Caisse nationale des monuments historiques et des sites, 1994) (hereafter referenced as *Guyane* in the main text).
7. Léon Gontran Damas, *Retour de Guyane: suivi de Misère noire: et autres écrits journalistiques* [1938] (Paris: J.-M. Place, 2003), p. 66.
8. Albert Camus, *Les Justes*, in *Œuvres complètes: théâtre, récits, nouvelles*, ed. by Roger Quilliot, Bibliothèque de la Pléiade (Paris: Gallimard, 1962), pp. 301–93
9. See Ève Morisi, 'Staging the Limit: Albert Camus's Just Assassins and the Il/legitimacy of Terrorism', in *Critical Concepts of Terrorism*, ed. by Peter Herman (Cambridge: Cambridge University Press, 2018), pp. 263–80 (p. 364).
10. Albert Camus, *L'État de siège* in *Œuvres complètes*, ed. by Quilliot, pp. 181–300 (p. 291)
11. See, for example, Albert Camus, *Carnets, mai 1935-février 1942* (Paris: Gallimard, 1962), p. 141. For a discussion of this, see Ève Morisi, *Capital Letters: Hugo, Baudelaire, Camus, and the Death Penalty* (Evanston, IL: Northwestern University Press, 2020), pp. 129–30.
12. Albert Camus, *Actuelles: écrits politiques* (Paris: Gallimard, 2017), p. 41.
13. Camus, *Les Justes*, p. 308; *L'Homme révolté*, in OC, III, 320.
14. Albert Camus, *Actuelles: chroniques 1944–1948*, in OC, II, 436–56.
15. On the history of the penal colonies and hard labour, see Jean-Lucien Sanchez, 'The French Empire, 1542–1976', in *A Global History of Convicts and Penal Colonies*, ed. by Clare Anderson (London: Bloomsbury, 2018), pp.123–56.

16. For an account of the conditions below deck, see Sénateur, Cognaud and Mauro, *Martinière*, pp. 101–02. Paul Mauro was a member of the crew of *La Martinière* from 1935 to 1938, and so was serving on the vessel at the time Camus described its passage via Algiers. The account of his three voyages on the ship is included in the volume (pp. 42–55).
17. See Michael Rothberg, *The Implicated Subject: Beyond Victims and Perpetrators* (Stanford, CA: Stanford University Press, 2019).
18. On the penal dimensions of dark tourism, see Jacqueline Z. Wilson, *Prison: Cultural Memory and Dark Tourism* (New York: Peter Lang, 2008).
19. Sénateur, Cognaud and Mauro, *Martinière*, p. 47.
20. See Danielle Donet-Vincent, *La Fin du bagne* (Rennes: Ouest France, 1992).
21. Robert Badinter, 'Le Bagne de Guyane: un crime contre l'humanité', *Le Monde*, 24 November 2017.
22. Bernard Cherubini, 'Imprisoning Ethnic Heritage in French Guiana: The Seduction of a Penal Colony', in *The Making of Heritage: Seduction and Disenchantment*, ed. by Camila de Marmol, Marc Morell and Jasper Chalcraft (New York & London: Routledge, 2015), pp. 79–98 (p. 83).
23. Jean Bernabé, Patrick Chamoiseau and Raphaël Confiant, *Éloge de la créolité* (Paris: Gallimard, 1989).
24. Mehdi Lallaoui, *Kabyles du Pacifique* (Bezons: Au nom de la mémoire, 1994), p. 9; *Les Kabyles du Pacifique* (dir. by Mehdi Lallaoui, 1994). Lallaoui's book and film are part of a sustained *travail de mémoire* that brings together Algerian, French and Kanak history; the volume was published by Au Nom de la mémoire, an organisation also instrumental in bringing to public attention the massacres of Front de libération nationale (FLN) supporters by the French authorities in Paris on 17 October 1961.
25. Linda Amiri, 'Exil pénal et circulations forcées dans l'Empire colonial français', *L'Année du Maghreb*, 20 (2019) <http://journals.openedition.org/anneemaghreb/4514> [accessed March 2022].
26. See Mustapha Hadj Ali, *Les Bagnards d'Algérie de Cayenne* (Paris: Vérone, 2019), p. 89.
27. Ibid., p. 90.
28. See Amiri, 'Exil pénal et circulations forcées dans l'Empire colonial français'.
29. Michel Pierre, 'Les Algériens au bagne de Guyane', in *Justices en Guyane: à l'ombre du droit*, ed. by Sylvie Humbert and Yerri Urban (Paris: La Documentation française, 2016), pp. 171–87 (p. 177).
30. Ibid., pp. 177–78
31. Ibid., p. 182.
32. See Marine Coquet, 'Bagnards, "arabes" et porte-clefs en Guyane: naissance et usages d'un rôle pénal et colonial (1869–1938)', *L'Année du Maghreb*, 20 (2019), 77–92.
33. Bill Marshall, *The French Atlantic: Travels in Culture and History* (Liverpool: Liverpool University Press, 2010), p. 236.
34. The author records his gratitude to Eddie Hughes, who first drew his attention to the 1938 article by Camus in *Alger républicain*, and to Ève Morisi and Mark Orme, who kindly provided advice on the place of the *bagne* in the author's wider *œuvre*.

CHAPTER 6

Empire, Memory and Language in Pierre Michon's 'Vie d'André Dufourneau'

Patrick Crowley

Qu'on songe à cette mutilation sans retour qu'à représenté la fin des paysans, cette collectivité-mémoire par excellence dont la vogue comme objet d'histoire a coïncidé avec l'apogée de la croissance industrielle. [...] À la périphérie, l'indépendance des nouvelles nations a entraîné dans l'historicité les sociétés déjà réveillées par le viol colonial de leur sommeil ethnologique. Et par le même mouvement de décolonisation intérieure, toutes les ethnies, groupes, familles, à fort capital mémoriel et à faible capital historique.

[Consider, for example, the irrevocable break marked by the disappearance of peasant culture, that quintessential repository of collective memory whose recent vogue as an object of historical study coincided with the apogee of industrial growth. [...]. Among the new nations, independence has swept into history societies newly awakened from their ethnological slumbers by colonial violation. Similarly, a process of interior decolonization has affected ethnic minorities, families, and groups that until now have possessed reserves of memory but little or no historical capital.][1]

The disappearance of peasant culture. The epigraph to this chapter is from Pierre Nora's introduction to the nine-volume *Les Lieux de mémoire* where Nora presents the dialectic of history and memory by juxtaposing the decline of France's peasant memory with the effects of colonisation on overseas societies. And yet where Nora's multi-volume work is an extensive enumeration and reflection on France's realms of memory, the entries are largely silent on sites that materially mark France's role in 'colonial violation'. Apart from Charles-Robert Ageron's chapter on the Exposition Coloniale of 1931, the entries do not reflect upon the relationship between French sites of memory and the colonial enterprise of the Third Republic. Algiers is not a *lieu de mémoire* yet the Tour de France is counted as such, as is Stendhal's *Vie de Henry Brulard*. These 'omissions and blindspots' have received their closest scrutiny and most expansive response in *Postcolonial Realms of Memory*.[2] The editors of this work acknowledge Nora's 'ground-breaking paradigm for rethinking the relationship between the nation, history and memory' but 'underline the urgency of asserting the central place of the colonial in the making of modern France, and of anchoring it in a collective memory that often evacuated traces of empire'.[3]

The absence, erasure or silence relating to *la plus grande France* is, however, marked by an inflection within Nora's structuring logic of centre and periphery.[4] He writes that on the periphery (not captured in the English translation above) the independence of new nations has brought overseas societies out of their 'ethnological sleep' and into history. The trope of (Western) societies forging history by overcoming nature through industry is a commonplace; beyond France and Europe lay societies caught up within nature's cycles, waiting to be awoken.[5] But what of the peasant within France's internal periphery? How did those distant, unnamed colonised nations across the seas inform or leave an imprint upon the thoughts and imagination of French peasants who represented, in Nora's view, the 'quintessential repository of collective memory'? Offering a critical reading of Pierre Michon's 'Vie d'André Dufourneau', this chapter examines the memory of empire that survives in the *imaginaire social* of peasant France as represented in this, the first chapter of *Vies minuscules* published in 1984, the same year as the first volume of Nora's *Les Lieux de mémoire*.

Pierre Michon (b. 1945) is a French author who with, and since, *Vies minuscules*, has consistently interrogated the uncertain terrain that exists between biography and fiction through canonical texts and images. He has written of Arthur Rimbaud, of Francisco de Goya, of Jean-Antoine Watteau, in a style that draws upon the narrative devices and possibilities of fiction and the constraints of biographical facts. His first publication, and in many ways his richest work, offers eight chapters — biographical sketches of farm labourers and family members from the Creuse region of his childhood; ordinary lives that Michon subsumes within a highly literary style. Each chapter, or biographical novella, of *Vies minuscules* is also about the writer, Michon, thus constituting an oblique autobiographical portrait of Michon's quest to become a writer beginning with his recollection of stories he heard as a child.

Michon's rural upbringing is central to his work. The writer and critic Pierre Bergounioux stresses the importance of Michon's rural experience and characterises the Creuse as a place where nothing or almost nothing comes to pass.[6] Even today, he notes, the western part of the Creuse where Michon grew up is called 'la Marche' which, like the English word 'marchlands', signifies lands on the margins or across an ill-defined frontier. The Creuse is a region which, earlier in its history, saw the fading prominence of the northern *langue d'Oïl* and the beginning of the *langue d'Oc*'s influence. It was where patois continued to be spoken into the 1940s when Michon's maternal grandparents came to live with the author and his mother. They spoke *patois*: 'C'est très important pour mon usage de la langue. Par rapport à ce patois, la langue littéraire est une langue étrangère' [It's very important to how I use language. Compared to patois, literary language is a foreign language].[7]

On this sense of being on the margins of France, Bergounioux writes that what redeemed Michon, or damned him further, was the legacy of the Jacobin desire to centralise the Republic through education and intensify its social cohesion through the promulgation of standard French within the schools of the Third Republic.

It was at school, argues Bergounioux, that Michon became aware of a different world that existed beyond the Creuse. Literature — extracts from Hugo's poetry, twenty lines or so from Flaubert, a few of La Fontaine's fables — was a conduit to an elsewhere yet its secrets were hidden within style and the high language of literature. The *école républicaine* represented 'le seul ferment d'universalité, de recul, de délivrance dans ces territoires séparés, misérables et toujours patoisants' [the only leaven of universality, of reflection, of deliverance in these isolated, impoverished territories where patois was still spoken].[8] But just as the *école républicaine* opened up a vista it also suggested a barrier: the destiny of the 'great men of letters' was refused to those from the Creuse who remained outside.[9] Paris was the centre — literary, economic and social — that defined the Creuse as provincial. The marchlands were neither within the 'ethnological slumbers' of the colonies nor peopled with the heroic agents of history.

Michon moved from the Creuse to university at Clermont Ferrand before abandoning his studies during the *événements* of May 1968. He joined the Maoist movement and, in 1969, the avant-garde theatre group Théâtre Kersaki, before going to Paris in 1971 where he registered as a student at the Institut des langues orientales.[10] He drifted between various odd jobs in the 1970s before the publication of *Vies minuscules*. 'Vie d'André Dufourneau' provides us with a representation of peasant memory of *la plus grande France* through images, text, memories and an author-narrator who negotiates the complex processes of memory and language. The narrative is based on the few details that remain of André Dufourneau's life: an orphan sent to work on Michon's maternal great-grandparents' farm at Les Cards in the Creuse in the opening decade of the twentieth century, he lived with the family where he was taught to read and write by Élise, Michon's grandmother. Sometime between 1919 and 1921, Dufourneau emigrated to that part of French West Africa which is now Côte d'Ivoire. He sought to make his fortune there and returned to France and to the farm in Les Cards just once, for a brief visit, in 1947. These are the bare events and the text emerges from Dufourneau's absence, Élise's subsequent attempts to keep his memory alive, and the author-narrator's embellishment of her stories. There are no direct accounts of Africa, few references to real experiences, only fictional constructs based on meagre traces that tenuously linked rural France to French West Africa.

'Vie d'André Dufourneau' has been the subject of significant critical attention with two works that attend, in particular, to the colonial dimension. Edward Hughes draws compelling attention to the way in which Michon, as narrator, seeks to transform the ordinary, peasant lives of the Creuse with the high rhetoric of *la belle langue* and through the powerful after-images of high art. Hughes is alive to the colonial dimension of Michon's 'Vie d'André Dufourneau' and to the function of 'Africa' as a metaphor for his writerly enterprise.[11] Though Dufourneau's departure is real, Côte d'Ivoire becomes lost within the embracing image of 'Africa' which, in turn, becomes a metaphor for the possibilities and limits of writing and being. Africa functions as a metaphor for Michon's exploration of language and the quest to be an author:

> Je ne savais pas que l'écriture était un continent plus ténébreux, plus aguicheur et décevant que l'Afrique, l'écrivain une espèce plus avide de se perdre que l'explorateur; et, quoiqu'il explorât la mémoire et les bibliothèques mémorieuses en lieu de dunes et forêts, qu'en revenir cousu de mots comme d'autres le sont d'or ou y mourir plus pauvre que devant — en mourir — était l'alternative offerte aussi au scribe.
>
> [I did not know that writing was so dark a continent, more enticing and disappointing than Africa, the writer a species more bent on getting lost than the explorer; and, although that scribe may explore memory and memory's libraries instead of sand dunes and forests, may return with words instead of gold, or die poorer than ever, 'to die of it' was the alternative offered to him as well.][12]

Africa, as metaphor, is not new. Even less so when it is described as dark, seductive and deceptive, yet in returning to this cliché, in re-writing it, Michon's text reminds us of the popular view of Africa and offers a metaphorical site that allows for broader engagement between memory and language, between colonisation and domination. Hughes notes that active here is Joseph Conrad's *Heart of Darkness* which is a commentary not only on the 'dark continent' of Africa but serves too as a metaphor for European civilisation. For Hughes, this 'ambiguity mutates in Michon's narrative, where the risks in colonialist undertakings give way to the dangers inherent in the enterprise of literarity' as seen in the 'clichéd colonialist impressionism' of Dufourneau's letters.[13] Where Hughes attends to how the metaphor leads into the wider question of the imbrication of a life and art in Michon's *œuvre*, this chapter explores the question of language and colonial memory and the imprint of empire upon the *imaginaire social* of rural France.

Oana Panaïté's reading of 'Vie d'André Dufourneau' also reflects upon the way in which the 'colonial imaginary is a distant mosaic, a literary re-membering of fragmented and shifting family stories', a colonial transfiguration of humble French lives.[14] Panaïté identifies Michon's opening 'life' within a convincing paradigm for reading French and Francophone literatures that feature the colonial. She names this analytical tool as 'paracolonial aesthetics', persuasively arguing that on the one hand it 'refers to the revival, resurgence and remanence of the colonial in today's political and cultural imaginary [...]. On the other, it addresses the reimagining, revisiting and reassessment of the colonial in works of literature'.[15] She concludes that writers such as Michon, Claude Simon and Régis Jauffret 'bring forward the ethical dilemma of contemporary fiction, which makes its political implications critically visible by exhibiting its most visceral aesthetic forms at the risk of reviving and potentially relegitimizing an obsolete colonial imagination'.[16] In what follows I analyse the relationship Michon that puts in play between the colonial imagination and peasant memory which results in a powerful *lieu de mémoire* constituted by language and the colonial *imaginaire social*.

The dissemination of the colonial idea was sponsored by a section of France's political and industrial elite. As Kate Marsh has convincingly written, 'an understanding of the vexed question of how the colonies are elided in French national history is not going to be achieved without the development of an historical awareness of how those in a dominant position imagined colonial contact'.[17] In his contribution to Nora's *Les Lieux de mémoire*, Charles-Robert Ageron asks the question: 'Oui ou non, l'exposition de Vincennes fut-elle ce lieu où s'enraciner pour l'avenir la mémoire de la République Coloniale?' [Yes or no, was the Vincennes exhibition a place where the future memory of the Colonial Republic took root?].[18] Ageron's conclusion is that 'l'Exposition de 1931 a échoué à constituer une mentalité coloniale: elle n'a point imprégné durablement la mémoire collective ou l'imaginaire social des Français' [the 1931 Exhibition failed to establish a colonial mentality: it did not leave an indelible imprint upon the collective memory or the social imagination of the French].[19] But if the Exposition failed to mark the *imaginaire social*, then in what way or how did the colonial expansion of the Third Republic leave its trace upon the imagination of *la France profonde*? Michon's text offers an answer: the Colonial Exhibition of 1931 was but one conduit for the colonial message, and there were many, ranging from forms of popular culture to high culture.

The diegesis of 'Vie d'André Dufourneau' is a complex interweave of Élise's memories and speculations and Michon's endeavour to rework the rudimentary, if part invented, accounts conveyed to him by his grandmother into a 'schème plus noble et bonnement dramatique qu'un réel pauvre' [a more noble, overtly dramatic theme than her impoverished reality] (*VM*, 20; *SL*, 18). Élise's account circulates around Dufourneau's announcement that he had decided to leave for Africa to make his fortune: '"J'en reviendrai riche, ou y mourrai": cette phrase pourtant bien indigne de mémoire, j'ai dit que cent fois ma grand-mère l'avait exhumée des ruines du temps' ['I will come back rich, or die there'. As unmemorable as it is, I have said how, a hundred times, my grandmother exhumed that phrase from time's ruins] (*VM*, 21; *SL*, 18). This simple sentence captures colonial French West Africa as a vocation for the aspiring provincial peasant hoping to make his fortune. Michon refers to letters Dufourneau sent in the 1930s to Élise and Félix and to the postmarks on the envelopes of places which, the narrator says, are now lost: Kokombo, Malamalasso, Grand-Lahou.[20] Though the names of real places in what is now Côte d'Ivoire, their function here seems to be as emblematic referents providing an exotic triad of faraway places of which his grandmother knew little. From the letters, she learns that Dufourneau worked first as a forester before becoming a planter. After his only return visit to Les Cards in 1947, Dufourneau sent one further letter and a bag of green coffee beans which remained in his absence and acted as collateral against the erosions of time. Michon writes that this bag of beans 'était le précieux alibi de ce souvenir, de cette parole: il était image pieuse ou épitaphe, rappel à l'ordre pour la pensée trop prompte à l'oubli' [It was the precious alibi of that memory, of that word; it was the devout image or epitaph, the call to order for minds too apt to forget] (*VM*, 28; *SL*, 24).

There followed an unbroken silence eventually interpreted as Dufourneau's death. Remembering his concerns about the atmosphere of mutiny arising with the emergence of 'les premières idéologies nationalistes indigènes' [the first indigenous nationalist ideologies] (*VM*, 29; *SL*, 25)], Élise believed that:

> Dufourneau avait succombé de la main des ouvriers noirs, qu'elle se représentait sous des traits d'esclaves d'un autre siècle mâtinés de pirates jamaïcains tels qu'ils figurent sur les bouteilles de rhum, trop éclatantes pour être pacifiques, sanglants comme leur madras, cruels comme leurs bijoux. (*VM*, 29)
>
> [Dufourneau had died at the hands of the black laborers, whom she imagined much like slaves from another century crossed with Jamaican pirates as they were depicted on bottles of rum, too dazzling to be peaceful, as bloody as their madras scarves, cruel as their jewels.] (*SL*, 25)

In attempting to visualise the indigenous peoples of French West Africa Michon's grandmother makes use of the images to hand. And just as she uses the image of Jamaican pirates on a rum bottle to provide her imagination with a figure, Michon, too, in recalling, interpreting and recasting Élise's stories of Dufourneau, wonders what images prompted the latter to leave for Africa. Both grandmother and writer create a *bricolage* of images and text from the representations of Africa that circulated at the time. Michon writes:

> Est-ce un homme, un livre, ou, plus poétiquement, une affiche de propagande de la Marsouille, qui lui révéla l'Afrique? Quel hâbleur de sous-préfecture, quel mauvais roman enlisé dans les sables ou perdu en forêt sur d'interminables fleuves, quelle gravure du *Magasin pittoresque* où des haut-de-forme luisants, noirs comme elles et comme elle surnaturels, passaient triomphalement entre de luisantes faces, fit miroiter à ses yeux le continent sombre? (*VM*, 18–19)
>
> [Was it a person, a book, or, more poetically a propaganda poster for the Marines that disclosed Africa to him? What bragging sub-prefect, what bad novel buried in the sands or lost in forests stretching over endless rivers, what magazine engraving of gleaming top hats passing triumphantly along gleaming faces, just as black and supernatural, made the dark continent sparkle with bright prospects?] (*SL*, 16)

How did 'Africa' enter into the *imaginaire* of the peasants in rural France and persist within memory? Michon's reference to recruitment posters for the French Marines, to the popular novels of the early twentieth century that had colonial backdrops and to local government windbags suggests the circuits of dissemination.[21] The author-narrator's mention of *Le Magasin pittoresque*, a review that contained popularising articles on exotic and historical subjects, is also striking. The illustrated magazine was first published in 1833 under Édouard Charton and continued until 1912. That Dufourneau's departure occurred some eight years after the last publication of *Le Magasin pittoresque* need not diminish its inherent interest. This magazine, and others such as *Le Petit Journal* and *Le Petit Parisien*, were critical to the dissemination of the colonial idea and the construction of the colonised Other.[22] Michon's reference can be read generically — illustrated magazines promoted colonialism — or as a recollection of such magazines stored like books, forgotten or perhaps not. Michon's weave of fact and fiction, though impossible to untangle, need not detract from the argument that such magazines did inform and colour the *imaginaire social* of rural France.

Michon's recasting of Dufourneau's departure is a further example of how French colonial Africa had seeped into the cultural imagination and was articulated within literary works. As Africa began to enter the popular imagination so too did it enter the imagination of poets and not for the first time. Dufourneau's '"J'en reviendrai riche, ou y mourrai"' and Élise's memory of his departure for Africa are recast by Michon with the arabesques of Rimbaud's poetry, in this case the line 'Je reviendrai [...] J'aurai de l'or' from 'Mauvais sang': 'Le voilà parti, André Dufourneau. "Ma journée est faite; je quitte l'Europe." L'air marin, déjà surprend les poumons de cet homme de l'intérieur' [And that was the departure of André Dufourneau. 'My day is set; I am leaving Europe.' Already the sea air shocks the lungs of this inlander] (*VM*, 22; *SL*, 19); 'Ma journée est faite; je quitte l'Europe. L'air marin brûlera mes poumons' [My day is done: I'm leaving Europe. The sea air will scorch my lungs].[23] Michon never explicitly mentions Rimbaud nor does he mention the title of the poem 'Mauvais sang', only the quotation marks indicate the intertextual graft that lifts Dufourneau's phrase, remembered by Élise, into the validation of literary language. But there is something else at play here. While the quotation marks signal the debt to Rimbaud, the next line — 'L'air marin, déja surprend les poumons de cet homme de l'intérieur' — is a borrowing and recasting of Rimbaud's poetry, drawing it into Dufourneau's prosaic life. In subsuming the language of the peasant into the literarity (and coloniality) of Rimbaud's work (and life), Michon's narrator draws our attention to the wider network of references that helped frame the impact, in France, of colonial expansionism and came to form part of an everyday life.

The account of Dufourneau's return visit provides an insight into Michon's view of memory through the way in which he represents the image and memory of colonial Africa. He writes of Dufourneau meeting Michon's mother and himself, then a baby in his mother's arms:

> Le biographe est au berceau et ne conservera aucun souvenir du héros; le héros ne voit dans l'enfant qu'une image de son propre passé. Si j'avais eu dix ans, sans doute l'eussé-je vu sous la pourpre d'un roi mage, posant avec une réserve hautaine sur la table de la cuisine les denrées rares et magiques, café, cabosses, indigo: si j'en avais eu quinze, il eût été 'le féroce infirme retour des pays chauds' qu'aiment les femmes et les poètes adolescents [...] hier encore, et pour peu qu'il fût chauve, j'aurais pensé que 'la sauvagerie l'avait caressé sur la tête', comme le plus brutal des coloniaux de Conrad; aujourd'hui, quel qu'il soit et quoi qu'il dise, j'en penserais ce que je dis ici, rien de plus, et tout reviendrait au même. (*VM*, 26)

> [The biographer is a babe in arms and will retain no memory of the hero; the hero recognizes in the child only an image of his own past. If I had been ten years old, no doubt I would have seen him in the royal crimson robes of Magi, placing rare and magical goods on the kitchen table with a haughty reserve, coffee, cacao, indigo. If I had been fifteen, he would have been 'the fierce, wounded soldier returned from the hot climes,' whom women and adolescent poets love, fiery eyes set in dark skin, with furious word and grip. Even yesterday, and especially if he was bald, I would have thought that 'savagery had caressed his head,' like the most brutal of Conrad's colonials. Today, whatever he may be or say, I would think what I say here, nothing more, and it would all amount to the same thing.] (*SL*, 23)

Here Michon acknowledges the fiction of his own text and how he puts in play a chain of colonial continuities that derive from literature and which frame Dufourneau and Africa through different textual filters each of which would have changed his perception of Dufourneau but all of which reduce him to narratives inflected by empire. We see how Michon, as a child influenced by his Roman Catholic culture, would have understood Dufourneau in terms of one of the Magi coming from the East but with gifts from colonial Africa; as a teenager influenced by his favourite poet he would have read Dufourneau's return in terms of Rimbaud's 'Mauvais sang' and how as an adult he would have viewed Dufourneau through the prism of Conrad's *Heart of Darkness*. In this way, Michon's text questions the extent to which we have access to the referent of France's colonial past beyond the screen of narratives that mediated empire and, in doing so, suggests that memories of French colonial Africa are based on popular images and literature that had both absorbed and served to circulate the propaganda of the colonial lobby, the colonial exhibitions of 1907 or 1931 and, more widely, Western European imperialism that left an imprint upon cultural production.

As with Dufourneau, the representation of Côte d'Ivoire is composed of both the imaginary and real. Michon, for example, imagines Dufourneau arriving at the Grand-Bassam sandbar at the mouth of Abidjan harbour but does so through the filter of André Gide's descriptions of Grand-Bassam in his novel *Paludes* (1895) which, he notes, 'est une image de l'ancien *Magasin pittoresque*' [is an engraving from an old magazine] (*VM*, 24; *SL*, 20). In suggesting that the cultural filters of popular forms such as the illustrated magazine also influenced writers (Gide did not travel to sub-Sahara Africa until 1926) as well as peasants, Michon presents the ways in which many French viewed and understood colonial French West Africa, and raises the question of how cultural forms and language continue to carry a colonial imprint. Indeed, language is the foundational conflict that underpins Dufourneau's departure for French colonial Africa.

The apotheosis of *la plus grande France*, around 1930, corresponded with the near perfect ascendancy of the French language taught in schools throughout France and in selected schools within parts of the colonies. And it is the French language, and the hierarchies that it helped underpin, that continues to carry the traces of empire. Modernity and the rise of literacy allowed reviews such as the *Le Magasin pittoresque* to flourish and Rimbaud's poetry to be popularised. Élise taught Dufourneau to read French, thus giving him access to a written culture distinct from the oral culture transmitted through *patois*. So quick was he to learn that neighbours made sense of his aptitude by imagining him to be the illegitimate son of the local gentry. Dufourneau, Michon imagines, believed the myth. However, during his military service in the city he became acutely aware of his social status through encounters with the officer class and the bourgeoisie, and how this status was linguistically inscribed. Language marked his social position, his place as a peasant whose French was not that of the urban middle class: 'c'était la langue qu'il tenait d'Élise, mais elle paraissait une autre tant ses indigènes, en connaissaient les pistes, les échos, les foueries. Il sut qu'il était un paysan' [It was the language he had learned from Elise, but it seemed like some other because its natives knew so many paths, echoes, clever turns. He knew he was a peasant] (*VM*, 18; *SL*, 15).[24] This crushed sense of self, mediated through language, is partly his spur to leave. 'Africa' offered him a place where his French appeared more elevated thus allowing him to maintain the fiction of his origins: 'là-bas un paysan devenait un Blanc [...] et, fût-il le dernier des fils mal nés, contrefaits et répudiés de la langue mère, il était plus près de ses jupes qu'un Peul ou un Baoulé' [over there a peasant became a White Man, [...] and, even if he was the last of ill-born sons, deformed and repudiated by the Mother Tongue, he was nearer to her skirts than a Fulah or an Akan] (*VM*, 19–20; *SL*, 17). In constructing himself as a White Man through language and the privileges and violence of the coloniser, Dufourneau had to blind himself to the marginal difference that separated his linguistic range from that of his workers. Brought up speaking *patois*, his competency in standard French was not that of the 'native' French yet, for Dufourneau, his French was superior to those whose language was Fulah or Akan. Michon writes that this self-image was to be his undoing:

> Dufourneau avait sans doute été d'autant plus impitoyable envers les humbles qu'il se défendait de reconnaître en eux l'image de ce qu'il n'avait jamais cessé d'être; [...] cette incertitude d'un langage mutilé qui ne sert qu'à dénier les accusations et parer les coups, avait été sienne; pour fuir [...] ce langage qui l'humiliait, il était venu si loin; pour nier avoir jamais aimé ou craint ce que ces nègres aimaient et craignaient, il abattait la chicotte sur leurs dos, l'injure à leurs oreilles; et les nègres, soucieux de rétablir la balance des destins, lui arrachèrent une ultime terreur équivalant leurs mille effrois, lui firent une dernière plaie valant pour toutes leurs plaies et [...] le tuèrent. (*VM*, 30–31)

> [Dufourneau, she knew, had undoubtedly been all the more pitiless toward the lowly in his efforts to keep himself from recognizing in them the image of what he had never ceased to be. [...] The uncertainty of a mutilated tongue that serves only to deny accusations and ward off blows had been his; he had come so far to flee the labours he loved, the language that humiliated him; to deny having ever loved or feared what those black men loved and feared, he brought the whip down on their backs, shouted abuses into their ears. And the blacks, concerned with re-establishing the balance of destinies, wrested from him one final terror to equal their thousand terrors [...] and, extinguishing forever that horrified stare in the instant when he finally admitted he was one of them, killed him.] (*SL*, 26)

Here 'colonialist and colonized are drawn together in a mortal encounter'.[25] Significantly, the violence is also marked by and within Dufourneau's inner drama enacted through language: his acute awareness of his 'mutilated tongue' and of 'the language that humiliated him'. If Michon's text seeks to flatten the asymmetrical relationship between coloniser and colonised, it works only to a point: this final encounter is between the named, French, anti-hero and 'the blacks'. It succeeds only in identifying the common domination of the French language, in establishing an analogical relation that, at the very least, asks the reader to consider the intersection of class and race within the matrix of a hegemonic language.

Panaïté rightly argues that Michon's writing 'while fully engaging with the mediated, indirect and therefore creative fascination with the colonial ideation, looks askance, as it were, at any form of explicit commitment or morality', and adds that this mirrors Dufourneau's 'inability to express the indescribable colonial experience'. She concludes: 'This ineptitude does not arise from a lack of words, however, but rather their excess'.[26] Panaïté's point is well made but it could be augmented: it is not simply the use of language and its excess but the values and traces embedded within it, what the language represents and how it is put to work within structures of power. Such structures are often veiled by language. In his contribution on the French language as a *lieu de mémoire*, Marc Fumaroli focuses on the evolution of the language towards clarity and universality prior to the Revolution. His final line unites nation and language and notes their separation from their roots in French royalty from 1784 on when they become 'abstractions prêtes à recevoir l'énergie nouvelle de la religion des droits de l'homme' [abstractions ready to receive the new energy of the religion of human rights].[27] Fumaroli, unsurprisingly, flags human rights but not the colonial republic to come.

Where Nora posits, and overstates, the demise of environments of memory and the ascendancy of history, linking them to the end of peasant culture in France and the rupturing of traditions in colonial countries, in contrast, the colonial references and backstory to Michon's text suggest that peasant memories continue. Michon's 'Vie d'André Dufourneau' might not have a biographical referent: Dufourneau could be the product of a transformation of the common noun (furnace/ *fourneau*) into a proper noun that doubles as a metaphor, but what is clear is that Michon's text works at the level of metaphor, of analogy, where French peasant is likened to colonised subject, each suffering beneath an apparatus of power that is embedded in, and reinforced by, language. It is the French language, with its cultural intertexts and colonial assumptions still enshrined in phrases such as *un français petit-nègre*, that carries within it a linguistic, and perhaps, structuring, *lieu de mémoire* commemorated by a majority in France that is still undergoing a reluctant process of decolonisation.[28] It is here, within this realm of memory, that peasant memories of *la République coloniale* continue to take form and it is this that Michon's text draws upon, explores and realises. The multi-layered analogical structure of colonial continuities linking Peasant-White Coloniser-Literary Author is constructed from the debris of colonial empire, drawn from the memorial traces of colony that are, once more, put to work. Yet in drawing from the *imaginaire colonial* of rural France, Michon's text delineates the imprint of French empire, language and violent coloniality and makes explicit what was silenced and largely erased in Nora's *Lieux de mémoire*. It is Michon's text that unwittingly awakens *Les Lieux de mémoire* from its own slumber and brings the reader into an encounter with the ongoing task of decolonisation.[29]

Notes to Chapter 6

1. *Les Lieux de mémoire*, ed. by Pierre Nora, 3 vols (Paris: Gallimard/NRF, 1984–92), I, xvii–xviii; 'Between Memory and History: Les Lieux de Mémoire', in *Memory and Counter-memory* (= special issue of *Representations*, 26 (1989)), 7–25 (p. 7). For an early critical review that offers a postcolonial perspective of the English translation of *Les Lieux de mémoire* [Realms of Memory], see Hue-Tam Ho Tai, 'Remembered Realms: Pierre Nora and French National Memory', *American Historical Review*, 106.3 (2001), 906–22 <http://www.historycooperative.org/journals/

ahr/106.3/ah000906.html> ([accessed November 2021]. See also Emily S. Apter, *Continental Drift: From National Character to Virtual Subjects* (Chicago: University of Chicago Press, 1999), p. 2.
2. Étienne Achille, Charles Forsdick and Lydie Moudileno, 'Introduction', in *Postcolonial Realms of Memory: Sites and Symbols in Modern France*, ed. by Etienne Achille, Charles Forsdick and Lydie Moudileno (Liverpool: Liverpool University Press, 2020), pp. 1–19 (p. 1).
3. Ibid., p. 2.
4. Roger Little writes that in the nineteenth and early twentieth century, the expression *la plus grande France* designated 'France plus the overseas territories which had come under her control, the meaning shifting slightly from an ambition following the defeat suffered in the Franco-Prussian war to the fait accompli celebrated notably by the Colonial Exhibition of 1931'. See Roger Little, '"La plus grande France": A Hypothesis', *French Studies Bulletin*, 26.95 (2005), 19–20 (p. 19).
5. On the theme of labour and history, see Eric R. Wolf, Europe and the People without History [1982] (Berkeley & Los Angeles: University of California Press, 1997). The trope of peoples outside history was infamously recycled by Nicolas Sarkozy in his speech to university students in Dakar in 2007. See Makhily Gassama, *L'Afrique répond à Sarkozy: contre le discours de Dakar* (Paris: Philippe Rey, 2008).
6. Pierre Bergounioux, 'Pierre Michon et la littérature passée', in *La Cécité d'Homère* (Strasbourg: Circé, 1995), pp. 73–93 (p. 76).
7. Cited in Thierry Guichard, 'Pierre Michon: au nom du fils', *Le Matricule des anges*, 5 (1994), 4–6 (p. 4). All translations are my own unless stated otherwise.
8. Bergounioux, 'Pierre Michon et la littérature passée', p. 78.
9. Ibid., p. 80.
10. There are traces of Orientalism in a number of Michon's texts that invite further analysis.
11. See Edward J. Hughes, 'Pierre Michon, "Small Lives", and the Terrain of Art', *Romance Studies*, 29.2 (2011), 68–80.
12. Pierre Michon, *Vies minuscules* [1984] (Paris: Gallimard, Folio, 1996), p. 22 (hereafter referenced as *VM* in the main text); *Small Lives*, trans. by Jody Gladding and Elizabeth Deshays (Brooklyn, NY: Archipelago Books, 2008), p. 19 (hereafter referenced as *SL* in the main text).
13. Hughes, 'Pierre Michon, "Small Lives", and the Terrain of Art', p. 70.
14. Oana Panaïté, *The Colonial Fortune in Contemporary Fiction in French* (Liverpool: Liverpool University Press, 2017), pp. 35–36.
15. Ibid., p. 4.
16. Ibid., p. 56.
17. Kate Marsh, *Narratives of the French Empire: Fiction, Nostalgia, and Imperial Rivalries, 1784 to the Present* (Lanham, MD: Lexington Books, 2013), p. 97.
18. Charles-Robert Ageron, 'L'Exposition coloniale de 1931', in *Les Lieux de mémoire*, ed. by Nora, I, 561–91 (p. 562).
19. Ibid., p. 590.
20. On the colonial post system and postage stamps as a *lieu de mémoire* see David Scott, 'Post and the Postage Stamp', in *Postcolonial Realms of Memory*, ed. by Achille, Forsdick and Moudileno, pp. 351–59.
21. On popular colonial culture (1925 to 1931) see Nicolas Bancel, 'Le Bain colonial: aux sources de la culture coloniale populaire', in *Culture coloniale: la France conquise par son Empire 1871–1931*, ed. by Pascal Blanchard and Sandrine Lemaire (Paris: Autrement, 2003), pp. 179–90.
22. Sandrine Lemaire and Pascal Blanchard, 'Exhibitions, expositions, médiatisation et colonies', in *Culture coloniale*, ed. by Lemaire and Blanchard, pp. 43–54 (p. 49).
23. Arthur Rimbaud, 'Mauvais sang', in *Œuvres complètes*, ed. by Antoine Adam, Bibliothèque de la Pléiade (Paris: Gallimard, 1972), pp. 95–96; 'Bad Blood', in *A Season in Hell. The Illuminations*, trans. by Enid Rhodes Peschel (New York & Oxford: Oxford University Press, 1974), p. 49.
24. See Eugen Weber, *Peasants into Frenchmen: The Modernization of Rural France 1870–1914* (London: Chatto & Windus, 1977), in particular Chapters 6, 'A Wealth of Tongues', and 18, 'Civilizing in Earnest: Schools and Schooling'. For an historical and analytical account of the thinking behind,

and the establishment of, colonial schools see Antoine Léon, *Colonisation, enseignement et éducation* (Paris: L'Harmattan, 1991).
25. Hughes, 'Pierre Michon, "Small Lives", and the Terrain of Art', p. 70.
26. Panaïté, *The Colonial Fortune in Contemporary Fiction in French*, p. 45.
27. Marc Fumaroli, 'Le Génie de la langue française', in *Les Lieux de mémoire*, ed. by Nora, III, 911–73 (p. 968). For a succinct contrapuntal view see Cécile Van den Avenne, 'French Language', in *Postcolonial Realms of Memory*, ed. by Achille, Forsdick and Moudileno, pp. 327–33.
28. *Petit-nègre* was defined in the 1996 edition of the *Petit Robert* as 'français à la syntaxe simplifiée (où les verbes sont à l'infinitif), parlé par les indigènes des anciennes colonies françaises. *Parler petit-nègre* (ex. Moi pas vouloir quitter pays). — PAR EXT. Mauvais français'. The clear issue of racial politics and emigration is perfectly conveyed in the example provided. The *Petit Robert*'s own process of decolonisation and critical self-reflection is signalled by the 2013 entry: '*Parler petit-nègre* (ex. Lui pas être content). "*Parler petit-nègre, c'est exprimer cette idée: 'Toi, reste où tu es*'" FANON'.
29. Both texts were published nearly forty years ago yet the resistance to decolonial thought remains. See the opinion piece co-written by Alain Mabanckou and Dominic Thomas titled 'Pourquoi a-t-on si peur des études postcoloniales en France?', published on 16 January 2020 <https://www.lexpress.fr/actualite/pourquoi-a-t-on-si-peur-des-etudes-postcoloniales-en-france_2115044.html> [accessed November 2021]. On the controversy surrounding the use of the term *Islamogauchisme* by the political right see Ishaan Tharoor, 'France and the Spectral Menace of "Islamo-leftism"', published 22 February 2021 <https://www.washingtonpost.com/world/2021/02/22/france-macron-islamo-leftism/> [accessed November 2021].

CHAPTER 7

Resnais's Kaleidoscope

Anna Magdalena Elsner

Alain Resnais's 1963 film *Muriel ou le temps d'un retour* turns around Muriel, a woman tortured by French soldiers in Algeria, a woman who is never seen and whose story only peripherally enters the film through diary entries, photographs and a mysterious film-within-a-film. *Muriel* stages various homecomings, or rather, attempts to return home, of its four main protagonists: Hélène, a middle-aged antiques dealer in Boulogne-sur-Mer; her stepson Bernard, who has recently returned from Algeria; Alphonse, an ex-lover of Hélène; and a young actress, called Françoise, who accompanies Alphonse on his trip to Boulogne-sur-Mer. Like Resnais's earlier *Hiroshima mon amour* (1959) and *L'Année dernière à Marienbad* (1961), the film is a memory-piece; its composition is a set of fractal-like images that induces a sense of growing anxiety about the accuracy of memory and impossibility of forgetting.

Film criticism has scrutinised *Muriel*'s specific visual presentation of memory, forgetting and the role Algeria plays in it, and has noted how the film thereby differs from or repositions the ways in which some of these themes are engaged with in Resnais's earlier work. As part of this, scholarship since Susan Sontag's reading of the film has pointed to Resnais's specific desynchronised editing in *Muriel*, the 'rapid cutting-away-from-scenes' which Sontag describes as 'a rhythm new in Resnais' films'.[1] The resulting non-linear structure of the film and what Laura McMahon calls the 'aesthetics of topological transformation — a pattern of morphing and redistribution visualized in space'[2] has in this context been repeatedly associated with the motif of the kaleidoscope.[3] The optical instrument is used to describe Resnais's visual practice, but also allows conceptual connections to be established between memory, forgetting and their role in French history. In *Muriel*, the kaleidoscope as both motif and metaphor is particularly poignant because the film itself contains an actual kaleidoscope as well as a shot where a view through that kaleidoscope briefly fills the screen.

This chapter proposes to scrutinise the role of the kaleidoscope as both an actual, material object and motif in *Muriel*. In its attempt to establish a connection between the material and the visual/ conceptual, I propose that some of the meanings emanating from the mechanical make-up of the kaleidoscope, and the visual experience it affords its user, allow us to highlight the pivotal role played by the tactile instrument and the virtual reality it creates in the film. In its mediating between an inner and an outer world, the kaleidoscope also, as I argue here, bears a particular closeness to the role played by the optical metaphor in Marcel Proust's *A la recherche du temps perdu*, which, as Edward J. Hughes has highlighted, always oscillates between 'introspection and social representation'.[4] Facing comparable criticism with regard to how their respective works engaged with history, the kaleidoscope as both object and motif affords Resnais and Proust a powerful way to anticipate and respond to such criticism.

Marie-Do's Kaleidoscope

The very brief scene of approximately ten seconds' duration in *Muriel*, in which the actual kaleidoscope appears, shows Marie-Do, Bernard's girlfriend, who picks up the object in Bernard's studio-like apartment in which he frequently takes refuge to edit films and photographs. As Marie-Do picks up the kaleidoscope, Bernard tells her 'Regarde-moi avec' [Look at me with it] and she proceeds to point the kaleidoscope at him. In the shot that follows, Marie-Do looks at Bernard through the kaleidoscope and the multiplied, dispersed, colourful, fragmented and continuously shifting images of Bernard produced by the instrument briefly take over the screen as Marie-Do turns the device and thereby creates ever-changing formations. We then cut to another scene unconnected to Bernard and Marie-Do and the kaleidoscope never appears in the film again.

According to Christine Quinan, the counterpart to this scene is the memorable sequence midway through the film when projected images of Algeria are accompanied by the voice-over recounting the torturing of Muriel, the mysterious Algerian woman who seems to dominate the film without ever appearing. Quinan proposes that the kaleidoscope scene constitutes a coda to the images of Algeria, thereby emphasising the effects of France's censoring approach to the country:

> In its kaleidoscopic approach, the entire project of *Muriel* might also, to use a Foucauldian framework, subvert the art of surveillance and refigure the diagram of power that existed during and after the war. Instead of setting up surveillance and power visually like a pyramid or hierarchical structure, *Muriel* constructs it as a kaleidoscope, or a circle, or a horizontal 'plane', perhaps in an effort to diffuse the all-seeing, fascist-like gaze that certainly existed in periods of censorship into a subjective, more democratic but, therefore, also less coherent visual experience.[5]

Quinan's reading of Resnais's 'kaleidoscopic approach' relates the fragmented and dispersed nature of such a method to the larger conceptual challenges with which the film engages. These provide a framework for linking the visual puzzlements of the film to the conceptual relations between memory, forgetting and history; yet, in this reading, as in many others that have commented on the kaleidoscopic nature of Resnais's filmmaking generally, the actual object of the kaleidoscope that appears in *Muriel* is quickly discarded in order to focus on the kaleidoscope as a metaphor that captures Resnais's aesthetics of distortion and reflection.

Without questioning this indisputably compelling metaphor for Resnais's filmmaking, the kaleidoscope's material grounding within the film also turns Marie-

Do's picking up of it and the sudden and brief vision of Bernard through it into a concentrated counterpoint to Resnais's opening of the film. This opening may be less overtly linked to what has been made out as the grand theme of the film than the projected images of Algeria, and yet, it visually anticipates the fractal-like formations that the kaleidoscopic shot brings into focus. The first image that fills the screen is a close-up of a hand on the doorhandle of Hélène's apartment, which, given that Hélène sells antiques out of that apartment, resembles a temporary showroom more than an inhabited space or a home. The camera then shifts to several further close-ups of different objects — a jug, a chair, a chandelier, some porcelain grapes on the table, the feet and shoes of Hélène and her client, who describes the furniture she is interested in buying. It is only approximately fourteen seconds into the film that the faces of Hélène and her client finally appear. Prior to that, the camera zooms in on material objects and body parts, shown in a kind of visual proximity that becomes almost unbearable as their wider role and overarching function in the apartment or the body remain blurred.

The opening scene's focus on things and parts, and the fact that discussions about specific items of furniture repeatedly re-enter the conversation of the protagonists, assigns a privileged role to the material and physical in *Muriel*. Hélène's apartment is stocked with various items of bourgeois nineteenth-century furniture, which are either already sold, need to be handled with care as they are about to be sold, or are waiting to be picked up by her clients. In terms of design, the kaleidoscope, itself an object of the nineteenth century, fits into the timeline of this interior. Taking the object as a point of departure for an excursion into the kaleidoscopic thinking of Resnais's montage, I want to propose that a detour via the history and etymology of the kaleidoscope and its mechanical make-up, as well as its brief but important rise as an object of diversion and play, allow us to shed new light on how Resnais's kaleidoscopic vision of memory, forgetting and cinema is interconnected with the ways in which the Proustian metaphor mediates between the narrator's interiority and the outer world.

Kaleidoscope Phenomenology

The kaleidoscope was invented at the beginning of the nineteenth century by the Scottish natural philosopher Sir David Brewster, who deposited a patent for a new optical instrument which he called 'the kaleidoscope for exhibiting and creating beautiful forms and patterns' in 1817.[6] The kaleidoscope, which Brewster had defined as a 'general philosophical instrument of universal application' soon turned into a highly successful parlour game.[7] Made from several mirrors that are positioned at angles to each other, with a tube surrounding the mirror assembly, a collection of colorful objects is positioned at one end and the light reflecting between the mirrors thereby produces a multitude of symmetrical images. Through an open lens, these can be observed as changing with every movement. In an instruction leaflet accompanying his kaleidoscope, Brewster described the ways in which the instrument aimed to enable a kind of out-of-body experience, while, however, being firmly grounded within the body. The media historian Erkki Huhtamo explains the holistic component of 'the kaleidoscope experience' in the following terms: 'it was produced by the encounter between the eye, the hand, the viewing apparatus and the traces of real life that were transformed through a kind of transfiguration of the commonplace'.[8] Tellingly, the three patents submitted only two years later in France for comparable devices called the instrument 'le transfigurateur ou la lunette française', thereby highlighting the kind of (national) metamorphosis the device sought to afford the one who was looking through it.[9]

It is only Brewster's neologism 'kaleidoscope', however, which pays tribute to the aesthetic element that is at stake in the invention. The etymology of the word derives from the Ancient Greek *kalos* [beautiful], *eidos* [form], *skopo* [seeing] and thereby denotes a tool for the observation of beautiful forms. The term 'kaleidoscopic' is often used interchangeably with 'fragmented', a term that foregrounds the visual distortion over the creation of beautiful forms that is explicit in the name. As such, the kaleidoscope seeks to enhance, rather than fragment, reality. Georges Didi-Huberman, who has written about the kaleidoscope in Walter Benjamin, has commented on the technical make-up of the kaleidoscope that shapes the viewer's experience. According to him, it is precisely the disjunction between the mechanical make-up of a kaleidoscope and the experience it affords, that captures the device's magic. As he remarks:

> Dans cette variété même, le spectateur ne peut jamais oublier, en secouant l'appareil pour une nouvelle configuration, que la beauté même des formes doit à la dissémination et à l'agrégat son principe constitutif, sa permanente condition de négativité dialectique. La magie du kaléidoscope tient à cela: que la perfection close et symétrique des formes visibles doive sa richesse inépuisable à l'imperfection ouverte et erratique d'une poussière de débris. Or, cette phénoménologie du kaléidoscope exprime non seulement la structure de l'*image* — sa dialectique, son double régime — , mais encore la condition même — condition également dialectique, double régime — du *savoir sur l'image* et sur l'art en général.[10]
>
> [In this variety itself, which the spectator can never forget while shaking the apparatus for a new configuration, even the beauty of the forms owes its constitutive principle, its permanent condition of dialectical negativity, to dissemination and aggregation. The magic of the kaleidoscope is based on this: that the closed and symmetrical perfection of visible forms owes its inexhaustible richness to the open and erratic imperfection of a dust of debris. Now, this phenomenology of the kaleidoscope expresses not only the structure of the *image*, its dialectic, its double regime, but also the very condition, also a dialectic condition, double regime *of the knowledge ab*out the image and about art in general.]

Didi-Huberman here alerts us to the fact that the particular appreciation of formal beauty which the kaleidoscope creates is always accompanied by the awareness that the device creates visual perfection from imperfection. What he calls the 'phenomenology of the kaleidoscope' is therefore a kind of double awareness, namely the impossibility for the spectator to forget the dialectic out of which the perceived symmetry emerges.

The way in which Didi-Huberman connects the specific kaleidoscope experience to its technological make-up sheds light on how aesthetic form and ethico-historical content are interconnected in *Muriel*. Unlike Sontag, who has claimed that 'there is nothing "behind" the lean, staccato statements one sees' in *Muriel*, Didi-Huberman's phenomenology of the kaleidoscope makes tangible the film's seemingly invisible object chamber.[11] Even if the film, as Sontag highlights, is invested in studying 'the *form* of emotions', the double awareness regarding what hides 'behind' form, is never fully erased.[12] The story of Muriel's torturing is one — perhaps the most explicit — reference to the failure of form to fully supersede the debris. Another instance, which directly references the kaleidoscope's unfinished dream of beauty, is captured when Hélène, early in the film, remarks to her guests that she always wanted to make her apartment beautiful but has never managed to do so. In the light of Didi-Huberman's kaleidoscope phenomenology, this seemingly insignificant remark takes on a new meaning, as the debris firmly hidden and seemingly invisible in the object chamber, uncannily pierces through the film's forms.

Portrait of the Artist as a Kaleidoscomaniac

While the kaleidoscope was initially viewed as a technological object, it soon adopted the status of an everyday object of diversion and play. As such, it offered a temporary erasure from the present through the immersion it asks the viewer to undertake by centering his or her vision through the lens. Huhtamo therefore compellingly presents the history and role of the kaleidoscope as a cluster of 'symptoms of a creeping transition into the cultural condition we call "media culture"'.[13] There are several nineteenth-century caricatures playing on the theme of the kaleidoscope that show the perils produced by the interjection of the technological device in modern city life. A particularly telling illustration from the weekly handwritten Viennese newsletter entitled 'Archiv des menschlichen Unsinns' [Archive of Human Nonsense] depicts the composer Franz Schubert looking through a kaleidoscope while crossing the street and colliding with a draisine. Schubert's full physical immersion, paired with the experience of the alternate virtual reality the device enables, is caricatured here as a potential impediment for the kaleidoscope user's relationship to the world.

Huhtamo poignantly calls these early nineteenth-century technology aficionados 'kaleidoscomaniacs', thereby highlighting how many of these caricatures focusing on kaleidoscope addiction anticipate contemporary smartphone usage. In line with Huhtamo's media historical reading of the kaleidoscope, the signification of the appearance of an actual kaleidoscope in *Muriel* — shown in its duality as both a material object and a visual effect afforded to the one looking through it — also points to a critical commentary on the ethics of media culture. While Quinan scrutinises the perspectival vision associated with the kaleidoscope and how such a vision may be read as criticism of France's media censorship, the scene's focus on Marie-Do's immersion in a virtual reality is also a symbol for how fundamentally the interjection of a technological device reshapes relationality.

Fig. 7.1. Damian Klex [Leopold Kupelwieser]: Franz Schubert looking through a kaleidoscope and Leopold Kupelwieser riding a draisine. Watercolour (1818).[14]

Muriel has been criticised for its seeming prioritising of aesthetics over ethics, in the sense that Resnais does not directly address the Algerian War of Independence, despite the timing of the film's release shortly after the culmination of the conflict. In the foreground of such discussions has been the film's refusal to show the tortured Muriel and the way in which the voice-over telling of, but not showing, her torture clashes with the images of Algeria that are effectively shown.[15] Yet, if we take seriously the material reality of the kaleidoscope, as well as the role that technological devices play in the film more broadly, the film itself may be said to anticipate and respond to that very criticism. The immersion afforded by, and the aesthetic distortion produced through, technology is a key theme of *Muriel* that is repeatedly connected to Bernard, who is shown to carry around a camera and a voice recorder in his attempt to document the life and torture of Muriel. Bernard uses these devices to capture what he has experienced. Yet, he tellingly answers Hélène, who asks him to show her his film: 'j'ai pas envie de faire du cinéma, j'accumule des preuves' [I don't want to make a film. I am accumulating evidence]. Documentation and evidence over aesthetics and diversion — and yet, in French, 'faire du cinéma' also has a telling double meaning. It can be translated as Bernard not wanting to make a film, but it can also be read as 'I don't want to act', thereby signalling that Bernard sees himself as both filmmaker and acting subject in his film.

Later, Bernard is shown throwing his camera into the sea, thereby openly refusing the aestheticisation of Muriel's torture and his witnessing of it. While this suggests a clear refusal of the aesthetic, it is also Bernard who asks Marie-Do to look at him through the kaleidoscope, thereby suggesting that the film he is undertaking is about himself as much as it is about Muriel. The kaleidoscopic image of the multiplied, almost indistinguishable Bernard thereby turns into an evocative image of Bernard's own role within his film and *Muriel*. He is the one documenting Muriel, the ultimate other of Resnais's film, yet Bernard is also the subject and object of his own documentation. Bernard is therefore in front of the camera as well as behind it, infinitely split between its aesthetic form and the ethical content with which it seeks to connect. His throwing-away of the camera may point to a refusal of the aesthetic, but the scene also inserts a *mise-en-abyme* of the simultaneously absent and present filmmaker in *Muriel*.

Proust's Kaleidoscopes

Resnais's genesis as a filmmaker is often specifically related to the work of Proust — Carol Mavor has pithily stated: 'Resnais received a movie camera from his parents for his twelfth birthday and discovered Marcel Proust when he was fourteen: with these tools in hand, he would spend a lifetime making work on not forgetting'.[16] On a thematic level and regardless of biographical intersections, the particular affinity between Proust's and Resnais's respective *œuvres* is grounded in their common engagement with memory and forgetting. A specific resonance of these themes, I want to claim here, is to be found in the role that the kaleidoscope plays in the imaginary of *A la recherche*.

Optical instruments have long been identified as playing a prominent role in Proust's work.[17] As material objects, they testify to the ways in which the novel pays tribute to a time marked by massive scientific and technological changes; as motif and metaphor, the kaleidoscope in particular is associated with shifting meanings connected to the narrator's experience of the inner and outer world. While this connection finds productive resonances in the central positioning of the kaleidoscope in *Muriel*, it needs to be highlighted that the kaleidoscope is never referred to qua material object in *A la recherche*; it is the magic lantern, another popular nineteenth-century optical instrument and technological forerunner of the kaleidoscope, which is assigned a more privileged role as an object of diversion that sets in motion the narrator's creative imagination in *Combray*.[18] The magic lantern and its transformation of reality also offer a specific link between *Muriel* and *Combray*. As the narrator witnesses the images produced by the magic lantern, the character Golo's body memorably takes over the form of the narrator's doorhandle:

> Le corps de Golo lui-même, d'une essence aussi surnaturelle que celui de sa monture, s'arrangeait de tout obstacle matériel, de tout objet gênant qu'il rencontrait en le prenant comme ossature et en se le rendant intérieur, fût-ce le bouton de la porte sur lequel s'adaptait aussitôt et surnageait invinciblement

sa robe rouge ou sa figure pâle toujours aussi noble et aussi mélancolique, mais qui ne laissait paraître aucun trouble de cette transvertébration.

[The body of Golo himself, being of the same supernatural substance as his steed's, overcame every material obstacle — everything that seemed to bar his way — by taking it as an ossature and absorbing it into himself: even the doorknob — on which, adapting themselves at once, his red cloak or his pale face, still as noble and as melancholy, floated invincibly — would never betray the least concern at this transvertebration.][19]

Just like Resnais's kaleidoscope, the magic lantern is here shown to both incorporate and transform the external world. And, just as in Resnais's memorable opening image, which focuses on the doorhandle of Hélène's apartment, the narrator's doorknob, a mechanical device allowing access to an inner, private space, is assigned a privileged role here.[20]

But even if no actual kaleidoscope is referred to in *A la recherche*, the figure of the kaleidoscope already makes an appearance in the first pages of the novel's *ouverture*, where the narrator, unable to fall asleep, comments:

> Je me rendormais, et parfois je n'avais plus que de courts réveils d'un instant, le temps d'entendre les craquements organiques des boiseries, d'ouvrir les yeux pour fixer le kaléidoscope de l'obscurité, de goûter grâce à une lueur momentanée de conscience le sommeil où étaient plongés les meubles, la chambre, le tout dont je n'étais qu'une petite partie et à l'insensibilité duquel je retournais vite m'unir. (*RTP*, I, 4)

> [I would fall asleep again, and thereafter would reawaken for short snatches only, just long enough to hear the regular creaking of the wainscot, or to open my eyes to stare at the shifting kaleidoscope of the darkness, to savour, in a momentary glimmer of consciousness, the sleep which lay heavy upon the furniture, the room, that whole of which I formed no more than a small part and whose insensibility I should very soon return to share.] (*SLT*, I, 2)

This 'kaléidoscope de l'obscurité', as Hughes comments, is 'formed by the clusters of private night-time memories and associations'.[21] Without light, however, kaleidoscopes cannot function, and in these opening lines of *A la recherche*, it is only due to the narrator's own 'lueur momentanée de conscience' that temporary forms can emerge from the diverse formations of fragmented darkness.

The *ouverture*'s kaleidoscope, and the way in which it casts the narrator's mind as the creative source of light, has therefore, as André Benhaïm observes, been read as pointing towards the narrator's own artistic genesis: 'kaléidoscope de l'obscurité: vision mosaïque — de l'ombre. Vision kaléidoscopique pour écriture fragmentaire et enveloppante, graphie illisible, graffite nocturnes' [kaleidoscope of the darkness: mosaic vision — of the shadow. Kaleidoscopic vision for fragmentary and immersive writing, illegible graphics, nocturnal graffito].[22] But before Proust's kaleidoscope turns into a poetic vision for the novel and allegory for the artist that Benhaïm and others see in it, the interplay of shadows and light affects how the narrator perceives his surroundings. The shifting kaleidoscope of darkness is perceived, in the first instance, as affecting the space — the room, the furniture — in which the narrator finds himself. The kaleidoscope of the *ouverture*, even if it is not referred to as an actual object, is thereby firmly grounded in the narrator's experience of the material world.

In its emphasis on darkness rather than light, the Proustian kaleidoscope turns into a visual variation on the opening shot of Resnais's *Muriel*: the film's opening sequence is not characterised by darkness, and yet different parts of the room are intermittently spotlighted and zoomed in on, which creates an effect similar to the insomniac narrator's impressions that define the *ouverture* of *A la recherche*. As seemingly randomly chosen details of objects, body parts and interactions are momentarily moved into focus only to be similarly arbitrarily cast aside, the opening scene of *Muriel* produces a sense of disorientation in space and overwhelming exposure to unconnected visual and relational details. Emma Wilson has pointed to the film's refusal of totality, commenting that 'Resnais chops up the diegetic reality we perceive, disorienting us and making the viewing process self-conscious'.[23] In a similar vein, the opening pages of *A la recherche* create a process of self-conscious refusal of totality in as much as the fragments of memories and imagination, as well as the interspersed images relating to the narrator's bedroom, confront readers with their own ever unsuccessful attempts to construct a linear narrative.

Later in the novel, the kaleidoscope motif further deepens the theme of introspection, as it moves from the domain of consciousness and exposure to the external world to the unfathomability and instability of human emotion and relationships. The jealous narrator, meditating on Albertine's suspected infidelity, remarks:

> Nous croyons savoir exactement les choses, et ce que pensent les gens, pour la simple raison que nous ne nous en soucions pas. Mais dès que nous avons le désir de savoir, comme a le jaloux, alors c'est un vertigineux kaléidoscope où nous ne distinguons plus rien. (*RTP*, IV, 100)
>
> [We imagine that we know exactly what things are and what people think, for the simple reason that we do not care about them. But as soon as we have a desire to know, as the jealous man has, then it becomes a dizzy kaleidoscope in which we can no longer distinguish anything.] (*SLT*, V, 593)

In *A la recherche*, the reader is invited to share the narrator's jealous meandering thoughts, to enter the ever-growing fractal-like vision of Albertine that emerges as the narrator plays through different ways in which he could read her behaviour. The 'vertigineux kaléidoscope' of emotional relationality is fleshed out in the Proustian text, as the different possible versions of events and emotions are minutely reviewed, compared and revised.

Muriel provides a negative of the Proustian image. Self and other are in constant interaction in the film and everything that is known about a character, is known merely through the brief, uninformative and always rushed interactions with others. Whenever the protagonists' lives outside these interactions move into the foreground, they immediately retreat. Exemplary in this regard is Alphonse's reply to the question of what precisely he did in Algeria, to which he responds: 'Ah il me faudrait beaucoup de temps de venir sur la question d'Algérie' [Ah it would take me a long time to address the issue of Algeria]. This inconclusive reply averts the question and moves from his particular situation to the general;

nobody ever broaches the subject of Algeria with him again. Yet, this open refusal of introspection paired with Resnais's aesthetics of visual deflection, makes the missing answer not less significant; instead, Alphonse's evasiveness sets up one of the film's many *blancs*, which together create what Wilson has called the particular 'unease of this post-war French community'.[24]

This leads to the perhaps most pertinent parallel between Proust and Resnais regarding the kaleidoscope, namely how the instrument comes to stand for a social dialectics of history and thereby pre-empts criticism of the ways in which their respective works engage with specific historical events and ideologies. It is through the kaleidoscope that Proust captures how we are to make sense of the seemingly arbitrary transformations of society. Any politico-historical event is hereby turned into a merely temporary disposition, because 'pareille aux kaléidoscopes qui tournent de temps en temps, la société place successivement de façon différente des éléments qu'on avait crus immuables et compose une autre figure' [like a kaleidoscope which is every now and then given a turn, society arranges successively in different orders elements which one would have supposed immutable, and composes a new pattern] (*RTP*, I, 507; *SLT*, II, 103). The Dreyfus Affair is one such example for when the social order assumes an erratic new shift, as the narrator already highlights in *A l'ombre des jeunes filles en fleurs*:

> Ces dispositions nouvelles du kaléidoscope sont produites par ce qu'un philosophe appellerait un changement de critère. L'affaire Dreyfus en amena un nouveau, à une époque un peu postérieure à celle où je commençais à aller chez Mme Swann, et le kaléidoscope renversa une fois de plus ses petits losanges colorés. Tout ce qui était juif passa en bas, fût-ce la dame élégante, et des nationalistes obscurs montèrent prendre sa place. (*RTP*, I, 508)
>
> [These new arrangements of the kaleidoscope are produced by what a philosopher would call a 'change of criterion.' The Dreyfus case brought about another, at a period rather later than that in which I began to go to Mme Swann's, and the kaleidoscope once more reversed its coloured lozenges. Everything Jewish, even the elegant lady herself, went down, and various obscure nationalists rose to take its place.] (*SLT*, II, 103)

Proust's position on shifting social identities and political ideologies can, of course, be read as emanating from a detached, apolitical position. And just as Resnais was criticised for refusing a more overt engagement with the Algerian War of Independence in *Muriel*, Proust, when being awarded the Prix Goncourt for *A l'ombre des jeunes filles en fleurs* in 1919, was held accountable for how such a view supposedly led him to prioritise aesthetics. Edward Hughes's book *Proust, Class, and Nation* has done much to disprove such readings, highlighting instead how the kaleidoscope captures Proust's 'tactic of working from the particular to the abstract'.[25] This tactic can anticipate and pre-empt criticism because the figure of the kaleidoscope, on the one hand, zooms in on, multiplies and enhances a certain image, but on the other hand, it also always recalls the arbitrarily shifted debris hiding behind the mirror image of a specific ideology and event.

As such, it bears a compelling affinity to an early scene in *Muriel*, where Alphonse and Françoise, after meeting Hélène at the station, are walking through

Boulogne-sur-Mer. Françoise remarks that the entire town seems to be rebuilt and asks whether that is because of the war. 'Une ville martyre' [A martyrised city], comments Alphonse, to which Hélène replies, 'Oui, il y a eu beaucoup de morts, de fusillés — je ne me souviens plus du nombre. 200? 3000? Je ne me souviens plus' [Yes, there were many dead, shot — I do not remember the exact number. 200? 3000? I do not remember.] The camera then shifts to several shots that focus on how the town is still marked by the architectural ruins of the Second World War. Accelerating images of half-destroyed buildings, street names and plaques seeking to commemorate the war, mainly shown in black and white, offer a contrast to the colourful images that the film otherwise employs. *Muriel* thereby sets up the Second World War and France's own complicated role within it, within a film that in its title bears the name of an Algerian woman tortured by the French. As the images create a mosaic of a town marked by the indelible scars of war, the debris of the kaleidoscope's chamber powerfully pierces through the ever-growing, ever-shifting formations of destruction. As Proust's and Resnais's kaleidoscopes mediate between the inner lives of their protagonists and the outer worlds they inhabit, the interconnections between the material and visual genealogy of the kaleidoscope enable us to untangle the ways in which their *œuvres* are caught in a continuous mirroring of ethics and aesthetics.

Notes to Chapter 7

1. Susan Sontag, 'Resnais' *Muriel*', in *Against Interpretation and Other Essays* (London: Farrar, Straus & Giroux, 1964), pp. 232–41 (pp. 239–40).
2. Laura McMahon, 'Untimely Resnais: Muriel's Disarticulations of Justice', *Film-Philosophy*, 20 (2016), 219–34 (p. 229).
3. See, for example, Emma Wilson, *Alain Resnais* (Manchester: Manchester University Press, 2006), pp. 97–98.
4. Edward J. Hughes, 'Proust and Social Spaces', in *The Cambridge Companion to Proust*, ed. by Richard Bales (Cambridge: Cambridge University Press), pp. 151–67 (p. 152).
5. Christine Quinan, 'Postcolonial Memory and Masculinity in Algeria: Alain Resnais's Absent Muriel', *Interventions: International Journal of Postcolonial Studies*, 19.1 (2017), 17–35 (pp. 28–29).
6. Erkki Huhtamo, '"All the World's a Kaleidoscope": A Media Archaeological Perspective to the Incubation Era of Media Culture', *Schermi/Screens*, 55 (2014), 139–53, n. 8 <https://journals.openedition.org/estetica/982> [accessed November 2021].
7. Ibid., para. 7.
8. Ibid., para. 11.
9. Ibid., para. 24.
10. Georges Didi-Huberman, 'Connaissance par le kaléidoscope: morale du joujou et dialectique de l'image selon Walter Benjamin', *Etudes photographiques*, 7 (2000), para. 16 <https://journals.openedition.org/etudesphotographiques/204?lang=en> [accessed November 2021]. All translations in this chapter are my own unless stated otherwise.
11. Sontag, 'Resnais' *Muriel*', p. 234.
12. Ibid., p. 235.
13. Huhtamo, para. 4.
14. In Eduard Anschütz, 'Archiv des menschlichen Unsinns: ein langweiliges Unterhaltungsblatt für Wahnwitzige', 2.26 (16 July 1818). Source: Wienbibliothek im Rathaus, H.I.N.-68011 <https://permalink.obvsg.at/wbr/AC15862881> [accessed November 2021].
15. For a summary of these discussions, see McMahon, 'Untimely Resnais', p. 220; Suzanne Gauch, 'Muriel, or the Disappearing Text of the Algerian War', *L'Esprit Créateur*, 41.4 (2001), 47–57.

A powerful counter-argument which highlights the many ways in which *Muriel* engages with the political context of the Algerian War is presented in Leo Bersani and Ulysse Dutoit, *Arts of Impoverishment: Beckett, Rothko, Resnais* (Cambridge, MA: Harvard University Press, 1993), pp. 181–208.
16. Carol Mavor, 'The Inconsolable, Insoluble Memory of Alain Resnais (June 3, 1922-March 1, 2014)' <https://dukeupress.wordpress.com/2014/03/26/the-inconsolable-insoluble-memory-of-alain-resnais-june-3-1922-march-1-2014/> [accessed November 2021].
17. See, for instance, Roger Shattuck, *Proust's Binoculars* (New York: Random House, 1963), particularly its opening section entitled 'Proust's Optical Figures' (pp. 3–20), and Anne Henry, 'Le Kaléidoscope', *Cahiers Marcel Proust 9 (Études proustiennes III)* (Paris: Gallimard, 1979), pp. 27–66. Proust's optics have also been explicitly linked to filmmaking and montage, see Miriam Heywood, 'True Images: Metaphor, Metonymy and Montage in Marcel Proust's *A la recherche du temps perdu* and Jean-Luc Godard's *Histoire(s) du cinema*', *Paragraph*, 33.1 (2010), 37–51.
18. Indeed, in 1866, David Brewster published a popular guidebook about the magic lantern in which he claims that while the device was initially viewed as a parlour game for children, its true purpose is 'conveying scientific instruction': *The Magic Lantern: How to Buy and How to Use it, By 'A Mere Phantom.'* (London: Houlston & Sons, 1866), p. 19.
19. Marcel Proust, *A la recherche du temps perdu*, ed. by Jean-Yves Tadié and others, 4 vols, Bibliothèque de la Pléiade (Paris: Gallimard, 1987–89), I (*Du côté de chez Swann*), 10 (hereafter referenced as *RTP* in the main text); *In Search of Lost Time*, trans. by C. K. Scott-Moncrieff and Terence Kilmartin, rev. by D. J. Enright, 6 vols (London: Vintage, 2000–02), I, 9 (hereafter referenced as *SLT* in main text).
20. Celia Britton, who has also pointed to the great emphasis on doors and doorways in *Muriel*, has highlighted the particular importance of the film's closing shot in this regard: 'the final shot, in which the flat is left not only empty but with the door open, is perhaps the most striking statement of this theme'. See 'Broken Images in Resnais's Muriel', *French Cultural Studies*, 1 (1990), 37–46 (p. 43).
21. Hughes, 'Proust and Social Spaces', p. 152.
22. André Benhaïm, *Panim: visages de Proust* (Villeneuve d'Ascq: Presses universitaires du Septentrion, 2006), p. 159. As such, the Proustian image recalls Baudelaire's memorable description of the artist-*flâneur* in *Le Peintre de la vie moderne* as 'un kaléidoscope doué de conscience' [a kaleidoscope endowed with consciousness]. Charles Baudelaire, *Œuvres complètes*, ed. by Claude Pichois, 2 vols, Bibliothèque de la Pléiade (Paris: Gallimard, 1975–76), II, 692.
23. Wilson, *Alain Resnais*, p. 98.
24. Ibid., p. 99.
25. Edward J. Hughes, *Proust, Class, and Nation* (Oxford: Oxford University Press, 2011), p. 248.

CHAPTER 8

Feeling the French-Algerian War: Male Vulnerability, Shame and the Wounds of Brotherhood in Yacine Balah's *Frères ennemis* (2013)

James S. Williams

How to do emotional justice to historical events? Or rather, what might it look like to 'feel' rather than to 'know' history? It's a question posed with singular force and originality by a short narrative film entitled *Frères ennemis* (2013) [Enemy Brothers] by young Maghrebi-French director Yacine Balah, which engages with the emotional toll of the French-Algerian War. Lasting barely twenty-two minutes, *Frères ennemis* has been entirely ignored by film scholars and historians, although it is readily available on-line with subtitles.[1] Such indifference is perplexing since the film already offers something rarely glimpsed in French cinema: an encounter between two Algerians on different sides. Set in central France in 1958, it follows an operative of the Front de Libération Nationale (FLN) on the run from the French army who finds temporary refuge in the home of a *harki*, that is, one of the many Algerian auxiliaries who sided with the French during the conflict and were regarded by the FLN as traitors.[2] Yet while the film observes some of the standard tropes and themes of narrative cinema about the conflict (racist violence, torture, martyrdom, the figure of the *porteur de valises*, generational strife), its primary focus is on human pain and suffering, from fear and vulnerability to shame and loss. Indeed, with an immediate, frontal, realist style and purposively minor mode (it limits itself to a matter of hours in an anonymous rural area far from the major sites of the conflict), *Frères ennemis* pursues a narrative arc that is fundamentally emotional: from the abject panic of men about to be shot to individual tears shed at the dreadful destruction of life.

Such raw, visceral attention to human trauma contrasts notably with Rachid Bouchareb's genre-driven *Hors la loi* (2010) [Outside The Law], a sweeping historical epic about the creation of an FLN network in Nanterre from the perspective of three Algerian brothers and which revels in hyper-stylised gangster violence, although the controversy the film aroused owed more to perceived historical inaccuracies.[3] *Frères ennemis* doesn't stint on violence, far from it, but concentrates more on its effects, both physical and mental, or what French historian Benjamin Stora has termed the material 'body of the war' which, he rightly claims, has been conspicuously lacking in French films about the conflict where, as the revolutionary idealist Abdelkader in *Hors la loi* puts it: 'Il n'y a pas de place pour des passions personnelles' [Personal passions should not get in the way].[4]

Frères ennemis clearly invites a biographical reading. In the few brief interviews he has given, Balah explains that while the film is based in large part on the stories of his father Messaoud (the name also of the FLN character) who served in the FLN in France (the film is dedicated at the end to his memory), his maternal grandfather was a *harki*.[5] Yet while *Frères ennemis* offers a determined counter-narrative of the war regarding the relations between the FLN and the *harkis*, it presents no explicit political agenda around memory and marginalisation typical of second-generation *harkis* who have identified themselves as 'les oubliés de l'histoire' [the forgotten of history], co-opting the political metaphor of 'memory wars' to frame their memory practices embracing the suffering and trauma experienced by their parents.[6] Indeed, what distinguishes *Frères ennemis* is its assiduously objective, linear, third-person narration and commitment to depicting at once the shared wounds of war and the conflicted feelings of identity and loyalty. Balah formalises his dual heritage specifically in terms of an emotional ache: 'ce tiraillement que j'ai porté en moi toute ma vie entre ma mère, fille de Harki, et mon père, ancien membre du FLN' [this gnawing tension I've carried inside me all my life between my mother, daughter of a *harki*, and my father, former member of the FLN].[7] This formative tension is reflected in the film's title, *Frères ennemis*: the *harki* is a 'false' brother, or fraternal enemy, not only of the FLN but also of the French.

In fact, *Frères ennemis* appears to suggest that beyond establishing the essential bare details of the French-Algerian War, the drive to acquire knowledge of the conflict in the absence of a full consideration of its emotional scars and ongoing trauma may be misplaced. Not only does the film powerfully exploit the advantages of the short form (brevity, economy, concision) and consciously withhold information (secrets are not revealed, elements are left vague or opaque), but also it engages at the start directly with the materiality and white heat of the audio archives of the French-Algerian war within a fictional format. In so doing, *Frères ennemis* raises important questions about the value of the archives for an understanding of the past and the role of affect in cinema's treatment of history. Such questions assume greater urgency with the recent declassification by President Macron of French military files and documents relating to the French-Algerian War. Macron's calculated balancing of 'historical truth' with legitimate 'national defence issues' led him to commission a report by Stora on the 'memories of colonisation and the Algerian War'.[8] Submitted and made public in January 2021, it highlighted the need for France to 'face up to its history' and suggested creating a 'Memories and Truth' commission (accordingly established) to reconcile 'the two shores of the Mediterranean'. The official hope is that a more complete understanding of the once undeclared *guerre sans nom* may now finally be possible, yet Macron has also made it clear that while France may acknowledge responsibility for torture and killing, it will not apologise for its role in the conflict, still less repent for it or offer recompense.[9] What, then, might the 'unofficial', artistic reason be for excavating the archives? Is it primarily to disentomb historical facts and data from the murk of history — often from under a mountain of denial — for political analysis, or does it also involve a search for some kind of resolution (personal, aesthetic, emotional)?

In what follows I will attempt to show that if *Frères ennemis* constitutes 'the creation of a "new, inclusive memoryscape"', it is one where emotion rather than memory and knowledge is the key determinant.[10] Further, by making the viewer experience directly the brutalising effects of violence and the body in crisis, *Frères ennemis* both reveals the scale of human wounding and opens up potent doubts about identity and the norms of masculinity. Finally, I will argue that the film's aesthetic creation of emotion has implications for the cultural healing of the transgenerational wounds of war within contemporary French society.

Framing War

Frères ennemis begins with a cascade of sounds from the archives over a black screen. We hear a recording of the famous words delivered by Charles de Gaulle during a press conference in Paris on 23 October 1958 when, prompted by reporters' questions about the French government's reaction to what appeared to be a halt in recent weeks to terrorist activities in France, he suddenly showed himself willing to discuss a cease-fire with the FLN. Of the 'Muslim rebels' de Gaulle declared: 'je dis, sans aucun embarras, que pour la plupart d'entre eux les hommes de l'insurrection ont combattu courageusement. Que vienne la paix des braves! Et je suis sûr que les haines iront en s'effaçant' [I say without confusion that, for the majority of them involved in the insurrection, they fought courageously [...] Let there be the peace of the brave, and I'm sure hatreds will continue to fade away].[11] This provocative call for a 'peace of the brave' is heard in disjointed fashion due to other competing, and much less familiar, recorded voices on the soundtrack that cut into, and occasionally talk over, de Gaulle's words. First, a news reporter is heard setting the scene outside the Ministry of Information in Paris where a crowd has gathered following an FLN attack. The event in question is not identified but is most probably the failed attempt by an FLN commando unit on 15 September 1958 on the life of the Information Minister, Jacques Soustelle. This came on the heels of the FLN attack in Marseille on 25 and 26 August and fifteen simultaneous attacks in cities across the country which initiated the FLN's temporary opening up of a new front on domestic French soil.

Two other separate male voices are then brought into the mix expressing distinctly different viewpoints: 'le droit de disposer librement de son destin est enfin reconnu au peuple algérien' [the Algerian people have finally been accorded the right to determine their own fate]; and, just audible, 'et la France ne reconnaîtra pas chez elle d'autre autorité que la sienne' [and France will not recognise at home any other authority than its own]. The first are the words spoken by the French Communist politician Jacques Duclos during a parliamentary session in the French Senate on 27 October 1959 — a response to de Gaulle's televised speech to the nation on 16 September 1959 announcing for the first time the once-taboo idea of Algerian self-determination.[12] The second statement is by François Mitterrand, then centre-left Minister of the Interior, on 7 November 1954, a week after the beginning of the conflict (the first, more familiar part of the declaration: 'L'Algérie, c'est la France', is omitted). As the final part of de Gaulle's 1958 call is heard, the words 'France, 1958' appear typewritten in white over the black screen.

What we are hearing in this dense, highly compressed concatenation of voices of varying status, volume and style are evolving historical viewpoints over a five-year period. Confusion is created by the mash-up of disembodied sounds and voices presented in counterpoint and with no captions or intertitles to identify them. The disorientation is increased by the brooding drums of the prowling, minimalist theme music (by Mohand Sahridj and Jérémie Tuil) which convey an ominous sense of foreboding reflecting the volatility of the moment when metropolitan France was on a knife-edge politically and militarily. At this mid-stage in the conflict de Gaulle is banking on a reconciliation between enemies — 'us' (the French forces) and 'them' (the Algerian rebels) — on the grounds of a mutual respect for military bravery, in the hope that what he calls the 'courageous personality of Algeria' might come to exist peacefully. The term 'the peace of the brave' signifies a peace accord or provision in honourable conditions and on consideration of the bravery of fighters. Yet de Gaulle's monumentalising argument is complicated and even undermined here by the other statements that disturb its flow, creating the effect of dissent and a *dialogue de sourds*. The result is to upend the idea of a shared, common conception of masculinity — the universal admiration of physical exploits, the legend of military prowess — around which men of all nationalities might unite (the FLN rejected de Gaulle's peace proposal three days later).

The auditory montage thus announces the theme of male relations and relationality, raising the question of what type of change or transformation is possible between men who may be defined as 'brothers' on an ethnic and cultural level, yet who are sworn enemies politically. At the same time, through its refusal to supply any contextualising details, the opening thirty-second barrage of sound fires a warning shot about the purpose of archival work. It took this listener many patient hours on Google Search to establish all the references, yet the film is suggesting that this may not be enough, or rather too much. For what matters more is an acute appreciation of the surge of raw emotions and sensations that are released in any reopening of the media archives of war with their recorded ferment and still-live wounds and fractures. Put differently, the archives are presented here less as a source of knowledge than as a zone of affective intensity, and the film will ensure through its various strategies of opacity that the viewer remains exposed to this cinematic body of affect by resisting our natural desire to identify and control material.

If the prologue provides the historical and conceptual frame for *Frères ennemis*, it also establishes the quickfire pace and taut, elliptical style of the film which now bursts into colour on the screen and breaks down into five discrete movements.

One, a slightly-built, scraggy-looking Arab man (Salem Kali) runs frantically through woodland undergrowth carrying a small suitcase as three blindfolded Arab men are lined up outside a farmhouse and summarily executed by a French soldier for refusing to divulge information. Two, the same fleeing man confronts a French solider pointing a gun at him and knifes him in the stomach before suffocating him, in the process sustaining a bloody wound to his leg. Three, the fugitive, now identified as Messaoud, arrives at an apparently deserted house where he collapses after being surprised by the owner, Belkacem (Abel Jafri). Four, the French executioner, lieutenant Messard (François-David Cardonnel), with his sergeant Marino (Thibaut Wacksmann), visits Belkacem who has hidden Messaoud and denies all knowledge of him, the ID check also revealing that Belkacem served as a corporal in the French army. Five, tipped off inadvertently by a French neighbour, the soldiers return and Belkacem is shot dead as Messaoud escapes limping into the woods.

Structured as a suspense thriller, the film presents a stark depiction of the actuality of violence and slaughter at ground level, captured with unflinching immediacy by cinematographer Ludovic Zuili and intensified by the real time effect of long takes. The proliferation of terror and horror creates a burden of trauma for the viewer who is forced to watch aghast, for there is no aesthetic filtering of the carnage through the conventions of genre, such as the invitation to identify formally with one side over another through subjective point-of-view shots (here rigorously denied). Further, the sensory overload generated by the restless back and forth between close-ups, hand-held tracking shots and momentary fades to black is matched on the soundtrack by the deliberately uneven shifts between different musical styles and tempos, including snatches of a percussive electronic score and plaintive North African strings. Yet for all the breathless build-up of multiple killings and graphic motifs (blood, rifle-pointing, gunfire, wounds, dead bodies), it is the tempestuous meeting between Messaoud and Belkacem that constitutes the film's most charged episode precisely because it throws easy notions of brotherhood into question and lays bare the appalling emotional and psychological costs of war.

Opening Up Wounds: Memory, Emotion, Release

Let us replay the encounter in detail. After a rifle edges into view behind Messaoud's head from right to left of screen and he is commanded to turn around slowly, he is astonished to behold the imposing face of an older Arab man. 'Écoute mon frère' [Listen to me, my brother], he pleads, to which Belkacem immediately responds with surly precision: 'Il n'y a pas mon frère' [I'm not your brother].[13] The fugitive tries again, 'Tire si tu veux, mais...' [Shoot if you like, but...], before falling to the ground. The film returns to black screen. A few seconds later Messaoud wakes up on a bed and discovers that a dressing has been put over his leg-wound. If Belkacem refuses to identify this unwelcome stranger as his brother, he still treats him with human dignity and care and is duly thanked. Yet Belkacem, it transpires, has also opened the suitcase while Messaoud was asleep and knows what it contains

FIG. 8.1. Facing the enemy: Messaoud (Salem Kali) appealing to his 'brother' Belkacem (Abel Jafri, off-screen) in *Frères ennemis* (2013), directed by Yacine Balah.
© Boogieman Production.

(information withheld from view). After trading some basic background details while smoking a cigarette (Messaoud states he was part of an FLN unit based in the hide-out of a French ally that was exposed; Belkacem does not deny he is Algerian), the men square up to each other in mutual suspicion. Their antagonism, accentuated by the use of shot/counter-shot, takes the form of a face-off between the generations. Messaoud addresses Belkacem derogatively as a 'veteran': you veterans gave in — you tried everything (votes, assemblies) and achieved nothing (the irony of Messaoud declaring himself a 'soldier who obeys' when manifestly he is not a professional is not lost on Belkacem). He even calls Belkacem contemptuously 'El Hadj', with a hint perhaps of Messali Hadj, leader of the rival Algerian National Movement (MNA).[14] Belkacem, meanwhile, adopts a thoroughly jaded stance: the promises of the leaders, even those fighting for independence, are all the same — empty.

It is after the visit by the fractious French soldiers, when Messaoud overhears Belkacem being grudgingly saluted as a veteran in the military sense, that the power relations between the two are dramatically reversed. Messaoud has already swiped Belkacem's rifle and, livid with rage, points it menacingly in his face (this time from left to right of screen) while accusing him of being a traitor, which Belkacem concedes. Yet rather than counter-attack, Belkacem, forced onto his knees, now implores Messaoud to shoot: 'Je ne suis plus rien. Aide-moi!' [I'm nothing anymore. Help me!]. He even tauntingly offers to help Messaoud undertake the task. But Messaoud doesn't shoot. Instead, despite the urgency of his situation, he grants Belkacem time to tell his story. What initially promised to be a political-philosophical dialogue about commitment between two men ideologically opposed has been short-circuited into an anguished confessional. Belkacem recounts he was serving in Guelma province in Algeria and was ordered to shoot at a crowd during an insurrection; among those in the crowd was his nephew. Sobbing, he describes how the experience left him in an unbearable state of distress and loss which he is visibly still living: 'Je suis un soldat ... J'exécute les ordres ... J'ai tout perdu' [I'm a

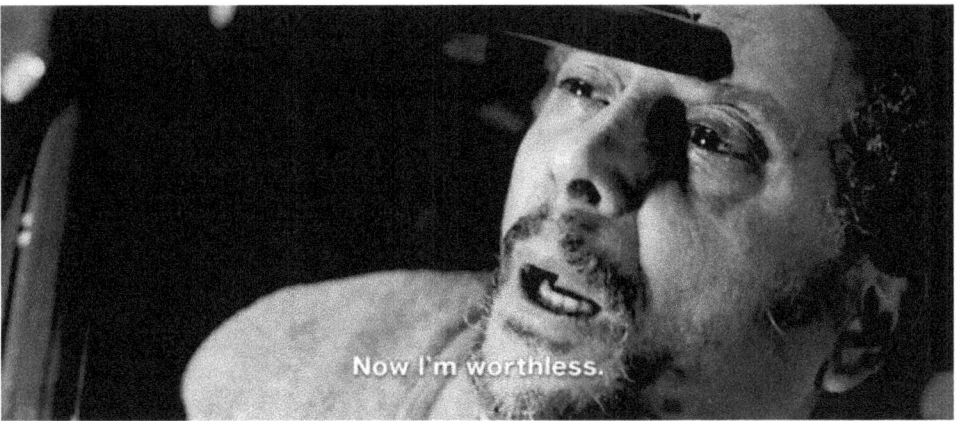

Fig. 8.2. The face of shame: Belkacem (Abel Jafri) beseeching Messaoud (Salem Kali, off-screen) to shoot him in *Frères ennemis* (2013), directed by Yacine Balah. © Boogieman Production.

soldier ... I execute orders ... I've lost everything]. We infer that he subsequently retired from the army and moved to France where he now lives alone, shorn of status and not fully accepted as French, with only his wounds of abject shame that remain glaringly open.[15] If Messaoud wished to humiliate Belkacem politically, Belkacem's own feelings of guilt and shame already run far deeper. Physical injuries may be neatly bandaged up to relieve the pain, but internal torment is much more difficult to treat, still less heal. The notion of wounds and woundedness has thus expanded from the purely physical to the emotional and existential, creating the sense of an all-consuming catastrophe.

Belkacem is still on the floor kneeling in submission when the French soldiers return. Holding first in his hands, then to his chest, a large photograph (of his nephew? — again, the viewer is denied confirmatory access), he begins chanting words in Arabic. These are no doubt religious verses from the Koran sighted earlier, but a translation of the words into French is not supplied. Messard points his gun down brutally towards Belkacem and appears ready to shoot. To Marino's concern that one can't simply kill a French soldier and that an interrogation is first required, Messard responds with pure racist hatred: 'they' (Arabs) are all 'the same dirty race'. The scene then cuts abruptly to a forward-tracking shot of Messaoud running into the woods, the camera hugging close behind, while Belkacem's chanting remains still audible. This is the first and only time in the film that different scenes are brought together through the migration of diegetic sounds from one sequence to another. Such intermixing links Belkacem and Messaoud formally as sound and image for six long, agonising seconds (0:19:26–0:19:31). When Messard finally pulls the trigger, the camera stays on Messaoud who stops dead in his tracks and turns around. He stares out in our general direction in a state of consternation, tears welling up in his eyes and falling slowly down his left cheek as the same spare, elegiac piano that accompanied Belkacem's breakdown returns. It is as if Messaoud were now facing head-on both the enormity of human loss and destruction and the fact that, as earlier, he owes his life to others being killed for keeping silent. Before,

Fig. 8.3. Face to face in shared loss: Messaoud (Salem Kali) looking back towards the viewer in *Frères ennemis* (2013), directed by Yacine Balah. © Boogieman Production.

focused solely on the safe passage of his suitcase, he had to suppress his emotions. Now, suddenly, he can take emotional stock of events and express, if only in silence, his feelings of relief, gratitude, fear, confusion and horror. He will eventually swivel back round and head off once more into the woods, the image fading in an abstract blur before a final return to black screen and the end-credits.

Again, the viewer, torn simultaneously between tracking Messaoud's passage to safety and having to anticipate the sonic shock of the lethal bullet, is intimately exposed to this shattering moment. Witnessing Messaoud and his outpouring of emotions in close-up, we find ourselves immersed in a circuit of agony and trauma. The film's insistence that we contemplate the wordless hurt and desolation in Messaoud's mute face recalls Judith Butler's attention in *Precarious Life: The Powers of Mourning and Violence* (2004) to the ethical implications of Levinas's notion of the face as something that communicates what is human and expresses the fragility and vulnerability that unite us. She writes: 'To respond to the face, to understand its meaning, means to be awake to what is precarious in another life or, rather, the precariousness of life itself'.[16] In other words, to respond to the face (which may not, of course, always literally be the face) is to understand the precariousness of the Other. Butler's further gloss on Levinas is significant here in light of the way the viewer is also placed in direct proximity with Belkacem's wailing: 'the face,' she continues, 'seems to be a kind of sound, the sound of language evacuating its sense, the sonorous substratum of vocalisation that precedes and limits the delivery of any semantic sense'.[17] Hence, if the French soldiers dismiss Belkacem indiscriminately as a faceless, 'jabbering' Arab (the verb *baragouiner* is used in the sense of speaking pidgin French), the film itself summons the viewer and makes an ethical appeal: that we register Messaoud's entangled emotions as our own and grieve, even for those like Belkacem who might have seemed beyond redemption. The film's burden of grief has been effectively transformed into a gift to be shared in relay: Belkacem's tears are Messaoud's tears are *our* tears.

In narrative terms, Belkacem's motives for again not betraying Messaoud to the French and delaying the soldiers just long enough for him to escape may be easily surmised: a wish to atone for past deeds out of a sense of extreme guilt and remorse, along with a realisation that he has nothing left to lose. By helping Messaoud escape he is re-engaging again with the French-Algerian war on his own terms which correspond ironically to those of the FLN. In a further tragic irony, this potentially momentous act of self-transformation cancels itself out as soon as it occurs since it demands his own death. Yet it is the affective force of this moment, when Belkacem's gentle yet pained chanting floods the visual image of the fleeing Messaoud, that is being prioritised here. For in a way entirely unforeseen, FLN and *harki* — young and old, political and religious — are now conjoined, creating an emotional unity all the more precious for being so unexpected and transitory. The cut or wound of montage thus functions here less as a means of fragmentation, as it did in the opening audio montage, than as a point of convergence, signalling that the naked face of common vulnerability may perhaps embody the true face of brotherhood.

Redefining the Masculine: Brotherhood Beyond Identity

By compelling the viewer so unremittingly to *feel* the body of the war, *Frères ennemis* is a blistering audiovisual experience. Jill Bennett has written eloquently about the power of images in their 'capacity to address the spectator's bodily memory: to touch the viewer who feels rather than simply sees the event, drawn into the image through a process of affective contagion'.[18] To this we may add the permeability of sound which, in *Frères ennemis*, not only underscores visible atrocity but also figures imagined terror and dread. Crucially, the film declines to complete the historical frame opened up at the beginning: there is no fast-forward return to history of the kind found in *Hors la loi* which is framed by archival images of collective jubilation (opening with newsreel images of the Liberation parade of May 1945 on the Champs-Élysées, it closes with images of the crowds in Algiers in July 1962). Such completion is arguably a way of closing off, or sublimating, the trauma of the war, as if it could instantly be healed through political catharsis. In the deliberately open-ended *Frères ennemis*, the cycle of 'impure' violence and death is decidedly not over and remains merely suspended in an indeterminate flux with all still to play (and die) for, like an interminable, gaping wound. In the spirit of its opening archival montage, the film is daring to suggest that it may be more important to avoid the temptation of closure and keep the transgenerational wounds of the French-Algerian war open until its continuing legacy of suffering and loss has been properly recognised and collectively confronted. For just as vital as the commitment to historical knowledge is the work of grief and mourning that must form part of any final cultural reckoning of the conflict. As we have seen, if the film demands an alert, emotionally engaged viewer attuned to the heightened acoustics of the archives, it consistently cautions against any complacent faith in the amassing of facts which may, after all, never be fully established (the contents of the suitcase — the motor of the drama — are made literally immaterial). It could even be that the best way forward is, as Lia Brozgal illustrates in her innovative cultural history of the 17 October 1961 Paris massacre, to reconceive the very notion of the archive (she employs the felicitous term 'anarchive'). This includes charting how literature and visual culture represent both the existence and erasure of history by complicating it, potentially by resisting reality while speculating on what might have been.[19]

Yet *Frères ennemis* also records the creation of unexpected, transformative feelings of brotherhood through the sudden realisation of new relationalities and affective affinities. Such fraternity translates more as kinship premised on commonality and empathy with a fellow human being in need, before terms like 'brother' and 'solidarity' come into ideological play. Belkacem may have unwittingly become a martyr to the Algerian cause, but his mortal act is presented as an instinctive, corporeal response to the situation at hand, one that cannot immediately be named or defined politically and which escapes the simplistic binaries of brother versus enemy. Hence, if a rapprochement between warring parties is ever to happen, it is not on account of masculine bravery and admiration in the field of battle, but rather as a result of compassion and sympathy in the shared face of horror, including, as here, listening attentively to another man's harrowing account of shame.

In tracing the turmoil of lone, lost, troubled men, *Frères ennemis* fails spectacularly to reproduce the cinematic norms of masculinity and insists on vulnerability and precariousness. In so doing, it not only offers a salutary rebuke to de Gaulle's lofty script of heroic masculinity and 'peace of the brave', but also contests the muscular masculinity displayed in most mainstream films about the Algerian Revolution with their sentimental macho posturings that forbid the open display of male emotions and fragility. In the case of *Hors la loi*, its celebratory portrayal of FLN virility and heroism harked back to the propagandistic Algerian films made in the aftermath of independence — works like Tewfik Farès's *Les Hors-la-loi* (1969) which, as Guy Austin has shown, present in their articulation of national identity 'the narrativisation of trauma as a means of remembering to forget, hence a "working through"'.[20] Men were placed in the centre of the frame as fearless warriors and martyrs in an express attempt to dispel the pervasive sexual concerns around masculine identity that characterised the conflict.[21] Through the enveloping affective folds of montage, *Frères ennemis* invites the viewer instead to speculate about softer, more fluid and provisional forms of masculinity born out of the very wounds of masculinity.

Such reframing of masculinity as embodied (inter-)subjectivity and kinship may be placed in the context of the period itself when, as C. L. Quinan has brilliantly shown, the French-Algerian War precipitated a dynamic in which the challenging of hegemonic notions of gender, sexuality and nationality occurred alongside a production of queer modes of subjectivity, embodiment and memory that subvert norms. Fictional works like Alain Resnais's 1963 film, *Muriel ou le temps d'un retour* (discussed in Anna Elsner's chapter in the present volume), Michael Haneke's *Caché* (2005) and Laurent Mauvignier's 2009 novel *Des Hommes* (*The Wound*), which explore the scarring of white masculinity haunted by postcolonial guilt, reveal particular anxieties about hybridity (racial, sexual, gendered, national). Yet, as Quinan compellingly argues, postcolonial subjects may also occupy multiple and conflicting identities, including different ways of inhabiting gender.[22] In the case of the Algerian author Jean Sénac, this entailed the formulation of a new, 'impure', hybrid identity through his marginal in-betweenness as French-Algerian and queer. In works like *Carnets inédits* (1955) Sénac proposed a new consciousness and relationality built on love and solidarity as the necessary first step to a 'new man' beyond the entrenched lines of racial, national and sexual identity.[23]

With *Frères ennemis* Balah is plainly working on a personal level through the rupture of his own split cultural and political identity, and one might surely interpret Messaoud's tears for Belkacem across the battlelines of generation and ideology as a gesture of gratitude by the director to his own mother and father who surpassed their opposed backgrounds (*harki* and FLN respectively) to raise a new hybrid French family. For this reason, the film may be said to honour Stora's wish for a proliferation of intersecting memories (or *mémoires plurielles*) that move beyond the common and often divisive rhetoric of a *guerre des mémoires* (memory war) that has mobilised the memorial landscape.[24] Yet by showing how the free expression of emotions in men may ultimately allow for different kinds of masculinity and engagement with others, *Frères ennemis* also moves beyond the need to fix the terms of identity and belonging which are always contingent and in a virtual state of becoming. At a time when the French-Algerian War still casts such a long shadow over France, in particular its Maghrebi population, and when French-Algerian subjectivities are still being reduced in identarian terms to republican assimilation (which assimilates by erasing history) versus *communautarisme* (the notion that French of Maghrebi background will never assimilate and always remain Arab), *Frères ennemis* stakes a claim on new hybrid identities — a France *métisse* — by pointing towards more open, inclusive, propitious forms of kinship and filiation no longer tied to the closed, binary regimes of identity and the alignments of community based on race and nationhood. Balah is currently writing the script for a feature film derived from his remarkable short, although he acknowledges it may take him many years.[25] Whatever this labour of love ultimately produces, it constitutes already a thrilling cultural and political project.

Notes to Chapter 8

1. See <https://www.youtube.com/watch?v=5A_fpRJJIvw> [accessed November 2021]. The film was produced by Boogieman Production.
2. *Harkis* were principally of rural origin, unskilled and motivated by a fear of FLN violence and the need to survive. Their numbers rose to 210,000 in 1958. See Michel Roux, *Les Harkis, ou, Les oubliés de l'histoire* (Paris: La Découverte, 1991).
3. Bouchareb was criticised for suggesting that the FLN brought the war officially to the metropole. Only once did this occur, briefly, in August and September 1958. For an incisive overview of the film's reception in France, see Julien Gaertner, 'We Could Be Heroes: "Arabs" Becoming Brave in Rachid Bouchareb's Cinema', in *ReFocus: The Films of Rachid Bouchareb*, ed. by Michael Gott and Leslie Kealhofer-Kemp (Edinburgh: Edinburgh University Press, 2020), pp. 116–30.

4. See Benjamin Stora, 'The Algerian War: Memory through Cinema', *Black Camera*, 6.1 (2014), 96–107. For more wide-ranging accounts of films engaging with the violence of the French-Algerian War, see Maria Flood, *France, Algeria and the Moving Image: Screening Histories of Violence 1963–2010* (Oxford: Legenda, 2017), and Nicole Beth Wallenbrock, *The Franco-Algerian War through a Twenty-First Century Lens: Film and History* (London: Bloomsbury, 2020).
5. Claire Diao, 'Yacine Balah, entre histoire et cinéma', interview with Yacine Balah, 11 October 2013, para. 2 <https://www.bondyblog.fr/culture/yacine-balah-entre-histoire-et-cinema/> [accessed November 2021]. All translations are my own.
6. Isolated in temporary housing camps when they arrived in France after the war and referred to as 'Français par le sang versé' (i.e. French only by virtue of spilled blood), *harkis* felt abandoned by the French. *Hors la loi* is not untypical in its disdainful presentation of the *harkis*, heroising the FLN when they engage in armed raids against *harki* soldiers relegated anonymously to the back of the frame.
7. Diao, 'Yacine Balah, entre histoire et cinéma', para. 2.
8. For the full original version of the report, which Stora has insisted is not political, see <https://www.lefigaro.fr/politique/document-rapport-de-benjamin-stora-sur-les-memoires-de-la-colonisation-et-de-la-guerre-d-algerie-20210120> [accessed November 2021].
9. Already in 2018 Macron had formally recognised the responsibility of the French state in the 1957 death of a dissident in Algeria, Maurice Audin. In March 2021 he acknowledged that French troops tortured and killed the Algerian independence activist Ali Boumendjel in 1957. In both cases, however, no official apology was issued.
10. I am borrowing the phrase from Susan Ireland in 'Moving Beyond the Legacies of War in Second-generation *Harki* Narratives', in *Post-migratory Cultures in Postcolonial France*, ed. by Kathryn Kleppinger and Laura Reeck (Liverpool: Liverpool University Press, 2018), pp. 112–27 (p. 125). Of particular relevance for our discussion is Ireland's key point, following Cathy Caruth, that *harki* is 'the inheritance of a wound that "cries out"' (p. 116).
11. See <https://fresques.ina.fr/de-gaulle/fiche-media/Gaulle00023/conference-de-presse-a-matignon.html> [accessed November 2021].
12. Duclos's statement echoes word for word the response to de Gaulle's speech by the Gouvernement Provisoire de la République Algérienne (GPRA) in a declaration published in *El Moudjahid* on 28 September 1959.
13. The subtitle here reads 'Don't call me fellow' which misses the force of Belkacem's counter-response to Messaoud's invocation of brotherhood.
14. In an ironic twist of nomination, Belkacem is also the name of the revolutionary FLN fighter and later Algerian politician, Krim Belkacem.
15. During the 1950s Algerians in France were colonial subjects and denied the rights reserved for citizens. In 1958, from being referred to as 'Français musulmans d'Algérie' they became 'Français de souche nord-africaine' (as opposed to 'Français de souche européenne').
16. Judith Butler, *Precarious Life: The Powers of Mourning and Violence* (London: Verso, 2004), p. 134.
17. Ibid.
18. Jill Bennett, *Empathic Vision: Affect, Trauma, and Contemporary Art* (Stanford, CA: Stanford University Press, 2005), p. 36.
19. See Lia Brozgal, *Absent the Archive: Cultural Traces of a Massacre in Paris, 17 October 1961* (Liverpool: Liverpool University Press, 2020).
20. Guy Austin, *Algerian National Cinema* (Manchester: Manchester University Press, 2012), pp. 33–60 (p. 35). Austin shows how Algerian 'freedom fighter cinema' employed a range of epic, mythic and symbolic elements.
21. For analysis of the common French perception of Arabs and Arabisation as unmanly and 'feminine' during the conflict, see Todd Shepard, *Sex, France, and Arab Men, 1962–1979* (Chicago: University of Chicago Press, 2017).
22. C. L. Quinan, *Hybrid Anxieties: Queering the French-Algerian War and its Postcolonial Legacies* (Lincoln: University of Nebraska Press, 2020), p. 186.
23. Jean Sénac, 'Carnets inédits (extraits)', in *Algérie: un rêve de fraternité*, ed. by Guy Dugas (Paris: Omnibus, 1997), pp. 845–54.

24. See Benjamin Stora, *La Guerre des mémoires: la France face à son passé colonial* (La Tour d'Aigues: L'Aube, 1977), p. 190.
25. Yacine Balah, interview with Adrian Kundi, 18 March 2016, para. 7 <https://www.thelondontree.com/interviews/director-yacine-balah-talks-of-history-france-algeria-and-freres-ennemis/> [accessed November 2021].

PART III

Works and Days:
Labour, Class, Society

CHAPTER 9

'Tu renonces à toi pour devenir tout le monde': Visions of Labour and Society in Blaise Cendrars and Fernand Léger

Eric Robertson

In his most recent monograph, *Egalitarian Strangeness*, Edward J. Hughes explores the points of intersection between representation and the social world through a series of penetrating literary case studies.[1] In the book's introduction, he cites the case of French artist Fernand Léger, whose work strove to challenge traditional distinctions between 'high' and 'low' artistic forms, and particularly between fine and applied art. Hughes reflects on a chance occurrence that Léger recounts in an essay and which, for all its apparent ordinariness, proved to have a defining and lasting impact on his work. The artist recalls exhibiting some paintings in the Salon d'Automne at the Grand Palais in Paris before the First World War.[2] During his visit to that exhibition, his attention was drawn to the sound of manual workers busy installing another exhibition, the Salon de l'Aviation, behind a partition in the museum. Léger was captivated by the powerful geometry of the machines on display there: these colourful metal constructions, functional and beautiful, seemed to encapsulate all he was striving to express in his painting.[3] The realisation that aviation engineering could be a potent new source of aesthetic beauty was nothing short of an epiphany, but there was more to come: on the same occasion in the Grand Palais, he observed a young manual worker dressed in colourful overalls, hands spattered in Prussian blue paint, who had stepped through a gap in the partition to stand, lost in thought, in front of a painting in the Salon d'Automne exhibition. As Hughes puts it, Léger 'relishes the symmetry and levelling that sees aircraft workers and artist-painter making discoveries on either side of the partition'.[4]

Léger's observation reminds us to what a large extent he understood his own artistic vocation in terms of just such a levelling. His work is innovative not only in its radical stylistic experimentation but also in its treatment of subject-matter; it frequently establishes analogies with other walks of life and other forms of production, especially those not conventionally deemed to belong in the realm of fine art. The same is true of the writer Blaise Cendrars, who befriended Léger before the First World War and collaborated closely with him on some memorable projects over the course of a friendship that lasted until Léger's death in 1955. Cendrars experienced poverty but had a complex attitude to work. His writing conveys an understanding of social inequality and disdain for entitlement; yet at times he enjoyed the material privileges of patronage, and he produced some exquisite artists' books that were well beyond the reach of the ordinary citizen.[5] His most illustrious collaborator was Léger, whose paintings continued to emphasise the dignity of labour even after commercial success had brought him considerable wealth. Both celebrate technology and express fascination with the machines that had transformed the modern era, even though that very same machinery had nearly killed both of them in the First World War. This chapter will explore some of these paradoxes.

★ ★ ★ ★ ★

'Les Pâques à New York' was the poem that compelled the twenty-four-year-old Frédéric-Louis Sauser to become the poet Blaise Cendrars; it also helped to launch him onto the avant-garde scene when he arrived in Paris in the summer of 1912. He had written the poem in New York that spring, impoverished, constantly hungry and unable to find lasting employment since arriving there the previous November.[6] The poem was inspired by a chance encounter on Easter Sunday 1912 with a performance of Haydn's *Creation* in a Presbyterian church. Sauser walked out during the performance because a member of the church harangued him several times to make a donation.[7] Written in a single draft and in a state of virtual hallucination, it is a modern-day epic in rhyming couplets in which the marginal figures of the city provide the cast for a meditation on faith in the modern world. The theme is a parable of its time and astonishingly prescient of the shape this still-young century would take: modern society, infatuated with corporate greed and intent on worshipping Mammon, has become detached from the symbolism of Easter and the compassion once associated with Christ. The poem is a cry of anger on behalf of the poor, the marginalised and the displaced; it bemoans the plight of New York's many disadvantaged communities:

> Il y a des Italiens, des Grecs, des Espagnols,
> Des Russes, des Bulgares, des Persans, des Mongols.
>
> Ce sont des bêtes de cirque qui sautent les méridiens.
> On leur jette un morceau de viande noire, comme à des chiens.
>
> [There are Italians, Greeks, Bulgarians,
> Spaniards, Persians, Russians and Mongolians.
>
> They're circus animals that leap meridians.
> They're thrown a piece of rotten meat, like dogs.][8]

In strident rhyming couplets the narrator urges Christ to protect the city's community of Jewish refugees, while expressing sympathy for other marginalised groups such as prostitutes, drunks, addicts and petty thieves.

Cendrars's disdain for any form of pigeonholing meant that he even rejected the label of poet to the extent that it might be construed as a discipline: 'Je ne suis pas poète. Je suis libertin. Je n'ai aucune méthode de travail. J'ai un sexe. Je suis par trop sensible' [I am not a poet. I am a libertine. I have no working method. I have a sex. I am too sensitive].[9] His resistance to the perceived status of poetry as inhabiting a more refined cultural space underpins his collaboration with Sonia Delaunay, the extraordinary 'simultaneous book' *La Prose du Transsibérien et de la petite Jehanne de France* of 1913. Cendrars explains: 'Poème semblait trop prétentieux, trop fermé. Prose est plus ouverte, populaire' [Poem seemed too pretentious, too closed, Prose is more open, popular].[10] Delaunay's vibrant watercolours that adorn this hybrid work have the appeal of advertising billboards and anticipate the bold fabric designs that she produced commercially over some decades. This eclecticism and immersion in life appealed to Cendrars, whose aim was to write an accessible form of everyday poetry encompassing 'tout le monde d'aujourd'hui, la vie de tous les jours, les annonces des journaux, les étiquettes des boîtes de conserves, les marques de fabrique, les horaires [...], en un mot nos richesses' [the whole of today's world, everyday life, newspaper adverts, the labels on jars, brand names, timetables [...], in a word, our treasures].[11]

Cendrars and Léger met in Paris in 1911 at the Salon de la Section d'or. They quickly became friends, and it was not long before their work started to show a mutual influence. Both men were already receptive to the stimuli of everyday life. Léger's experimentation with subject-matter, while broadly influenced by the Cubism of Picasso and Braque, differed in significant ways from theirs: the latter were primarily preoccupied with questions of form that insulated them from the world outside the studio, whereas Léger's experiments mostly began with outdoor subjects and sought to express the chromatic diversity of the modern world by means of dissonant colours. His fragmented forms reflect the fact that the early twentieth-century European city was often experienced at volume and at speed. In 1914 he expressed scorn towards the denigrators of billboards and telegraph poles, claiming, 'cette affiche jaune ou rouge, hurlant dans ce timide paysage, est la plus belle des raisons picturales qui soient; elle flanque par terre tout le concept sentimental et littéraire et elle annonce l'avènement du contraste plastique' [this yellow or red poster, howling in this timid landscape, is the most beautiful of all pictorial reasons; it throws the whole sentimental and literary concept to the ground and announces the arrival of plastic contrast].[12]

A similar impulse to record the colourful minor occurrences of daily life defines Cendrars's 1919 collection of 'poèmes de circonstance' [circumstantial poems] entitled *Dix-neuf poèmes élastiques*. Mostly written before the war, these are much briefer than his earlier poems and employ language more disruptively.[13] They are explicitly topical and provide snapshots of everyday life:

> Chez le bistro
> Les ouvriers en blouse bleue boivent du vin rouge
> Tous les samedis poule au gibier
> On joue
> On parie.

> [At the bar
> The workers in blue overalls drink red wine
> Every Saturday, the numbers game
> You play
> You bet].[14]

Paradoxically, their extreme syntactic reduction renders some lines resistant to straightforward interpretation and reminds us that, however rooted in everyday life his subjects may be, Cendrars has no intention of patronising his reader: 'Gong tam-tam zanzibar bête de la jungle rayons X express bistouri symphonie' [Gong tom-tom zanzibar jungle animal X-rays express scalpel symphony]; or 'Des cosaques le Christ un soleil en décomposition' [Cossacks Christ a shattered sun].[15] In these poems, words often appear as momentary sensations that refuse to coalesce into a clear mental image, like colours flashing before our eyes on a screen or glimpsed from the window of a moving train. In this respect, they have a fragmentary quality that brings them close to the atmosphere of Léger's paintings in the immediate aftermath of the Great War. Crucially, their radical experimentation is neither an end in itself, nor intended to signal art's detachment from life, but a means to express the modern world in all its vibrant complexity.

First-hand experience of the First World War had a huge impact on the work of both figures. When war was declared in the summer of 1914, Cendrars enlisted in the French Foreign Legion and served as a corporal. In September 1915, during an attack on the fields of Champagne, his right arm was shot to pieces and had to be amputated above the elbow. His 'phantom hand' haunted him for the rest of his life, but he avoided addressing the specific circumstances of his wound for some thirty years. Claude Leroy has argued that after his amputation, Cendrars's left-handed writing became 'plus dérangeant, plus subversif, plus moderne, en un mot' [more disturbing, more subversive, in a word, more modern] as he engaged the right hemisphere of his brain.[16]

Léger enlisted in the French army and served in the Argonne and at Verdun, first as a sapper and then a stretcher-bearer, until he was invalided out in early 1917 after being gassed on the Aisne front. He was scornful of his peers who used the war as an opportunity to pursue their artistic experimentation. He firmly believed that his duty to fight was his main priority and that to pursue artistic experimentation would be an abdication of his responsibility to his fellow soldiers. Cendrars similarly refrained from writing until his time at the front had abruptly ended. As he later put it, 'Quand on écrit, on ne combat pas à coups de fusil et quand on tire des coups de fusil, on n'écrit pas, on écrit après. On aurait bien mieux fait d'écrire avant et d'empêcher tout ça' [When you're writing, you're not fighting with a rifle and when you're firing a rifle, you're not writing, you do the writing afterwards. We'd have done much better to write first and prevent all that].[17]

Léger did eventually produce some drawings during his time at war, and these tell us much about how the experience shaped his understanding of his social position as an artist. Made variously during lulls between periods of intense service, the drawings continue his pre-war practice of reducing forms to a geometric essence. But in contrast to his earlier work, they are much more firmly rooted in identifiably real subjects, most commonly scenes of daily life in the trenches that he directly observed. Above all, these drawings reflect the impulse to record war's new reality of machinery and men-machines.[18] After Léger's discharge from the war, his work underwent a fundamental transformation. The war had brought him into contact with 'crude reality', and this encounter had entailed an entire series of levellings: as Anna Vallye notes, the war had made Léger aware of the equivalence 'between himself and the common soldiers, the lower-class *poilus*, or infantrymen; and between the soldier's body and the gear, muck and weaponry around him. The "real" was a matter of base material equality'.[19] The return to civilian life allowed him to transpose this new understanding into pictorial form.

For Cendrars, too, the experience of war had a profound and lasting effect on his writing. Appropriately, the closing poem of *Dix-neuf poèmes élastiques*, and the only one written after his recuperation from his war wound, focuses on Léger. Its title is 'Construction', which seems remarkably prescient given that some of Léger's best-known paintings of the inter- and post-war years focused on construction workers (as illustrated on the cover of the present volume). For Cendrars writing in 1919, the titular term serves as a metonymic cipher for the artist himself, and by omitting the article from the poem's title, he knowingly plays on the word's double status as something made ('*une* construction') and as an ongoing process of creation ('*la* construction'). In an essay on contemporary art written around the same time as this poem, Cendrars states: 'le bloc cubiste s'effrite' [the cubist block is crumbling]. Without naming any artists, he implicitly aligns himself with Léger in welcoming colour as a means of moving beyond the predominantly cerebral concerns of Cubism and bringing experimental art more closely in touch with lived reality: 'La réalité du monde est avant tout une sensation. C'est pourquoi les nouveaux peintres sont des sensuels et la nouveauté qu'ils apportent c'est: la couleur! J'annonce donc beaucoup de couleur et de la couleur toute neuve' [The reality of the world is above all a sensation. That's why the new painters are sensual and the novelty they are bringing is colour! So I announce a lot of colour, brand new colour].[20] As if to confirm that Léger was on his mind when he wrote these words, Cendrars's poem opens with a line that echoes the terms of his own essay. The poem's simple syntax and minimalist structure create rhythmic tensions between its long and short lines and between images of stasis and movement. The industrial imagery and geometric forms of Léger's work appear modern yet as old as the Earth itself: 'De la couleur, de la couleur et des couleurs... | Voici Léger qui grandit comme le soleil de l'époque tertiaire' [Colour, colour, and more colours... | Here's Léger who grows like the sun in the tertiary epoch.][21] The closing lines shift from the natural realm to that of manufactured artifacts:

> La peinture devient cette chose énorme qui bouge
> La roue
> La vie
> La machine
> L'âme humaine
> Une culasse de 75
> Mon portrait.

> [Painting becomes this great thing that moves
> The wheel
> Life
> The machine
> The human soul
> A 75 mm breech
> My portrait.][22]

Indeed, around 1918, Léger did produce a portrait of Cendrars. Drawn in black ink, it depicts the writer's face in close-up: his hair is cut short, his eyes obscured by dark shadows, his expression sober. But the 'portrait' in question could equally well relate to the last seven lines of the poem, in which the act of painting — and by extension creative representation more broadly — is suggestively and elliptically shown to be bound up with the wheel (of life? or even the rotating Earth itself?) and all life forms, but also with modern technology and the machinery of large-scale destruction. Seen in these terms, the portrait in question could equally well relate to Cendrars or to Léger himself, so closely aligned were their artistic stimuli at the time. It seems particularly fitting that the two closing lines should establish an implicit analogy between the 75 mm cannon and the portrait: the foundational experience of combat, the community of life in the trenches and the constant proximity of death had brought to both men a more profound realisation of what gives life its value. All their work from that point on would be marked by that chapter of their lives.

It is unsurprising, then, that Cendrars and Léger's first collaborative work engaged in the most graphically direct way with the war. The essay *J'ai tué* appeared in November 1918, just days before the armistice, with colour lithographs that Léger produced while recovering from his war wound. Their experience of combat strengthened their affinity, as too did their shared weariness with the Parisian avant-garde scene. As Christopher Green notes, 'In 1915 and 1916, in the Argonne and at Verdun, Léger not only saw modern reality in all its mechanised dynamism as never before, but identified with a group of men utterly alien to the avant-garde "elite" from which he had come in Paris'.[23] The opening sentences of the text adopt a panoramic perspective that hints at the huge scale of the conflict: 'Ils viennent de tous les horizons. Jour et nuit. 1000 trains déversent des hommes et du matériel' [They're coming from every horizon. Day and night. A thousand trains spew out men and material].[24] Léger's illustration on this page employs just one colour, the same orange-red ink in which Cendrars's text is printed. The picture plane is tightly organised and fragmented into a network of repeated interlocking straight-edged and curved lines. Rhythmic striations flatten perspective by denoting indiscriminately the shadows on the soldiers' faces, the surface of their equipment and the row of hills in the distant background. The principle of metonymy is at work: dense arrangements of minimal lines hint at serried rows of troops' helmets, cannon barrels and armoured machines with rivet heads forming repeated arcs.

The text zooms in progressively to conclude with a graphic close-up, a first-person account of a hand-to-hand fight to the death. In Léger's corresponding image, paradoxically, magnification has accentuated its ambiguity, an effect he later harnessed in his own experiments with cinema.[25] Its indeterminate metallic fragments reflect Cendrars's allusion to the war's 'machinerie anonyme, démoniaque, systématique, aveugle' [anonymous, demonic, systematic, blind machinery]. While Cendrars likens the human to an ape, Léger's machines all but eclipse the soldiers, apart from a few parallel lines that suggest fingers. Together they anticipate Paul Virilio's observation that the First World War marked the transition from proximate hand-to-hand combat to remote warfare, waged on a cinematically fragmented landscape, viewed through a camera.[26] When Cendrars's war ended, cinema had offered a possible lifeline. In 1918, shortly before he and Léger collaborated on *J'ai tué*, he had worked as assistant to director Abel Gance on his war film *J'Accuse*, even appearing as an extra, and worked again two years later on Gance's next film, *La Roue*. Léger too embarked on film-making a few years later, but in the meantime he took some important stylistic lessons from Cendrars, whose literary and cinematic experimentation seems to have shaped the artist's approach of constructing rhythmic compositions consisting of shard-like cuts and flat planes.[27]

As we have seen, Cendrars was keen to celebrate poetry as a manifestation of the vibrant diversity of city life, teeming with energy, enlivened by electricity and advertising billboards that adorned the streets and squares of Paris. He and Léger often frequented the place de Clichy in the first years of their friendship as it had the biggest billboards in the city.[28] But Cendrars also saw dangers in the modern metropolis, particularly its dizzying capacity, by virtue of its sheer scale, to engulf the individual and erode one's sense of self. His writing on this subject seems prescient a century later, when global brands have become commonplace. His 1917 essay *Profond aujourd'hui* articulates wariness towards the pernicious effect of consumer culture on our individuality: 'Tu te perds dans le labyrinthe des magasins où tu renonces à toi pour devenir tout le monde' [You get lost in the labyrinth of stores where you renounce yourself to become everyone].[29] And not only consumerism, but the city itself, huge, imposing, alienating, threatens to undermine our sense of selfhood. The melting pot allows us to shed our inhibitions but also carries the threat of dissolving our identity: 'Tu fais partie de ce grand corps anonyme qu'est un café. Je ne me reconnais plus dans la glace, l'alcool a effacé mes traits' [You are part of the great anonymous body of a café. I no longer recognise myself in the mirror, alcohol has blurred my features].[30] A close correspondence emerges with his contemporaneous writing on cinema, the archetypal art form for the modern era in the way it concentrates and intensifies the incessant movement, fragmented and augmented sensory awareness that the city encapsulates. The most striking parallel between *Profond aujourd'hui* and his essay *L'ABC du cinéma* lies in their shared identification of a particular state of collective experience that is a form of communion, paradoxically accompanied by the isolation that often characterises life in the metropolis: 'Tu vis. Excentrique. Dans la solitude intégrale. Dans la communion anonyme' [You live. Off-centre. In integral solitude. In anonymous communion].[31]

From this it is clear that Cendrars saw the relationship of the individual to the metropolis as one of conflicting forces: the city affords us greater autonomy, but in so doing, it can also loosen the ties that might bind us to other humans and to a stable sense of place. In this respect, his vision is akin to the phenomenon of urban modernity that Georg Simmel had analysed in his short but influential essay of 1903, *Die Großstädte und das Geistesleben* [The Metropolis and Mental Life]. Simmel defined the psychological foundation of the metropolitan sensibility in terms of the '*intensification of nervous stimulation* that results from the swift and uninterrupted change of external and internal stimuli'.[32] Cendrars encapsulates the tensions arising from this intensity and in turn foreshadows the work of Walter Benjamin, who in his *Arcades Project* would identify the city as a site of spectacle but also as one of alienation.[33] For Cendrars, the advent of cinema is nothing short of a revolution akin to the invention of a standardised alphabet and the printing press centuries before. His cinema essay ends with a vision of crowds all over the world simultaneously emerging from cinemas in a stream that could crush palaces and prisons.[34]

After the Great War, Léger's paintings of the city began incorporating anonymous human figures who resemble robots or simulacra rather than identifiable individuals. These have an ambiguous status: in the monumental oil on canvas, *La Ville* (1919), the human form appears in two distinct guises, both of which locate it within a visual syntax of fragmentation, disjuncture and machine-like anonymity and reproducibility.[35] The first of these typologies is visible in two robotic figures in the centre close to its lower edge, whose entire bodies seem to be constructed in grey metal. The second type of human figure is truncated, flattened into a two-dimensional silhouette and duplicated in nearly identical form, both iterations appearing inside square-edged frames, seemingly mediated as billboards. Troublingly, their one visible arm ends above the elbow. Both typologies, unmistakably human yet literally faceless and lacking individual features, are difficult to read: it is impossible to determine whether they are celebrating our interconnectedness with the urban environment whose characteristics they share, or internalising the oppressive rhythm of modern life that threatens to engulf the individual and strip away all vestiges of humanity. They suggest both of these conditions, mirroring the modern city's capacity to exhilarate and unsettle in equal measure.

The year in which Léger painted *La Ville*, 1919, also saw the publication of his and Cendrars's next and arguably greatest collaborative work, *La Fin du monde filmée par l'Ange N.-D.*, which Cendrars had begun writing in September 1917 around the time of his close involvement with cinema. As he was recovering from the loss of his writing arm, the quasi-prosthetic capacity of the 'machine of vision' to enhance sensory perception and create new forms of discourse beyond words alone must have appealed strongly.[36] As he later put it, 'Dès 1917 je me suis jeté à corps perdu dans le cinéma' [From 1917 on, I threw myself headlong into cinema].[37] In *L'ABC du cinéma*, he strives to characterise the dizzying power of this new visual language that seems capable of usurping literature and transforming society. Augmented by the movie camera, aided by a Bergsonian intuition, our perceptive faculties transcend intellectual activity and come into contact with life in its purest state: 'Remue-ménage d'images. L'unité tragique se déplace. Nous apprenons. Nous buvons. Ivresse. Le réel n'a plus aucun sens. Aucune signification' [An uproar of images. Tragic unity is displaced. We learn. We drink. Intoxication. Reality no longer makes any sense. It has no significance].[38]

Labelled a 'roman' or novel, *La Fin du monde* is a stunning *livre d'artiste*, but it also merits the label *ciné-roman*, since it embraces so many structures and tropes of cinema. Cendrars designed the title page, which Léger completed; the abbreviation of Notre Dame to the initials 'N.-D.' announces the narrative's terse, telegraphic style: written almost entirely in the present tense, it is divided into fifty-five numbered short scenes, some a mere sentence in length. As Léger later recalled, this project reflected their shared fascination with typography, and its aesthetic derived directly from the specific environment of Paris.[39]

Like *J'ai tué*, this story conveys a vision of war, but set in the future and on an interplanetary scale. It is also, and perhaps above all, an attack on capitalism and the American dream, and an indictment of those societies that will stop at nothing, even war, in their pursuit of financial gain. The main character is God, cast as a Hollywood-style director complete with fat cigar and green sun shield; the Angel of Notre-Dame is his cameraman. God has made a huge profit from nearly a century of conflict. He starts another war, against Mars this time, and is forced into hiding. In an attempt to make this war pay too, he sends a telegram to 'quelques vieux coquins de l'Ancien Testament' [some old rascals from the Old Testament] requesting them to carry out the prophecies.[40] The Angel of Notre-Dame blows his horn and the earth goes into meltdown. So too, literally, does the roll of film that is figuratively showing us all this action. The projector catches fire, and we witness the entire film rewinding, sequence by sequence, to the starting-point. We return to the opening scene with God as film director at his desk; but this time, he is bankrupt. So too, by implication, is any society that lays great store on commercial exploitation and territorial expansion at the expense of humanity.

Léger's designs evoke the profusion of visual and verbal signs that assault the senses in a busy city. Stencilled lettering and fragmented, geometric forms connote a modern, multilingual environment of industry and commerce.[41] The opening double page relies equally on its visual, verbal and graphic signs which overlap and partially cancel each other out. Only with some effort do we decipher in Léger's composition specific elements that appear in the opening lines of the text: as if adjusting to a dark room, our eyes gradually make out fragments such as God at his desk, wearing a sunshade and smoking a fat cigar. Seen as a whole, this double page invites us to alternate repeatedly between reading and viewing, but prevents us from settling in either mode. Léger imports strings of Cendrars's text into his design, such as the words 'il se lève | allume un gros cigare'. Other textual fragments help the reader decipher elements of the visual image: in front of God is a book of prayers or psalms, identifiable by the words 'PRIEZ DIEU' [pray to God]; the positioning of the latter word across God's chest doubles as a label identifying him for the reader's benefit. By an act of Cubist fragmentation, the initial letter of 'priez' is lopped off to become 'riez' [laugh], forewarning us that this god may have comic overtones. Léger's lettering is painted in a style imitative of industrial stencilling, which further connotes the world of commerce.[42] The book's design also blurs the boundaries that usually assign separate, self-contained spaces to a text and its illustrations.

The fragmented, pared-down forms of Léger's illustrations reflect the same principle of montage that defines Cendrars's text, and both repeatedly hint at the capacity of optical devices such as the camera lens to provide a prosthetic extension of human vision, which became a trope of French avant-garde film in the 1920s.[43] But the book also reflects the fascination of both men for popular cinema, and especially Chaplin's silent comedies, which they had first seen on periods of leave from the war. Like *La Fin du monde*, Chaplin's 1917 film *The Immigrant* portrays the converse of the American Dream: as their ship arrives in New York, the immigrants gaze at the Statue of Liberty, but what awaits them is poverty and intolerance. Chaplin's protagonist, whose nationality we never learn, fails to understand the menu in the restaurant and resorts to ordering his food by means of hand gestures.

Cendrars claimed that 'Charlot' had helped the Allies win the war by boosting their morale and helping them through its darkest times.[44] And Léger too found in Chaplin a vital antidote to the war: as Jennifer Wild observes, Charlot 'rose up, over the carnage, as utterly distinct from the diffuse space of the waking dream of war'.[45] Three years after his collaboration with Cendrars, Léger paid tribute to Chaplin by having his animated model of a cubist Charlot appear at the start of his experimental film *Ballet mécanique* (1924). But the illustrations in *La Fin du monde* already hint at Léger's admiration for Charlot: the double-page illustration that introduces Chapter 2 features a large face squinting behind a large round object which could be a monocle or the barrel of a large gun (the figure is wearing a medal and appears to be squeezing a trigger); but the circular form could also signify a camera lens. To the left is a small line drawing of an unmistakably Chaplinesque splay-footed figure in a bowler hat who appears to be carrying a cane. Chaplin is the archetype of the 'little man', continually battling adversity and fighting society's injustices; but in other ways too, Léger's image hints at the vital role of ordinary people in the machinery that makes societies work. In the lower portion of the same illustration are hints of classical and modern architectural forms; one column is cut off mid-way down its length, and standing immediately underneath it, propping it up, are three small human figures. Léger seems to be suggesting that the Everyman is the prop that holds up the entire edifice of society but goes unnoticed by it.

The chapter in which the Angel brings about the end of the world is called 'L'Ange N.-D. Opérateur': in the twentieth century, the term *opérateur* came to denote not only a camera operator or cameraman, but also a telegraph operator and typesetter: in this sense, the Angel as 'opérateur' is the perfect symbol for this intermedia work that combines literature, fine art, typography and cinema into an aesthetic whole. The word *opérateur* also retained more archaic meanings, including someone who conducts surgical operations, an analogy that anticipates Walter Benjamin's observations on the camera's capacity to penetrate the body like a surgeon's knife.[46] For Cendrars and Léger, however, the camera operator, the telegraph operator and the typesetter are the new heroes of modern art and poetry in the age of mechanical reproduction: their work represents the ideal symbiosis of human labour and technology, and their efforts create new modes of communication as well as new forms of art that are accessible to the masses.

The importance of Léger's collaborations with Cendrars should not be underestimated. They drew his attention to the expressive potential of incorporating isolated fragments of stencilled lettering into the artwork, a practice he later adopted in some important paintings including *La Ville*. In 1919, he again summed up the importance of technical *opérateurs* by making the typographer the entire subject of a painting.[47] Preparatory sketches reveal that this painting originated in a study of a wounded *poilu*; the definitive version succeeds in transforming an image of violence and suffering into a celebration of skilled labour enhanced by machines.

★ ★ ★ ★ ★

In the inter-war years, Cendrars broke decisively with the Parisian avant-garde scene and pursued a more independent literary path, travelling to Brazil and establishing strong bonds with that country's Modernists. For some years, he and Léger seem to have drifted apart for reasons that are not known but can be inferred; Cendrars expressed resentment about the celebrity status of some of his artist peers who had become wealthy despite the fact that, in his opinion, they lagged decades behind the poets in terms of originality.[48]

After the Second World War, Léger and Cendrars asserted their commitment to social issues as they had done after the previous war. Cendrars produced four long volumes of heavily autobiographical prose constituting a form of autofiction *avant la lettre*. The first of these, *L'Homme foudroyé* (1945), deals with the writer's life in the interwar years, but almost entirely eclipses his well-known literary and artistic acquaintances, focusing instead on those with a lower social profile such as his erstwhile camera operator and a woman who cleaned the house he rented in 1927. Léger does appear, albeit relatively briefly, and this because one day in 1923 he asked Cendrars to introduce him to his friends in the Roma community in the 'Zone' of Kremlin-Bicêtre on the outskirts of Paris.

In *La Banlieue de Paris* (1949), Cendrars engages critically with factory life and its perpetuation of dehumanising working conditions in the mid-twentieth century. Likening these institutions to prisons, he argues that whether they are in public or private hands, the end result for the worker is forced labour.[49] But when he visited the Royal Arsenal in London in March 1940 as war correspondent for the British army, its extraordinary cleanliness and calm atmosphere confounded all his expectations of a factory. He notes the pride that the workers take in their job and the presence of personal mementos such as family photographs that bring touches of humanity into the workplace.[50] Yet Cendrars acknowledges that he has never succumbed to the tyranny of alienated labour: 'je n'ai pas honte de le dire, j'ai fui, j'ai déserté la grande peine des hommes, le travail industriel, le travail maudit' [I'm not ashamed to say it, I fled, I deserted the great struggle of men, industrial work, accursed work].[51] Yet nor did the life of the writer bring happiness:

> Ecrire ce n'est pas réellement vivre, ce n'est pas la vie du corps. [...] C'est donc un vice, c'est une mauvaise habitude. C'est pourquoi ça me dégoûte neuf fois

sur dix. Je n'aime pas du tout écrire, et je ne suis pas le seul parmi les écrivains qui ait dit ça.[52]

[Writing isn't really living, it's not being physically alive. [...] it's a vice, a bad habit. That's why it disgusts me nine times out of ten. I don't like writing at all, and I'm not the only writer to have said that.]

Despite his distaste for the writer's vocation, he acknowledges that authors are privileged compared to the vast majority of people who live 'comme des pièces dans une mécanique' [like parts in a mechanism].[53]

Léger, for his part, looked to art as a means of improving the worker's lot. In 1953, he exhibited some twelve paintings including his monumental 1951 canvas *Les Constructeurs* in the Renault car plant in Boulogne-Billancourt, provoking the bemusement of some of its workers and the admiration of others.[54] He hoped for the popularisation of visual art akin to the expansion that music had enjoyed since radio had brought it into people's homes, and argued that a shorter working day and more leisure time would enable the working class to enjoy art. As he put it in an interview, 'Il est aussi fin, l'homme du people, pour lui aussi s'éduquer très rapidement — peut-être plus rapidement que les autres. Mais il n'a pas le loisir' [The man of the people is clever enough to educate himself very quickly — perhaps even more quickly than others. But he doesn't have the time].[55] Léger sustained a phenomenal work rate into his seventies, as Cendrars attests in *Paris ma ville*, the collaborative book on which they were working when Léger died in 1955.[56] Cendrars too, despite his oft-professed hatred of the writer's task, managed around this time to finish what proved to be his last novel, *Emmène-moi au bout du monde* [*To the End of the World*], bringing his total published output to over forty books.

In a chapter of *Egalitarian Strangeness* devoted to the 'dramas of manual knowledge', Edward J. Hughes discusses one of Léger's preparatory drawings for *Les Constructeurs* depicting a construction worker gripping a rope; Hughes observes how, in Léger's treatment, the worker's fingers have become an extension of its strands.[57] In the same chapter, Hughes examines Thierry Beinstingel's 2010 novel *Retour aux mots sauvages* and its exploration of contemporary tensions engendered by the loss of manual skills, the alienating impact of 'the new form of mass labour that is the call centre', and the 'sensory amputation' of those who have to endure working in one.[58] These observations prompt us to reflect on the ways in which the potentially liberating technologies heralded by Cendrars and Léger have given way to newer and more pernicious forms of alienated labour in the twenty-first century. Yet for all their championing of modernity, Cendrars and Léger already anticipate the nostalgia for lost manual effort that Hughes examines in contemporary fiction. Cendrars claimed to have created his 1929 novel *Les Confessions de Dan Yack* entirely on a tape recorder, but in fact he had written it by more conventional means; the book *Blaise Cendrars vous parle...* originated in a series of radio interviews recorded in 1950, but the published book contains enough modifications and edits for Claude Leroy to describe it as 'une véritable seconde version originale' [a veritable second original version].[59] And by the 1950s Cendrars was wary of the consequences of mass industrialisation:

Quand un garçon comme moi, qui a foi dans la vie moderne, qui admire toutes ces belles usines, toutes ces machines ingénieuses, se rend compte et voit à quoi cela aboutit, il ne peut que condamner car, réellement, cela n'est pas encourageant.[60]

[When a lad like me, who has faith in modern life, who admires all these beautiful factories, all these ingenious machines, realises and sees what it leads to, he can only condemn it because, really, it is not encouraging.]

Despite the idealism of Léger's portrayal of manual labour and the contradictions in Cendrars's attitude to the world of labour, their persistent championing of the hand at work is a compelling affirmation of the creative act. In his written correspondence throughout the inter-war and post-war years, it is telling that Cendrars frequently signed off with the words 'ma main amie'.

Notes to Chapter 9

1. Edward J. Hughes, *Egalitarian Strangeness: On Class Disturbance and Levelling in Modern and Contemporary French Narrative* (Liverpool: Liverpool University Press, 2021).
2. Christopher Green concludes that this was likely to have occurred in 1912. Christopher Green, *Léger and the Avant-garde* (New Haven, CT, & London: Yale University Press, 1976), p. 84.
3. Fernand Léger, 'L'Esthétique de la machine: l'objet fabriqué, l'artisan et l'artiste', *Der Querschnitt*, 3.3–4 (Autumn 1923), 122–23 (repr.: *Bulletin de l'Effort moderne*, January 1924); reproduced in Ferdinand Léger, *Fonctions de la peinture* (Paris: Gallimard, 2009), pp. 87–102.
4. Hughes, *Egalitarian Strangeness*, p. 2.
5. The eight copies of *La Prose du Transsibérien* printed on vellum cost five hundred francs in 1913, which was several months' average wages in France at the time. The copies printed on Japon and simili Japon cost one hundred francs and fifty francs respectively. The few extant copies to be auctioned in recent years have fetched six-figure sums.
6. Cendrars was briefly taken on as a pianist, an abattoir worker and a tailor. See his conversation with Joël Curchod, 2 July 1954, in 'Sous le signe du depart: entretiens de Blaise Cendrars', 1, Radio Télévision Suisse <https://open.spotify.com/album/7qIJqRW5D8cXBCmiFUTYm7> [accessed October 2021].
7. Blaise Cendrars, *Blaise Cendrars vous parle... suivi de Qui êtes-vous? Le Paysage dans l'œuvre de Léger et de J'ai vu mourir Fernand Léger*, ed. by Claude Leroy (Paris: Denoël, 2006), pp. 159–60.
8. Blaise Cendrars, *Œuvres romanesques, précédé des Poésies complètes*, ed. by Claude Leroy, Jean-Carlo Flückiger and Christine Le Quellec Cottier, 2 vols, Bibliothèque de la Pléiade (Paris: Gallimard, 2017), I, 10; *Blaise Cendrars: Complete Poems*, trans. by Ron Padgett (Berkeley, Los Angeles, CA, & London: University of California Press, 1992), p. 6 (translation slightly modified). I am grateful to Adam Watt for his thoughtful insights into the translation.
9. Cendrars, *Œuvres romanesques*, I, 209. Translations, unless otherwise indicated, are my own.
10. Cited in Antoine Sidoti, *Genèse et dossier d'une polémique: La Prose du Transsibérien et de la Petite Jehanne de France. Blaise Cendrars — Sonia Delaunay novembre-décembre 1912-juin 1914* (Paris: Minard, 1987), pp. 107–08.
11. Blaise Cendrars, letter to Georges Sauser-Hall, 22 December 1913, cited in Claude Leroy, 'Notice' in Cendrars, *Œuvres romanesques*, I, 1209.
12. Léger, *Fonctions de la peinture*, p. 42.
13. Cendrars, *Dix-neuf poèmes élastiques*, in *Œuvres romanesques*, I, 51–72.
14. Ibid., I, 56; *Complete Poems*, p. 56.
15. Ibid., I, 56, 59; pp. 56, 61.
16. Claude Leroy, *La Main de Cendrars* (Villeneuve d'Ascq: Presses universitaires du Septentrion, 1996), p. 321.
17. Cendrars, *Blaise Cendrars vous parle...*, p. 154.

18. Green, *Léger and the Avant-garde*, p. 100.
19. Anna Vallye, 'The Painter on the Boulevard', in *Léger: Modern Art and the Metropolis*, edited by Anna Vallye, exhibition catalogue (Philadelphia: Philadelphia Museum of Art, 2013), pp. 1–47 (p. 2).
20. Blaise Cendrars, 'Quelle sera la nouvelle peinture aux Indépendants 1919?', in *La Rose rouge*, 1, 3 May 1919. Reproduced as 'Modernités: quelle sera la nouvelle peinture ?', in *Aujourd'hui, suivi de Jéroboam et la Sirène, Sous le signe de François Villon, Le Brésil et Trop c'est trop*, ed. by Claude Leroy (Paris: Denoël, 2005), pp. 53–54 (p. 53).
21. Cendrars, *Œuvres romanesques*, 1, 71; *Complete Poems*, p. 80.
22. Ibid., 1, 71–72; p. 80.
23. Green, *Léger and the Avant-garde*, p. 103.
24. Blaise Cendrars, *J'ai tué* (Paris: La Belle Edition, 1918), unpaginated; *I Have Killed*, in *Modernities and Other Writings*, ed. by Monique Chefdor, trans. by Esther Allen with Monique Chefdor (Lincoln & London: University of Nebraska Press, 1992), p. 9.
25. Léger, 'Autour du *Ballet mécanique*', in *Fonctions de la peinture*, p. 134.
26. Paul Virilio, *Guerre et cinéma: logistique de la perception* (Paris: Cahiers du cinéma, 1984).
27. Green, *Léger and the Avant-garde*, p. 166.
28. Blaise Cendrars, *Le Paysage dans l'œuvre de Léger*, in *Blaise Cendrars vous parle...*, p. 262.
29. Blaise Cendrars, *Profond aujourd'hui*, in *Œuvres romanesques*, 1, 337–43 (p. 340); *Profound Today*, in *Modernities and Other Writings*, pp. 3–6 (p. 4).
30. Ibid.
31. Ibid., 1, 342; p. 6.
32. Georg Simmel, *The Metropolis and Mental Life*, in *The Urban Sociology Reader*, ed. by Jan Lin and Christopher Mele (London: Routledge, 2013), pp. 23–31 (p. 25).
33. Walter Benjamin, 'Paris, the Capital of the Nineteenth Century' [1935], in *The Arcades Project*, trans. by Howard Eiland and Kevin McLaughlin (Cambridge, MA, & London: Belknap Press at Harvard University Press, 2002), pp. 3–13.
34. Cendrars, *Œuvres romanesques*, 1, 747.
35. The painting is reproduced here: <https://philamuseum.org/collection/object/53928> [accessed November 2021].
36. The term is taken from Paul Virilio, *La Machine de vision* (Paris: Galilée, 1988).
37. Unpublished manuscript, cited in Cendrars, *Œuvres romanesques*, 1, 1458. 'A corps perdu' has the literal sense of losing one's body.
38. Cendrars, *Œuvres romanesques*, 1, 743–44; *Modernities and Other Writings*, pp. 25–26.
39. 'Fernand Léger: entretien avec Georges Charbonnier', radio interview recorded in the series 'Couleur du temps — couleurs de ce temps', Radio France, 1950 <https://www.youtube.com/watch?v=m1IG_pC7jBY&list=PLiN-7mukU_RGuwZV-kK2cNwWlnU1ZngAm&index=7> [accessed November 2021].
40. Blaise Cendrars, *La Fin du monde filmée par l'Ange N.-D.*, illus. by Fernand Léger (Paris: La Sirène, 1919); *Œuvres romanesques*, 1, 351–72 (p. 362).
41. Some pages of the original edition can be viewed on the website of the Koninklijke Bibliotheek in The Hague: <https://www.kb.nl/en/themes/koopman-collection/la-fin-du-monde-filmee-par-lange-n-d> [accessed November 2021].
42. See Maria Gough's illuminating essay, 'New in Print', in *Léger*, ed. by Vallye, pp. 119–25.
43. See the opening frames of Man Ray's *Emak Bakia* (1926), in which an eye is superimposed onto the camera's lens. Later, human eyes are superimposed over car headlights and painted onto the lenses of driving goggles.
44. See, for example, Blaise Cendrars, 'La Naissance de Charlot', in *Aujourd'hui*, ed. by Leroy, pp. 125–27.
45. Jennifer Wild, 'What Léger Saw: The Cinematic Spectacle and the Meteor of the Machine Age', in *Léger*, ed. by Vallye, pp. 145–50 (p. 149).
46. Walter Benjamin, 'The Work of Art in the Age of Mechanical Reproduction' [1935], in *Illuminations*, ed. by Hannah Arendt, trans. by Harry Zohn (London: Pimlico, 1999), pp. 211–44 (p. 227).

47. Fernand Léger, *Composition (Le Typographe)* [1919], reproduced in *Léger*, ed. by Vallye, p. 119.
48. Cendrars, *Blaise Cendrars vous parle...*, pp. 30–31.
49. Blaise Cendrars, *La Banlieue de Paris*, illus. by Robert Doisneau (Lausanne: Guilde du Livre, 1949), p. 47.
50. Ibid., pp. 49–50.
51. Ibid., p. 47.
52. Blaise Cendrars, interviewed by Michel Manoll as part of the series 'En bourlinguant avec Blaise Cendrars', recorded for Radio France, 14–25 April 1950 <https://open.spotify.com/album/3leLFghJ5yovh6jDWCYmuC> [accessed November 2021].
53. Cendrars, *Blaise Cendrars vous parle...*, p. 27.
54. *Les Constructeurs* was exhibited again in 2014 in Renault's plant in Flins on the outskirts of Paris. See <https://www.renaultgroup.com/en/news-on-air/news/les-constructeurs-by-fernand-leger-exhibited-at-renault-flins-plant/> [accessed November 2021].
55. 'Fernand Léger: entretien avec Georges Charbonnier'.
56. Blaise Cendrars and Fernand Léger, *Paris ma ville* (Paris: Bibliothèque des Arts, 1987).
57. Hughes, *Egalitarian Strangeness*, p. 63.
58. Ibid., pp. 61, 66.
59. Claude Leroy, 'Notice', in *Blaise Cendrars vous parle...*, p. 327.
60. *Blaise Cendrars vous parle...*, p. 28.

CHAPTER 10

'Le naufrage de l'homme profane': Genet and the Anecdotal

Richard Mason

Writing on Rembrandt's late portraits, Jean Genet praises the Dutch painter's ability to rid 'le sujet de ce qu'il a d'anecdotique et le placer sous une lumière d'éternité' [the subject of whatever anecdotal quality it has and position it under a light of eternity].[1] Genet's appraisal can be situated within a constellation of statements, disseminated across different periods and textual genres, in which he expresses disdain for the anecdotal and for anecdotes. This chapter will interrogate this stance, drawing primarily on Genet's writing on art, as well as on his challenging and rarely examined text *Fragments...*, produced when he was undergoing a creative crisis in the early 1950s. I will argue that Genet's refusal of the anecdotal is both partial and ambivalent, and that this ambivalence indexes an exploration of writing's capacity to bear witness to marginal lives and erotic experience, as well as a reflection on hierarchies of subject matter across a range of artistic disciplines and genres.

Early on in Genet's first novel, *Notre-Dame-des-Fleurs*, the narrator evokes the collapse and dissolution of anecdotes in the inconsistency of dreams and erotic fantasy: 'le soir les préliminaires du sommeil dénudent les environs de moi, détruisent les objets et les anecdotes, me laissant au bord du sommeil aussi seul que je pus l'être un soir au milieu d'une lande orageuse et vide' [in the evening, the preliminaries of sleep strip my surroundings of my self, destroying objects and anecdotes and leaving me, at the edge of sleep, as solitary as I was one night in the middle of a stormy and barren heath].[2] With an ambivalence that typifies Genet's treatment of the category, the announcement of the anecdotal's collapse, as a principle of narrative production, is itself couched 'anecdotally' ('aussi seul que je pus l'être un soir au milieu d'une lande'). Elsewhere, the narrator of Genet's 1948 text *Journal du voleur* draws a stark contrast between the realm of the anecdote, conceived of as the raw material of experience, and that of art:

> Ce qui, m'étant un enseignement, me guidera, ce n'est pas ce que j'ai vécu mais le ton sur lequel je le rapporte. Non les anecdotes mais l'œuvre d'art. Non ma vie, mais son interprétation. C'est ce que m'offre le langage pour l'évoquer, pour parler d'elle, la traduire: réussir ma légende. (*RP*, 1250)

[What will guide me, as something learned, is not what I have lived, but the tone in which I tell it. Not anecdotes but the work of art. Not my life, but its interpretation. It is what language offers me to evoke it, to talk about it, to translate it: to achieve my legend.]³

From the early 1950s onwards, Genet's allusions to the anecdotal become more starkly negative, as if he had doubled down on his resistance to the category. Genet's biographer, Edmund White, talks of Genet having a 'new contempt for the mere anecdote' around this time, which, along with an increased interest in abstraction, White connects to Genet's reading of Mallarmé.⁴ In *Fragments...*, Genet's only substantial publication from the period, Genet voices a fear that his reflections amount to nothing more than banal anecdotes and dismisses the experiential grounds of the text — an unhappy love affair — as a failure 'sur le plan du fait anecdotique' [on the level of anecdotal fact] (*RP*, 1359; *FA*, 31). Towards the end of the 1950s, in a letter to his agent and translator Bernard Frechtman describing his struggles with his writing for the theatre, Genet denigrates the anecdotal as a symptom of artistic deficiency:

> Dès la première scène, il faudrait que toute la pièce soit déjà absolument totalement déroulée dans l'esprit du spectateur. Que le spectateur aille alors à la rencontre de lui-même et non de péripéties extérieures. Le remue-ménage anecdotique est là pour masquer la pauvreté du dramaturge.⁵

> [From the very first scene, the entire play should already be absolutely, completely unfolded in the spectator's mind. The spectator can then encounter himself rather than external incidents. Anecdotal comings-and-goings serve only to conceal the failings of the playwright.]⁶

Genet's readers have added weight to this stance. Jean-Paul Sartre evokes Genet's disdain for the anecdotal on multiple occasions in his long study of the writer, *Saint Genet: comédien et martyr*, published in 1952 as the first volume of Genet's complete works. Sartre connects Genet's refusal of the anecdotal to what he terms Genet's 'recherche austère et maniaque de l'être' [austere and feverish quest for Being].⁷ It is in this context that the philosopher claims that Genet:

> N'a pas plus de regards pour son aventure individuelle — qu'il nomme avec mépris: l'anecdote — qu'un Égyptien antique pour son histoire nationale; il ne daigne prêter attention aux circonstances de sa vie que dans la mesure où elles paraissent répéter le drame originel du paradis perdu.⁸

> [No more cares about his individual adventure — which he contemptuously calls 'the anecdote' — than did an ancient Egyptian about his national history. He deigns to take notice of the circumstances of his life only insofar as they seem to repeat the original drama of the lost paradise.]⁹

Sartre goes as far as to claim that a 'mépris de l'anecdote' [contempt for anecdote] is one of Genet's most consistent traits. In Sartre's characterization, Genet views his life as a 'une suite de historiettes négligeables' [a succession of negligible sketches]; the anecdotal matter of everyday existence must be transformed through an act of poetic distillation oriented towards a governing absence: 'Cette poésie brute, c'est la plus prodigieuse tentative pour sauver le sacré au sein du naufrage de l'homme profane' [This raw poetry is a prodigious endeavour to save the sacred amidst the shipwreck of profane man].[10]

Genet's stance towards the anecdotal in the early 1950s can be situated in relation to the creative and affective crisis he underwent following his intense period of literary production in the 1940s, as well as to transformative encounters with the work of Rembrandt and Giacometti, upon whom he would later publish essays. Strikingly, Genet's various allusions to the anecdotal almost always connect to questions of artistic vision and practice. By the early 1950s, Genet was experiencing a creative impasse, exacerbated, if not originally provoked, by Sartre's monumentalizing biography. In the 1957 essay 'Le Funambule', a meditation on the figure of the artist, Genet alludes to this period of sterility: 'après une période brillante, tout artiste aura traversé une désespérante contrée, risquant de perdre sa raison et sa maîtrise' [after a brilliant period, every artist will cross a desperate land, risking the loss of his reason and his mastery] (*OC*, v, 26; *FA*, 83, translation modified). Significantly, in a later interview with *Playboy*, Genet dismissed these years of creative struggle and depression by evoking the repetition of insignificant daily acts:

> Je suis resté six ans dans cet état misérable, dans cette imbécilité qui fait le fond de la vie: ouvrir une porte, allumer une cigarette... Il n'y a que quelques lueurs dans une vie d'homme. Tout le reste est grisaille. (*OC*, vi, 26)
>
> [For six years I remained in this pitiful state, in that imbecility which forms the backdrop to a life: opening a door, lighting a cigarette... There are only a few glimmers within a man's life. The rest is greyness.] (*FA*, 83, translation modified)

The anecdotal, then, as the quotidian remains of creativity's failure.

Genet's first significant encounter with Rembrandt's paintings came in 1952 when he visited the National Gallery in London. As he gazed at them, not only in the National Gallery, but also, in the following years, in Amsterdam, Berlin and Vienna, Genet was clearly thinking about Rembrandt's own artistic trajectory, and how this might shed light on his own creative predicament. Genet's two published texts on Rembrandt, fragments of a wider project on the painter that was abandoned, provide ways in to understanding what Genet means by a stripping back of the anecdotal.

Genet is particularly interested in the later period of Rembrandt's life and career, when, following the loss of his mother and his wife, the painter sought to disappear socially, and his work took on a new intensity. In his essay 'Le Secret de Rembrandt', Genet saw in the ageing Rembrandt an artist striving for creative reinvention, which was also a form of divestment and asceticism, an established artist ready to 'tout apprendre [...] sans jamais se risquer à la virtuosité' [learn everything [...] without ever venturing virtuosity] (*OC*, v, 35; *FA*, 87). In 'Ce qui est resté d'un Rembrandt', Genet reflects on what it means to '[vouloir] n'être rien' [to want to be nothing]. In this context, Genet considers how an individual might 'cherche à perdre, à laisser se dissoudre ce qui, de quelque manière, le singularise *banalement*' [seek to lose, to let dissolve, what in some way *banally* singularizes him] (*OC*, iv, 22–23; *FA*, 93). It is in connection with this desire that Genet praises Rembrandt's ability to strip his subjects of their anecdotal attributes.

Genet's discussion of Rembrandt emphasises the painter's shifting treatment of 'faste', which might be translated as abundance, splendour or pomp, initially detectable in Rembrandt's depictions of jewels and luxurious fabrics, but emerging in his later work, almost paradoxically, as the effect of a levelling, egalitarian gaze: 'il va le faire passer [cet éclat] dans les matières les plus misérables, si bien que tout sera confondu' [he will cause this brilliance to manifest in the most wretched materials, so that everything will be confused] (*OC*, v, 34; *FA*, 87). This levelling gaze undoes his sitters of their particularities — the particular having a close alignment with the anecdotal for Genet — to reveal a universal vulnerability or 'wound' (*blessure*) that corresponded to a focus of Genet's reflections in the period, famously described in both 'Ce qui est resté d'un Rembrandt' and his essay 'L'Atelier d'Alberto Giacometti' as a consequence of an encounter with an ugly old man in a third-class carriage of a train.[11] Whilst Rembrandt's portraits are rich in *physiological* traits — and in particular in fleshy decrepitude — Genet argues that they rarely reveal *character* traits ('nous livre rarement un trait de caractère du modèle', *OC*, v, 33; *FA*, 86). Provoked by his grief at the loss of his wife Saskia, Rembrandt's late vision tended towards a cancellation of difference and hierarchy, a corollary of his flight from the social sphere and its vanities:

> Cet effort l'amène à se défaire de tout ce qui, en lui, pourrait le ramener à une vision différenciée, discontinue, hiérarchisée du monde: une main vaut un visage, un visage un coin de table, un coin de table un bâton, un bâton une main, une main une manche. (*OC*, v, 37)

> [This effort brings him to rid himself of all that could lead him back to a differentiated, discontinuous, hierarchic vision of the world: a hand has the same value as a face, a face as the corner of a table, a table corner as a stick, a stick as a hand, a hand as a sleeve.] (*FA*, 89)

The stripping of the anecdotal names Rembrandt's refusal of the 'pittoresque' [picturesque], of the individual's 'écorce particulière' [particular shell] (*OC*, IV, 27; *FA*, 97), of a vision of the world predicated on surface ornamentation, by which Genet also means social identity. In his writing on Rembrandt, but also in his essay on Giacometti, who similarly became a model of artistic commitment for the writer in the 1950s, Genet has frequent recourse to a lexical field of stripping or undoing — *(se) défaire, (se) dénuder, enlever, écarter, (se) dépouiller* — designating an ontological starkness and the universal vulnerability, or wound, that Genet had intuited in his encounter on the train. Genet often mirrors this ontological starkness, in his own creative practice, through stark deployments of the verb *être* ('la décrépitude est. Donc belle' [decrepitude is. Therefore, is beautiful], *OC*, v, 32; *FA*, 85, translation modified) which might be framed as an 'anti-anecdotal' technique.

Genet's growing disdain for the anecdotal can also be linked to the shifting status, in his writing, of erotic description, which had been prominent in his novels. The left-hand column of 'Ce qui est resté d'un Rembrandt', describing Genet's encounter in the train, evokes a series of renunciations: '"D'ici peu, me dis-je, rien ne comptera de ce qui eut tant de prix: les amours, les amitiés, les formes, la vanité, rien de ce qui relève de la séduction"' ['Soon,' I told myself, 'nothing of what used to be so precious will count: love affairs, friendships, forms, vanity, everything that has to do with seduction'] (*OC*, IV, 27–28; *FA*, 98). Genet then announces that 'l'érotisme et ses fureurs me parurent refusés, définitivement. [...] "La recherche érotique, me disais-je, est possible seulement quand on suppose que chaque être a son individualité, qu'elle est irréductible et que la forme physique en rend compte"' [Eroticism and its furies seemed denied to me, utterly. [...] 'The search for the erotic,' I told myself, 'is possible only when one supposes that each being has its individuality, that it is irreducible and that physical form is aware of it and only of it'] (*OC*, IV, 30; *FA*, 100–01). The stripping of the anecdotal, an artistic aspiration orientating Genet's creative reassessment in this period of crisis, was simultaneously framed as a collapse of the erotic as a principle of differentiated forms.

I have suggested that Genet's disdainful stance towards the anecdotal served as a quilting point for the artistic and affective crisis he underwent at the start of the 1950s, and it is through a consideration of the stakes of the anecdotal that I will approach his idiosyncratic work *Fragments...*, the one substantial text he published during this period. Characterised by discontinuity and fragmentation and, at times, 'tortuous and hard to follow' in White's characterization, this work has largely been avoided by critics.[12] The text juxtaposes a dark, universalising vision of homosexuality as sterility and isolation with a series of intimate scenes and addresses to a lover. The origins of the text lie partly in a letter sent by Genet to Sartre, who likely encouraged him to develop these ideas for publication in *Les Temps modernes* in 1954 (*RP*, 1568). In an apparent riposte to the existentialist account of homosexuality offered by Sartre in *Saint Genet*, Genet characterises homosexuality as a curse, oriented towards death and destruction, claiming that homosexuality 'm'isole, me coupe à la fois du reste du monde et de chaque pédéraste. Nous nous haïssons, en nous-mêmes et en chacun de nous. Nous nous déchirons' [isolates me, cuts me off both from the rest of the world and from every pederast. We hate each other, within ourselves and within each of us. We destroy each other] (*RP*, 1350; *FA*, 23). Simultaneously, *Fragments...* bears witness to Genet's infatuation with a tubercular Roman sex worker named Decimo Christiani, and a first version had been announced in 1953, though not published, under the title 'Lettre ouverte à Decimo' [Open Letter to Decimo].[13] Decimo is never named in the extant text, however. More broadly, *Fragments...* can be situated in the context of a wider project, associated with various titles including *La Mort*, *Le Bagne* and *L'Enfer*, towards which Genet was working in this period, but which he ultimately abandoned (*RP*, 1564). White summarises *Fragments...* as 'bits and pieces of this major work comprising autobiography, aesthetic reflections and abstract, universal speculations'.[14] The text's interest for a consideration of the anecdotal resides partly in the interplay between these different modes of writing. In a note in the Pléiade edition, Gilles Philippe comments:

> La figure et la maladie de Decimo hantent [...] le texte [...], que l'on ne saurait plus considérer, dès lors, comme de simples ruines du Livre à venir, mais comme l'infléchissement, voire le détournement de son objet dans un cadre plus circonstanciel, celui de l'échec de l'amour. (*RP*, 1565)

[Decimo and his illness haunt the text, which can no longer be considered as the mere ruins of the Book to Come, but rather as that work's inflection by, or diversion into, a more circumstantial setting: a failed love affair.]

My discussion of this fragmentary and elusive work will consider how Genet's gestures towards the legendary or mythic come to be 'inflected by the circumstantial', as Philippe puts it.

In *Fragments...* there are two explicit references to the anecdotal. The first, describing an older lover's feelings of insecurity and inadequacy, evokes Genet's failed courtship of Decimo:

> S'agit-il donc d'une simple anecdote réductible à ceci: un pédéraste s'amourache d'un jeune garçon qui le berne? Le pédéraste se désole, enrage, s'enfonce. Ironique et souverain, l'enfant se croit fort. Il trompe et se trompe. Il est subtil et cruel par l'indifférence. Voilà des données simples. Le jeu en est banal et facile. (*RP*, 1357)

> [Is this just a question of a simple anecdote reducible to: a pederast becomes infatuated with a young boy who deceives him? The pederast grieves, becomes enraged, hides. Ironic and sovereign, the child thinks he is strong. He fools and is fooled. He is subtle and cruel out of indifference. Those are the simple givens. The game is banal and easy.] (*FA*, 30)

The second describes an act of transformation:

> Enfin cette aventure qui sera, sur le plan du fait anecdotique, un échec à la fois désiré et imposé, se change en une poursuite logique qui s'oppose à la morale du monde, et cependant qu'elle veut la nier, elle lui emprunte toutes ses notions, ses termes de comparaison — qui sont pleins — afin de les vider. (*RP*, 1359)

> [Finally this adventure that, on the level of anecdotal fact, will be a failure at once wished for and compelled, changes into a logical pursuit that is opposed to the morality of the world, and although it tries to deny it, it borrows from it all its notions, its terms of comparison — which are full — in order to empty them.] (*FA*, 31, modified)

These efforts at creative transformation serve as the horizon for Genet's reflections on how, in a movement away from a realm of anecdotal particularity, the lover-in-writing might become legendary, a kind of pure signifier, evoking the notion, frequent within Genet's *œuvre*, of the poem as a form of deathly apotheosis or consecration. White highlights Genet's exploration in *Fragments...* of an art 'consecrated to death', where words serve as empty tombs.[15] Frequent allusions to marching, processions or steps in *Fragments...* trace, I would argue, the passage from an anecdotal, experiential realm to artistic representation. One can imagine this feature of the work catching Giacometti's attention when he read the text with keen interest, subsequently compelled to meet the writer in person and to produce a series of portraits of him (*RP*, xliv).[16] The introductory note to the fragments describes them as 'un des nombreux brouillons d'un texte qui sera *démarche lente, mesurée, vers le poème*' [one of several drafts of a text that will be the *slow, measured progress* toward the poem] (*RP*, 1343; *FA*, 19, my emphasis), evoking a mourning procession and aligning the finished work, perhaps that work entitled *La Mort*, with the tomb and with death. This is the petrifying movement from the realm of particularity and individuality to the legendary realm of the signifier, cast as a refuge for the dying lover — but one that 'saves' through its negation of particular attributes, subsumed to mythic and legendary qualities. The endgame, here, is language as evacuated, mortuary abstraction; 'type' or 'archetype' as the stripping back of particularity: 'Deviens: une putain, puis la grue sublime, la reine — toi lope aux crachats sanguinolents la déesse, une constellation puis le nom seule de cette constellation, et ce nom un signe usé que le poète utilise' [Become: a whore, then the sublime slut, the queen — you, faggot of the bloody spittle, the goddess, a constellation, then the name alone of that constellation, and that name a used-up sign that a poet can use] (*RP*, 1361–62; *FA*, 34). At the threshold both of death and of written representation, Decimo's gestures are captured within a series of discontinuous, statuesque poses: 'Habile à te ciseler, ton cœur s'arrêtant de battre, en n'importe quelle posture la mort te définit. Monumental, à tout moment achevé, tu es cerné par elle' [Deftly capturing your form, your heart ceasing to beat, death portrays you in any which posture. Monumental, finished off at every moment, you are surrounded by death] (*RP*, 1346; *FA*, 20, modified).[17] Mapping onto a wider interrogation in his work of language's capacity to capture and contain the object of desire, Genet enumerates in *Fragments...* phrases that might stand in for the dying lover: 'Voici, pour te définir, de sournois propos: s'en aller de la caisse, sentir le sapin, dégueuler ses poumons, mollarder des huitres... merveilles.' [Here, to define you, are some insidious suggestions: a cough will carry you off, one foot in the grave, vomit your lungs, spit oysters... marvels!] (*RP*, 1348; *FA*, 22, modified).[18] Elsewhere, Genet invokes a form of poetic reason 'qui recule l'événement et le fixe au ciel immobile du langage' [that thrusts away the event and fixes it in the motionless sky of language] (*RP*, 1361; *FA*, 33). This distancing movement denotes a form of effacement that subsumes the events of a particular life to an abstracting idea: 'De toute vie que demeure-t-il? Son poème. À l'extrême un signe: le nom devenu exemplaire. Qu'à leur tour s'effacent le nom et l'exemple, et que demeure "une idée de misère infinie"' [From any life, what remains? Its poem. At most a sign: the name become exemplary. In turn, the name and the example vanish, and an 'idea of infinite misery' remains] (*RP*, 1353; *FA*, 26).

Several allusions to tragedy as dramatic genre within the fragments develop this aspect of the text, notably repeated comparisons between Decimo and the tragic heroines Phaedra and Antigone, the latter resonating powerfully with Genet's characterization of poetic language as tomb through her commitment to burying her brother, as well as her own living entombment.[19] Later in the text, in a fragment of dialogue, Decimo expresses his sadness that a friend has given his only suit to a dead friend to be buried in, recalling the concern for burial rites at the heart of Sophocles's plot. On the surface of things, the tragic would seem a particularly apt genre for Genet's flight from the realm of the anecdotal and the everyday. In an essay entitled 'Tragedy and the Whole Truth', Aldous Huxley reflected on the ways in which 'tragedy omits all the everyday parts of life that dilute its effect'.[20] Through his meditations on the lover's transfiguration into writing, Genet could be seen to be exploring just such a tragic distillation. Genet's allusions to tragic heroines call to mind, furthermore, hierarchies of subject matter to which tragedy as a genre has always been particularly attentive. This finds a formal correspondence, I would argue, in the typographical presentation of Genet's text, which consists of short fragments displaying variations in font size, embedded sections of text, shifts to the margin and dense and digressive footnotes.[21] This exploration of marginalia and typographical 'hierarchy' — implied subordination of footnotes and smaller font — resonates with the text's meditations on the anecdotal, inviting considerations of 'dominant' and 'marginal' subject matter and rhetorical modes. An attentive reading of *Fragments...*, however, suggests the typographical cues provided by Genet constitute a lure. White comments, in this regard, that the fragmentary and typographically irregular presentation 'render[s] a contradictory sense of subordination and a complete collapse in the hierarchy of literary elements'.[22]

In *Fragments...*, then, Genet reflects on how the individual life might be stripped bare of its anecdotal particularity to assume the full force of the sign: Decimo's transfiguration into an 'assemblage [...] scintillant de lettres' [a gleaming collection of letters] (*RP*, 1346; *FA*, 20), abstracted from the humdrum specificity of everyday eroticism and suffering. Significantly, the middle section of *Fragments...*, outlining the autobiographical circumstances by which Genet arrived at his wider reflection on homosexual sterility, is entitled 'Le Prétexte', as if Genet were signposting erotic and affective experience as 'pretextual' in some sense. Through a sentence that seems to rise from its dejected, autobiographical point of departure, Genet charts the desiring movement towards the signifier:

> J'étais las, encore que pointât, lancinant, le souci d'éternité qui, chez moi, ne pouvant se traduire par la pérennité dans les générations, ni par la notion de continu gonflant mes actes, s'exprimait par la recherche d'un rythme — ou loi interne à mon seul système — ou section d'or, qui fussent éternels c'est-à-dire capables d'engendrer, lier et boucler le poème achevé, parfait signe évident, intouchable et ultime de cette aventure humaine, la mienne. (*RP*, 1356)
>
> [I was weary, yet the tormenting concern for eternity still made itself felt, a concern incapable in my case of being translated through the sequence of generations, or by the notion of continuity filling out my acts, a concern I expressed through my search for a rhythm — or a law within my system alone — or a Golden Section, eternal, that is to say, capable of engendering, connecting, and completing the finished poem, the perfect and obvious sign, untouchable and final, of this human adventure, my own.] (*FA*, 28–29, modified)

There is an echo, here, of Genet's opening note to the fragments, in which the poem served to consecrate both life and writing: 'le poème, justification de ce texte comme le texte le sera de ma vie' [the poem, justification of this text as the text will be of my life] (*RP*, 1343; *FA*, 19). Yet the eternalizing horizon to which Genet's poetic act tends never wholly escapes its origins within the intimate and the 'circumstantial', his disavowal of writing's anecdotal origins being both partial and ambivalent. This ambivalence emerges especially in his dramatization of the erotic, that category he ostensibly sought to attenuate in his work from the late 1940s onwards, and which his later reflections on art would align with the anecdotal.[23]

As we have seen, Genet was fascinated with the levelling, egalitarian gaze that he saw at work in Rembrandt's late portraits, achieving an effect whereby 'une main vaut un visage, un visage un coin de table, un coin de table un bâton, un bâton une main, une main une manche' [a hand has the same value as a stick, a face as the corner of a table, a table corner as a stick, a stick as a hand, a hand as a sleeve] (*OC*, v, 37; *FA*, 89). An undifferentiated perceptive field was suggestive, for Genet, of the collapse of erotic interest; the stripping back of anecdotal attributes, in Rembrandt's painting as in Genet's transformative encounter in the train carriage, simultaneously a divestment of 'les amours, les amitiés, les formes, la vanité, [...] de ce qui relève de la séduction' [love affairs, friendships, forms, vanity, everything that has to do with seduction] (*OC*, IV, 27–28; *FA*, 98). In his texts on Rembrandt, however, Genet does not wholly commit to his disavowal of the erotic, following up his comment on the collapse of eroticism with a confession: 'Pourtant, j'écrivais ce qui précède sans cesser d'être inquiété, travaillé par les thèmes érotiques qui m'étaient familiers et qui dominaient ma vie' [Yet I wrote the preceding without ceasing to be unsettled, worked on, by the erotic themes that had been familiar to me and that had dominated my life] (*OC*, IV, 30; *FA*, 101). In the earlier text, *Fragments...*, an ambivalence regarding the transfiguration of the anecdotal, or of the *circonstanciel*, to deploy Philippe's similarly inflected phrase, can be traced through the text's dramatization of erotic scenes.

Genet enumerates in *Fragments...* the visible markers of Decimo's presence that, he claims, will not outdo the abstractions of death and a mythologizing mode of writing: 'Slip, sueur, souliers, larmes, — ou que tu te mouches — n'empêcheront pas que le vide ne t'isole' [Underwear, sweat, shoes, tears — or when you blow your nose — will not prevent the void from isolating you] (*RP*, 1346; *FA*, 20). Nonetheless, Genet frequently returns in *Fragments...* to the lover's distinguishing attributes: a gesture, a characteristic pose or mannerism, a part of the body. The text opens, indeed, by focusing the reader's attention on an isolated part of the body: 'La paupière morose — où la chimère est frappée, tu guettais' [The morose eyelid — where the chimera was broken, you were keeping watch] (*RP*, 1345; *FA*, 19). Elsewhere, there is an exclamatory reference to 'cette tache velue sur ta cuisse!' [that hairy spot on your thigh!] and then again, a little later, to the same 'tache presque violette, plaquée sur ta cuisse, [qui] donne à ta beauté le cachet singulier' [an almost purple mark, spread across your thigh, that gives your beauty its unique seal] (*RP*, 1347, 1349; *FA*, 21, 22, modified). Sometimes the isolation of sexual attributes is amplified by the omission of a main verb: 'Derche offert au chibre des vieux' [Rump presented to old men's dicks] (*RP*, 1347; *FA*, 21). In a way that resonates with Genet's evocation of marching and processions, there are several allusions to the lover's feet, which assume an exemplary function: 'Chacun de tes pas — tes longues pattes nerveuses — pourrait porter ton nom' [Each of your steps — your long, nervous strides — could bear your name] (*RP*, 1346; *FA*, 19). Genet adds: 'Une ankylose subtile détache chacun [de tes pas] d'une démarche qui te porte au cercueil' [A subtle ankylosis distinguishes each step from a walk that carries you to the coffin] (*RP*, 1346; *FA*, 19–20). Given the imbrication of marching, death and writing in *Fragments...* this seems to suggest that the individuating feature (the 'ankylose subtile') does not fall into step with the eternalizing poetic gesture, the lover's singularity causing the consecrating movement of poetic language to stumble. The recurrent emphasis on the individuating attribute serves as a marker of ongoing erotic efficacy, I would argue, in the wider economy of Genet's reflections on the erotic. This is decidedly *not* the undifferentiated realm that Genet discovered in Rembrandt's painting, in which 'une main vaut un visage'.

The remanence of the encounter's experiential ground can also be felt in the fragments' rhetorical form, and in Genet's deployment of *tutoiement* to evoke intimate, if opaque, erotic encounters. In Genet's writing, a characteristically antagonistic and oppositional rhetorical stance is often marked using *vous*, notably in his first novel, *Notre-Dame-des-Fleurs*, in which the narrator takes his distance from the narratee with 'Weidmann *vous* apparut dans une édition de cinq heures' (*RP*, 3) [Weidmann appeared before you in a five o'clock newspaper].[24] Yet within that novel, the contrasting tonality of *tutoiement* signals a different rhetorical and relational stance, albeit one inflected by death:

> Tu ne bougeais pas, tu ne dormais pas, tu ne rêvais pas, tu étais en fuite, immobile et pâle, glacé, droit, étendue raide sur le lit plat comme un cercueil sur la mer, et je nous savais chastes, tandis que j'étais attentif à te sentir t'écouler en moi, tiède et blanc, par petites secousses continues. (*RP*, 5)
>
> [You did not move, you were not asleep, you were not dreaming, you were in flight, motionless and pale, frozen, straight, stretched out stiff on the flat bed like a coffin on the sea, and I knew that we were chaste, while I, all attention, felt you flow into me, warm and white, in continuous little jerks.][25]

Michael Lucey observes that *Notre-Dame-des-Fleurs* 'has as one of its generating principles the contrast between a social *vous* and a personal *tu*'.[26] Indeed, Genet acknowledged his attentiveness to the pronouns and forms of address that he used in the text in a late interview with Bertrand Poirot-Delpech (*OC*, VI, 231). As in *Notre-Dame-des-Fleurs*, *tutoiement* in *Fragments...* indexes intimate yet stubbornly opaque erotic encounters. More broadly, the interplay between Genet's pronouncements about language's 'capture' of the erotic event and the opacity with which he strives to mark erotic encounters in the text dramatises the 'push and pull' between experience and representation, between life and writing, posing, if not answering, a question about art's capacity to bear witness to marginal experience.

I want to suggest, then, that the anecdotal continues to exert a pressure within the textual dynamics of *Fragments...*, often against the grain of the text's surface pronouncements concerning the transfiguration of experience into poetry. The border territory between the encounter and its consecration finds expression in the text, I would argue, through a description of Decimo in the bathhouse, a space of indeterminacy and liminality, in which steam seems to function as a metaphor for writing's powers of abstraction, the younger man appearing 'pieds nus sur les dalles, habillé d'une serviette-éponge, dans la buée qui, avec la honte, te recule et t'abstrait' [feet bare on the tiles, dressed in a terrycloth towel, in the condensation that pushes you back and abstracts you] (*RP*, 1347; *FA*, 21, modified). Even within this vapour, distinctive attributes once more counter the forces of abstraction: 'je t'observe dans ces bains turcs [...] parcourant en silence et l'illuminant par: tes dents, tes yeux, ton cynisme, cette masse de vapeur blanche et moite' [I watch you in the Turkish baths [...] travelling silently through that mass of white, sweaty steam and illuminating it by: your teeth, your eyes, your cynicism] (*RP*, 1347; *FA*, 21, modified). Genet's poetic transformations of Decimo as dying lover, then, never wholly follow through on the evacuating movement promised by the writer, signalling the remanence, within his work, of the 'anecdotal' as a principle of erotic differentiation and interest, as well as an index of marginal lives. Genet's ambivalence about the anecdotal offers a way not only of framing the 'désespérante contrée' that the writer traversed between 1948 and 1955, but also his wider interrogation of the passage between marginal experience and writing.

Notes to Chapter 10

1. Jean Genet, 'Ce qui est resté d'un Rembrandt déchiré en petits carrés bien réguliers et foutu aux chiottes', in *Œuvres complètes*, 5 vols (Paris: Gallimard, 1951–91), IV, 22–23 (hereafter referenced as *OC* in the main text); 'What Remains of a Rembrandt Torn into Equally Sized Little Pieces and Flushed Down the Toilet', in *Fragments of the Artwork*, trans. by Charlotte Mandell (Stanford: Stanford University Press, 2003), p. 93 (hereafter referenced as *FA* in the main text).
2. Jean Genet, *Notre-Dame-des Fleurs*, in *Romans et poèmes*, ed. by Emmanuelle Lambert and Gilles Philippe with Albert Dichy, Bibliothèque de la Pléiade (Paris: Gallimard, 2021), p. 66 (hereafter referenced as *RP* in the main text); *Our Lady of the Flowers*, trans. by Bruce Frechtman (New York: Grove Press, 1963), p. 128 (modified).
3. Jean Genet, *The Thief's Journal*, trans. by Bernard Frechtman (New York: Grove Press, 1964), p. 205, modified.
4. Edmund White, *Jean Genet* (London: Chatto & Windus, 1993), pp. 448–49.
5. Jean Genet, *Théâtre complet*, ed. by Michel Corvin and Albert Dichy, Bibliothèque de la Pléiade (Paris: Gallimard, 2002), pp. 927–28.
6. Unless stated otherwise, all translations are my own.
7. Jean-Paul Sartre, *Saint Genet: comédien et martyr* (Paris: Gallimard, 1952), p. 21; *Saint Genet: Actor and Martyr*, trans. by Bernard Frechtman (New York: Pantheon Books, 1963), p. 12.
8. Sartre, *Saint Genet*, pp. 12–13.
9. Ibid., pp. 12–13; p. 5.
10. Ibid., p. 338; p. 330.
11. See Carl Lavery, 'Ethics of the Wound: A New Interpretation of Jean Genet's Politics', *Journal of European Studies*, 33 (2003), 161–76; Ian Fleishman, 'Ce qui est poussé repousse: Jean Genet, Hélène Cixous, the Wound, and the Poetics of Omission', *French Studies*, 69 (2015), 190–204.
12. White, *Jean Genet*, p. 448.
13. Ibid., p. 428.
14. Ibid., p. 447.
15. Ibid., p. 449.
16. See, too, Thierry Dufrêne, *Giacometti, Genet: masques et portrait moderne* (Paris: Éditions l'insolite, 2006), p. 7.
17. For a discussion of writing as sculpture in Genet's work see Mairéad Hanrahan, 'Sculpting Time', *Paragraph*, 27 (2004), 43–58 (pp. 47–53).
18. For a discussion of the erotics of the phrase in Genet's work, and its relationship to mastery and capture, see Richard Mason, 'Érotique de la phrase: la mise en scène de la parole de l'autre chez Proust et Genet', in *Marcel Proust, roman moderne*, ed. by Vincent Ferré and Raffaello Rossi (= special issue of *Marcel Proust Aujourd'hui*, 14 (2018)), 116–29.
19. Dumas's *La Dame aux Camélias*, also about a tubercular lover, is another frequent reference (*RP*, 1576, n. 6).

20. Aldous Huxley, 'Tragedy and the Whole Truth', in *Music at Night, and Other Essays* (London: Chatto & Windus, 1949), pp. 3–18 (pp. 3–4).
21. This anticipates Genet's later typographical experimentation in 'Ce qui est resté...', which Derrida would in turn explore in his engagement with Genet in *Glas* (Paris: Galilée, 1974).
22. White, *Jean Genet*, p. 449
23. For a discussion of Genet's 'censorship' of sexual elements within his texts see *RP*, xlvi.
24. Genet, *Our Lady of the Flowers*, p. 51 (modified).
25. Ibid., p. 54.
26. Michael Lucey, 'Genet's *Notre-Dame-des-Fleurs*: Fantasy and Sexual Identity', in *Genet: In the Language of the Enemy*, ed. by Scott Durham, (= special issue of *Yale French Studies*, 91 (1997)), 80–102 (p. 86).

CHAPTER 11

Late-life Care and the Labours of Attention in Contemporary Women's Writing

Shirley Jordan

We turn to literature as a place where the complexity of hard-to-articulate experience finds expression. In reading written accounts of relationships, we interrogate in turn the bonds within our own, mull over the ethical dilemmas with which they present us and reconsider the ways in which we are responsible for one another. Given this fundamental truth, it seems surprising that explicit accounts of late-life care have to date found relatively little place in literature. Care is arguably the most universal of human needs from birth through to death, and the provision of care one of the most challenging and potentially enriching of relational experiences. As Madeleine Bunting notes in *Labours of Love: The Crisis of Care*, 'care is usually regarded as menial, unimportant or too closely associated with bodily processes to be worthy of description in literature'.[1] The narrative arc of care is repetitive, slow and unexciting; its practices, as Lisa Baraitser remarks, are 'mostly arduous, boring, and mundane, or simply unbearable'.[2] A repeated caress in the context of a romantic narrative makes for pleasurable reading; the same gesture within the context of late-life care is trickier to read and more demanding. The silencing of care in the literary field indicates our deeply rooted reluctance to engage with the concrete implications of our common vulnerability and dependency. It is also evidence of a shared fear of the complexity of care. Thus, notes Bunting, we make the labour of care invisible in a willed 'cultural blindness', showing 'a profound refusal to recognize and value the work that sustains human well-being'.[3]

This chapter explores the current volume's overarching ideas of labour and attention in relation to the pressing and timely question of care. Its focus is on two powerful testimonies that emphasise in micro detail the ethical and practical requirements of care in late life, Simone de Beauvoir's *Une mort très douce* [A Very Easy Death] (1964) and Chantal Akerman's *Ma mère rit* [My Mother Laughs] (2013), both of which are written by a woman grappling with the imperatives of late-life care for her vulnerable mother.[4] In both, the mother is cared for by diverse professionals, in hospitals and/or at home. The processes are recorded by daughter-narrators who become alert to the needs of an ailing person and must help consider how to make her safe, comfortable and pain-free. Care in these texts is at its most personally challenging for several reasons. First, the narrators are inexperienced care givers who are not only interfacing with professional support but working out how to be carers themselves. Second, the caring situation assumes distinctive existential and affective freight on account of its involvement in the already intractably complicated mother-daughter relationship. This produces a special slant on vulnerability as both daughter and mother straddle carer/cared-for positions and grapple with the unwanted reversal which, in Annie Ernaux's wrenching *Je ne suis pas sortie de ma nuit* [I Remain in Darkness] (1997), produces the oft-quoted protestation against her shifting sense of self: 'Je PEUX pas être sa mère' [I CANNOT be her mother].[5] As they home in on care's fleshly and emotional realities, these works raise difficult yet essential questions about the kinds of attention that care requires, the ways in which care shapes human relationships and how to establish boundaries within care giving. They also prompt us to ask how writing and reading are implicated within relations of care, and ultimately whether acts of attention in literature can lead to re-valorisation of care's labours. Exploring such questions requires a short foray into some recent thinking about care.

Care theory, a rapidly expanding critical framework for interrogating our relationship with everything that *needs* care, is permeating numerous fields of enquiry, its relevance bolstered by the COVID-19 pandemic which has opened to scrutiny the startling crisis of care provision in care-less neoliberal systems. The labour of care is being freshly highlighted in ways that validate and connect with the concerns of early thinkers on care ethics such as Carol Gilligan, Nell Noddings and Joan Tronto. Attention to care has permeated French critical thinking, giving rise to Sandra Laugier's study of care ethics as a politics of the ordinary,[6] to Cynthia Fleuri's impassioned claim, spurred by the pandemic, that 'le soin est la seule manière d'habiter le monde' [care is the only way of living in the world],[7] or to Fabienne Brugère's investigation of and investment in '[le] travail de la sollicitude' [the labour of solicitude].[8] Care as a structuring paradigm in literature is newly evident in the upsurge of interest in the health humanities: in Alexandre Gefen's influential insistence that French literature at the start of the twenty-first century is vitally connected to repair;[9] in Régine Detambel's exploration of reading and being read to as therapy;[10] and in analyses of a '(re)turn' to care in French cultural production.[11]

In this chapter, explorations of the labour of care by Beauvoir and Akerman are set in dialogue not only with overarching ideas emerging from care theory, but more specifically with a concept elaborated by philosopher and psychoanalyst Anne Dufourmantelle in *Puissance de la douceur* [Power of Gentleness].[12] 'Gentleness' is interesting because it prompts a canny side-step from 'care', allowing us to nuance and disturb the ways we think with a term muddied by marketisation and by negative association with, for example, an under-rated employment sector, or an undesirable kind of 'home'. In French, *la douceur* is similarly distinct from the neoliberal terminology of the care industry. 'Gentleness' asks us to examine instead an elusive quality that is played out in the relational activities of caring; one that assents to a decelerated relationship to time and that foregrounds the embracing of vulnerability and the heightened acceptance of our common fragility to which care theory alludes. For Dufourmantelle this acceptance is a force which 'fait de la douceur un degré plus haut, dans la compassion, que le simple soin' [makes gentleness a higher degree of compassion than simple care] (*PD*, 26; *PG*, 13). There is a tough realism in gentleness, allowing it to invent relationships that accommodate negativity, confusion and fear. Dufourmantelle sets it at the centre of a paradigm of resistance, as a soft power requiring strength and endurance. As a form of embodied intuition, gentleness binds together sensation, tactility and affect in response to, for example, 'La palpitation d'une veine qui affleure sous la peau' or 'Une peau très âgée comme un galet translucide' [The throbbing of a vein that surfaces from under the skin. Very aged skin like a translucent pebble] (*PD*, 39; *PG*, 23). Gentleness is slippery, not to be instrumentalised, yet at the same time it is an ethical praxis and not simply an innate quality. In her preface to the English translation of *Puissance de la douceur*, 'Philosophy in Furs', Catherine Malabou notes that 'since rigid conceptual determination does not suit it, gentleness appears gradually through a series of tableaux that shape it' (*PG*, xii). This too is how the labour of care emerges, heuristically, within our chosen texts, both of which are informed in different ways by gentleness.

One further factor motivates the harnessing of gentleness in a reading of these works: the relevance of its emphasis on embodied care to daughter-mother caring. Philosophers of care such as Maurice Hamington note how care is learned in early life through bodily contact and argue that what care *feels* like is stored in haptic and muscle as well as emotional memory. Thus, care is 'embodied as a form of ethics which we understand through our bodies in ways which we can't always articulate. We start learning of care through the body as babies before we have language'.[13] Similarly, Dufourmantelle locates the origin of gentleness in pre-natal contact: 'Sans doute dort-il dans chacune de nos cellules, nous invitant au retour impossible à ce monde perdu qui fut, bien avant les bras maternels, un bercement' [The touch of gentleness undoubtedly sleeps in each one of our cells, beckoning us to return, impossibly, to this lost world that rocked us long before maternal arms did] (*PD* 133–34; *PG*, 96). The generosity and persistence of this protective contact are, of course, unrealisable as something willed. Such contact remains as aspirational a horizon as Derrida's notion of unconditional hospitality, yet gentleness labours to keep it in mind.

Dufourmantelle's reading of gentleness as tough and resistant raises — and seeks to overcome — the insidious feminising of care. Care theory, and care itself, are undoubtedly gendered. Feminist care theory has sought to validate the hidden, everyday caring undertaken by women which remains de-valued, under-researched and under-articulated. This is essential work. In her preface to *Service ou servitude: essai sur les femmes toutes mains* [Service or Servitude: Essay on Women as 'Dogsbodies'] Geneviève Fraisse explores how care, as well as those who provide and receive it, are routinely marginalised and shamed, how society has constructed 'care' as a dirty word, how this contaminates carer and cared for and how that contamination is feminised.[14] Yet it is imperative to make the case for care not as women's labour but as a species activity. Similarly, while the ethical concept adopted by Brugère to think about care, *la sollicitude*, is routinely feminised, Brugère argues that it must be wrenched away from this entanglement and democratised. Arguably, texts such as those explored in this chapter contribute powerfully to the de-contaminating of care, help to open for fresh scrutiny care's gendered parameters and above all underscore our common vulnerability as individuals who will almost inevitably need or be involved in providing care of various kinds throughout our adult lives whatever our gender. My drawing together here of *Une mort très douce* and *Ma mère rit* is partly driven by the very different starting-points on shared vulnerability that they exemplify, and the contrasting processes of coming to care that they explore.

Une mort très douce

Une mort très douce is an arresting account of a thirty-day period of care, written in 1963 shortly after the death of the author's mother. Following a fall in her bathroom, Françoise de Beauvoir is hospitalised with a broken femur. After several tests and operations, she is diagnosed with intestinal cancer and dies without ever leaving the hospital. The rise of the medical humanities has prompted some new, care-focused readings of Beauvoir's testimony;[15] indeed, it has recently been re-cast as an important harbinger of contemporary care theory, with Beauvoir once again writing ahead of her time.[16] It is also a litmus test of attitudes to literary accounts of care: upon publication its care-driven focus prompted critiques of inappropriacy, morbidity, even sensationalism. Further, such critiques disregarded the difficult labour of writing about care. Beauvoir was charged precisely with being *un*-caring in taking notes at the bedside of her dying mother, charges she later rebuts.[17] My own short analysis focuses on *Une mort très douce* as a powerful, performative account of coming to care, and on how this entails a radical existential re-situating of the self.

Une mort très douce is dense with meticulously detailed accounts of the labour of care. Beauvoir is at once an observer of care and an auxiliary carer within the organised structures of a hospital system, ultimately assisting in the collective task of her mother's dying as the latter becomes 'une chose sans défense, tout entière à la merci de médecins indifférents et d'infirmières surmenées' [a defenceless thing, utterly at the mercy of indifferent doctors and over-worked nurses] (*MD*, 111; *ED*, 94). She is sharply observant on professionalised care as provided by various players, alert to objectifying discourse and keen to tease out the gendered distinctions between the technologically ambitious male doctors who plan and execute interventions, reducing patient to pathology and reading her body for confirmation of their own expertise, and the female nursing staff whose 'minutieuse sollicitude' [greatest care] (*MD*, 18; *ED*, 13) is comparatively devalued. Beauvoir records the comment by 'Le professeur B' that on leaving hospital her mother 'pourra reprendre sa petite vie' [will be able to potter around again] (*MD*, 20; *ED*, 15), cleverly leaving her reader to absorb the impact of this chillingly ageist and gendered observation before returning to critique it later. Conversely, she sympathises with the nurses who are 'liées à leur malade par la familiarité des corvées' [linked to their patient by the extreme closeness of [...] necessary tasks] (*MD*, 28; *ED*, 22) and show friendly interest in the patient's life. Consistent with feminist care theory, *Une mort très douce* teases out the patriarchal appropriation of medicine, critiquing its production of an uncaring, depersonalised care driven by technology and ambition.

The labour required from female carers is both physical and emotional. They cut the mother's meat at mealtimes and help her to eat, dab her with eau de cologne, dust her with talc and carefully move her to ease her bed sores. Beauvoir is struck by the gentleness of Mlle Leblon who does not concede to cut the patient's hair but instead restores its beauty, taking time to unplait, brush and carefully re-plait it, arranging the tresses in a crown around her head (*MD*, 58; *ED*, 48). Such care entails waiting, sustained attention and a reading of small signs, both voluntary and involuntary, made by the patient and her body. The labour entailed for Beauvoir herself, described as a 'vigilance têtue' [obstinate watchfulness] (*MD*, 110; *ED*, 94) which reduced considerably her mother's suffering, consists in attending (listening, reassuring, validating, dispelling fear) and in physical assistance. She helps move and hold her mother when she is being changed. The increasing difficulty of gentleness — of intended gentleness being *felt* as gentleness when the body is sensitive and wracked with pain — is noted, as are the patient's fear, powerlessness and trepidation that 'on va me trimbaler, me bousculer [...] me secouer, me transbahuter' [They are going to hustle me and push me about [...] shake me about and trundle me around] (*MD*, 30–31; *ED*, 23–24). Care's routines demand a giving-over of the self to a differently elastic temporality, as long swathes of waiting and watching are interspersed with repetitive business:

> Il fallait aider maman à cracher, lui donner à boire, arranger ses oreillers, ou sa natte, déplacer sa jambe, arroser ses fleurs, ouvrir, fermer la fenêtre, lui lire le journal, répondre à ses questions, remonter sa montre qui reposait sur sa poitrine, suspendue à un cordonnet noir. (*MD*, 67)

> [I had to help Maman to spit; I had to give her something to drink, arrange her pillows or her plait, move her leg, water her flowers, open the window, close it, read her the paper, answer her questions, wind up the watch that lay on her chest, hanging from a black ribbon.] (*ED*, 56–57)

Remarkable in this work is the quality of writing care. Care for her mother is not only the thematic driver of the text; more than this, the gestures of care shape Beauvoir's prose. We are witness, through the author's notations, to the way that she scrutinises anxiously her mother's face, repeatedly noting her colour, any signs of tension, fear or pain, whether her eyes are half-closed or open, the contractions of her brow. The position of her body, its smallest movements and the sound of her breathing are also captured. Notations such as 'Son front, ses mains brûlaient' [Her forehead and hands were burning hot] (*MD*, 15; *ED*, 11) indicate touch. Such detail, with which the text is thick, exceeds narrative function and is the pure writing of care. Beauvoir notes frequently her mother's mouth, remarking on a downward twist, the sucking movement of her lips dampened with water. She deciphers in this movement a palimpsest of suggestive expressions and, explaining it in detail to Sartre, imitates it with her own mouth despite herself: 'j'avais posé [la bouche] de maman sur mon visage [...] la compassion me déchirait' [I had put Maman's mouth on my own face [...] compassion wrung my heart] (*MD*, 39; *ED*, 31).

I began by arguing that *Une mort très douce* is a narrative about coming to care. We see how the text is informed by prevailing responses to older age which characteristically work to 'other' older people, keeping them at a distance and discounting their experiences. Yet a tension rapidly emerges between dispassionate distancing and intimate identification. Beauvoir's own early reference to her mother as 'cette alitée' [this patient in bed] is challenged by the intense proximity, empathy and sense of shared vulnerability that progressively seep into and take over the text, and such distancing is overtly critiqued through Beauvoir's observations on the alienating and reductive gaze of the doctors, who frame her mother as 'cette vieille femme mal peignée, un peu hagarde' [this ill-kempt, rather wild-looking old woman] (*MD*, 27; *ED*, 21).

Especially salient in this work is how the labour of care challenges and re-shapes Beauvoir's sense of self. Ultimately the challenge of care is a challenge to our reliance on the notion of autonomous subjecthood, and on the transcendent, future-oriented view of the individual that is the engine of Beauvoir's existentialist view of self-in-time. *Une mort très douce* records the emergence of Beauvoir's recognition of her own vulnerability, mirrored in that of her mother, and this recognition surfaces precisely through her close connection with the repetitive labour of care. She makes us witness to the onset of a shift from individualism, and from a certain position on old age and late life which is detached and pragmatic, to an entanglement in new emotions and a new sense of interdependency. Thus, she progresses from statements about her mother such as: 'Je m'émus peu [...] somme toute, elle avait l'âge de mourir' [I was not very much affected [...] after all, she was of an age to die] (*MD*, 17; *ED*, 13), to profound identification and a reckoning with new, unrecognisable forms of pity and 'désarroi' [disturbance] (*MD*, 27; *ED*, 21). Her understanding of care relationships becomes more subtle as she notes the sweetness her mother sometimes finds in dependency: 'Elle prenait plaisir à cette dépendance et réclamait sans répit notre attention' [She took a pleasure in her dependence and she called for our attention all the time] (*MD*, 67; *ED*, 57). The knowledge of this undoes Beauvoir's earlier unquestioned declaration that the intimate labour of care is automatically humiliating for the patient and repugnant for the carer (*MD*, 28; *ED*, 22); the relationship is more ambivalent than this allows for, and more rewarding. Through such observations, Beauvoir makes herself vulnerable to us. This is an unaccustomed position for her as a writer and it is one of the features that draws readers into this text in a new way. Terry Keefe, commenting on the absence of didacticism in *Une mort très douce*, notes that 'for once [Beauvoir's] readers are not told what to think on the underlying issues'.[18] Instead, the writer's disarray leaves the work open, inviting us to 'participate in the text and explore its meanings'.[19] The text is an instantiation of Dufourmantelle's suggestion that gentleness may visit us without our consent, may not be willed, and may usher in experiences that are ungraspable 'dans les frontières de votre moi ancien' [within the boundaries of [one's] former self] (*PD*, 114; *PG*, 81). Dufourmantelle speaks of accepting gentleness's invitation to 'entrer dans ses marées [...] parcourir ses chemins creux [...] se perdre pour que quelque chose d'inédit survienne' [enter its tides, tread its hollow paths, get lost so that something unprecedented may arise] (*PD*, 114; *PG*, 81), and this process is in evidence in *Une mort très douce*.

Arguably the above process begins even as Beauvoir imaginatively reconstructs the scene of her mother's fall in the text's opening paragraph, drawing on witness statements of those who came to her aid. Here one detail stands out which already opens tellingly to care. Her mother was found lying on the floor 'dans sa robe de chambre rouge en velours cotelé' [in her red corduroy dressing gown] (*MD*, 14; *ED*, 9). Within the tableau of personal devastation being constructed by Beauvoir, a tableau through which she at once holds at bay and begins to nudge empathically into the suffering of her mother, this detail has an equivalent narrative force and emotional impact to the punctum that pricks and wounds Roland Barthes as he surveys selected photographs. Does it matter, after all, which dressing gown her mother was wearing? The red dressing gown is redundant, except as a spur to proximity and a marker of solicitude. Beauvoir seems to be inviting us to consider the feel of corduroy next to the skin, a softness perhaps countering the blow or the coldness of the bathroom floor; it is as if enrobing her mother in it once more via the text were a gesture of protection, of gentleness. The daughter will come to detest this garment, which hangs uselessly in the hospital cupboard and which will not be worn again.

One further important perspective on the labour of care in *Une mort très douce* is its relationship to Beauvoir's subsequent ground-breaking work on the marginalisation of older people both in *La Vieillesse* (1970) [*Coming of Age*] and in the interconnected documentary film made with Marianne Ahrne *Promenade au pays de la vieillesse* (1974) [*A Walk in the Country of Old Age*]. In the former, Beauvoir stands in more comfortable, scholarly relation to the 'scandalous' subject matter of ageing and care; the latter offers graphic and distressing depictions of the un-met need for care and gentleness in later life and of the inhumane regime of social care that prevailed in 1960s France. We may speculate that forced attentiveness to the micro-detail of the labour of late-life care as recorded in *Une mort très douce* was at least in part responsible for prompting these major, overarching critiques. Not only does her testimony prepare the ground for her determination to break society's 'conspiration du silence' [conspiracy of silence] about ageing; it also shows the emergence of her sharp personal awareness that ageing, vulnerability and the need for care are the common lot and that we need urgently to recognise our future selves in older people: 'Il le faut si nous voulons assumer dans sa totalité notre condition humaine' [It is essential if we are to assume our human condition in its totality].[20]

Ma mère rit

Chantal Akerman's phototext *Ma mère rit* is an intimate self-portrait that slides between loosely connected memories from different time periods, touches upon key relationships within and beyond Akerman's family and has at its core the evolving forms of dependency within a specific mother-daughter relationship, notably the practices of late-life care. As is customary, Akerman focuses on the quotidian and records, often without comment, the mundane incidents and interactions that constitute the stuff of life. If Beauvoir's narrative represents a coming to care and the seeping in of vulnerability, Akerman's is steeped in vulnerability and begins and ends in the thick of care's labours. Here the writing is spontaneous, focalised by the daughter as overwhelmed carer, driven by and saturated in affect and plunging us into the micro detail of everyday care without pausing to address us explicitly about the text's remit or contours. While *Une mort très douce* is a carefully controlled, analytic and chronological account, *Ma mère rit* is immersive, fragile, reiterative, temporally unmoored and entirely bound up in the unrelenting problematic of care. In *Enduring Time*, Baraitser observes that caring requires habituating ourselves to a temporal regime made up of 'modes of waiting, staying, delaying, enduring, persisting, repeating, maintaining, preserving and remaining — that produce felt experiences of time *not passing*'.[21] Caught up in the suspended time of care, *Ma mère rit* is entirely consistent with Baraitser's contention.

The text begins with a rush of present-tense observations made by the author during several winter days when she comes to stay with and help care for her eighty-five-year-old mother in the run up to the latter's heart operation. Although she is making a good recovery from a previous operation, Natalia Akerman is in constant pain from a broken shoulder and sharply aware of her own frailty and mortality. Throughout the text we see her catapulted into various new situations of care, including a protracted period in hospital following a pulmonary embolism. Increasingly incapacitated, she can no longer wash or dress herself, or prepare her own food. Her Brussels flat sees the comings and goings of an array of women, some from social services, some family friends, who form part of a network of long-term formal and informal care. Such care is regarded as the only viable solution by the author who protests vehemently when the possibility of a care home is mooted: 'il n'en est pas question. Ma mère, ce sac d'os, se sent encore une personne et pour elle, les seigneureries, c'est pour se débarrasser des gens, c'est pour les gens qui attendent la mort' (*MMR*, 68–69) [it's out of the question. My mother, this bag of bones, still feels herself to be a person and for her, care homes are for getting rid of people, for people who are waiting to die]. For family carers such as Akerman, part of the labour of care entails negotiating the competing needs of carer and cared-for and establishing an equilibrium whereby care is not so all-consuming that it overrides the imperative of self-care. This tension is foregrounded and exacerbated in *Ma mère rit* for the author too is fragile: 'je prends plein de médicaments, je suis obligée à cause de ma maladie chronique et de mes insomnies' (*MMR*, 185) [I take loads of medication, I have to because of my chronic illness and my insomnia]. Psychologically and emotionally vulnerable, she feels ill-equipped for the labour required of her and her already fragile sense of stability is further imperilled by her mother's needs. Akerman's exposed and raw account exemplifies the difficult labour of boundary negotiation, repeatedly rehearsing the challenges of gentleness as the multiple ways in which mother and daughter are entwined in attempts at mutual care complicate the care scenario. Dufourmantelle notes: 'la bonne distance qu'invente la douceur permet à chacun d'exister dans son propre espace; elle est le contraire de l'effraction' [the right distance as invented by gentleness allows everyone to exist within his or her own space; it is the opposite of intrusion] (*PD*, 122; *PG*, 87). Yet this immersive mother-child relationship makes such invention exceptionally challenging. Helping to dress her mother, for instance, is not neutral for the daughter; instead, she fleetingly recalls the thrill when, as a child bedazzled by her mother's loveliness, she helped zip up one of her beautiful dresses. The right distance is hard to find, let alone sustain. The text often focuses, performatively, on the daughter's struggle to attain it while providing the consistency of care, most especially emotional care, that her mother requires.

One notable characteristic of this text is that it is constructed not only around what the author does to help, sustain and heal, but also by numerous instances of the withdrawal of care, producing a Fort-Da rhythm in her engagement with her mother. Akerman notes the vicious cycle produced by the latter's palpable anxiety: as this emotion is contaminating, family carers need to detach themselves from it, yet such detachment produces a sense of disconnection that leaves her feeling 'qu'on la traite comme un meuble' (*MMR*, 93) [that she is being treated like a piece of furniture], which in turn heightens her own anxiety. The phenomenon is intensified in interactions with Akerman: when the care assistants arrive, she notes, her mother stops groaning: 'Elle réserve ça pour moi' (*MMR*, 66) [she reserves that for me]. A repeated complaint from mother to daughter is 'tu me fuis' [you're avoiding me]. Such avoidance is often connected to writing, an act manifestly linked to care and explicitly presented as a form of self-care. Each of Akerman's scrambling, associative notations is a *point de repère* helping to hold together self and world in momentary respite from her mother's invasive needs: 'Quand j'écris j'entends moins ses gémissements' (*MMR*, 63) [When I am writing I don't hear her moaning as much]. The labour of attention entailed in writing is salvific, providing the carer with an activity that, while related to care, is also apart from care, differently immersive, and that allows her to record her own, competing need for care.

The upbeat title of Akerman's text, *Ma mère rit*, not only underscores the mother's ongoing capacity for pleasure, but the author's determination to affirm this capacity. It also denotes listening as integral to care. Akerman's recording of speech, laughter, sighs, moans and the regularity or raggedness of breathing allude to listening as an important way of taking the emotional and physical pulse of her mother's well-being and needs. Dufourmantelle explicitly connects gentleness and listening. She focuses on listening in the psychoanalytic encounter, wherein the analyst 'essaie d'*entendre* autrement' [tries to *hear* differently] (*PD*, 111; *PG*, 79), but her thoughts are also relevant to the labour of care. How should a carer listen? In part, through relinquishing the urgency and goal-driven imperatives that typically characterise our relationship to time, giving the self over to a free-floating attention to 'celui qui [...] parle, se plaint, souffre, s'essoufle' [the one who is speaking, complaining, suffering, faltering] (*PD*, 111; *PG*, 79) and to the nuances arising from tone, hesitations and tics. Listening as care and remaining open to what is un-articulated and un-translatable, is a strain for the author. Akerman's mother's utterances are important indicators, but they are also intrusive: 'Elle gémit à intervalles réguliers. Sans cesse [...] Elle gémit. Si seulement ses gémissements pouvaient s'arrêter' (*MMR*, 178) [She moans at regular intervals. Incessantly [...] She moans. If only her moaning could stop], as is her intensifying requirement for communication: 'Moi j'adore parler. Oui, je sais maman' (*MMR*, 182) [I love talking. Yes, I know Mum]. For the taciturn daughter, reluctant to talk about her own life, this dimension of care is a struggle and results in protracted negotiations. A further dimension of care's labour entails conceding to narrative practice *as* care, through articulating and ordering the mother's illness: 'Ma mère demandait sans arrêt des détails sur ce qui lui était arrivé' (*MMR*, 98) [My mother was perpetually asking for details of what had happened to her], reminding us that re-establishing the order of events as part of care, as well as assuring that 'tu te remettras' (*MMR*, 95) [you will recover] may be integral to a positive outcome. Strategies of communicative kindness, such as exploring what can be easily shared (making a shopping list together is a recurring example) are also integral to care.

Ultimately, however, *Ma mère rit* says as much about the failure of care, the need for care unmet and the tussle with the all-consuming nature of care as it does about care's labours. One of the empathic observations which see Akerman imaginatively inhabiting her mother's position as dependent contrasts her rational appraisal of the care her mother receives with knowledge of her emotional sense of abandonment. While knowing that Akerman's sister, for example, is doing 'tout ce qu'il faut pour la garder en vie à n'importe quel prix' (*MMR*, 107) [everything necessary to keep her alive at any cost], there is a deficit in terms of being listened to and above all in terms of physical contact: 'et c'est surtout ça dont ma mère a envie et besoin, qu'on la serre contre son propre corps et qu'ainsi elle s'oublie ou le contraire, qu'elle se sente exister' (*MMR*, 107) [and it is above all this that my mother wants and needs, to be held closely by another body and thus to forget herself, or conversely to feel that she exists]. This fleeting observation abruptly asks us to revisit touch as integral to care. It reads as the culmination of the text's many passing mentions of how Akerman's mother has been supported, washed or manipulated into her clothes. It reminds us that touch, as integral to care's labour, must be more than functional and not collude in reducing the cared-for person to their sickness, frailty or advanced age.

A further distinguishing feature of care as explored in *Ma mère rit* is its wholescale alertness to vulnerability. In an important episode, both mother and daughter widen our perspective on the need for care, discussing how their attention is drawn to it by the mattresses they see lying in doorways or on pavements in their respective cities (Brussels and New York). Both express concern for what these material signs imply in terms of living conditions, and imaginatively inhabit the physical and emotional experience of homelessness and dispossession evidenced in the stark materiality of these makeshift beds. What, asks Akerman's mother, should the individual do in the face of such yawning need for care? Briefly, she considers inviting destitute people into her home. After all, her flat is roomy. Mother and daughter share stories of how they ultimately glance away, overwhelmed by this evidence of human need and of the fragile fabric of care provision. This glancing away is a distinguishing feature too of the images that punctuate Akerman's text. Their overarching quality of discretion, their focus on the mundane, their obliqueness and what they imply about the woman who took them are eloquent on the issues of both care and care-avoidance, although there is not space to pursue such analysis in detail here.

The testimonies briefly examined in this chapter offer powerful examples of a growing determination, especially on the part of women writers, to attend to the minutiae of late-life care in their work. A wider study would assess other extraordinary testimonies such as Noëlle Châtelet's *La Dernière Leçon* [The Final Lesson], or Hélène Cixous's *Homère est morte* [Mother Homer is Dead (The Frontiers of Theory)].[22] My analysis constitutes a small gesture towards mapping the evolution of this determination. Reading *Une mort très douce* and *Ma mère rit* explicitly for care helps us to re-valorise the marginalised and hidden labour of care, to reclaim the practical, emotional and ethical intricacies of day-to-day care as viable literary subjects, to calibrate as we read our own capacity to engage in care's labour, and to reinforce one of care theory's most important messages: the need for enhanced attentiveness to vulnerability as a universal human characteristic. My tentative thinking with Dufourmantelle's idea of gentleness points to a further dimension of care theory: the layered complexity of care as a term, and the need to tease out explicitly what it encompasses by focusing on the specific and slippery forms of yielding and resistance that effective care requires.

Notes to Chapter 11

1. Madeleine Bunting, *Labours of Love: The Crisis of Care* (London: Granta, 2020), p. 58.
2. Lisa Baraitser, *Enduring Time* (London: Bloomsbury, 2017), p. 2.
3. Bunting, *Labours of Love*, p. 4.
4. Simone de Beauvoir, *Une mort très douce* (Paris: Gallimard, 1964) (hereafter referenced as *MD* in main text); *A Very Easy Death*, trans. by Patrick O'Brian (New York: Pantheon Books, 1965) (hereafter referenced as *ED* in main text). Chantal Akerman, *Ma mère rit* (Paris: Mercure de France, 2013) (hereafter referenced as *MMR* in main text). All translations in this chapter are my own unless stated otherwise.
5. Annie Ernaux, *Je ne suis pas sortie de ma nuit* (Paris: Gallimard, 1997), p. 29.
6. Sandra Laugier, 'The Ethics of Care as a Politics of the Ordinary', *New Literary History*, 46.2 (2015), 217–40.
7. Cynthia Fleuri, *Le Soin est un humanisme* (Paris: Gallimard, 2019), p. 5.
8. Fabienne Brugère, *Le sexe de la sollicitude* (Paris: Seuil, 2008), p. 14.
9. Alexandre Gefen, *Réparer le monde: la littérature française face au XXIe siècle* (Paris: Éditions Corti, 2017).
10. Régine Detambel, *Les Livres prennent soin de nous: pour une bibliothérapie créative* (Paris: Babel, 2017).
11. *The Care (Re)Turn in Contemporary French and Francophone Cultural Production*, ed. by Loïc Bourdeau, Natalie Edwards and Steven Wilson (= special issue of *Australian Journal of French Studies*, 57.3 (2020)).

12. Anne Dufourmantelle, *Puissance de la douceur* (Paris: Payot & Rivages, 2013) (hereafter referenced as *PD* in main text); *Power of Gentleness: Meditations on the Risk of Living*, trans. by Katherine Payne and Vincent Sallé (New York: Fordham University Press, 2018) (hereafter referenced as *PG* in main text).
13. Maurice Hamington, *Embodied Care: Jane Addams, Maurice Merleau-Ponty and Feminist Ethics* (Champaign: University of Illinois Press, 2004), p. 36.
14. Geneviève Fraisse, *Service ou servitude: essai sur les femmes toutes mains* (Paris: Seuil, 2021), pp. 15–28.
15. For example, Jordan McCullough, 'Bien accompagner la fin de vie: Medical, Religious and Spiritual *accompagnement* in Simone de Beauvoir's *Une mort très douce*', in *The Care (Re)Turn in Contemporary French and Francophone Cultural Production*, ed. by Bourdeau, Edwards and Wilson, pp. 365–80.
16. By Fabienne Brugère in 'L'Heure bleue', France Culture, 19 October 2020 <https://www.franceinter.fr/emissions/l-heure-bleue/l-heure-bleue-19-octobre-2020> [accessed November 2021].
17. See Simone de Beauvoir, *Tout compte fait* (Paris: Gallimard, 1978), p. 168.
18. Terry Keefe, *Simone de Beauvoir: A Study of her Writings* (London: Harrap, 1983), pp. 57–58.
19. Ibid., p. 57.
20. Simone de Beauvoir, *La Vieillesse* (Paris: Gallimard, 1970), pp. 8, 12; *Coming of Age*, trans. by Patrick O'Brian (New York: W. W. Norton, 1996).
21. Baraitser, *Enduring Time*, p. 2.
22. Noëlle Châtelet, *La Dernière Leçon* (Paris: Seuil, 2004); Hélène Cixous, *Homère est morte* (Paris: Galilée, 2014); *Mother Homer is Dead (The Frontiers of Theory)*, trans. by Peggy Kamuf (Edinburgh: Edinburgh University Press, 2020).

CHAPTER 12

Proustian Afterlives: Paolo Sorrentino's *La grande bellezza* (2013)

Marion Schmid

To compare Paolo Sorrentino's Oscar-winning *La grande bellezza* [*The Great Beauty*] (2013) to Proust's *A la recherche du temps perdu* (1913–27) may seem far-fetched, if not downright sacrilegious. What does Sorrentino's garish portrayal of Rome's *bella gente* in the wake of the Berlusconi era have to do with Proust's vast fresco of French life from the Belle Époque to World War I and its aftermath? Where, beyond superficial commonalities, is the connection between an Italian art film satirising the frivolous pursuits of the city's decadent elites and Proust's minute dissection of privilege, class and artistic taste? What is there to link Sorrentino's dandyish protagonist Jep Gambardella (Toni Servillo) to the extraordinarily introspective Narrator of *A la recherche*? And, not to forget artistic form, in what ways might a postmodern director renowned for his hyper-aestheticising, glossy style be considered an heir to Proust's elegant, sinuous prose?

Sorrentino's sixth feature, the visually and aurally sumptuous *La grande bellezza* met with immediate international success at its release in 2013. Crowned with the Academy Award for Best Foreign Language Film and numerous other prizes, the film has been praised for its acerbic critique of Roman high society, even if the director's apolitical stance and predilection for spectacular images are often criticised in his native Italy.[1] In the complex landscape of contemporary Italian cinema, Sorrentino's film stands out as a postmodern successor to the work of Antonioni, Scola and Fellini, whose famous portraits of Rome during the post-war economic miracle traced the emergence of what Guy Debord has termed the 'society of the spectacle'.[2] Sorrentino's self-acknowledged affinity with Fellini in particular reverberates throughout the film in its combination of realism and illusionism, flirtation with the grotesque and the oneiric, as well as its many nods to the great Italian director: note, for instance, Jep's evocation of the sea monster from the closing sequence of *La dolce vita* (1960) in a playful dialogue with his partner Ramona (Sabrina Ferilli); his failed attempt to talk to a mysterious neighbour while sharing the lift, which recalls the scene in *8½* (1963) where Guido Anselmi (Marcello Mastroianni) tries to strike up a conversation with the entourage of a bishop; or the surreal procession of prelates parading in front of a missionary nun, reminiscent of the ecclesiastical fashion parade in *Roma* (1972).³ Beyond its rich filmic intertextuality, *La grande bellezza* also extensively references modern literature from Flaubert to Breton, Pirandello and Moravia, not to forget a quotation from Céline's *Voyage au bout de la nuit* at the start of the film. Indeed, not only are intertextuality and intermediality ubiquitous in Sorrentino's films, but as essential features of the director's aesthetic, they afford a deeper understanding of his work.⁴

Given the centrality of intermediality to Sorrentino's cinematic strategies, it is surprising that few commentators so far seem to have noted *La grande bellezza*'s sustained engagement with another key modern author, Proust, all the more so since the film offers us some repeated hints.⁵ The first reference to the author of *A la recherche du temps perdu* occurs nine minutes into the story, during the lengthy sequence of Jep's birthday party, whose decadent excess and flamboyant visuality set the tone for the rest of the film. A budding stage actress and a television actor flirtatiously converse about their current projects: 'Io mi dedico al mio primo romanzo, una cosa proustiana' [I'll write my first novel, a Proust-style piece], she boasts, to which he responds a not very credible 'Sai che Proust è il mio scrittore preferito?' [Really? Proust is my favourite writer!], upon which the two walk off together, much to the chagrin of the actress's aspiring boyfriend.⁶ The use of Proust as a chat-up line here is ironically emblematic of the self-promoting trend-setters that traverse Sorrentino's film, not dissimilar to one of the characters describing her new hair colour as 'Pirandelloesque' in a comic confusion between the playwright and the Renaissance painter Pisanello. A darker reference to Proust is made halfway through the film, when Andrea (Luca Marinelli), the mentally unstable son of one of Jep's friends, confides in him, 'Proust scrive che la morte potrebbe coglierci questo pomeriggio. Mette paura Proust. Non domani, non tra un anno, ma questo stesso pomeriggio, scrive' [Proust says that death may come to us this afternoon. Proust is scary. Not tomorrow, not in a year, but this afternoon, he writes]. Trying to calm him down, the socialite replies, 'Non li prendere troppo sul serio questi scrittori' [Don't take these writers so seriously], only to be scolded, 'Se non prendo sul serio Proust chi prendo sul serio?' [If I don't take Proust seriously, who should I?]. Taking Proust seriously or not, then, becomes a question that divides the characters into, on the one hand, name-dropping hedonists and, on the other, true readers of literature grappling with the fragility of human existence. In a bitter afternote to the conversation, only a few scenes later, Andrea perishes in a suicidal car crash, while Ramona, who had listened to the young man's words with visible emotion, succumbs to an incurable illness.

But Proust provides more than just a barometer of the characters' interiority and an indicator of their destiny in *La grande bellezza*. Beyond the postmodern game of citation that Sorrentino shares with directors such as Godard, Tarantino or Greenaway, the film ties an intricate web of relations with the Proustian universe, that manifests at the level of its themes, as well as its wider narrative structure and aesthetic. In what follows, I want to investigate the diffuse, often subterranean, ways in which Sorrentino draws on Proustian tropes and figures, actualising a modernist heritage which, like the Italian cinema that precedes him, constitutes an important reference point in his work. It is helpful to draw on the director's own attitude with regard to artistic influence to refine the approach that will govern this chapter. Questioned about the impact of Fellini on *La grande bellezza*, Sorrentino answers cautiously:

> *Roma* and *La Dolce Vita* are works that you cannot pretend to ignore when you take on a film like the one I wanted to make. They are two masterpieces, and the golden rule is that masterpieces should be watched but not imitated. I tried to stick to that. But it's also true that masterpieces transform the way we feel and perceive things. They condition us, despite ourselves. So I can't deny that those films are indelibly stamped on me and may have guided my film.[7]

Similarly, what will interest me here is not so much the question of any direct influence, but, rather, that of the mark left by Proust on a film that was released exactly one hundred years after the publication of the first volume of *A la recherche*. In other words, what is at stake here is to trace a Proustian afterlife in a work that gravitates around a strikingly different temporal, cultural and social context and is, above all, shaped in a different medium.

The Perils of *mondanità*

La grande bellezza centres on an ageing Roman socialite, Jep Gambardella, who idles away his time at parties when he is not writing articles for a magazine devoted to celebrity culture and fashionable art events. Connected to everybody who's anybody, Jep is the self-pronounced 're dei mondani' [the king of the high life], a cultural trend-setter who is not only in demand at the most exclusive gatherings, but decides who is 'in' and who isn't. Having come to Rome from his native Naples aged twenty-six, the protagonist has, in his own words, fallen into 'il vortice della mondanità' [the whirlpool of the high life]. A talented writer, who won critical acclaim for his first and only novel, *L'apparato umano* [The Human Apparatus], he has not written anything serious for forty years, having let himself become absorbed in mundane distractions. Loosely organised into episodes, the film unravels to the festivities of a medley crowd of (pseudo-)celebrities: heiresses, artists, media tsars, wannabe stars, plus, *Rome oblige*, a *papabile* more disposed to the pleasures of gastronomy than questions of spirituality.

The overarching theme of *mondanità*, the love of society life, instantly places *La grande bellezza* in the tradition of Proust, who, from his first book *Les Plaisirs et les jours* [Pleasures and Days], warned of the dangers of social dissipation for the aspiring artist. If, according to Albert Sbragia, Jep is 'a throwback to the dandies and flâneurs of an earlier age of aristocratic leisure', his idle lifestyle is also reminiscent of the Proustian Narrator, who similarly compromises his literary vocation in rubbing shoulders with the upper classes — and let us not forget that Proust himself started out as a newspaper chronicler of high society gatherings.[8] In the mode of late capitalism, the wild parties, select dinners and trendy art events of Jep's social set recall the Belle Époque salons of the Verdurins or the Guermantes, equally prone, as the Narrator discovers to his disappointment, to vulgar chit-chat and the

Fig. 12.1. Jep Gambardella (Toni Servillo), 'il re dei mondani'
(*La grande bellezza*, dir. by Paolo Sorrentino, 2013)

absurd rites of social comedy.[9] Where Proust's novel, spanning a period of some fifty years, from the Third Republic to the early 1920s, traced the decline of the aristocracy and ultimate triumph of the bourgeoisie, in Sorrentino's film set in the immediate aftermath of the Berlusconi era, social distinction — once linked to titles, history and habitus — has long been replaced by the short-lived fashions of 'in-ness'. Beautiful people and wannabe celebrities brashly posture as the new elites, while elderly aristocrats are furtively glimpsed playing cards in their *palazzi* or, in one particularly emblematic scene, hired to impersonate another couple at a dinner party. Sorrentino's garish pop video aesthetic, restless (ever zooming, tilting or swirling) camera, fast editing and eclectic sound track give audio-visual expression to the obsession with visibility and mediatic notoriety of a society where, to paraphrase Debord, *having* has declined into merely *appearing*.[10]

When asked by Ramona why he didn't write another novel, Jep blames the distractions of Rome for his lack of productivity, his words 'scrivere richiede molta concentrazione, tanta calma' [writing requires focus and peace], resonating with Proust's famous dictum 'les vrais livres doivent être les enfants non du grand jour et de la causerie, mais de l'obscurité et du silence' [real books should be the offspring not of daylight and casual talk but of darkness and silence].[11] Yet, as he himself comments ironically, his sensitivity to sensory impressions makes him stand out among his superficial entourage: 'Ero destinato alla sensibilità. Ero destinato a diventare uno scrittore' [I was destined to sensibility. I was destined to become a writer]. In its narrative construction, the film juxtaposes the protagonist's social dissipations with quieter moments, when he takes solitary strolls across the city or observes life from the seclusion of his terrace. Cinematographer Luca Bigazzi's vertiginously mobile camera relaxes into a more contemplative pace here, in tune with Jep's absorption into the sights, sounds and textures of Rome. Point-of-view shots immerse us in his tactile, visual and aural experiences as he refreshes himself in a fountain, watches a nun picking oranges in the lush cloister of a monastery or observes a flock of birds swirling in the sky. With their rich soundscape of gushing water, chirping birds and the chatter of children at play, scenes such as these capture the sensory pleasures of more secret parts of the city, afforded to the solitary *flâneur*.

Throughout the film, Sorrentino pits two strikingly different visions of Rome: on the one hand, the commodified eternal city, infamous 'seat of the debased and banalised image regime of our contemporary society of the spectacle'; on the other, a more secret, magical Rome that offers itself to those who are sensitive to its hidden charms.[12] As is ironically hinted at in the opening scene, where a tourist suffers a heart attack while photographing the celebrated view of the city from the Janiculum, Rome's beauty is impossible to capture in images. Its sublime vistas elude the facile consumption favoured by neo-capitalism. Yet, beneath its glossy, post-card-like images of famous monuments and sites, *La grande bellezza* offers glimpses of genuine 'great beauty', most poetically so in the sequence where Jep and Ramona are taken on a private nocturnal tour to some of the city's most arresting sites, thanks to a friend who holds their (symbolic) keys. Consisting of a montage of several locations, the sequence begins with the famous view of St Peter's Basilica through the Aventine keyhole — an optical reframing that hints at the different regime of vision that will be afforded here — before segueing into the artistic collections of the Capitoline Museums, Borromini's Baroque colonnade of the Palazzo Spada and the Renaissance gardens of the Villa Medici. As the trio wander through the rooms of the Musei Capitolini (presented as a private *palazzo* in the film), emerging from the darkness, Roman busts and sculptures seem to take on a life of their own, their solid forms given greater plasticity through a combination of tilting and zoom shots. The chiaroscuro effects created by the soft, flickering light of a candle chandelier endow the marble surfaces with a skin-like tactility. Inversely, Annachiara Mariani observes, Jep's 'head mingles with and petrifies among the sculptures of the Roman emperors' heads, creating the illusion that he is, in fact, becoming one of them'.[13] In stark contrast to Ramona, who seeks to capture, and thus commodify, this almost mystical experience in photographs, Jep is the only one who truly communicates with the artworks; yet, despite his manifest sensibility to art, he neither has the resolve nor the persistence to fix transient artistic impression into impermeable written form.

Finding Time Again

In Proustian fashion, the protagonist has to first undergo the painful experience of death and ageing before he can take stock of his life and confront the book that had lain dormant in him for so long. Tellingly, we first encounter Jep during a rooftop party on the Via Veneto, one of the iconic sites of Fellini's *La dolce vita*, celebrating his sixty-fifth birthday. While this wild bacchanal, unravelling to the tunes of 1970s Eurotrash, seems worlds apart from the princesse de Guermantes's refined musical *matinée* in *Le Temps retrouvé*, a series of close-ups of the frenzied revellers, their faces distorted by lascivious grimaces or deep age lines, evokes the Proustian *bal de têtes*, where the aged appearance of old friends and acquaintances sensitises the Narrator to the destructive force of time, the close-up here becoming a cinematic equivalent to Proust's famously detailed descriptions. As Jep, framed centrally, comes into view among the dancers, his grey-haired, balding head and lined face contrast sharply with the youthful traits of the woman he kisses voraciously. In later scenes, we see him using beauty products and a belly belt to maintain his looks, though, in a candid moment, he confesses 'Mi sento vecchio' [I feel old].

Where the Proustian Narrator has to experience the deaths of his lover Albertine and friend Saint-Loup to shake him out of his stale, superficial existence, Jep, within a short amount of time, suffers the loss of two people with whom he had a close relationship. The day after his birthday, he learns of the death of his former girlfriend Elisa (Annaluisa Capasa), which prompts flashbacks of their romance some forty years earlier. Shortly thereafter, his new partner Ramona, with whom he had begun a caring relationship, succumbs to a mysterious illness. A highly elliptical sequence, reminiscent of the temporal compressions and ellipses of the Proustian narrative, alludes to Ramona's death without ever addressing it head-on. Her fate is foreshadowed by a disturbing circular take of her lying motionless on the bed, not responding to Jep's worried calls. An ominous close-up of her foot framed against a slowly closing window leads into a slow-motion scene of Jep, dressed in funereal black, in a working-class bar, one of the rare instances of working-class life in the film. To the elegiac sounds of Damien Jurado's folk song 'Everything Trying', a visibly stunned Jep makes his way through this dream-like space, when a strange-looking woman — half Fellini, half Tarantino — asks him in a voice reminiscent of Ramona: 'E ora chi si prende cura di te?' [Who's going to look after you now?]. The sequence ends with a montage of shots of Andrea's mother Viola (Pamela Villoresi) mourning her late son, Ramona's father (Massimo De Francovich) receiving the condolences of a friend and Jep looking down onto the wreckage of the Costa Concordia, all of which brutally convey the protagonist's predicament: 'Sta morendo tutto quello che mi sta intorno' [Everything around me is dying].[14]

In what is perhaps the most evidently Proustian borrowing in the film, the protagonist experiences a series of epiphanies that restore lost time to him. A first involuntary memory, rendered in strikingly cinematic terms, occurs as Jep muses about a conversation with Elisa's widower. Thanks to a digital trick, the ceiling of his bedroom morphs into a seascape, its screen-like surface — self-reflexively alluding to the cinema — serving as a portal to the past, as he relives the memory of a near-miss accident on the Isola del Giglio. We see the present-day Jep diving underwater to escape an approaching motorboat, before reappearing as his eighteen-year-old younger self (played by Flavio Mieli), applauded by a group of young women with at their centre Elisa. As the story unfolds, past and present (embodied by the two different actors) become increasingly intertwined and eventually merge. Thus, during an intimate conversation with Ramona, Jep reminisces of the night at the lighthouse when he first made love with Elisa, but gets so lost in thought that he stops halfway through his evocation. Extreme close-ups of his moved face, intercut with shots of the young lovers, offer another, more conventional, visualisation of the process of memory. Accompanied by Arvo Pärt's haunting musical setting of

FIG. 12.2. and 12.3. Jep, present (Toni Servillo) and past (Flavio Mieli) selves (*La grande bellezza*, dir. by Paolo Sorrentino, 2013)

Robert Burns's 'My Heart's in the Highlands', the scene is infused with a plaintive nostalgia, echoed in the 'Farewell' refrain of the lyrics. Heard again in a later, fuller flashback, 'the song, despite its cultural and musical specificity, becomes a kind of leitmotif for his [Jep's] character as he re-experiences his most formative experience in flashback-heightened memory'.[15]

In a turn of events that evokes the 'miracle' of *La dolce vita*, Jep's fulfilment of his literary vocation is precipitated through his burlesque meeting with a missionary, Sister Maria, called 'La Santa' (Giusi Merli). Like Ramona before her, Sister Maria asks why he never wrote another book, yet this time he replies more lucidly: 'Cercavo la grande bellezza, ma non l'ho trovata' [I was looking for great beauty, but I didn't find it]. Inscribed in the film's title, 'la grande bellezza' is emblematic of the protagonist's quest for an aesthetic ideal that is incompatible with his worldly lifestyle. Like the Proustian Narrator, who becomes aware of his vocation at a stage when he has lost faith in his creative powers, a final epiphany makes the protagonist realise that the material for his writing does not come from the outside, but needs to be found within himself. While reporting on the sinking of the Costa Concordia off the Isola del Giglio, the sight of the lighthouse triggers a final flashback. A sustained parallel editing juxtaposes Jep's remembrance of his first night of love with Elisa with Sister Maria painfully ascending the Scala Santa, that is, the steps which, according to Christian tradition, Christ climbed when he appeared before Pontius Pilate. In provocative fashion, then, and emphasised by the accompanying music, John Tavener's 'The Lamb', two types of passion are being confronted here: on the one hand, Christ's spiritual and physical suffering during the final stages of his Passion, emulated by pilgrims who ascend the Scala Santa; on the other, the sexual and amorous passion of the young couple. In this tortured analogy, Elisa's revealing of her breasts to the young Jep is likened to divine revelation, the re-found memory of their love leading not only to his spiritual redemption, but also to his rebirth as a writer. Problematic as this ending may be in its depiction of the dead woman as the 'eschatological force of his [the protagonist's] salvation' and its 'object-image of desire [...] so culturally *overcoded*, *nostalgic* and *banalised*', it is not without irony, conveyed in visual terms by the cross-cutting between kitschy images of the young lovers haloed by the rays of the lighthouse and extreme close-ups of Sister Maria's wrinkled face beaming with spiritual ecstasy.[16]

Though markedly different from Proust in tone and style, the final sequence recalls *A la recherche du temps perdu* in its articulation of an aesthetic programme that announces the *œuvre* to come: a voice-over monologue delivered by the present-day Jep, standing in the exact place where we previously saw his younger self, outlines a poetics which *La grande bellezza* 'invites us to interpret [...] as the film's own'.[17] Reminiscent of *A la recherche*'s circular *mise en abyme* structure, but also of Fellini's *8½* which similarly folds in on itself, the book Jep is finally going to write is none other than the film we have just seen.[18]

Art and Aesthetics

The doubling of the art work as a self-reflexive aesthetic treatise that underpins *A la recherche du temps perdu* and *La grande bellezza* finds its wider expression in both works in a sustained meditation on the nature and function of art. Stretching from medieval painting and architecture via Rembrandt, Vermeer and the Impressionists to Wagner and the Ballets Russes — to name only some of the cornerstones of his *œuvre* — the Proustian novel offers a dazzling panorama of artistic creation. Referenced, woven into metaphors or transformed into ekphrastic word pictures, painting, music, literature and the performing arts are omnipresent in *A la recherche*, with the influence of imaginary artists such as Bergotte, Vinteuil and Elstir playing a crucial role in the development of the Narrator's artistic sensibility. If these artists impart to the Narrator lessons on the importance of vision and style in the creation of a work of art — indeed, on style as a direct expression 'non de technique, mais de vision' [not of technique, but of vision] (*RTP*, IV, 474; *SLT*, VI, 254) — they are also instrumental to Proust's investigation of artistic fashions and tastes, which, like the shifting dynamics of power and class, are central to the novel's enquiry. Thus, in the later volumes, we see the writer Bergotte, once dismissed as a 'joueur de flûte' [a flute-player] (*RTP*, I, 464; *SLT*, II, 51) by the pompous Marquis de Norpois, attain the greatest glory (*RTP*, III, 141; *SLT*, IV, 165); the composer Vinteuil, quasi unknown in his lifetime, is hailed as one of the greatest contemporary musicians (*RTP*, III, 263; *SLT*, IV, 309); and the paintings of Elstir, formerly detested by Mme de Guermantes, are acquired by the Musée du Luxembourg (*RTP*, III, 905; *SLT*, V, 462). For Proust, as evidenced by the changing fortunes of these artists, 'tout art véritable est classique, mais les lois de l'esprit permettent rarement qu'il soit, à son apparition, reconnu pour tel' [all true art is classical, but the laws of the mind rarely allow it to be recognised as such when it appears].[19]

Yet, while *A la recherche* demonstrates that it is only a matter of time before the public appreciates truly original art, the novel also cautions against poseurs and dilettantes, whose antics are not to be confused with genuine art. As a breeding ground for the avant-garde, the Verdurin salon is particularly ambivalent in this respect: it has nurtured the great Elstir, but also harbours mediocrities such as the sculptor Ski, an Elstir 'en moins bien' [a less satisfactory version] who 'peignait tout ce qu'on voulait, sur des boutons de manchette ou sur les dessus de porte' [would paint anything you asked, on cuff-links or on lintels] and 'passait pour merveilleusement intelligent, mais ses idées se ramenaient en réalité à deux ou trois, extrêmement courtes' [was regarded as being marvellously intelligent, but as a matter of fact his ideas boiled down to two or three, extremely limited] (*RTP*, III, 266–67; *SLT*, IV, 314). Having become princesse de Guermantes by marriage, the former Mme Verdurin facilitates the second-class actress Rachel's triumph over the great Berma, yet her protégée's gestural excesses and extravagant intonations continue to provoke politely concealed hilarity (*RTP*, IV, 577; *SLT*, VI, 388). Not easily fooled by short-lived fashions, in the theoretical reflection about art contained in 'Matinée chez la Princesse de Guermantes' the Narrator derides a type of criticism that puts superficial mannerisms before true talent (*RTP*, IV, 472; *SLT*, VI, 251–52). To the self-promoted, modish artist he opposes the true creator, who alters the way in which we perceive the world:

> Grâce à l'art, au lieu de voir un seul monde, le nôtre, nous le voyons se multiplier, et autant qu'il y a d'artistes originaux, autant nous avons de mondes à notre disposition, plus différents les uns des autres que ceux qui roulent dans l'infini. (*RTP*, IV, 474)
>
> [Thanks to art, instead of seeing one world only, our own, we see that world multiply itself, and have at our disposal as many worlds as there are original artists, worlds more different one from another than those which revolve in infinite space.] (*SLT*, VI, 254)

In a twenty-first century context, *La grande bellezza* shares with *A la recherche* a similar interrogation of what constitutes true originality in the arts, forming part of its larger inquiry into the nature, and pitfalls, of 'great beauty'. In one of the film's recurrent thematic tropes, Sorrentino weighs the enduring classical art of

Fig. 12.4. The child performance artist Carmelina (Francesca Amodio) (*La grande bellezza*, dir. by Paolo Sorrentino, 2013)

Rome — valorised by the spectacular camera work — against the ephemerality of a certain type of performance or body art. Some twenty minutes into the narrative, the camera cuts from shots of a novice, wearing a white veil, playing tag with children in a cloister to children dressed in angel costumes veiling the head of the otherwise-naked concept artist Talia Concept (Anita Kravos), in preparation for her head-butting run against the ruins of the Appian Aqueduct. Recalling the opening scene of *La dolce vita*, where a helicopter transports a statue of Christ over the Parco degli Acquedotti, the juxtaposition of 'true' and 'false' religious imagery here demystifies the performance as a fake: the artist's vacuous talk is subsequently taken apart in Jep's art column and her trickery involving foam rubber exposed by his editor. More sinister, at a fashionable art dealer's party, we see the child prodigy Carmelina (Francesca Amodio) being forced by her mercenary parents to perform for a group of invitees. A grotesque mixture of Jackson Pollock's drip paintings and Hermann Nitsch's *Schüttbilder* [Poured Paintings], her action consists in flinging pots of paint against a white canvas before aggressively rubbing the colour into the surface with her body. The girl's frenzied motion, distraught cries and fragile adolescent figure dripping with paint ask urgent questions about the ethical limits of performance, and about spectators' perverse complicity with child exploitation. The only person who is genuinely disturbed by Carmelina's tears is Ramona — a stripper by profession, who knows what it means to commodify the body — yet Jep cynically reassures her that 'la ragazzina guadagna milioni' [the girl earns millions].

In one of the film's many ironic twists, even the Fellini-esque ceremony where religious dignitaries of all confessions pay their homage to 'La Santa' has a distinct performance-like character. The parallel montage of shots of dignitaries walking up to the missionary and onlookers watching her every move for signs of her (dis-)approval creates a sense of acute anticipation, indeed risk, heightened by close-ups of Sister Maria's outstretched hand and dangling feet. Emphasis is laid on the bodily actions of the 'saint', whose public appearances are managed by an assistant, resembling an art agent, who speaks on her behalf. While the *papabile* passes the test, a Greek Orthodox dignitary mysteriously falls to the ground after kissing her hand, and a representative of the Jacobite Syrian church is symbolically ostracised by the thunderous sound of her dropped sandal. The question of what is authentic and what is fake, who exploits whom and for what purpose, is further complicated in a surreal scene on Jep's terrace where a flamboyance of flamingos have flocked around the 'saint', before being blown away by her 'holy' breath. Is this a miracle or just another trick? Albert Sbragia notes astutely:

> In the secularisation of the society of the spectacle, miracles lose their status as 'supernatural mysteries' of faith and transcendence; they yield to the magic trick, 'technological' enchantments that are ephemeral simulations, signs detached from depth, existing solely at the surface.[20]

Indeed, here, the garish colours and magnified sound effects of the digitally created 'fake' image ironically foreground the apparatus behind cinematic 'miracle'-making.

But where does all of this leave us with regard to Proust's and Sorrentino's aesthetics and their respective visions as artists? As Hugues Azérad reminds us, Proust's seeming predilection for classicism should not blind us to the resolutely modernist aesthetic that underpins his writing. Not only was Proust well aware of the early twentieth-century avant-gardes that transformed the art world, but, in its emphasis on perception, time and perspectivism, the revolution in writing he ushered in shares a strong affinity with the two most prominent movements of the time: Cubism and Futurism.[21] The importance accorded to temporality — 'the fourth dimension' of Cubist painters — in *A la recherche*, its self-reflexive structure which draws attention to writing itself, and the emphasis on vision and sensation place the novel firmly in the camp of European Modernism. Likewise, if Sorrentino derides a certain type of performance art that colludes with the society of the spectacle, he is not averse to contemporary art as such, as is evidenced by Jep's reviewing of a photographic installation, which leaves him deeply moved. As the protagonist slowly walks along a wall of photographs, made up of portraits capturing every single day in the artist's life, point-of-view shots of these images, ranging from early childhood to middle age, unravel before our eyes like a motion picture. In another instance of self-reflexivity in the film, the photographs not only allude to the art of cinema, grounded in the single frame, but gesture towards an implicit manifesto for a cinematic art of temporality. Seeing them unfold one after the other in a poignant visualisation of the self's inexorable journey through time, we are reminded of Proust's famous metaphor of people as 'des géants plongés dans les années à des époques, vécues par eux si distantes, entre lesquelles tant de jours sont venus se placer' [like giants plunged into the years, they touch the distant epochs through which they have lived, between which so many days have come to range themselves] (*RTP*, IV, 625; *SLT*, VI, 451).

More explicitly, *La grande bellezza* resonates with *A la recherche* in its setting out of an, albeit rather rambling, poetics in Jep's final monologue. His realisation that the purpose of writing is above all to excavate genuine human experience and affect beneath 'il chiacchiericcio e il rumore' [the chitter chatter and the noise] echoes the Proustian endeavour to cut through superficial social life to convey the deeper essences of our experience. Like the Proustian Narrator, who realises that even the most insignificant episodes of our life can become the source of creation, Sorrentino's protagonist eventually rejects the elusive 'grande bellezza' he had been striving for in favour of 'gli sparuti, incostanti sprazzi di bellezza' [the haggard, inconstant splashes of beauty]. Albert Sbragia explains what is at stake in this final programmatic monologue:

> It is a modernist poetics, one that ascribes a depth model to the film, a breaking through the surface chatter and awkward banality of life to capture in the work of art the manifold truth, beauty, and suffering of the human condition. At the same time and paradoxically, Jep's words affirm the film's ironic postmodern poetics of re-enchantment, since, after all (as the camera focuses one final time on Elisa's face), it is just a *trick*.[22]

In the final analysis, then, Sorrentino seems to owe as much to the modernist Proust as he does to the magician Fellini. Echoing major Proustian tropes such as the conflict between *mondanité* and artistic vocation and resonating with the Proustian aesthetic of time, memory and perception, *La grande bellezza* also clearly inscribes itself in the lineage of Fellini, signalled not only in the many references to the Italian director, but in the film's wider espousal of cinema as an art of the spectacle. Perhaps there is no clearer hint at this indebtedness than the scene in the Baths of Caracalla — iconic site of Marcello's (Marcello Mastroianni) dance with Sylvia (Anita Ekberg) in *La dolce vita* — where a magician friend of Jep makes a giraffe disappear before his eyes, avowing that his performance is, of course, 'solo un trucco' [just a trick]. As in so many of Fellini's films, trickery and enchantment become the very means by which the inauthentic living of the society of the spectacle can be ironically unveiled.[23] Yet, if there is much that links these three artists, and to return to the interview with Sorrentino I quoted at the outset, the director in no way seeks to imitate Fellini, nor, for that matter, Proust. Richly intertextual and intermedial, Sorrentino is a '*post*modernist filmmaker in the most meaningful sense of one who comes *after* as the knowing heir to a rich cultural tradition — both in relation to cinema's own modernist period and also modernity per se'.[24] It is in this sense of an assumed 'after-ness' that radiates and remediates the works of the past, playfully making them present to new audiences, that we can truly speak of an 'afterlife'.

Notes to Chapter 12

1. While Sorrentino has been criticised for his apparent lack of political positioning, critics such as Russell J. A. Kilbourn and Millicent Marcus have sought to reclaim the director's postmodern aesthetic and pervasive irony as a form of political engagement. See Russell J. A. Kilbourn, *The Cinema of Paolo Sorrentino: Commitment to Style* (New York: Columbia University Press, 2020), p. 175, and Millicent Marcus, 'The Ironist and the Auteur: Post-realism in Paolo Sorrentino's *Il Divo*', *The Italianist*, 30.2 (2010), 245–57.
2. Guy Debord, *La Société du spectacle* (Paris: Gallimard, 1992). On the film's place in Italian film history, see Albert Sbragia, 'The Spectacular Commodification of Rome in Paolo Sorrentino's *La Grande Bellezza*', *The Italianist*, 40.2 (2020), 276–95 (pp. 278–79); Giuseppina Mecchia, 'Birds in the Roman Sky: Shooting for the Sublime in *La Grande Bellezza*', *Forum Italicum*, 50.1 (2016),

183–93 (p. 184), and Kilbourn, *The Cinema of Paolo Sorrentino*, p. 88.
3. See Sbragia, 'The Spectacular Commodification of Rome in Paolo Sorrentino's *La Grande Bellezza*', p. 290.
4. On the highly intermedial nature of Sorrentino's films more widely see Kilbourn, *The Cinema of Paolo Sorrentino*, pp. xxi–xxiii and *passim*.
5. Since the time of writing this chapter, another article which brings these two figures together has been published. See Enrico Palma, 'L'identità proustiana de *La grande bellezza*', *E|C: rivista dell'Associazione italiana di Studi Semiotici*, 33 (2021), 196–206.
6. I would like to thank my friend Loreta Gandolfi for her help with the transcription of the Italian dialogue. The translations are taken from the subtitles.
7. Gary Crowdus, 'In Search of "The Great Beauty": An Interview with Paolo Sorrentino', *Cineaste*, 39.2 (2014), 8–13 (p. 10).
8. Sbragia, 'The Spectacular Commodification of Rome in Paolo Sorrentino's *La Grande Bellezza*', p. 281.
9. For a rich assessment of this dimension of Proust's novel, see Edward J. Hughes, 'Proust and Social Spaces', in *The Cambridge Companion to Proust*, ed. by Richard Bales (Cambridge: Cambridge University Press, 2001), pp. 151–67.
10. Debord, *La Société du spectacle*, p. 22.
11. Marcel Proust, *À la recherche du temps perdu*, ed. by Jean-Yves Tadié, 4 vols, Bibliothèque de la Pléiade (Paris: Gallimard, 1987–89), IV, 476 (hereafter referenced as *RTP* in main text); *In Search of Lost Time*, trans. by C. K. Scott-Moncrieff and Terence Kilmartin, rev. by D. J. Enright, 6 vols (London: Vintage, 2000–02), VI, 257 (hereafter referenced as *SLT* in main text).
12. Sbragia, 'The Spectacular Commodification of Rome in Paolo Sorrentino's *La Grande Bellezza*', p. 278.
13. Annachiara Mariani, 'Experiencing Panismo in Sorrentino's *The Great Beauty*, *Youth* and *Loro*', *Italica*, 96.3 (2019), 481–505 (p. 488).
14. Sorrentino mobilises the Costa Concordia disaster, which claimed thirty-two lives, as a metaphor for personal loss as well as a potent allegory of Italy's ruin during the Berlusconi era. See Carlotta Fonzi Kliemann, 'Cultural and Political Exhaustion in Paolo Sorrentino's *The Great Beauty*', *Senses of Cinema*, 70 (2014) <https://www.sensesofcinema.com/2014/feature-articles/cultural-and-political-exhaustion-in-paolo-sorrentinos-the-great-beauty/> [accessed November 2021].
15. Kilbourn, *The Cinema of Paolo Sorrentino*, p. 99.
16. Ibid., p. 101; Sbragia, 'The Spectacular Commodification of Rome in Paolo Sorrentino's *La Grande Bellezza*', p. 292.
17. Sbragia, 'The Spectacular Commodification of Rome in Paolo Sorrentino's *La Grande Bellezza*', p. 292.
18. On the similarity with Fellini, see ibid.
19. Marcel Proust, 'Classicisme et romantisme', in *Contre Sainte-Beuve, précédé de Pastiches et mélanges et suivi de Essais et articles*, ed. by Pierre Clarac and Yves Sandre (Paris: Gallimard, 1971), pp. 617–18 (p. 617).
20. Sbragia, 'The Spectacular Commodification of Rome in Paolo Sorrentino's *La Grande Bellezza*', pp. 290–91.
21. Hugues Azérad, 'Paris and the Avant-garde', in *Marcel Proust in Context*, ed. by Adam Watt (Cambridge: Cambridge University Press, 2013), pp. 59–66. On Proust's relationship to the contemporary avant-gardes, see also Luzius Keller, 'Proust au-delà de l'impressionnisme', in *Proust et ses peintres*, ed. by Sophie Bertho (Amsterdam: Rodopi, 2000), pp. 57–70.
22. Sbragia, 'The Spectacular Commodification of Rome in Paolo Sorrentino's *La Grande Bellezza*', p. 292.
23. For a discussion of the spectacularisation of Fellini's cinema and its relation to *La grande bellezza* see Sbragia, 'The Spectacular Commodification of Rome in Paolo Sorrentino's *La Grande Bellezza*', pp. 279–81.
24. Kilbourn, *The Cinema of Paolo Sorrentino*, p. xxvii.

PART IV

Marcel Proust: Labours of Language

CHAPTER 13

Along the rue Jean de La Fontaine: The *Fables* in *A la recherche du temps perdu*

Michael Moriarty

When Edward Hughes joined Queen Mary, University of London, I was a member of the French department there. Some time before he arrived, I had devised and taught a course on *A la recherche du temps perdu*. There had been a course on Proust before, but the colleague who had taught it (Maya Slater, an expert, as it happens, on La Fontaine) had retired, and I thought that the gap should be filled. I enjoyed teaching the course very much, but when Eddie arrived, I turned it over to him. With typical graciousness, he said that he was quite willing to teach in other areas — his range of expertise was quite wide enough for that — but I felt that the students must profit far more from being taught by a proper Proustian than by an amateur like myself. This piece is a tribute from that amateur to the consummate professional.

Its title alludes to Proust's first connection with the seventeenth-century fabulist Jean de La Fontaine: he was born in his uncle's house, 96 rue de la Fontaine, in the sixteenth *arrondissement*. But in this most literary of novels, it is not surprising to find allusions to the poet's work. They are sufficiently numerous to suggest that they play a role in the overall design of *A la recherche du temps perdu*. I attempt here to pick out some of the threads of meaning they contribute to the text.

Moralistes

La Fontaine is sometimes put together with the early modern so-called *moralistes*, writers whose significance for Proust has often been explored. As one of the finest of all Proust critics, Malcolm Bowie, observes, much of Proust's psychological reflection, on such central topics as 'the multiplicity of the self, forgetfulness, psychical numbness, de-personalisation, and the inconstancy or contradictoriness of desire', has 'deep roots in the French intellectual tradition: in the work of Montaigne, Descartes, Pascal, La Rochefoucauld and La Bruyère'.[1] All of these writers can plausibly be characterised as *moralistes*, in line with this definition from a leading authority:

> Nous appellerons moraliste *l'écrivain qui traite des mœurs et (ou) s'adonne à l'analyse, en ne s'interdisant pas de rappeler des normes; qui adopte très généralement pour forme*

*soit le traité, soit le fragment; dont l'attitude consiste à se maintenir avant tout à hauteur d'homme, du fait du vif intérêt qu'il porte au vécu.*²

[By 'moralist', I shall mean *a writer who deals with human behaviour and/or is concerned to analyse it, who does not always refrain from invoking norms; who, as regards form, most commonly adopts either the treatise or the fragment; whose attitude consists in remaining first and foremost on the human level, on account of his or her keen interest in lived experience.*]

To read La Fontaine as a *moraliste* is central to Odette de Mourgues's influential interpretation.³ Moreover, if we recall that La Fontaine wrote two fables addressed to La Rochefoucauld, one of which, he states, derives both its subject-matter and its substantial content ('ce qu'il a de solide') from the work of the author of the *Maximes*, then to link him to the *moralistes* seems prima facie eminently reasonable.⁴

Those scholars who have explored Proust's connections with the *moralistes* have concentrated, however, on La Rochefoucauld or La Bruyère (and sometimes Pascal). This is true of Nicola Luckhurst's subtle analysis of Proust's use of the maxim.⁵ It is true also of two recent studies of Proust in relation to the moralists, by Rainer Warning and Uta Felten, whose analyses are more concerned with themes and worldview.⁶ Luc Fraisse has suggestively explored Proust's relationship to La Rochefoucauld. Proust can be seen, he argues, as rethinking La Rochefoucauld's *Maximes* from the point of view of a novelist, that is, by embodying moral truths in situations and characters. But Fraisse finds the deepest connection between the two writers in their shared concern with the complexities and opacities of the human mind.⁷ In another study, exploring Proust's relationship to the language of French classicism, Fraisse connects the discussion of the difference between Bergotte and the writers who imitate him with two fables of La Fontaine that attack plagiarists and imitators: 'Le Geai paré des plumes du paon' [The Jay Bedecked with the Peacock's Feathers] (IV.9) and 'Le Singe' [The Ape] (XII.19).⁸ Fraisse is not concerned here, however, with La Fontaine as a moralist, and his key references in the chapter are Saint-Simon, Mme de Sévigné and Racine.

One could certainly indeed try to factor La Fontaine into the analysis of Proust's relationship to the *moralistes*; to do for La Fontaine what Fraisse has done for La Rochefoucauld, reading *A la recherche du temps perdu* with an eye to themes and concerns, or to a vision of human nature, common to the twentieth-century novelist and to the seventeenth-century fabulist. But that is not what I propose to do here. Instead, I propose to look at references to the *Fables* on two levels. First, that of the discourse of the characters; secondly, and more briefly, in terms of their contribution to the overall design of the novel.

Characters

All of Proust's characters, those brought up in France at any rate, would have been familiar with La Fontaine's fables from their schooldays.⁹ No doubt, therefore, Mme de Morienval, one of the guests at the climactic reception held by the princesse de Guermantes, is not alone in thinking of them as children's stuff (*RTP*, IV, 579; *SLT*, VI, 391; I will come back to this passage). In any case, the *Fables* linger in the mind of many of the characters, though sometimes only on a superficial level. Some have not so much an aesthetic appreciation of the *Fables* as an awareness that to know them counts as a sign of the possession of cultural capital. M. de Cambremer is one such. To display a knowledge of La Fontaine is, he thinks, a useful way of pointing out to men of science that the aristocratic lifestyle from which they are excluded is compatible with the cultural competence of which they might wish to claim a monopoly. Unfortunately, his repertoire of fables is limited so he always quotes the same ones (*RTP*, III, 307; *SLT*, IV, 363).[10] One of them is 'L'Homme et la couleuvre' [The Man and the Snake] (x.1), which he brings up in the course of a discussion of place names. He mentions a place called Pont-à-Couleuvre which he knows well, and where, despite the name, he has never seen a snake. But this allows him to make a reference to La Fontaine's praise of snakes, from which he dissents (*RTP*, III, 317; *SLT*, IV, 374–75). In point of fact, there is no praise of snakes in the fable at all: the point of it is the snake's criticism of human nature. The mention of 'Le Chameau et les bâtons flottants' [The Camel and the Floating Sticks] (IV.10), is equally laboured (*RTP*, III, 353–54; *SLT*, IV, 419); but the moral of the fable (more or less, 'familiarity breeds contempt') perhaps rebounds on M. de Cambremer, whose allusions to La Fontaine are bound to impress less and less with each repetition. In referring to the author on both occasions as '[le] bon La Fontaine' [good old La Fontaine] M. de Cambremer not only betrays his tendency to repeat himself, but reproduces a patronising cliché about the fabulist's character, endorsed by a reference of Sainte-Beuve to 'le bonhomme La Fontaine' [dear old La Fontaine]. Since we have already learned that the Narrator's mother finds this latter expression unbearable, we know what to think of those who speak of La Fontaine in this way.[11]

The particular man of science that in the first case M. de Cambremer wishes to impress is Brichot. Brichot himself includes La Fontaine in his arsenal of cultural references, making use of him in a particularly pretentious speech in which he reports a possibly entirely fictitious exchange with Charlus: 'Comme dit La Fontaine, mon example était tiré "d'animaux plus petits"' [as La Fontaine says, my example was taken 'from smaller animals'] (*RTP*, III, 833; *SLT*, V, 376). The words quoted come from the start of 'La Colombe et la fourmi' [The Dove and the Ant] (II.12), making the link with the previous fable 'Le Lion et le rat' [The Lion and the Rat] (II.11).[12] However, the expression is used by the Narrator in his own person (*RTP*, II, 824; *SLT*, III, 618), and Proust was given to using it freely in his correspondence.[13] It is not therefore the choice of the allusion that reflects badly on Brichot so much as the way it features in a string of pretentious references. In any case, it shows that, even for a man of genuine learning like Brichot, a knowledge of La Fontaine is a sign of distinction.

The case of M. de Cambremer's brother-in-law, Legrandin, is even more instructive. An engineer by profession, he is cited by the narrator as an example of a man of science who possesses a deep knowledge of literature and art, and who has indeed some reputation as a writer. His speech is characterised by its perhaps excessive bookishness and by its repeated diatribes against the aristocracy (*RTP*, I, 66–67; *SLT*, I, 78–79). He refers to the fable of 'Le Paysan du Danube' [The Peasant of the

Danube] (XI.7), in one of these diatribes, directed at the Narrator, who runs into him on his way to meet Saint-Loup. Observing the Narrator's frock coat, Legrandin accuses him of betraying his soul by frequenting polite society, and exposing himself to its nauseating atmosphere, which he himself would find irrespirable. It is a pity, he says, that the aristocrats were not all wiped out in the Terror. He excuses his old-fashioned frankness as that of the 'paysan de la Vivonne qui est aussi resté le paysan du Danube' [peasant of the Vivonne who has also remained a peasant of the Danube] (*RTP*, II, 452; *SLT*, III, 172). But in using La Fontaine's fable to vindicate his rugged independence Legrandin is only partly successful. To be sure, he is identifying with the peasant of the title, who is sent to Rome as a representative of his people to denounce Roman oppression. The question the peasant asks of the Roman senators could well have been asked by a Jacobin condemning aristocrats to the guillotine: 'Quel droit vous a rendus maîtres de l'univers?' [By what right did you become masters of the world?] (l. 41). Like Legrandin with the Narrator, the peasant seems to expect his listeners to take exception to his frankness ('une plainte un peu trop sincère' [a complaint somewhat too sincere], l. 84). But Legrandin's identification with the peasant goes deeper; for the peasant's reward is to be made a Roman aristocrat (l. 88), entirely in keeping with Legrandin's social fantasies. In this case, it is not that the allusion to La Fontaine betrays pretentiousness and superficiality; it is that it reveals more of the genuinely cultured speaker than he would have wished. The moral of the fable, that one should not judge people by appearances (l. 1) is eminently applicable to the hypocritical snob.

Returning to the aristocratic characters, or rather the genuine aristocrats, since by the end of the novel Legrandin is calling himself 'comte de Méséglise' (*RTP*, IV, 250–51; *SLT*, V, 774–75), we observe that the duchesse de Guermantes also uses her knowledge of La Fontaine to impress. But she impresses all the more because she seems, unlike Brichot, not to be straining to. She has the kind of knowledge that permits real inventiveness in conversation — not untinged with malice. When she remarks that the Queen of Sweden has put on a great deal of weight, Mme de Villeparisis reminds her that she once compared the queen to a frog. In that case, says the duchesse, 'c'est la grenouille qui a réussi à devenir aussi grosse que le bœuf' [she's the frog that has succeeded in swelling to the size of an ox] (*RTP*, II, 507; *SLT*, III, 239). The joke here is that La Fontaine's fable 'La Grenouille qui se veut faire aussi grosse que le bœuf' [The Frog Who Wanted to Become as Big as the Ox] (I.3) is intended to show the impossibility of the frog's aspiration.[14] The explicit moral of the fable is about social pretension:

> Tout bourgeois veut bâtir comme les grands seigneurs,
> Tout petit prince a des ambassadeurs;
> Tout marquis veut avoir des pages. (ll. 12–14)

[Every bourgeois wants to build like a great lord. | Every princeling has ambassadors; | Every marquess wants to have pages.]

The general theme could not be more Proustian, but it is possible, more particularly, that the duchesse has the moral of the fable in mind. The current Swedish royal dynasty was founded by one of Napoleon's marshals, Bernadotte. To the duchesse it would appear positively frog-sized in origin, compared to other royal families she could name. In any case, having thought of one frog-fable, she now thinks of another: the queen is much livelier since the death of her husband, and thus does not resemble 'Les Grenouilles qui demandent un roi' [The Frogs Who Asked for a King] (III.4) (*RTP*, II, 508; *SLT*, III, 239). In aristocratic society, a witty allusion to La Fontaine is an exhibition of distinction.

This is borne out by another anecdote, which turns on the title of 'Le Meunier, son fils, et l'âne' [The Miller, his Son and the Donkey] (III.1). An aristocrat snobbishly refuses an invitation to dinner from his wife's grandfather, who has made a fortune in the flour trade, and whom he dismissively refers to as a 'miller'. The grandfather's reply uses the title of the fable to imply that the aristocrat is an ass. But since the alleged snob is M. de Luxembourg, whom he knows from personal experience to be incapable of behaving so crassly, the Narrator rejects the anecdote as a clumsy fabrication (*RTP*, II, 827; *SLT*, III, 622).[15]

There is one aristocrat, however, who has a real appreciation of La Fontaine as something more than an asset in a portfolio of cultural capital: Charlus. It is true that on occasion he uses his familiarity with La Fontaine in the service of his snobbery and spite. In a vicious diatribe against the comtesse Molé, who is, by his standards, a mere *bourgeoise*, he accuses her of trying to imitate the manners of the duchesse de Guermantes, like the jay in *Fables*, IV.9, who bedecks itself in the cast-off plumage of the peacock, and follows up by comparing her to the frog that wants to be as big as an ox (I.3) (*RTP*, III, 739; *SLT*, V, 264). The fact that we have seen the duchesse herself citing this latter fable reinforces the point that a knowledge of La Fontaine can feature in an aristocratic arsenal of weapons of class self-assertion. Elsewhere, however, we see Charlus responding to La Fontaine at a very different level. When Mme de Villeparisis speaks of Mme de Sévigné's expressions of affection for her daughter as insincere, he demurs altogether. In Mme de Sévigné's day, such feelings, he explains, were well understood. As witness he cites two fables of La Fontaine:

> L'habitant du Monomotapa de La Fontaine courant chez son ami qui lui est apparu un peu triste pendant son sommeil, le pigeon trouvant que le plus grand des maux est l'absence de l'autre pigeon, vous semblent peut-être, ma tante, aussi exagérés que Mme de Sévigné ne pouvant pas attendre le moment où elle sera seule avec sa fille. (*RTP*, II, 121)

> [The inhabitant of La Fontaine's Monomotapa, running round to see his friend who had appeared to him in a dream looking rather sad, the pigeon finding the greatest of evils in the absence of the other pigeon, seem to you perhaps, my dear aunt, as exaggerated as Mme de Sévigné's impatience for the moment when she will be alone with her daughter.] (*SLT*, II, 395)

The fables in question are 'Les Deux Amis' [The Two Friends] (VIII.11) and 'Les Deux Pigeons' [The Two Pigeons] (IX.2). (The titles by themselves suggest the theme of reciprocity, and by contrast its absence, that so permeates the whole novel.) 'Monomotapa' in 'Les Deux Amis' is the name of a real place (a former kingdom in Africa). But the lines 'Les amis de ce pays-là | Valent bien dit-on ceux du nôtre' [The friends in that country| Are just as good friends, so it's said, as those in ours] (ll. 3–4) suggest, rather, by understatement, that it is an ideal world, in which friendship is more authentic than here. These two friends have all things in common. In the fable, one friend gets up in the middle of the night and rushes to the other's house. The second friend asks him why he has come: is he in need of money? He offers his purse. Does he need a second to fight a duel? He offers his sword. Is he lonely? He offers his slave-woman. No, none of these things, says the first man: it was just that he had a dream in which his friend appeared to be sad, and he wanted to find out if he was really in trouble.

The fable actually takes the form of a problem: 'Qui d'eux aimait le mieux? que t'en semble, lecteur? | Cette difficulté vaut bien qu'on la propose' [Which of them loved the better? What do you think, reader? | This question is one well worth asking] (ll. 24–25). The moral points to two aspects of friendship (ll. 26–31), each embodied by one of the two men: a friend anticipates his friend's wants without having to be asked for help, and is easily frightened by the thought of something bad happening to his friend. Charlus, then, has simplified the message, focusing on the anxious and sensitive friend rather than the practical and helpful one. The same is true as regards 'Les Deux Pigeons'. The pigeon whose words Charlus quotes ('L'absence est le plus grand des maux' [Absence is the worst of evils], l. 7) is the one left behind to grieve at home, rather than the one who sets off to see the world, and nearly never comes back.[16]

This literary discussion with Mme de Villeparisis is explicitly presented as an important stage in the characterisation of Charlus. He was first mentioned as devoted to physical exercise, in particular long-distance walking (*RTP*, II, 107–08; *SLT*, II, 379), and this seems to be part of a cult of virility that involves scorn for anything effeminate (*RTP*, II, 121; *SLT*, II, 395). But the views he expresses here are presented as a sign of a refined sensibility esteemed by the Narrator's grandmother, which she and the Narrator are inclined to interpret as a sign of a woman's influence on his life. An alternative explanation is provided by his voice, which, when he talks in this way, takes on surprisingly feminine overtones (*RTP*, II, 121–23; *SLT*, II, 395–97). Clearly, his response to the two fables is in keeping with his yearning after a special friendship, as expressed to the Narrator, even if that relationship, as he conceives it, is markedly unequal compared to those of the fables (*RTP*, II, 581–92; *SLT*, III, 326–40).

An important theme of the passage is that love is specified as such by its intensity rather than its objects ('L'important dans la vie n'est pas ce qu'on aime,' says Charlus, 'c'est d'aimer' [But what matters in life is not whom or what one loves, it is the fact of loving]). Mme de Sévigné's love for her daughter, he says, has more in common with Racinian passion than her son's dealings with his mistresses (*RTP*, II, 122; *SLT*, II, 396). The fables quoted by Charlus bring this out. The relationships do not fall into conventional patterns. Obviously, both the friends and both the pigeons are male. The intensity of the friends' concern of each for the other is more redolent of standard conceptions of love, as the question 'Qui d'eux aimait le mieux?' suggests.[17] The pigeons are stated to love each other 'd'amour tendre' [with a tender love] (l. 1). When the stay-at-home pigeon tries to persuade his companion to stay, his language is reminiscent of Dido's pleas to Aeneas.[18] They see their relationship as between brothers (ll. 6, 16, 24). But the moral of the story is addressed to lovers, and the poet's idyllic reminiscences concern his love for a young shepherdess (l. 75).

Clearly, the reference to Mme de Sévigné is paramount in the conversation as a whole, but that of La Fontaine is scarcely less important.[19] Both are relevant to the Narrator's grandmother's judgement that Charlus has a better understanding of certain works of literature than his aunt Mme de Villeparisis, and that he has something in him that sets him far above most men-about-town ('gens de club', *RTP*, II, 122; *SLT*, II, 397). What these examples show is that a character's relationship to La Fontaine serves as a touchstone of his or her intellectual and, to some extent, moral worth.

But even if there is a significant difference between the person who quotes La Fontaine as a form of self-promotion, an index of their cultural capital, and the one who can respond imaginatively and affectively to his work, this latter capacity is not the same as having an aesthetic appreciation of the *Fables*. For this we must turn to Bergotte. A passage from typescript no. 2 deals with his appreciation for classic authors, such as Racine, Molière and La Fontaine. This occasionally involves finding expressions in their work of ideas and sensations of which the authors themselves would not have thought. But it is the authors' language itself that makes such associations possible. The example Proust gives is from 'Le Jardinier et son seigneur' [The Gardener and his Landlord] (IV.4): 'Il avait de plant vif fermé cette étendue. | Là croissait à plaisir l'oseille et la laitue' [He had bordered this space with young plants. | There sorrel and lettuce grew freely] (ll. 5–6).[20] What Bergotte savours is, apparently, the very concrete and specific vocabulary that creates a precise visual image. This is entirely in keeping with his tendency to evaluate a work in terms of local details: 'quelque scène faisant image, quelque tableau sans signification rationnelle' [some scene that furnished the reader with an image, some picture that had no rational meaning] (*RTP*, I, 546; *SLT*, II, 150); and the little patch of colour in a rural garden is echoed by the little patch of yellow wall in the picture by Vermeer that is the last thing Bergotte sees before his death (*RTP*, III, 692; *SLT*, VI, 207–08). (For all that, one could argue that the concrete detail in La Fontaine conveys the gardener's love and concern for his garden more effectively than any reference to these feelings could.)

Performance

One of the main features of the reception given by the princesse de Guermantes in *Le Temps retrouvé* is a recitation of poems by the now famous actress Rachel, including fables by La Fontaine (*RTP*, IV, 562, 569; *SLT*, VI, 368, 377). At the same time as the reception, La Berma, now old and incurably ill, is holding a tea party for her son and daughter-in-law. But all those she has invited have also been invited to the reception, and that is where they decide to go, in the belief that it is really Rachel's party (*RTP*, IV, 572–73; *SLT*, VI, 382–83). No one comes to La Berma's party except one young man. Even he, after a time, heads off to the princesse de Guermantes, to be followed eventually by the son and daughter-in-law themselves (without an invitation), leaving La Berma at home spitting blood (*RTP*, IV, 575–76, 590–91; *SLT*, VI, 386–87, 405–07).

Society, then, has pronounced in favour of the fashionable actress, and against the old one. But the Narrator does not share this view. His judgement that La Berma is far superior to Rachel is borne out by the description of the latter's 'modernist' technique when she recites the poems (*RTP*, IV, 580–81; *SLT*, VI, 392–93). The damning adjective 'intelligent' is applied to it, and it involves extravagant gestures and tones of voice — each word is uttered as if it were a groan (*RTP*, IV, 576–77; *SLT*, VI, 387–88). Rachel draws attention to herself in a manner directly opposed to the art of La Berma, who disappears into the text and the character (*RTP*, I, 440; *SLT*, II, 22). And this is the gravamen of Gilberte's criticism of Rachel's rendering of 'Les Deux Pigeons': 'Un quart est de l'invention de l'interprète, un quart de la folie, un quart n'a aucun sens, le reste est de La Fontaine' [One quarter is the invention of the actress, a second is lunacy, a third is meaningless and the rest is La Fontaine] (*RTP*, IV, 579–80; *SLT*, VI, 391–92).[21] (The role of La Fontaine in establishing the contrast between La Berma and Rachel would have been even stronger if Proust had kept the passage that refers to La Berma giving a recitation of 'Les Animaux malades de la peste' [The Animals Sick with the Plague] (VII.1) in *Esquisse* IV (*RTP*, I, 1002).)

The prominence of Rachel with her aberrant rendering of La Fontaine is cited taken by the Narrator as an explicit sign that there is no necessary progress in the arts over time. Time has brought recognition to the genius of Elstir, but it has also brought celebrity to the mediocre Rachel (*RTP*, IV, 580–81; *SLT*, VI, 392–93). But it is also, more generally, one of the changes that have shaken the foundations of the Narrator's former picture of the world — not quite on a par with the transformation of Mme Verdurin into the princesse de Guermantes, but in keeping with it — changes that are to be incorporated into his future work, alongside the impressions that belong to a realm outside time (*RTP*, IV, 510–11; *SLT*, VI, 302).

But we might ask in conclusion why 'Les Deux Pigeons'? The mention of it must be significant since Rachel recites more than one fable and this is the only one named.[22] Insofar as it is a fable about love, which can also be read as a fable about friendship, it surely affirms two values that the novel relegates to inferiority, as distractions from the project of writing. We can, however (if, like Bergotte, we are willing to find meanings in a classic work of literature of which the author never thought), read the poem another way, as the story of a homecoming that is symbolic rather than literal. One of the pigeons leaves home in quest of new experiences to be shared in future conversations:

> Mais le désir de voir et l'humeur inquiète
> L'emportèrent enfin. Il dit: Ne pleurez point:
> Trois jours au plus rendront mon âme satisfaite;
> Je reviendrai sous peu conter de point en point
> Mes aventures à mon frère.
> Je le désennuierai: quiconque ne voit guère
> N'a guère à dire aussi. (ll. 20–26)

[But the desire to see, and a mood of restlessness
Prevailed in the end. He said, 'Do not weep.
Three days at the most, and my soul will be satisfied.
I'll be back before long, to share every single one
Of my adventures with my brother.
I shall keep him entertained; whoever has little to see
Has little to say as well.']

His experiences are traumatic and nearly fatal: he is caught in a storm, trapped in a net, nearly carried off by a vulture and nearly killed by a stone from a child's catapult, at which point he heads for home. In a sense he is like the Proustian protagonist, who subjects himself to the vicissitudes of travel through different social milieux and relationships, exciting in prospect, fruitless when experienced, and who returns home disillusioned — but who is, all the same, bringing back his experiences to share with his other self, the creative self, 'l'autre moi, celui qui avait conçu son œuvre' [the other self, the one which had had a glimpse of the task that lay before it] (*RTP*, IV, 617; *SLT*, VI, 441).

Notes to Chapter 13

1. Malcolm Bowie, *Freud, Proust and Lacan: Theory as Fiction* (Cambridge: Cambridge University Press, 1987), p. 70.
2. Louis Van Delft, *Le Moraliste classique* (Geneva: Droz, 1982), p. 108. All translations are my own unless stated otherwise. I retain the French term *moraliste* in the text, since it is an accepted label for a certain group of French writers, though I do not agree with the view that the *moraliste* is not a moralist in the ordinary sense. As Van Delft's definition acknowledges, the *moralistes* sometimes invoke norms, like any moralist; their aim is not simply to describe, but to evaluate.
3. Odette de Mourgues, *La Fontaine: 'Fables'* (London: Edward Arnold, 1963); *Ô muse, fuyante proie: essai sur la poésie de La Fontaine* (Paris: José Corti, 1962).
4. Jean de La Fontaine, *Fables*, 'L'Homme et son image' [Man and his Image] (I.11), and 'Discours à M. Le duc de La Rochefoucauld' (X.14). I shall refer to particular fables, as here, by their title, the book from which they come (in roman numerals) and their number within the book (in arabic numerals). The edition used is Jean de La Fontaine, *Œuvres complètes. I: Fables, Contes et nouvelles*, ed. by Jean-Pierre Collinet, Bibliothèque de la Pléiade (Paris: Gallimard, 1991). Translations from the *Fables* are my own.
5. Nicola Luckhurst, *Science and Structure in Proust's 'A la recherche du temps perdu'* (Oxford: Oxford University Press, 2000), pp. 6–30.
6. Rainer Warning, 'Proust et la pensée moraliste', *Revue d'études Proustiennes*, 9.1 (2019), 43–62; Uta Felten, 'L'Éloge de la curiosité moraliste: Proust et la reception de la philosophie moraliste', *Revue d'études Proustiennes*, 9.1 (2019), 33–42.
7. Luc Fraisse, 'Perles de la pensée: Proust et La Rochefoucauld', in *La Petite Musique du style: Proust et ses sources littéraires* (Paris: Classiques Garnier, 2011), pp. 113–33.
8. Luc Fraisse, 'La Feuille qui chante, ou l'imaginaire de la langue classique', in *La Petite Musique du style*, pp. 93–112 (p. 93). Marcel Proust, *A la recherche du temps perdu*, ed. by Jean-Yves Tadié, 4 vols, Bibliothèque de la Pléiade (Paris: Gallimard, 1987–89), I, 540–41 (hereafter referenced as *RTP* in main text); *In Search of Lost Time*, trans. by C. K. Scott-Moncrieff and Terence Kilmartin, rev. by D. J. Enright, 6 vols (London: Vintage, 2000–02), II, 143–44 (hereafter referenced as *SLT* in main text).
9. For a study of the place of La Fontaine in Third Republic education, see Ralph Albanese, 'Le Discours scolaire au dix-neuvième siècle: le cas La Fontaine', *The French Review*, 72.5 (1999), 824–38.
10. The passage poses various problems. First of all it says that M. de Cambremer would freely cite

one fable by La Fontaine and one by Florian (the eighteenth-century fabulist Jean-Pierre Claris de Florian) and that he barely knew more than two ('il n'en connaissait guère que deux', *RTP*, III, 307; *SLT*, IV, 363). In fact he mentions two by La Fontaine: 'L'Homme et la couleuvre' (x.1) (*RTP*, III, 317; *SLT*, IV, 374); and 'Le Chameau et les bâtons flottants' (IV.10) (*RTP*, III, 353–54; *SLT*, IV, 419). The apparent reference to Florian is to a fable called 'La Grenouille devant l'aréopage' (*RTP*, III, 317; *SLT*, IV, 374–75), but there is no fable by him of that name. See the note in *RTP*, III, 1517, n. 2. Elsewhere we are told that a few fables of La Fontaine's constitute the whole of M. de Cambremer's acquaintance with literature (*RTP*, III, 740; *SLT*, V, 265).

11. *RTP*, III, 167; *SLT*, IV, 197, and the corresponding note (*RTP*, III, 1437, n. 3).
12. The Pléiade note incorrectly puts 'XII.2' (*RTP*, III, 1771, n. 3).
13. As indicated in *RTP*, II, 1801, n. 1. It is just possible that the Narrator is implicitly quoting the Turkish ambassador's wife; since we are told that has a real gift for assimilating what she hears (*RTP*, II, 823; *SLT*, III, 618), she might have picked up the phrase from other people's use of it.
14. In *Esquisse* XII for *Le Temps retrouvé*, Charlus compares Italy, with its expansionist ambitions, to the frog in fable 1,3 (see 'M. de Charlus pendant la guerre', *RTP*, IV, 777).
15. M. de Luxembourg (then conte de Nassau) had regularly written to the Narrator during his grandmother's illness (*RTP*, II, 625; *SLT*, III, 378–79). The anecdote does actually have a basis in reality; see the note on the passage (*RTP*, II, 1805, n. 1), referring to George Painter's biography of Proust.
16. This episode is discussed in Sylvaine Landes-Ferrali, *Proust et le grand siècle: formes et significations de la référence* (Tübingen: Gunter Narr, 2004), pp. 246–47.
17. The reference to the slave woman (ll. 17–18) implies that they practise heterosexuality; but it hardly needs pointing out that this does not exclude homoerotic attachments.
18. See, *La Fontaine, Œuvres completes I*, ed. by Collinet, p. 1222, n. 3.
19. Charlus also mentions La Bruyère, quoting *Les Caractères*, 'Du cœur', 23 (*RTP*, II, 122; *SLT*, II, 396).
20. See *RTP*, I, 1391–92, n. 4. The Pléiade editors correct Proust's quotation (from 'fermé' to 'semé') but Proust's text corresponds to that in modern scholarly editions such as those of Collinet and Marc Fumaroli: Jean de La Fontaine, *Fables*, ed. by Marc Fumaroli, illus. by Marie Hugo, 2 vols (Paris: Imprimerie nationale, 1985).
21. Gilberte says this to Mme de Morienval, who is incapable of appreciating her irony, and who believes, as we saw, that La Fontaine's *Fables* are suitable only for children; she therefore concludes that what she has just heard is a new work which simply incorporates bits of La Fontaine, and when she says this to other people no one has the knowledge to correct her. This is offered as a damning comment on the ignorance of members of fashionable society (*RTP*, IV, 579–80; *SLT*, VI, 391–92). Gilberte of course understandably dislikes Rachel as the former mistress of her dead husband Robert de Saint-Loup, but that does not detract from the force of her criticism.
22. See *RTP*, IV, 562 and 579 (*SLT*, VI, 368 and 391), where it is clear that she recites one nameless fable before 'Les Deux Pigeons'.

CHAPTER 14

Proust's Prosopopoeias

John O'Brien

Towards the end of the Balbec episodes in *A l'ombre des jeunes filles en fleurs*, Albertine produces a letter Gisèle has sent her, containing a copy of an essay Gisèle had to write for her 'certificat d'études' [examination].[1] Gisèle reports that she had to choose between two topics: either 'Sophocle écrit des Enfers à Racine pour le consoler de l'insuccès d'*Athalie*' [Sophocles, from the Shades, writes to Racine to console him for the failure of *Athalie*] or 'Vous supposerez qu'après la première représentation d'*Esther*, Mme de Sévigné écrit à Mme de La Fayette pour lui dire combien elle a regretté son absence' [Suppose that, after the first performance of *Esther*, Mme de Sévigné is writing to Mme de La Fayette to tell her how much she regretted her absence] (*RTP*, II, 264–65; *SLT*, II, 567). She chose the first of these, the more difficult topic, and so impressed the examiners that she was awarded fourteen out of twenty, a score of seventy per cent in today's terms, although Albertine acidly remarks that Gisèle was merely lucky and that anyway her French teacher had got her to mug up on that topic. Andrée then picks up this idea at some length, criticising, correcting and improving on Gisèle's attempt. In the midst of these snide exchanges, the composition in question is quoted in full; written in the present, perfect and imperfect tenses, it gives voice and immediacy to the characters in question, while nonetheless being mediated through a particular literary form as well as through the letter Albertine is reading out: these are all significant features, as we shall see in due course.

The device which Gisèle is set as her topic for imitation is prosopopoeia, a familiar part of the rhetorical repertoire from classical antiquity onwards. This anthropomorphic figure, which bestows a face (*prosopon*) and a voice on distant animate or inanimate objects, is a way of 'manipulating time and space', creating an illusion of immediacy and presence.[2] Its history is rich and long, and attains 'sophisticated' treatment in the Roman writer Quintilian who notably develops its scope and may serve as the representative of the rhetorical tradition.[3] One of prosopopoeia's aspects, he writes, is to allow imaginary conversations between historical figures.[4] In the scene from Proust, the words 'Vous supposerez' [Suppose that] point precisely to this function. Quintilian then goes on to show that prosopopoeia has a range of other flexible applications: it can display inner thoughts, it can introduce conversations between ourselves and others, it can supply characters for words of advice, reproach, complaint; it can raise the dead, and allow cities and nations to acquire utterance; it can also portray 'an imaginary speech with an undefined speaker' or even 'a speech without any person'.[5] In short, prosopopoeia gives a voice not only to things to which nature has not, but also to things of a purely imaginary or fictitious character. This last attribute is of special significance, for 'the power to conjure up human presences and endow them with speaking voices is not just a momentary trick of the orator but is the basis of the making of fictions'.[6]

Such prosopopoeic fictions are plentiful in French literature before Proust and an inspection of their character bears out the spectrum described in the classical tradition: inanimate objects such as houses, bridges, pyramids and dolls, collectives such as universities, assemblies and towns, abstractions such as nature and peace, can all be given their own voice.[7] Some of these we would now think of personifications, with which prosopopoeia is contiguous, as Quintilian observes, the *Roman de la rose* being a major early French example of a vastly extended personification sustained over the course of 21,000 lines, shaped into an allegory of love.[8] Yet the most striking instances of prosopopoeia remain those where the dead are resurrected and endowed not just with features and a voice, but with the ability to address and converse with an interlocutor.[9] The departed return as a more than ghostly presence.

Running alongside literary practice, French rhetorical theory similarly added to this tropological debate. A turning-point of particular importance was reached with the work of the nineteenth-century rhetorician Pierre Fontanier, whose work on tropes and figures (1821–27) distinguishes sharply between personification and prosopopoeia. The first, he claims, 'consiste à faire d'un être inanimé, insensible, ou d'un être abstrait et purement idéal, une espèce d'être réel et physique, doué de sentiment et de vie, enfin ce qu'on appelle une personne' [consists of turning an inanimate, insensible entity or an abstract and purely ideal entity into a sort of real physical being, imbued with feeling and life, ultimately what is called a person].[10] By contrast, prosopopoeia, for him, is emphatically not to be confused with personification or apostrophe, although they may accompany it. Its purpose is to:

> Mettre en quelque sorte en scène, les absens, les morts, les êtres surnaturels, ou même les êtres inanimés; à les faire agir, parler, répondre, ainsi qu'on l'entend; ou tout au moins à les prendre pour confidens, pour témoins, pour garans.[11]
>
> [As it were to dramatise the absent, the dead, supernatural beings or even inanimate entities; to make them act, speak, reply, as one intends; or at the very least to take them as confidants, as witnesses, as guarantors.]

While Fontanier's definitions are not as clear-cut as might be hoped, in essence two essential characteristics emerge: if personification is merely a lively figure of speech, a manner of speaking, a 'so to say', prosopopoeia is a scheme of thought and Fontanier agrees with a long French tradition that it is often the trope of the dead, the absent, given face and voice. Fontanier was enthusiastically championed by scholars of rhetorical theory such as Gérard Genette and Tzvetan Todorov,[12] and of linguistic theory such as Michael Riffaterre who quotes Fontanier in his discussion of prosopopoeia.[13] He also fed into post-structuralist thought, particularly through the writings of Paul de Man who offers the densest reflections about prosopopoeia, radically broadening its deconstructive scope to make of it, as Jeffrey Mehlman has noted, the 'dominant figure' of autobiography, the 'master trope' of poetry and the 'very figure of the reader and of reading'.[14] Indeed, as James Paxson comments, in De Man's hands, prosopopoeia 'gets expanded to characterize all human cognition'.[15] It becomes the arch figure of a particular post-structuralist modernity.

Although both De Man and Riffaterre acknowledged the link between prosopopoeia and personification, they had their intellectual reasons for following Fontanier in distinguishing between them and preferring the former to the latter. Other recent critics, however, have taken a less austere approach. For instance, J. Hillis Miller, while firmly in the post-structuralist camp, makes no hard-and-fast distinction between the two tropes.[16] Paxson, who shares many of the same theoretical sympathies as Miller, follows the same approach. Indeed, he, and more recently still Walter Melion and Bart Ramakers, go further and see the two terms as interchangeable, beginning their discussions with the identical phrase, 'personification or prosopopoeia'.[17] Melion and Ramakers, like Paxson, acknowledge the formal properties of prosopopoeia — its significant relationship with personification and allegory on one hand and apostrophe on the other — but while recognising and welcoming the rich potential of prosopopoeia's scope, they follow the most recent critical trend in being willing to entertain a less rigid approach to its application.[18]

The exam exercise which Gisèle undertakes thus stands in a long-established tradition of critical reflection and literary practice which highlights the special salience of prosopopoeia and will help contextualise Proust's own adventures with it. Some aspects of this topic, notably concerning art and artworks, have already received analysis and will not be re-examined here.[19] One general finding of these critical studies, though, has been to underscore Proust's liking for giving voice to inanimate objects, 'complete with addresses and apostrophes'.[20] That penchant had already been evident in *Jean Santeuil*, but it undergoes considerable expansion and refinement in *A la recherche* and will be the focus of the remainder of the present chapter.[21]

An instructive example is to be found in *Le Côté de Guermantes* when the narrator visits his friend Robert de Saint-Loup at Doncières. Before preparing to sleep in an unfamiliar hotel room, he sets out to explore 'tout mon féerique domaine' [the whole of my enchanted domain]. That phrase is the harbinger of what follows. He describes the contents of a long gallery, including 'dans un cadre ancien le fantôme d'une dame d'autrefois' [in an old frame, the phantom of a lady of long ago] (*RTP*, II, 383; *SLT*, III, 89), before abruptly coming to a halt. He then resumes his narrative in a new vein:

> Arrivé au bout, son mur plein où ne s'ouvrait aucune porte me dit naïvement: 'Maintenant il faut revenir, mais tu vois, tu es chez toi', tandis que le tapis moelleux ajoutait pour ne pas demeurer en reste que si je ne dormais pas cette nuit je pourrais très bien venir nu-pieds, et que les fenêtres sans volets qui regardaient la campagne m'assuraient qu'elles passeraient une nuit blanche et qu'en venant à l'heure que je voudrais je n'avais à craindre de réveiller personne.

Et derrière une tenture je surpris seulement un petit cabinet qui, arrêté par la muraille et ne pouvant se sauver, s'était caché là, tout penaud, et me regardait avec effroi de son œil-de-bœuf rendu bleu par le clair de lune. (*RTP*, II, 383)

[When I came to the end, the bare wall in which no door opened said to me simply: 'Now you must go back, but you see, you are at home here', while the soft carpet, not to be outdone, added that if I could not sleep that night I could perfectly well come in my bare feet, and the unshuttered windows looking out over the countryside assured me that they would keep a sleepless vigil and that, at whatever hour I chose to come, I need not be afraid of disturbing anyone. And behind a hanging curtain I came upon a little closet which, stopped by the outer wall and unable to escape, had hidden itself there shamefacedly and gave me a frightened stare from its little round window, glowing blue in the moonlight.] (*SLT*, III, 89)

This passage fields a series of prosopopoeic techniques distributed among the constituent elements of the scene: the wall which apostrophises the explorer, the hyperbolical transfer of sleeplessness from him to the windows, the words of the carpet reported in indirect speech and finally the anthropomorphised closet with its startled reactions. Reinforced by the ghostly presence of a lady from yesteryear and the reference to an enchanted domain, prosopopoeia skilfully orchestrates the mixing and fusing of the animate and the inanimate in a dreamy atmosphere which is already that of sleep even before the narrator has climbed into bed.[22] More broadly, the empathy between the narrator and his background here is also a way of emphasising the porosity of Proustian thought to its objects of attention, fostering the interpenetration between inner world of consciousness and the outer world of things.

That same porosity can be seen in a later episode from *Le Côté de Guermantes* in which the narrator reflects on Robert de Saint-Loup and the aristocratic ideals which have sculpted his physical form. This episode, in fact, situated just before the important encounter with the artist Elstir, expands on the 'agilité morale et physique' [moral and physical agility] (*RTP*, II, 96; *SLT*, II, 365) which the narrator had so admired in his friend on first meeting him. Now, extending the idea of Saint-Loup as 'une œuvre d'art' [a work of art] (*RTP*, II, 96; *SLT*, II, 366), the animate human is transformed into the inanimate artefact, both through a comparison with horsemen in a frieze and more particularly through an imaginary dialogue with Saint-Loup, which is also one of the functions of prosopopoeia.[23] Framed by a twofold linguistic marker of hypothesis, 'Hélas, eût pensé Robert [...]. Voilà ce que je crains aujourd'hui que Saint-Loup ait quelquefois pensé' [Alas! Robert might have thought [...]. This is what I now fear that Saint-Loup may at times have thought] (*RTP*, II, 707–08; *SLT*, III, 478), Saint-Loup's imagined words portray his dismay at the results of his scorn of wealth and aristocratic status in favour of close friendship with someone not of his class: he has been turned into an object of artistic pleasure, intellectual and detached, something he had not anticipated and never wanted. The friend as another self — a topos of friendship literature — has been eschewed in favour of an aesthetic ideal. To this conjectured outcry, the narrator invents a lengthy reply. Distinction of mind and physical distinction are not incompatible, he argues, and it is more than just a work of art that he admires in the suppleness of Saint-Loup's limbs: it is also his genuine moral humility which has been absorbed into his physical frame alongside his upper-class values. It is that nobility of mind and body that he finds so noteworthy, bestowed on him as a token of Saint-Loup's sovereign freedom which achieves through its lithe movement the highest expression of what Proust, using another commonplace of the literary tradition, styles perfect friendship. Thus while Saint-Loup takes the stage through the voice the narrator lends him, his material presence is interwoven with the reflections about fluidity and motion. The prosopopoeia has gradually merged with its commentary, the physical body with the body of the text.

It is clear even from these initial soundings that prosopopoeia, for Proust, is more than a device of vividness or *présentéité* [presentness], refined though his handling of this may be. Rather, it enables him to stage encounters between thought and extension, interfusing subject and object; it also acts thereby as a *mise en abyme* of the distinctive, transmogrifying powers of writing in respect of fictions of the person.[24] In other words, prosopopoeia is more than just a figure of speech; it fits in with an entire scheme of thinking, a whole way of conceptualising and writing about the interlinking of rhetoric and metaphorics, in line with the most expansive theoretical reflections on this oratorical device. Yet the occurrences of prosopopoeia in Proust can be more than just isolated episodes, however replete with significance and symbolism. They can also be formed into long-range sequences spread over more than one part of *A la recherche*. To key instances of such sequences we shall now turn.

One celebrated set of instances of prosopopoeia and the energised inanimate concerns the narrator's artistic vocation associated with an epiphany in a mnemonic landscape. It begins with his account of his vision as he rides in a carriage past the Martinville and Vieuxvicq steeples whose characterisation, however, extends no further than personification: they 's'étaient jetés [...] au-devant d'elle [i.e. the carriage]', [flung themselves in our path], they 'nous regarde[nt] fuir' [watch our flight], they wave goodbye; they are three maidens (*RTP*, I, 179; *SLT*, I, 217). That Martinville episode is then expressly recalled during yet another journey by carriage, this time with Mme de Villeparisis outside Balbec in the 'Noms de pays: le pays' [Place-Names: The Place] section of *A l'ombre des jeunes filles en fleurs*. At Hudimesnil, the narrator is suddenly overwhelmed by the same profound sense of joy that he had experienced in that earlier scene. Slightly beforehand he had seen a group of three trees and he feels they conceal a hidden meaning. But what? He struggles to recall and that struggle is embodied for us on the printed page by an extensive series of questions giving dense verbal form to his intellectual puzzlement. Are the trees a memory of something specific or of something general? Or does the memory lie so deep that it cannot be retrieved? Do they come from a dream, recent or past? (That sleep motif, once again.) 'Je crus plutôt que c'étaient des fantômes du passé,' he concludes [I chose rather to believe they were phantoms of the past] (*RTP*, II, 78; *SLT*, II, 344). (That ghost theme, once more.) The carriage then starts to pull away and it is at this point that Proust introduces the vocalisation fundamental to prosopopoeia:

> Je vis les arbres s'éloigner en agitant leurs bras désespérés, semblant me dire: 'Ce que tu n'apprends pas de nous aujourd'hui, tu ne le sauras jamais. Si tu nous laisses retomber au fond de ce chemin d'où nous cherchions à nous hisser jusqu'à toi, toute une partie de toi-même que nous t'apportions tombera pour jamais au néant'. (*RTP*, II, 79)
>
> [I watched the trees gradually recede, waving their despairing arms, seeming to say to me: 'What you fail to learn from us today, you will never know. If you allow us to drop back into the hollow of the road from which we sought to raise ourselves up to you, a whole part of yourself which we were bringing to you will vanish forever into thin air'.] (*SLT*, II, 345)

Here, Proust goes a stage further than he had with his encounter at Martinville. As the anthropomorphism of 'leurs bras désespérés' [their despairing arms] suggests, the trees now combine personification with prosopopoeia, but it is their vocal presence above all which is prominently highlighted and purposely sustained long enough to convey their crucial message in images of rising and then falling. These images signify, in turn, the oblivion of self and memory swallowed up by time's devouring power if the narrator cannot grasp their significance; the careful parallelism and echoing of 'retomber/ tombera' 'au fond/ au néant' (not replicated in the English translation) underline the stakes involved. Yet as the narrator feels compelled to confess, he cannot understand their meaning and this failure of anamnesis is as much vocational as ontological.

The sequel to this episode then reverses the angle of vision. Much later in the narrative, in the opening section of *Le Temps retrouvé*, the narrator is once again in a moving vehicle, in this case a train taking him back to Paris after an extended stay in a sanitorium. It stops in the middle of the countryside where he glimpses the play of sunlight on a row of trees. Now it is his turn to address them, but in internal monologue:

> 'Arbres,' pensai-je, 'vous n'avez plus rien à me dire, mon cœur refroidi ne vous entend plus. Je suis pourtant ici en pleine nature, eh bien, c'est avec froideur, avec ennui que mes yeux constatent la ligne qui sépare votre front lumineux de votre tronc d'ombre'. (*RTP*, IV, 433)
>
> ['Trees,' I thought, 'you no longer have anything to say to me. My heart is grown cold and no longer hears you. I am in the midst of nature. Well, it is with indifference, with boredom that my eyes register the line which separates your radiant foreheads from your shadowy trunks'.] (*SLT*, VI, 202)

Nature, the erstwhile purveyor of moments of seeing and being, no longer holds out the promise of revelation. In the rest of this monologue — it is emphatically not a dialogue nor an empathetic communion — the narrator tries to comfort himself with the thought that human beings may inspire in him what nature cannot. Yet he knows this is a delusion. All the components of transformation are present, but the scene remains resistant, despite the residual personification ('say', 'hear', 'foreheads') and even though he also notices, a little later, the evocative pattern of colour and light on two houses. Once again, it confirms for the narrator his lack of literary ability, his failure to grasp in perception, understanding and word the inner meaning of the fleeting, contingent impressions and sensations.

The finale of this sequence involves one of the most famous moments in *A la recherche*, the uneven paving stones in the courtyard of the hôtel de Guermantes. While set in a townscape rather than a landscape, this incident is expressly linked to the narrator's travels in the countryside around Balbec and to the Martinville steeples (*RTP*, IV, 445; *SLT*, VI, 216) because it imparts the same sensations, but now also dispels his doubts about his literary gifts, which had seemed insuperable on his train journey back to Paris. On this occasion, the sensation is of coolness and dazzling light and he stands there with a foot on either paving stone wondering what recollection is being stirred:

> Chaque fois que je refaisais rien que matériellement ce même pas, il me restait inutile; mais si je réussissais, oubliant la matinée Guermantes, à retrouver ce que j'avais senti en posant ainsi mes pieds, de nouveau la vision éblouissante et indistincte me frôlait comme si elle m'avait dit: 'Saisis-moi au passage si tu en as la force, et tâche à résoudre l'énigme de bonheur que je te propose'. (*RTP*, IV, 446)

> [Every time that I merely repeated this physical movement, I achieved nothing; but if I succeeded, forgetting the Guermantes party, in recapturing what I had felt when I first placed my feet on the ground in this way, again the dazzling and indistinct vision fluttered near me, as if to say: 'Seize me as I pass if you can, and try to solve the riddle of happiness which I set you'.] (*SLT*, VI, 217)

The personified vision here offers a revelation similar to the trees at Hudimesnil, no less teasing, but nonetheless more positively phrased. And now the Narrator does recognise the source of the vision: two equally uneven flagstones in the baptistery at St Mark's in Venice, forgotten but now resurrected through 'un brusque hasard' [a chance happening] (*RTP*, IV, 446; *SLT*, VI, 218), connect the past with the present. Although more abstract, less strikingly characterised than previous instances and not inanimate in quite the same way, the vision here, rooted in a physical action and sensation, nevertheless constitutes a decisive example of the rhetorical scheme of interest to us, for it is clear that this whole chain of prosopopoeias and personifications constitutes, in fact, an allegory of the writer's development and vocation; and allegory, we recall, features as an ingredient in the dynamics and interpretation of prosopopoeia. Occurring at nodal points over the entire span of *A la recherche*, interlinked by references and echoes back and forth, these episodes are thus embedded into one of the most critical themes in the novel and help illuminate its workings and significance.

Alongside this emphasis on the writer's calling sits a no less crucial thematic strand in which prosopopoeia likewise has a role to play: love. It is a sphere in which some of Proust's most innovative forays into prosopopoeia and the inanimate occur. For our present purposes, the focus will be on two objects, the letter and the telegram, and their interplay, relating to one major incident, the disappearance and death of Albertine.[25] The importance of the letter was already underscored in our opening instance of prosopopoeia in which Gisèle recounts and transcribes her exam question. This new sequence starts at the beginning of *Albertine disparue* (a title whose ambiguity nicely captures both disappearance and death) when the narrator receives a letter from Albertine expressly designed to say in mediated form what she cannot bring herself to say in person, namely that she is leaving (*RTP*, IV, 5; *SLT*, V, 477). The letter, quoted in its entirety, is her surrogate and stands in for her absence; words — voice rather than face — speak where she cannot or will not. The letter plunges the narrator into a frenzy of hypothesis, as he tries to speculate at length on when or whether or how Albertine might return and to conjecture whether or not she had planned to leave long before it happened. Moreover, this letter itself is the counterpart of another he had previously opened by mistake and erroneously supposed it to be a coded message to his mistress, whereas in fact that letter was genuine but delivered to the wrong address (*RTP*, IV, 10; *SLT*, V, 485–86). In both cases, the narrator's inferences are wide of the mark, yet they continue to feed his own tortured thoughts and hyperbolical feelings, despite being punctuated at regular intervals by the stark realisation encapsulated in Françoise's repeated factual phrase: 'Mademoiselle Albertine est partie' [Mademoiselle Albertine has gone] (*RTP*, IV, 3, 8, 12, 18; *SLT*, V, 477, 483, 488, 495).

The next stage of the narrative alternates the media of communication, mixing letters with telegrams, both forms in which address and apostrophe, as well as the sense of immediacy, are dominant. Two telegrams arrive from Saint-Loup who has offered his discreet assistance in the search for Albertine. The first, brief and quoted verbatim in capitals, informs the narrator that the women have gone away for three days (*RTP*, IV, 32; *SLT*, V, 512) and the second, paraphrased, that Saint-Loup has met Mme Bontemps, Albertine's aunt, but in so doing has been spotted by Albertine herself and has had his mission exposed (*RTP*, IV, 34–35; *SLT*, V, 515–16). The medium then switches rapidly to and fro between a telegram from Albertine, offering to return (*RTP*, IV, 36; *SLT*, V, 517), and correspondence between the two lovers in which the narrator ends by declaring that he intends to turn his attentions to Andrée. These missives are typically set out in full and are arranged so that the stream of exchanges with their contradictory leitmotifs of passion and indifference, yearning and distance, appears not just sequentially but at times contrapuntally. During a subsequent stay in Venice, the narrator himself sends Albertine a telegram, the content of which is summarised, begging her to return on any terms. His fantasy that she might agree is cut off by a brief sentence in the stark past historic, 'Elle ne revint jamais' [She never came back] (*RTP*, IV, 58; *SLT*, V, 544). However, no sooner has the telegram been sent than he receives one from Mme Bontemps, reporting grave news:

> MON PAUVRE AMI, NOTRE PETITE ALBERTINE N'EST PLUS, PARDONNEZ-MOI DE VOUS DIRE CETTE CHOSE AFFREUSE, VOUS QUI L'AIMIEZ TANT. ELLE A ÉTÉ JETÉE PAR SON CHEVAL CONTRE UN ARBRE PENDANT UNE PROMENADE. TOUS NOS EFFORTS N'ONT PU LA RANIMER. QUE NE SUIS-PAS MORTE A SA PLACE! (*RTP*, IV, 58)

> [My poor friend, our little Albertine is no more. Forgive me for breaking this terrible news to you who were so fond of her. She was thrown by her horse against a tree while she was out riding. All our efforts to restore her to life were unavailing. If only I had died in her stead!] (*SLT*, V, 544)

Yet this is not quite the end it seems. At that moment, in an apparent *coup de théâtre*, two letters arrive from Albertine herself, the second urgently making the same point as before — that she is eager to return. The contents of the letters are thus at variance with the telegram, since both derive from sources with a claim on credibility. The narrator quickly realises, however, that these letters must have been written before her riding accident; so that Albertine has scarcely been conjured back into precarious life through the vagaries of the postal system before she is consigned once more to the void. The whole episode thus appears definitively closed: Albertine is dead.[26] Or, in a further twist, perhaps not.

At a later point in the narrative, when the narrator has made his long-planned visit to Venice with his mother, he receives a telegram. The name of the recipient is uncertain and he is made to sign for it by way of confirmation. He opens it and reads: 'MON AMI VOUS ME CROYEZ MORTE, PARDONNEZ-MOI, JE SUIS TRÈS VIVANTE, JE VOUDRAIS VOUS VOIR, VOUS PARLER MARIAGE, QUAND REVENEZ-VOUS? TENDREMENT. ALBERTINE' [My dear friend, you think me dead, forgive me, I am quite alive, I long to see you, talk about marriage, when do you return? Affectionately. Albertine] (*RTP*, IV, 220; *SLT*, V, 736). Throwing the narrator back into introspective ruminations, these words do not nevertheless have the effect of rekindling his love because, he explains, the self that loved Albertine is itself dead and cannot be revived. A little later, in conversation with his mother about Saint-Loup's forthcoming wedding, about which they have both received letters, he rapidly sees that the telegraphist had wrongly deciphered the name of the telegram's sender; the sender was in reality Gilberte, whose florid signature he had transliterated into the name of Albertine. 'Combien de lettres lit dans un mot une personne distraite et surtout prévenue, qui part de l'idée que la lettre est d'une certaine personne? [...] On devine en lisant, on crée' [How many letters are actually read into a word by a careless person who knows what to expect, who sets out with the idea that the message is from a certain person. [...] We guess as we read, we create] (*RTP*, IV, 235; *SLT*, V, 753–54). 'On crée'. Yet this purely illusory creativity has a direct impact on the function of the message the narrator receives. The telegram-prosopopoeia of 'Albertine' speaks, apostrophising him, but ultimately remains a dead letter, with the result that the voice from beyond the grave — one prominent feature of the classical understanding of prosopopoeia — can no longer fulfil its promise, the *disparue* [dead/ disappeared] can no longer return. And the confusions over the names of the sender and of the recipient only serve to underline that this episode, like those that precede it, is not a comedy of errors but a drama of mis-communication and mis-reading.[27]

Although not by any means an exhaustive tally of the instances of telegraphic and epistolary exchange, actual or projected, in this section of *Albertine disparue*, the above account is intended to highlight not only the prevalence and intensity of their combinations and variations, each succeeding each with sometimes dizzying speed, but also the fact that such quoted communications (usually in capitals in the French text) take on a substantial visual presence on the printed page and are effectively the focus of and trigger for the action which flows from them. At the same time, the conventional attributes of prosopopoeia — the 'face', the features, the anthropomorphism it imparts — are now reduced to their basic dimension, the prominence of the voice, audible in telegrams and letters.[28] Designed to guarantee a speaking presence, such devices appear to bring the interlocutors closer together while in fact pushing them further apart and thereby sparking yet more convulsions in the narrator's parabola of desire, hope and despair, and indifference. In this way, Proust draws attention to the paradox of prosopopoeia as explored here: its illusion works as long as one believes that voice itself is an extension of the human, that it can be linked to a defined source, locatable, ascertainable, even if (in this case, especially if) that source is absent or dead. However, Proust's most radical experiments with this rhetorical form — apparent in the last few examples studied — leave the reader without that certainty; despite the presence of the voice, its putative source remains permanently empty, a ghost haunting the novel, a hollow signifier. In the end, prosopopoeia, in the love dimension of *A la recherche*, can present itself as an enigma rather than as a solution.

Boldness and innovation are the hallmarks of Proust's overall handling of prosopopoeia and inanimate objects. While he makes no observable hard-and-fast distinction between prosopopoeia and personification, he has a clear preference for the most audacious strains of rhetorical idiom which can serve his most ambitious purposes. Prosopopoeia is an ideal candidate for such purposes and Proust exploits its flexibility to the full. Whether in the misprisions of love or the struggles of the artist, he expands the range of work it is expected to carry out. It can act variously as a metatextual language for literature itself through its foregrounding of fictions of face, person and voice; as an instrument for exploring the interlacing of the self and the world; as a device which develops salient additions to the literary and rhetorical repertoire, such as the telegram and the postal services; and as a conduit for exposing the stateliness of rhetoric to the lability of writing. If prosopopoeia is not — could there ever be one? — Proust's modernist master trope, after the style of De Man, it nevertheless achieves in his hands a distinctiveness, a singularity, as a prime illustration of speculative thinking intrepidly 'flowing outwards to encompass the world's curiosities'.[29]

Notes to Chapter 14

1. All references incorporated in the text are to Marcel Proust, *A la recherche du temps perdu*, ed. by Jean-Yves Tadié and others, 4 vols, Bibliothèque de la Pléiade (Paris: Gallimard, 1987–89), II, 264 (hereafter referenced as *RTP* in main text). In 1999, Eddie Hughes gave me a copy of the first volume of this edition. The present essay is my tardy repayment of that compliment. Except where noted, English translations are taken from *In Search of Lost Time*, trans. by C. K. Scott-Moncrieff and Terence Kilmartin, rev. by D. J. Enright, 6 vols (London: Vintage, 2000–02), II, 567 (hereafter referenced as *SLT* in main text).
2. James J. Paxson, *The Poetics of Personification* (Cambridge: Cambridge University Press, 1994), p. 14.
3. 'Sophisticated' is the description given by Paxson, *Personification*, p. 17. For Quintilian, see also William J. Kennedy, ' "Voice" and "Address" in Literary Theory', *Oral Tradition*, 2 (1987), 214–30 (pp. 216–18), and Blandine Perona, *Prosopopée et 'persona' à la Renaissance* (Paris: Garnier, 2013), pp. 7–8.
4. Quintilian, *The Orator's Education (Institutio oratoria)*, trans. by Donald A. Russell, 5 vols, Loeb Classical Library (Cambridge, MA: Harvard University Press, 2001), IV, 9.2.29–37 for this and the examples that follow.

5. Ibid., IV, 9.2.37.
6. Gavin Alexander, 'Prosopopoeia: The Speaking Figure', in *Renaissance Figures of Speech*, ed. by Sylvia Adamson, Gavin Alexander and Katrin Ettenhuber (Cambridge: Cambridge University Press, 2007), pp. 97–112 (p. 108).
7. The Catalogue collectif de France under 'prosopopée' gives plentiful examples. The pamphlet literature of the Fronde is an especially rich source of prosopopoeia.
8. Quintilian, *The Orator's Education*, IV, 9.2.36. See further *La Personnification du Moyen Age au XVIIIe siècle*, ed. by Mireille Demaules (Paris: Garnier, 2014).
9. See, for example, Michel Simonin, 'Poétique(s) du politique: Montaigne et Ronsard prosopographes de François de Guise', in *Ronsard et Montaigne, écrivains engagés?*, ed. by Michel Dassonville (Lexington, KY: French Forum, 1989), pp. 83–101.
10. Paxson, *Personification*, p. 26. All translations are my own unless stated otherwise.
11. Ibid., p. 27.
12. Ibid., p. 28.
13. Michael Riffaterre, 'Prosopopeia', *Yale French Studies*, 69 (1985), 107–23 (pp. 107–08).
14. Jeffrey Mehlman, *Genealogies of the Text: Literature, Psychoanalysis and Politics in Modern France* (Cambridge: Cambridge University Press, 1995), pp. 131–38 (p. 131), quoting De Man's own definitions of prosopopoeia. Cf. Paxson, *Personification*, pp. 33–34, 169.
15. Paxson, *Personification*, p. 167.
16. Ibid., p. 34.
17. Ibid., p. 1; Walter S. Melion and Bart Ramakers, 'Personification: An Introduction' in *Personification: Embodying Meaning and Emotion*, ed. by Walter S. Melion and Bart Ramakers (Leiden: Brill, 2016), p. 1.
18. Melion and Ramakers, 'Personification', p. 1.
19. For example, Cormac Newark and Ingrid Wassenaar, 'Proust and Music: The Anxiety of Competence', *Cambridge Opera Journal*, 9.2 (1997), 163–83 (p. 172); Stéphane Chaudier, 'Le Moyen Âge remis à sa place', in *Proust et les 'Moyen Âge'*, ed. by Sophie Duval and Miren Lacassagne (Paris: Hermann, 2015), pp. 335–62 (p. 351); Luzius Keller, 'Ekphrasis, prosopopée et pastiche: rhétorique de la description des tableaux chez Proust', in *Lire, traduire, éditer Proust* (Paris: Garnier, 2016), pp. 175–85.
20. Riffaterre, 'Prosopopeia', p. 116.
21. Marcel Proust, *Jean Santeuil, précédé de Les Plaisirs et les jours*, ed. by Pierre Clarac with Yves Sandre, Bibliothèque de la Pléiade (Paris: Gallimard, 1971), p. 395: 'donnaient au sable même l'air de lui dire: "Nous ne vous connaissons pas" [...] la figure des lieux change moins vite que les hommes et celle des flots ne changera jamais — qui semblent nous dire: "C'était hier"' [gave the very sand the appearance of saying to him, 'We don't know you'. [...] the shape of places changes less quickly than humankind and the shape of the waves will never change — seeming to say to us, 'That was yesterday'].
22. For more on this episode, from the standpoint of the theme of sleep, see Sarah Tribout-Joseph, *Proust and Joyce in Dialogue* (Oxford: Legenda, 2008), pp. 83–85.
23. Cf. Quintilian, *The Orator's Education*, IV, 9.2.31.
24. Cf. Riffaterre, 'Prosopopeia', p. 113: 'for Proust [...] both subject and object are the same textual entity'.
25. Another candidate, not considered here, is the telephone.
26. In French, the expression 'Albertine est/ était morte' runs like a refrain through this section of *Albertine disparue*.
27. See Malcolm Bowie, *Proust Among the Stars* (London: HarperCollins, 1998), p. 293, on the 'faulty communications network' in this scene, by which 'meaning is arbitrarily cancelled, distorted and restored'; see also Adam Watt, *Reading in Proust's 'A la recherche': 'le délire de la lecture'* (Oxford: Oxford University Press, 2009), pp. 123–29.
28. On this topic, see Béatrice Athias, *La Voix dans 'A la recherche du temps perdu' de Marcel Proust* (Paris: Classiques Garnier, 2021), and Anne Penesco, *Oralité du texte et écriture des voix dans 'A la recherche du temps perdu'* (Paris: Classiques Garnier, 2021).
29. Bowie, *Proust Among the Stars*, p. 245.

CHAPTER 15

Proust's House of Fiction

Patrick O'Donovan

Proust's *œuvre cathédrale* opens in what seems a modest bedroom. At a point in the darkness of the night when the Narrator is fully awake, he can at least approximately situate its contents: a chest of drawers, a desk, the fireplace, a window overlooking the street, the room's two doors. The novel's first sentences recall the regular habits of sleep of a bygone past. They carry a number of discreet indications as to period: the Narrator recalls extinguishing his candle, and a while later striking a match and consulting his watch. His own accustomed room, with its fireplace, its desk and so on, belongs to an undisclosed place and time, and now becomes the site of a series of abrupt turns. Scenes of childhood come to the surface. He finds that his mind can substitute for the 'plan du lieu' [the map of the place] where he is in fact sleeping, the sensation of being in other more or less familiar rooms.[1] At first, he struggles to identify the dwelling in which he seems to find himself as he shifts between 'mondes désorbités' [dislocated worlds] (*RTP*, 1, 5; *SLT*, 1, 4, translation modified). The configuration of these other rooms then becomes more immediate. In them he can discern nothing less than 'les traits originaux de mon moi' [my self's original features] (*RTP*, 1, 6; *SLT*, 1, 4, translation modified). Certain items come more sharply to mind: a four-poster bed, a nightlight, a marble fireplace. For these, he realises, form part of the arrangement of his bedroom in Combray. But then, all at once, he is as if in his *chambre* at Mme de Saint-Loup's property at Tansonville. This is a setting that is close in space if not in time to the childhood scenes that the Narrator is about to broach, most pressingly the fateful evening visit of Swann.

The emblematic metaphor to which both Proust and his Narrator appeal, as the architectural model for a book grounded in a simple room, is indeed that of the cathedral.[2] As Luc Fraisse has minutely shown, this figure is one key to the project's highly propitious design. It gives expression to Proust's earliest intuition, 'à la fois très obscure et très nette' [all at once very opaque and very distinct], of the complete blueprint of his book and it sustained him in pursuing it right to its conclusion.[3] The depiction of space and time as these impinge on the half-awake, half-asleep Narrator has long been proclaimed to be one frame of reference for the novel's architecture.[4] These initial fluctuating reminiscences, though transient, are sufficient to encompass much of the plot that will follow. The Narrator's visit to Gilberte at Tansonville spans the end of *Albertine disparue* and the beginning of *Le*

Temps retrouvé. He recalls by way of contrast that house's more permissive regimen, where 'on dînait maintenant [...] à une heure où jadis on dormait depuis longtemps à Combray' [one dined now [...] at an hour at which in the past one had long been asleep at Combray] (*RTP*, IV, 266; *SLT*, VI, 1). He remembers the bedroom, again candlelit, in which, again on the point of falling asleep with book in hand, he reads Edmond de Goncourt's purported journal. He concludes that his ambition to become a writer is at a dead end. But then the novel is reframed. When the Narrator returns some years later to Paris, he makes his way to an altogether new house, that of the new princesse de Guermantes, where what will finally be disclosed to him is the outline of his novel or, better, its 'scaffolding'.[5]

If the model of the cathedral can be applied to the novel it is because of its multiplicity, its extreme plasticity. So argues Jacques Rancière. But this cannot be regarded as a fully premeditated prototype, he claims, given that the wartime expansion of the novel resulted in the increasingly anarchic absorption of elements of life into its architecture.[6] Perhaps, then, another approach could be taken to the novel's 'écrivain bâtisseur' [writer-builder].[7] One alternative is to look more expressly at rooms and houses. It is, after all, of these and of their configurations that the novel speaks to begin with. The Proustian estate will extend to many such structures, with a proliferation of discrete and diverse settings, diurnal as well as nocturnal, often particularised, but sometimes not. And despite Proust's affinity with the image of the cathedral, there is also scope to gauge his novelistic practice in the light of Henry James's no less graphic metaphor, that of the fiction as a house — in which, precisely, houses, real or imaginary, are at issue.[8] As Anna Kornbluh observes, James's 'constructivist conceit' gives rise to 'buildings [that] confound all who enter, defamiliarizing space itself', just as the disparate environments sensed by the Proustian Narrator in the dark can be dislocated and dislocating.[9] Proust's novel, for its part, generates its own even more grandiose reflexive tropes: of an imposing cake as a Ninevite palace, a lone house framed and illuminated so perfectly as to transmute into a venerable shrine, or the craving induced by Elstir's vaporous seascapes for beauties in nature that are if anything architectural.[10] This dual dimension of the 'patchwork novel' — *A la recherche* as the depiction of an array of architectures and at the same time as itself a consummate work of architectural contrivance — is a call to the labours of speculative attention, prompting the question: just how are its spaces, literal and figurative, to be connected to the 'multiple and accumulating interpretive and phenomenological possibilities' that it contains?[11]

The Narrator opens with a statement of his marked residual affinity with rooms: in the long reveries that followed his awakening he claims that he was able to remember all those where he had ever slept. But the same may not be true of the houses in which they are situated. These must await the *madeleine*. After the novel's early scenes, the settings of its proliferating story will emerge more tangibly from a cup of tea, along with its 'personnages consistants et reconnaissables' [people, solid and recognisable] (*RTP*, I, 47; *SLT*, I, 55). Though this part of the novel remains largely confined to Combray, already a varied distribution of social spaces can be detected on the horizon. It is not for nothing that Samuel Beckett refers to Swann as 'the corner-stone of the [novel's] entire structure'.[12] Like the Narrator's parents, he divides his time between Combray and Paris. It is he who connects not only the city and the country but also realms of the metropolitan world from which the Narrator's family seems largely exempt: high worldly contacts with the aristocracy, indeed with royalty, together with associations that are a good deal more dubious. Even in the provincial milieu of Combray, reports of an improbably diverse circle of connections hint at new manifestations of the two ways, those of Swann and of the Guermantes, but also more mixed settings. When the focus switches to Paris it quickly emerges that this transition comes with an architecture, social as well as material, to match. The person to whom these places and their construction will be of paramount concern is the Narrator as protagonist: his experiences of them account for much of the substance of the story, as the contrasting depictions of Balbec and Venice show. And shifting sites will herald further shifts, major and minor, in prevailing collective norms. Far from being banished to his bedroom, the hero dines with Norpois alongside his parents in Paris.

When the Narrator reports that what he apprehends in his teacup is the solid form of the surroundings of his childhood, it is to invoke a now augmented range of architectural bearings: here, Léonie's old grey house adjoining his parents' summer pavilion, there, Monsieur Swann's park with its gardens in flower, and so on. Jonathan Culler has argued that, rather than reproducing a given reality, a fiction 'inscribes its own context, institutes its own scene'. Rooms, modest or not, give instituting something to go on and represent also a figure of construction, so illustrating Culler's conclusion: as well as what it institutes, a fiction 'gives us to experience [its] instituting'.[13] The places to which the Narrator refers have a twofold significance. They represent a much more substantive step in the direction of the novel's foreshadowed topography. More significantly, their miraculous appearance seems to unleash an architectural agency that proves to be as potent as it is far-reaching. Tansonville at the outset is more a garden than a house: it exists to present the hero with his first sighting of a 'fillette d'un blond roux' and 'un monsieur habillé de coutil' [little girl with fair, reddish hair, a gentleman dressed in twill]. He is also afforded a glimpse of 'une dame en blanc' [a lady in white], whom he does not recognise as the 'dame en rose' [lady in pink] (*RTP*, I, 139–40; *SLT*, I, 168–69; translation modified). The 'partie irréelle' [unreal aspect] (*RTP*, III, 788; *SLT*, V, 321) intrinsic to the serial incarnations of the Verdurins' salon can be sensed for real in their amiably mobile furniture.[14] And near the end of the novel, each of the Narrator's prized final disclosures of involuntary memory is abetted by a house, in the first instance by its 'pavés assez mal équarris' [rather uneven paving-stones] (*RTP*, IV, 445; *SLT*, VI, 216; translation modified).

What Culler terms 'instituting', Kornbluh, for her part, identifies with the novel's form: what is at issue in the 'rigorous formalism' that she advances is 'the being of form'. The novel's 'formalization,' she claims, 'entails a certain priority of the spatial over the temporal'.[15] Its depiction of what James would name the 'right relations' between a dwelling and its inhabitants is, in Kornbluh's terms, a 'projection': not only a representation of some pre-existing 'constituted reality', but also a path to 'the construction of other visions'.[16] Rooms or houses in fiction are instances of a formalisation that is architectural in the sense that it brings about a 'rupture'. For this is ultimately what any architecture does: 'it wields power on the ground'. If it is deployed on the ground of a fiction, it is as a means of mastering 'the practice of "space as the fundamental category of politics"'.[17] This multidimensional affinity of novelistic form with space rather than time, and by extension with politics, emerges from a distinctive aspect of the experience of reading, namely its retrospectivity. Citing the example of Dickens's *Bleak House*, Kornbluh argues that the time of reading is simply a 'correlate' of the novel's length. Being spatial, form generates, by contrast, a 'synthetic thought'. What makes this architectural conception of form strictly literary is the condition under which it can be perceived. For it is 'after the time of reading' that it can be apprehended, 'as a blueprint or model'.[18]

A vivid illustration of such an effect is provided by the 'petite église' [little church] (*RTP*, I, 185; *SLT*, I, 225) of the Verdurins in *Un amour de Swann*. This setting does not, of course, form part of the Narrator's initial oneiric inventory, though the not so '"joli milieu"' ['nice lot of people'] (*RTP*, I, 196; *SLT*, I, 239) is known to his family. It also launches a distinct architectural cycle, as the Verdurin plot will extend into new rooms and houses, and not only in Paris. The insistent reprise of past bedrooms at strategic points in the novel is thus sharply offset, as Edward J. Hughes argues, by a discontinuity, if not a rupture, in the plot, first with this switch to the Verdurins' '"petit noyau"' ['little nucleus'] (*RTP*, I, 185; *SLT*, I, 225) and then in turn to Balbec, with 'its crucial broadening in the socialization of the novel's hero'.[19] The architecture of the novel is affected too. The ceaseless efforts of Madame Verdurin, up to her final incarnation as the princesse de Guermantes, 'à "faire clan"' [to 'make a set'] (*RTP*, IV, 562; *SLT*, VI, 369, translation modified) frame the novel's social plot: they exhibit the extreme versatility of the social spaces in which it unfolds.[20] Though Swann, dining out now among the Verdurins, remains a constant, the insertion of a mutable new interior into the narrative means that a house of fiction, or '*fabula*', comes to be erected within the house of fiction. The Narrator, in the guise of 'protagonist *as* storyteller', attaches his history to that of Swann, whose 'belated follower' he will continue to be until the very end of the novel.[21] Swann provides a blueprint for the Narrator's own experience of a social world that continues to metamorphose long after his death. It is in his everlasting apartment, with its paintings displayed in an 'arrangement de "collectionneur"' [a typical 'collector's' arrangement], that the 'caractère démodé' [unfashionable character] of the liaison between the very 'Restoration' duc de Guermantes and the altogether 'Second Empire' Odette becomes unmistakable (*RTP*, IV, 596; *SLT*, VI, 413). It is thus through retelling, replication and reframing that the novel shapes and reshapes its spatial coordinates and with them its social meanings, or, to apply Kornbluh's formulation, that it 'actuate[s] a projection of the social space in its world'.[22]

These and other settings disclose and connect unanticipated worlds: they point to the many-sided co-existence of high and low, public and private, the decorous and the indecent. It was in Proust's own lifetime that the 'private' room emerged as a 'truly secluded space' in domestic architecture. This development led in turn to the reinvention of spaces of circulation: 'the application of the corridor to domestic architecture not only affected the use of rooms — giving them a specific purpose — but reinforced the division between the upper and the lower ranks of society'.[23] In the novel, the portrayal of space is not restricted to 'served' or principal rooms like those brought into being by the Verdurins or the Guermantes. Its projections can be connected to the operation of a 'concept of social order' in the architecture of these more complex interiors, one that advances a distinction in the design and deployment of 'served' and 'servant' spaces.[24] For the narrative extends also to 'servant' or ancillary areas, including hallways, corridors, entrances and above all stairs. When the hero makes his furtive visit to his uncle Adolphe, he hears Odette's voice and her laughter from the staircase; some years later, he can scent her all-pervading perfume as he mounts the steps of her new home near the Bois de Boulogne. Odette herself, during her affair with Swann, faithfully ascends the 'escalier raide, obscur et fétide' [steep and dark and fetid staircase] (*RTP*, I, 238; *SLT*, I, 291) leading to the room of her seamstress friend. Françoise's loudest complaints on moving to the hôtel de Guermantes are brought on by its '"satanés escaliers"' ['confounded stairs'] (*RTP*, II, 334; *SLT*, III, 31). It is through the window on the staircase where the Narrator awaits the duc and duchesse de Guermantes that he spies 'un Charlus que je ne soupçonnais pas' [a Charlus whose existence I did not suspect] (*RTP*, IV, 353; *SLT*, VI, 104). Stairways prove to be transitional spaces in more ways than one. By definition, they are intermediate settings, lending particular significance to thresholds. They bridge distinct social milieux and assume a heightened import at moments where characters migrate between them. They acquire an exemplary symbolic significance among the characters themselves: as Swann mounts the 'escalier monumental' [monumental staircase] leading to Madame de Saint-Euverte's salon, he feels acutely his separation from Odette. For all the magnificence of the scene, it is on the 'étages noirs, malodorants et casse-cou de la petite couturière retirée' [dark, evil-smelling, breakneck flights to the little dressmaker's] that he broods (*RTP*, I, 319; *SLT*, I, 390–91).[25] Stairs are also paramount sites of incident. The discoveries that result from the chance encounters they bring about can lead to irreversible and far-reaching cognitive shifts. On the other hand, stairs can also have a more decidedly public orientation. In describing his slow descent of the steps leading away from the princesse de Guermantes's soirée, it is as 'tout un tableau vivant et comme une scène historique' [a complete tableau vivant, and, as it were, a historical scene] (*RTP*, III, 118; *SLT*, IV, 139) that the Narrator relives the moment and recounts the social performance of those who surrounded him. And finally the motif of the stairway proves also to have a structural function. From start to finish, the plot of *Le Côté de Guermantes* takes the Narrator up and down stairs and it is a delayed return to this same locus that will give *Sodome et Gomorrhe* its initial impetus, bringing about a pivotal reorientation of *A la recherche* as a whole.

 James's legendary preface to *The Portrait of a Lady* long postdates the novel. It is a 'very clever' retrospective panorama and draws on an intermittent if potent thread in the novel itself.[26] As she experiences the revival of innumerable 'disconnected visions' from her own past, Isabel Archer endures a moment in which 'the truth of things, their mutual relations, their meaning and for the most part their horror, rose before her with a kind of architectural vastness'.[27] Proust's much longer novel is different. The origins and growth of his plot are rooted in a sequence of rooms, houses and locales all at once more variegated, more multifaceted, more specific — in a word, more architectural. No less decisively, the Narrator's experience of self connects throughout to his volatile experience of these environments. As Walter Benjamin says of Proust, 'he built a house for the swarm of his thoughts'.[28] In the novel's very earliest drafts, it is amidst the objects in a family home in the countryside that the anxious hero feels he is 'entouré d'étrangers' [surrounded by strangers]. By contrast, his bedroom in Paris, whose furniture forms part of an habitual everyday ensemble, is as if 'enfermé en moi' [enclosed within me].[29] This dimension of the novel is central to what Rancière terms its '"forme de l'art"' ['form of art'], the means by which it brings about a 'union' between an '*impression*', like that of sleeplessness in his unfamiliar hotel room in Balbec, and its form, or '*architecture*'.[30] And unlike James's reappraisal of his own novel, the kind of self-reference implied by a treatment of space that is vertiginously connotative is wholly internal to *A la recherche*. As Rancière recalls, the work is at once essay and novel. It combines these two centrifugal forces within a single 'scène ambiguë' [ambiguous scene], in which the 'mythes qui l'absolutisent' [myths that confer an absolute status on it] are juxtaposed with the 'discours critiques qui en démontent le mécanisme' [critical discourses that lay bare its mechanisms].[31]

Repeatedly in *The Arcades Project*, Benjamin returns to the opening scene of *A la recherche*. What makes the novel exemplary in his eyes is its act of staking an entire life on the 'supremely dialectical point of rupture: awakening'. It is exemplary in that it pinpoints the ideal condition of 'every presentation of history': that it should begin in just this way. 'In fact,' Benjamin claims, 'it should treat of nothing else'. The historical dimension comes into play via the dynamics of consciousness: 'there is a not-yet-conscious knowledge of *what has been*: its advancement has the structure of awakening'.[32] In truth, the beginning of the novel is also an anticipatory awakening, opening onto a spatial universe that is considerably wider and even more protean in scope than the opening pages suggest. The connection to '*what has been*', the true 'dividing point of life'[33] for the 'dormeur-architecte' [sleeper-architect], comes about only when he tastes the *madeleine*.[34] It is then that he begins to undergo his full architectural regeneration. He will be able to go beyond the 'décor strictement nécessaire' [the bare minimum of scenery] of the drama of his going to bed, beyond the 'deux étages reliés par un mince escalier' [two floors joined by a slender staircase] (*RTP*, I, 43; *SLT*, I, 50) of the opening scenes. This awakening will continue to revitalise the Narrator: it motivates his account of the many other sites over which the narrative will extend. And at its close, he will draw his own trenchant conclusion regarding the relationship between people and places. A narrative in which, as he declares, 'tous mes passés' [all my various pasts] are to be blended into one must be architectural in scope: 'nous ne pourrions pas raconter nos rapports avec un être, que nous avons même peu connu, sans faire se succéder les sites les plus différents de notre vie' [it would be impossible to depict our relationship with anyone whom we have even slightly known without passing in review, one after another, the most different settings of our life] (*RTP*, IV, 608; *SLT*, VI, 429).

Rancière too recalls the Narrator in his room, poised between wakefulness and the state of dreaming. The former he aligns with habit, but also the potentially deceptive practice of representation, the latter with 'la nuit des dislocations et des terreurs' [the night of dislocation and terror] with which the novel opens.[35] In Rancière's view, Proust displays an unusually versatile grasp of the constant tension that exists between all of these forces: this is what distinguishes his work from that of Flaubert and Mallarmé, and accounts for its impact as 'un art qui s'examine lui-même, qui fait fiction de cet examen' [an art that scrutinises itself, which makes fiction out of this scrutiny].[36] For what Rancière shares with Benjamin and also with Proust himself is a sensitivity to the enduring urgency of the kind of critical attention that liminal moments like these demand. This attitude can be compared to what Proust referred to as an act of 'sauvetage' [rescue]: a special variety of intelligent labour, all at once 'prudent, docile, hardi' [prudent, docile, daring]. It is to be brought to bear on precisely the fluctuations that occur between the states of sleep and wakefulness, 'sans que cette intervention amenât le réveil' [but without this intervention bringing about an awakening]. Such an act of attention calls upon all of the reserves of the mind and the body, but Proust concludes that this contradictory task, while it demands special precautions, does not belong in the realm of the impossible.[37] Here is what Rancière considers the central enigma of a work in which the Narrator's own spatial intuitions pinpoint the fragile boundary that separates poetic dissolution of self from schizophrenic dissociation.[38] Rancière gives an unsparing account of the ambiguities that beset several of the architectural models that Proust himself invokes, including those of the cathedral and the dress, yet does conclude by offering a redesigned model of the former as the basis of the novel's 'réussite paradoxale' [paradoxical success].[39] The work, he argues, draws ultimately on the cathedral as a twofold metaphor. Its first function is to serve as a 'machine fictionnelle' [fictional machine]: it must reconcile the novel's contradictory appeal to the primacy of a pre-ordained plan and its openness to the chaotic contingencies of its plot. And secondly it is a 'machine théorique' [theoretical machine], one that makes the 'impossible accord de la nécessité du langage et de l'indifférence de ce qu'il dit' [the impossible accord between the necessity of its language and the insignificance of what it says] into the matter of a fiction.[40]

These readings conspicuously refashion the nocturnal scene in which *A la recherche* originates. In fact, the novel's fertile embellishment of this room of portents continues inevitably to haunt its reception, creative as well as critical, as a number of responses to the work confirm. Hughes, in the first of these, touches on the novel's protracted composition, which prompted adaptations to the original structural principle of cross-reference spanning the volumes in which Proust intended to publish *A la recherche*. The virtue of the model of the cathedral lay in its uncanny adaptability to large shifts in the novel's plot, many of them unforeseen.[41] But, as Hughes points out, the work's expanding scope also led Proust to unmake and redesign its key structural bearings, by displacing retrospective references to 'the well-established thematics of the dream life and [...] the incipit of *Combray*', especially at the beginning of *Le Côté de Guermantes*, and in the scene in *Sodome et Gomorrhe* devoted to the Narrator's exchange with the operator of the lift in the Grand-Hôtel on his return from La Raspelière and his broken sleep in the hours that follow. The effect is to accentuate the growing place of 'subaltern culture' in the novel.[42] As Hughes goes on to show, the ideological density that results from the novel's long composition comes to be matched not only by alterations to the structural blueprint that Proust had initially adopted but also by a much-expanded tonal range. Where in its earlier parts 'medievalism works as an antidote to dialectical materialism', the novel will later be subjected to a social awakening that makes its reflections 'by turn ludic, moralizing, inconsequential, sceptical, erotic, cynical and campaigning'. A progressive expansion of spatial reference produces the opposite and, as Hughes argues, quite salutary effect from that of the Gothic: it takes the novel in the direction of 'a conscious, architectonic framing of social exchange'.[43] In brief, the success of the work in deploying its spaces and its clamorous emergent registers lies in its resistance to the lures of the *œuvre cathédrale*.

The mutability of the Proustian edifice proves to be a reference point if not the basis for later no less diversely experimental gestures. These substantiate and extend James's intuition that houses and their rooms have something to tell us about fiction. Raymond Bellour remarks that from the eighteenth century onwards the bedroom has become 'l'espace réservé de nos enfances' [the reserved space of our childhoods]. What results is a to-and-fro between this intimate domain and what lies beyond it, in which 'le dehors [...] revient pour s'illuminer d'être réfléchi et incorporé' [what is outside returns in search of the illumination of reflective and incorporated being]. Compared to the room in film or television, the 'chambre littéraire [...] est en même temps plus réelle et flotte plus, et a par là peut-être plus de virtualité encore' [literary chamber is at the same time more real and floats more, and for this reason possesses perhaps a yet greater degree of virtuality]. This is its peculiar privilege. The example of the Narrator's childhood bedroom in *A la recherche*, with its magic lantern, leads Bellour to conclude that 'la chambre de fiction renvoie alors souvent à l'irréel de la chambre "réelle"' [the bedroom in fiction thus often evokes what is unreal about rooms in 'reality']. This and other rooms resonate, as he says, in the truly unreal bedroom — the one lined with cork and sealed off from the outside world — where the '"vrai"' ['true'] Proust composes his novel.[44] Bellour's mention of the novel's nocturnal plot is not incidental. Far from the tranquil chamber to which Blaise Pascal enjoined his reader to retire, the instances that he cites, ranging over works by Franz Kafka, Henri Michaux and Samuel Beckett among others, encompass an intertextual and intermedial horizon within which the dislocated rooms of one's own typified by *A la recherche* come to be unmade, remade and reinhabited. Proust's own instituting was also to resonate architecturally in the rooms and houses, themselves highly assorted, of Georges Perec — even though Perec early on concluded that in the era of the mass media the writer could no longer live enclosed 'dans le silence de son cabinet, parfois tapissé de liège' [in the silence of his study, sometimes lined with cork].[45] A certain 'Parcel Mroust' equips Perec with an epigraph for a chapter on the bed in *Espèces d'espaces*: 'Longtemps je me suis couché par écrit' [For a long time I put myself to bed in writing].[46] In the chapter that follows, on 'La chambre' [the bedroom], he remarks on his 'mémoire exceptionnelle' [exceptional memory] and echoes the awakening Proustian Narrator in saying that he can recall practically all of the rooms in which he ever slept.[47] He includes a fragment from a work in progress that was intended to document these *chambres*, a project he described as 'une sorte d'autobiographie vespérale' [a sort of vesperal autobiography].[48] Not the least suggestive outcome of his reinvention of the unassuming bedroom in these and others of his works is the possibility they afford of projecting back into *A la recherche* the egalitarian promise of 'la petite madeleine pour tous' [the little *madeleine* for one and all].[49]

But the last word goes to Roland Barthes, who considers the *chambre* an inordinate paradox: it is structured but independent of any norm.[50] He refers in *Roland Barthes par Roland Barthes* to his personal mania for prolepsis. At several points in his writings, he announces grand syntheses of his own to follow, ventures that live on even if they will never be finally brought to completion.[51] Yet here again, Proust offers a redeeming precedent. Barthes detects in *A la recherche* a cryptic architecture applicable to such projects, leading him to conclude that 'l'œuvre n'est jamais que le méta-livre (le commentaire prévisionnel) d'une œuvre à venir, qui, *ne se faisant pas*, devient cette œuvre-ci' [the work is only ever a meta-book (the prefigurative commentary) of a work still to come, which, *by not being actually realised*, becomes this very work]. This dual characterisation — of the work as prototype and self-anticipating edifice — calls for amended spatial archetypes. The alternative for which Barthes would reach is one that recalls in this context the salience of shifts, transitions and transformations among the many settings of *A la recherche*, and in turn the element of liminality that pervades its construction from start to finish: 'En un mot, l'œuvre est un échelonnement; son être est le *degré*: un escalier qui ne s'arrête pas' [In a word, the work's progress is step-wise; its mode of being is to proceed by *degree*: as in an unending staircase].[52] If the hermetic narratorial room is definitively the setting in which the novel will or will not come to be written, steps and stairs are a new emblem for the house of thresholds that may result. In this, one can trail the Narrator himself, who first appears on the point of mounting the 'escalier détesté' [hateful staircase] (*RTP*, I, 27; *SLT*, I, 31) in Combray and takes his precarious leave as he descends a stairway that will bring him finally to 'le grand repos' [the great rest] (*RTP*, IV, 618; *SLT*, VI, 443) of death.[53] It remains for his prospective readers to give effect for themselves to the work's open '*proposition*', as they wish to and as best they can[54] — an enterprise in which they may follow the methodical lead of Proust as labourer, 'tantôt tourmenté, tantôt exalté, de toute manière modeste' [sometimes tormented, sometimes elated, in any event modest].[55]

Notes to Chapter 15

1. Marcel Proust, *A la recherche du temps perdu*, ed. by Jean-Yves Tadié, 4 vols, Bibliothèque de la Pléiade (Paris: Gallimard, 1987–89), I, 5 (hereafter referenced as *RTP* in the main text); *In Search of Lost Time*, trans. by C. K. Scott-Moncrieff and Terence Kilmartin, rev. by D. J. Enright, 6 vols (London: Vintage, 2000–02), I, 4, translation modified (hereafter referenced as *SLT* in the main text). All other translations are my own.
2. Marcel Proust, *Correspondance de Marcel Proust*, ed. by Philip Kolb, 21 vols (Paris: Plon, 1970–93), XVIII, 359; *RTP*, IV, 610; *SLT*, VI, 431–32. See also Richard Bales, *Proust and the Middle Ages* (Geneva: Droz, 1975), pp. 117–38.
3. Luc Fraisse, *L'Œuvre cathédrale: Proust et l'architecture médiévale* [1990], 2nd edn (Paris: Classiques Garnier, 2014), p. 10.
4. Jean-Yves Tadié, *Proust et le roman: essai sur les formes et techniques du roman dans 'A la recherche du temps perdu'* (Paris: Gallimard, 1971), p. 236.
5. Samuel Beckett, *Proust and Three Dialogues with Georges Duthuit* (London: Calder, 1965), p. 11.
6. Jacques Rancière, *La Parole muette: essai sur les contradictions de la littérature* (Paris: Fayard/Pluriel, 2010), p. 164. See also Edward J. Hughes, '"Les lignes vaines et solitaires de mon écriture": "Word" and "World" in Proust's *Recherche*', *Romanic Review*, 105.3-4 (2014), 201–13 (pp. 201–02).
7. Fraisse, *L'Œuvre cathédrale*, p. 9.
8. Henry James, *The Portrait of a Lady*, ed. by Philip Horne (London: Penguin, 2011), pp. 628–40.
9. Anna Kornbluh, *The Order of Forms: Realism, Formalism, and Social Space* (Chicago: University of Chicago Press, 2019), p. 41.
10. Proust also extols the disjointed houses of Baudelaire's poems, with their hallways like greenhouses, divans as deep as tombs and their balmy porticos, in *Essais*, ed. by Antoine Compagnon, Christophe Pradeau and Matthieu Vernet, Bibliothèque de la Pléiade (Paris: Gallimard, 2022), p. 1243.
11. Hannah Freed-Thall, *Spoiled Distinctions: Aesthetics and the Ordinary in French Modernism* (New York: Oxford University Press, 2015), pp. 36–37.
12. Beckett, *Proust and Three Dialogues with Georges Duthuit*, p. 34.
13. Jonathan Culler, 'The Most Interesting Thing in the World', *Diacritics*, 38.1-2 (2008), 7–16 (p. 14).
14. On the Verdurins' 'successive salons [as] a mindscape in time [...] strictly indistinguishable from works of art', see Malcolm Bowie, *Proust Among the Stars* (London: HarperCollins, 1998), p. 113.
15. Kornbluh, *The Order of Forms*, p. 40.
16. James, *The Portrait of a Lady*, p. 630; Kornbluh, *The Order of Forms*, pp. 40, 10.
17. Kornbluh, *The Order of Forms*, p. 42, quoting Fredric Jameson (who quotes in turn Henri Lefebvre), 'Architecture and the Critique of Ideology', in *Architecture, Criticism, Ideology*, ed. by Joan Ockman (Princeton, NJ: Princeton Architectural Press, 1985), pp. 51–87 (p. 53).
18. Kornbluh, *The Order of Forms*, p. 40.
19. Edward J. Hughes, *Proust, Class, and Nation* (Oxford: Oxford University Press, 2011), pp. 89, 111.
20. On the volatility of social value in the novel as exemplified by Madame Verdurin, see Edward J. Hughes, 'Proust and Social Spaces', in *The Cambridge Companion to Proust*, ed. by Richard Bales (Cambridge: Cambridge University Press, 2001), pp. 151–67 (pp. 155–56); Hughes notes also the increasing heterogeneity of social milieux at further pivotal points of the narrative.
21. Peter Brooks, *Reading for the Plot: Design and Intention in Narrative* (Cambridge, MA: Harvard University Press, 1984), pp. 261–62.
22. Kornbluh, *The Order of Forms*, p. 40. On the architecture of Venice as vehicle for psychological projection on the Narrator's part, see Bowie, *Proust Among the Stars*, pp. 95–96.
23. Dogma, *The Room of One's Own: The Architecture of the (Private) Room* (Milan: Black Square, 2017), p. 24.
24. Louis Kahn, 'Order in Architecture', *Perspecta*, 4 (1957), 58–63 (p. 59).
25. As Mauricio R. Narváez notes, the particularisation of stairs consolidates their kinesic and other functions in the novel; see 'L'Esprit de l'escalier: fonctions de l'"escalier" dans *A la recherche du temps perdu*', *Marcel Proust aujourd'hui*, 11 (2014), 125–41 (pp. 128–32).

26. Virginia Woolf, *The Diary of Virginia Woolf*, ed. by Anne Olivier Bell and Andrew McNeillie, 5 vols (London: Hogarth, 1982), IV *(1931–35)*, 241.
27. James, *The Portrait of a Lady*, p. 590. See Kornbluh, *The Order of Forms*, p. 34.
28. Walter Benjamin, 'The Image of Proust' [1929], in *Illuminations*, ed. by Hannah Arendt, trans. by Harry Zohn (New York: Schocken Books, 2007), p. 203.
29. Marcel Proust, *Les Soixante-quinze Feuillets et autres manuscrits inédits*, ed. by Nathalie Mauriac Dyer (Paris: Gallimard, 2021), p. 36.
30. Rancière, *La Parole muette*, p. 155.
31. Ibid., p. 173.
32. Walter Benjamin, *The Arcades Project*, trans. by Howard Eiland and Kevin McLaughlin (Cambridge, MA: Harvard University Press, 1999), pp. 464, 844, 883.
33. Ibid., p. 844.
34. Fraisse, *L'Œuvre cathédrale*, p. 61.
35. Rancière, *La Parole muette*, p. 159.
36. Ibid., p. 175.
37. Proust, *Correspondance*, XX, 497. See also Proust, *Essais*, p. 1267.
38. Rancière, *La Parole muette*, p. 159. See also Edward J. Hughes, *Marcel Proust: A Study in the Quality of Awareness* (Cambridge: Cambridge University Press, 1983), pp. 186–88.
39. Rancière, *La Parole muette*, pp. 153–54, 166.
40. Ibid., pp. 165, 173.
41. See Nathalie Mauriac Dyer, who insists on Proust's unbroken commitment to his project for a fully composed work, however disjointed the labour of its construction, in *Proust inachevé: le dossier d''Albertine disparue'* (Paris: Champion, 2005), pp. 251, 260. By contrast, Suzanne Guerlac concludes that 'the very being of the work' is affected by its progressive expansion, meaning that the sense of its architecture is problematised: see 'Rancière and Proust: Two Temptations', in *Understanding Rancière, Understanding Modernism*, ed. by Patrick M. Bray (London: Bloomsbury, 2017), pp. 161–77 (p. 173).
42. Hughes, *Proust, Class, and Nation*, p. 189.
43. Ibid., pp. 76, 275, 167–68.
44. Raymond Bellour, *L'Entre-images 2: Mots, images* (Paris: P.O.L, 1999), pp. 281, 304, 307. Olivier Wickers notes the paradox by which Proust's strange room 'nous est devenue naturelle, telle une bizarrerie supplémentaire à côté du grand roman qui l'est tellement plus' [has come to seem natural to us, like an additional incongruity alongside a great novel that is more incongruous yet]; see *Chambres de Proust* (Paris: Flammarion, 2013), p. 28. See also Jean-Pierre Richard, for whom the reading of Proust is likewise a form of *enfermement*, or self-enclosure in the infinity of meaning, and for this reason, he contends, a liberation; see 'Proust et la demeure', *Littérature*, 164 (2011), 83–92 (p. 92).
45. Georges Perec, 'Écriture et mass-media', in *Entretiens et conférences*, ed. by Dominique Bertelli and Mireille Ribière, 2 vols (Paris: Joseph K, 2003), I, 94–104 (p. 96).
46. Georges Perec, *Œuvres*, ed. by Christelle Reggiani, 2 vols (Paris: Gallimard, 2017), I, 564. As Adam Watt notes, *W ou le souvenir d'enfance* similarly begins with a 'three-fold echo of Proust's fabled opening'; see 'Marcel Proust's *A la recherche du temps perdu*', in *The Cambridge History of the Novel in French*, ed. by Adam Watt (Cambridge: Cambridge University Press, 2021), pp. 456–72 (pp. 469–70). See also Georges Perec and others, *35 Variations* (Bordeaux: Le Castor astral, 2000).
47. Perec, *Œuvres*, I, 569.
48. Georges Perec, *Je suis né* (Paris: Seuil, 1990), p. 61. An excerpt from Perec's unfinished *Lieux où j'ai dormi* is reproduced under the Proustian title 'Trois chambres retrouvées', in *Penser/ Classer* [1985], 2nd edn (Paris: Seuil, 2003), pp. 25–29.
49. Philippe Lejeune, *La Mémoire et l'oblique: Georges Perec autobiographe* (Paris: P.O.L, 1991), p. 236, referring to *Je me souviens*. On Chris Marker and the 'humble' *madeleine*, see Bellour, *L'Entre-images 2*, p. 348.
50. Roland Barthes, *Comment vivre ensemble*, ed. by Claude Coste (Paris: Seuil, 2002), p. 90. On Proust, Barthes and the room, see Michael Sheringham, *Everyday Life: Theories and Practices from Surrealism to the Present* (Oxford: Oxford University Press, 2006), pp. 205–07.

51. Roland Barthes, *Roland Barthes par Roland Barthes*, in *Œuvres complètes*, ed. by Éric Marty, 5 vols (Paris: Seuil, 2002), IV, 575–772 (p. 745).
52. Ibid., IV, 746–47.
53. On the terrors of the death-framed novel, see Bowie, *Proust Among the Stars*, pp. 268–70.
54. Barthes, *Œuvres complètes*, IV, 746–47. This conception strikingly anticipates the emphasis placed by Rancière on the reader's access to the text as 'a democratic space'; see Edward J. Hughes, *Egalitarian Strangeness: On Class Disturbance and Levelling in Modern and Contemporary French Narrative* (Liverpool: Liverpool University Press, 2021), p. 275. See also Thomas Baldwin, who argues that if the reading of *A la recherche* is in any sense vertical its construal does not amount to the search for a settled hermeneutic solution, in *Roland Barthes: The Proust Variations* (Liverpool: Liverpool University Press, 2019), p. 3.
55. Roland Barthes, '"Longtemps, je me suis couché de bonne heure"', in *Œuvres complètes*, V, 459–70 (p. 459).

CHAPTER 16

Des 'parasites précieux': impureté et antinationalisme dans le roman proustien

Marisa Verna

Des mannequins sublimes

Depuis son exil londonien, Albert Cohen imaginait un 'Proust russe', qui 'ne donnerait nullement envie aux soldats russes de mourir pour leur patrie'. Certes Proust ne peut pas être rangé parmi ces 'mannequins sublimes' dont auraient 'faim' les combattants,[1] et même si on comprend l'état d'âme de Cohen en 1942, il vaut la peine de renvoyer dos à dos ses affirmations et le récit d'une victime de ces mêmes soldats, une victime que Proust aida à survivre.[2] Dans le camp de Gryazovets, où quatre cents officiers polonais (des quinze mille qui avaient été arrêtés par la police politique de l'Union Soviétique et qui furent presque tous tués), Józep Czapski tint une série de conférences à ses camarades sur l'œuvre de Marcel Proust. Son témoignage vaut une longue citation:

> I can still see my companions, worn out after having worked outdoors in temperatures dropping as low as minus forty-five degrees, packed together underneath portraits of Marx, Engels, and Lenin, listening intently to lectures on themes very far removed from the reality we faced at that time. I thought with emotion about Proust, in his overheated cork-lined room, who would certainly have been amazed and maybe even touched to learn that, twenty years after his death, some Polish prisoners, following a whole day spent in the snow and cold, would be listening with keen interest to the story of the Duchesse de Guermantes, the death of Bergotte, and anything else I could bring myself to recall of his world of precious psychological discovery and literary beauty.[3]

Bien que décoré de la médaille 'Virtuti militari' pour son héroïsme pendant le conflit russo-polonais, Czapski ne percevait donc pas la *Recherche* comme une évasion, mais plutôt comme un port de salut, un véritable acte de résistance qu'il partagea avec ses compagnons d'emprisonnement et de douleur.[4] Proust savait pertinemment que ses livres étaient 'soudés très étroitement à la guerre et à la Paix', et que c'était justement le refus d'une idéologie précise qui leur donnait un redoutable pouvoir.[5] Rien n'est plus perturbant, en effet, qu'une langue vraiment vivante, plutôt qu'explicitement militante, apte à 'mettre en valeur, dans l'espace d'un texte unique, le caractère hybride, ubiquiste et incertain de notre relation au monde'.[6]

Contre la pureté

Si la méduse visqueuse et répugnante de la plage de Balbec peut devenir 'une délicieuse girandole d'azur', c'est en effet grâce à une machine analogique qui ne cesse de reproduire et de recréer le vivant dans son irrépressible disposition au mélange et au métissage.[7] Certains lecteurs de ces pages 'would accuse the text of failing to provide a theoretical basis for a political program of gay liberation', mais en fait, comme Darwin, Proust 'defines nature as exuberantly, impossibly, revolutionarily, and even *queerly heterosexual*'.[8] La conjonction du bourdon et de l'orchidée n'est pas moins 'miraculeuse' (*SG*, III, 9) que la reproduction du bernacle que Darwin a étudié des années durant, lequel ne devient hétérosexuel que par une 'highly improbable, unlikely, contingent, and nevertheless sustained, aberrance'.[9]

Chez Proust comme chez Darwin, en effet, pureté rime avec stérilité, dans le monde naturel comme dans la langue. La conversation de Madame de Guermantes, 'délicieusement et purement française', est comparée à 'un vrai musée d'histoire de France' (*P*, III, 544–45), témoignage de ce côté 'conservateur' de la noblesse, 'avec tout ce que ce mot a à la fois d'un peu puéril, d'un peu dangereux, de réfractaire à l'évolution', tout en étant 'amusant pour l'artiste' (*P*, III, 546). Comme le parler de la duchesse, le restaurant de Dives (le 'Guillaume le Conquérant'), où l'on sert de la nourriture 'purement' normande dans un décor tout aussi authentique, 'also reminds us that, after all, the main *linguistic* result of the Norman conquest of England was not the preservation of '"purity" but its opposite'.[10]

Les langues évoluent comme les organismes, par le plus improbable des hasards, comparable à 'celui qui fit germer en France une mauvaise herbe d'Amérique dont la graine prise après la peluche d'une couverture de voyage était tombée sur un talus de chemin de fer' (*CG*, II, 533). Mais variation n'est pas métamorphose, et les conversations — surtout celles de ces 'êtres d'actions minuscules, microscopiques', que sont les gens du monde (*P*, III, 548) — tournent à vide, prises dans une série d'usages dont le goût et la fantaisie n'ont rien de substantiel, ne 'traduisent' pas le fonctionnement de la vie, ni d'ailleurs celui du langage lui-même. L'art seul est capable de véritable métamorphose, et par conséquent d'agir sur la langue de manière consistante et vitale, comme une nourriture. Cette métamorphose est du côté de l'écrit, car pour Proust 'conversation et écriture apparaissent comme les deux visages de ce nouveau Janus qu'est le langage: vanité et stérilité d'un côté, vérité et création de l'autre'.[11] Cette prééminence de l'écrit sur l'oral dans la pensée proustienne de la langue représente en elle-même un enjeu idéologique de taille. Ou plutôt un enjeu anti-idéologique, ce qui revient au même.

Une langue vivante

En attaquant le 'dogme grammatical' dans sa célèbre lettre à Madame Straus, Proust s'en prend certes à l'idéologie classique de la clarté,[12] mais il n'en est pas moins loin du 'purisme populiste' des défenseurs de la langue parlée comme seule véritable 'langue vivante'.[13] En se démarquant de la vocation universaliste de la langue classique, le purisme du xixe siècle (dont s'inspirera la pensée linguistique des années 1930), se voue à retrouver une mythologique langue populaire qui 'jaillirait' directement du sang du peuple, un 'chant naturel' qui s'opposerait à la 'cantilène apprise' de la langue savante.[14] Comme le rappelle Philippe Roussin (qui se réfère ici à Gourmont):

> La langue originaire qu'est la langue populaire a pour trait essentiel d'être originale et de n'être qu'elle-même. Elle ne reçoit rien et n'emprunte rien [...] contrairement à la langue de l'élite, savante et volontiers cosmopolite [...] elle est pure d'influences et soustraite par sa nature même au cosmopolitisme.[15]

Mais si 'la réalité se reproduit par division comme les infusoires, aussi bien que par amalgame', il est évident que pour Proust une langue qui ne 'reçoit ni n'emprunte rien' est une langue morte.[16] Une 'chanson populaire' et un 'vocabulaire plus pur' n'existent dans la *Recherche* que dans le 'musée' des conversations d'Oriane. Les défenseurs de l'oral (de Gourmont à Ramuz jusqu'à Céline) se réfèrent d'ailleurs à la langue parlée comme à la seule langue 'motivée', qui aurait 'la capacité de faire exister des rapports naturels entre les noms et les choses'.[17] Tant qu'il se débat dans le piège de 'l'Âge des Noms', le jeune héros de la *Recherche* semble bien baigner dans une croyance similaire, mais l'on sait depuis Genette que 'le héros cratyliste devient [...] le narrateur hermogéniste, lequel aura nécessairement le dernier mot, puisqu'il tient la plume. Critique du langage, triomphe de l'écriture'.[18]

Le cratylisme des partisans de l'oral était, cependant, moins naïf que celui du jeune Marcel fasciné par les noms de pays normands. Dans cette idéologie linguistique, en effet, le refus du français classique (et de la tradition de l'écrit) allait de pair avec une définition de l'identité française qui n'était plus 'politique et universaliste mais ethnique de l'ensemble national'.[19] La langue populaire est motivée, mais par le sang. En effet, Remy de Gourmont théorise une soi-disant homogénéité du lexique, un 'dictionnaire primitif' qui serait biologiquement inscrit dans la chair du peuple, à tel point que dans l'*Esthétique de la langue française* on peut lire l'affirmation inouïe que 'les peuples bilingues sont presque toujours des peuples inférieurs'.[20] Nous retrouvons les mêmes concepts chez Charles Maurras et, sans surprise, chez Édouard Drumont, qui considère que le Juif n'a pas 'sucé en naissant le vin de la patrie', n'est pas 'sorti du sol'.[21] En effet, 'le purisme change de nature, la pureté est maintenant évaluée en termes ethniques et raciaux',[22] et la question de Proust à Daniel Halévy, s'il est 'd'un bien bon français, de parler de "race française"?' n'en paraît que plus lourde de sens.[23]

La lettre où Proust pose cette question est un document précieux pour comprendre sa pensée (politique) de la langue. Il s'agit du refus à signer le manifeste 'Pour un parti de l'intelligence' promu par une cinquantaine d'écrivains de droite en juillet 1919, et comme l'observe très finement Edward Hughes, dans ce refus

Proust 'recoiled from the highly rhetorical posturing inherent in the very genre of the manifesto and appears vexed by the sanctimonious nationalist posturing' de ses auteurs: l'irritation de Proust était donc 'as much stylistic as political'.[24] Et si selon Stéphane Chaudier le roman de Proust est '*impolitique*', sa vision de la réalité sociale du monde correspondant à 'cette attitude qui aménage à l'écart du politique un espace qui le conteste et le vivifie, tout en dépendant de lui', la langue même dans laquelle cette attitude s'exprime est au contraire politique, car son 'impureté' s'oppose naturellement à une idéologie linguistique qui ne voit pas d'incorrection dans le syntagme 'race française'.[25]

Une langue étrangère

La défense du français populaire, ou plutôt l'affirmation de sa supériorité sur la langue cultivée et soi-disant élitaire s'accompagne du refus de la traduction, qui déracine, 'déterritorialise' une littérature supposée devoir revenir aux origines du terroir. La traduction est attaquée par les écrivains du 'français authentique' aussi bien comme pratique de passage d'une langue à une autre que comme expression de ce français classique, qui selon Céline (et avant lui Ramuz) ne correspond pas au sentiment profond de la langue française. Le français classique, en effet, serait une *traduction* de la pensée grecque et latine (des langues mortes), que le peuple français ne comprend pas, et qu'il est obligé d'apprendre: la langue de la tradition écrite serait donc une 'langue étrangère'. Dans ce simple syntagme nominal s'ouvre le véritable clivage entre la pensée de la langue de Marcel Proust et l'idéologie linguistique qui était en train de se développer dans les années mêmes où il écrivait son roman, et qui deviendra dominante dans les années 1930.

On se souvient, en effet, que pour Proust 'tous les beaux livres sont écrits dans une sorte de langue étrangère', mais cette langue étrangère n'est pas un idiome que l'on apprendrait à l'école ou pour comprendre lequel on consulterait un dictionnaire.[26] Elle est beaucoup trop étrangère pour cela, et en fait elle constitue la dénégation nette de la langue nationale telle que la conçoivent Gourmont et Céline après lui. Quand il parle de 'langue étrangère', Proust se réfère à un 'idiolecte individuel', et opère de ce fait une véritable 'désinscription nationale de la perspective langagière'. Or cette conception de la langue et du style a contribué à faire de Proust un étranger, 'un-French'.[27] Sa langue est 'du barbaros, l'étranger absolu'.[28]

Pour critiquer la langue de Proust dans le premier compte-rendu français de *Du côté de chez Swann*, paru en 1914 dans les pages du *Temps*, Paul Souday attribue les nombreuses 'erreurs' du nouvel écrivain à son activité de traducteur de Ruskin. S'il y a tant d'incises dans la prose de ce roman, si tous les 'menus faits' y sont rapportés, la faute en est à l'influence de la littérature anglaise: 'il y a, dans ses copieuses narrations, du Ruskin et du Dickens. Il est souvent embarrassé par un excès de richesse'. Traduire n'est pas un bon exercice pour un écrivain français: 'Français et Latins, nous préférons un procédé plus synthétique'.[29] Nathalie Mauriac-Dyer ne s'y trompe pas, quand elle identifie les véritables raisons de cette diatribe contre cette 'décomposition' de la langue française: 'The subtext here might be, of course, the unutterable half-Jewishness of the author'.[30]

Juif, cosmopolite par 'nature', Proust ne possède pas — ou plutôt il refuse — ce 'fameux monolinguisme que Derrida jalousait tant [...] qui n'est jamais accessible aux locuteurs mélangés, hybrides, congénitalement polyglottes, par trop cosmopolites et impurs'.[31] En fait, Proust cherche une langue 'plus que natale' (Esquisse XIII, SG, III, 1040), qu'il s'agit de 'traduire' (au sens étymologique de transporter, transférer) de son propre corps. Impure, nécessairement, car la vie est impure par définition.

Des parasites précieux

Dans son *Marcel Proust: A Study in the Quality of Awareness*, Edward Hughes identifie des passages du manuscrit de *Jean Santeuil* où Proust insère des observations télégraphiques sur la vie animale, telles que: 'Insectes — Mouvements de la femme qui accouche — le poumon, le cœur et la pensée — le requin et le pilote — un petit oiseau'.[32] Hughes met ce texte en relation avec le caractère mystérieux de l'activité artistique, et le met en regard avec cette observation de l'article sur Chardin et Rembrandt, qui vaut une longue citation ici:

> Ainsi le gynécologue pourrait étonner une femme qui vient d'accoucher en lui expliquant ce qui s'est passé dans son corps, en lui décrivant le processus physiologique de l'acte qu'elle a eu la force mystérieuse d'accomplir, mais dont elle ignore la nature; les actes créateurs procèdent en effet non de la connaissance de leurs lois, mais d'une puissance incompréhensible et obscure, et qu'on ne fortifie pas en l'éclairant. (*CSB*, 382)

Pour faire parler les poissons pilote, ou pour accoucher d'une nouvelle vie — d'un 'livre essentiel' (*TR*, IV, 469) — la pureté n'est d'aucun usage: ni celle de l'ordonnancement classique, ni, encore moins, celle des 'romanciers du parlé', pour lesquels la langue n'est qu''une substance, un trésor à disposition dans lequel il suffirait de puiser'.[33] En effet, comme Hughes l'observe justement, le langage de Proust 'will often stretch its resources [du langage] to the limit in an effort to capture a state that, by its very nature, outgrows the normal constrains of any linguistic system'.[34]

Pour dépasser les limites du langage, et entrer dans le secret du vivant, l'impureté est nécessaire. La pureté, même morale, est inféconde, comme Proust le rappelle à Lionel Hauser dans une lettre de 1918:

> Je *vois* les fils des doctrinaires, élevés dans un esprit de solidarité et d'entière pureté morale, la descendance des Broglie si tu veux, devenir d'académiques fruits secs qui ne servent à personne, et en revanche la parole nouvelle qui découvre une parcelle encore inconnue de l'esprit, une nuance supplémentaire de la tendresse, jaillir de l'ivrognerie d'un Musset ou d'un Verlaine, des perversions d'un Baudelaire ou d'un Rimbaud, voire d'un Wagner, de l'épilepsie d'un Flaubert.[35]

Parmi les idées, il n'y en a aucune qui 'n'ait été d'abord en véritable parasite demander à une idée étrangère et voisine le meilleur de la force qui lui manquait' (*JF*, I, 473). Il s'agit dans ce passage de l'idée du talent de la Berma (et de la carrière artistique du Narrateur), qui est venue au jeune Marcel en lisant dans le journal les mots 'la plus pure et haute manifestation d'art' à propos de la représentation de la mise en scène de *Phèdre*. Malgré le 'plaisir imparfait' (*JF*, I, 472) qu'il avait éprouvé au théâtre, l'idée que l'actrice est une 'grande artiste' se forme par 'agglutination', et se montrera plus tard imprévisiblement fertile. Encore une fois comme le bernacle que Darwin croyait entièrement hermaphrodite mais 'par hasard' a fini par être fécondé par un autre exemplaire, le Narrateur finira par comprendre que la Berma est vraiment une grande artiste, et surtout que lui-même est appelé à le devenir. Notre individu, d'ailleurs, n'étant pas une subjectivité complètement distincte des autres (ni du reste des créatures) une langue discontinue (formée d'unités clairement agencées les unes aux autres) ne saurait le décrire: il n'est, en effet, qu'un 'un polypier [...] où l'intestin, parasite enfoui, s'infecte sans que l'intelligence l'apprenne' (*TR*, IV, 516).

L'instrument de la métaphore rend possible le croisement des espèces, et c'est 'dans sa souple fourrure, avec les beaux yeux d'une bête' que 'quelque promeneuse rapide' surgit d'une futaie du Bois de Boulogne, alors que le parfum des acacias annonce 'l'approche et la singularité d'une puissante et molle individualité végétale' et que 'des centaines de fleurs' s'abattent sur les arbres 'comme des colonies ailées et vibratiles de *parasites précieux*' (*CS*, I, 410). Dans l'esthétique proustienne, la langue se nourrit du réel, mais le nourrit en retour: parasite, elle l'enrichit ou plutôt en dévoile ce qui sans elle n'aurait pas été visible. Comme les études d'Anne Simon l'ont démontré:

> Hibou voyant à travers la nuit, poule pondant son œuf ou guêpe fouisseuse surnourissant sa larve, c'est vers une hybridation entre création artistique et procréation animale, entre culture et nature, que nous mène un auteur pourtant réputé pour sa focalisation *quasi* exclusive sur l'humain.[36]

Comme Darwin, plongé dans les 'schemes and wonders' de la sexualité du bernacle, Proust ne relativise le moi humain que pour mieux s'émerveiller de l'individualité des espèces végétales.[37] Le fonctionnement métonymique des métaphores proustiennes permet la traduction linguistique d'une évolution qui n'est que variation incessante, car 'metonymy ensures that nothing can ever be alone' et que 'any one form will, sooner or later, be reflected in, and reflect, an adjacent form'.[38] L'étrangeté de la langue de Proust en devient radicale, ainsi que son impureté: non seulement elle n'organise ni ne hiérarchise la pensée, mais elle n'est d'aucun 'territoire', elle ne s'enracine pas.

Forcheville?

Józep Czapski termine sa série de conférences au camp de Griazowietz avec la description de Proust, mort dans son lit, à côté duquel aurait été trouvé un petit bout de papier tâché de tisane, sur lequel Proust aurait griffonné avec ses dernières forces le mot 'Forcheville'. Czapski cite ici l'article de François Mauriac, publié à la mort de Proust, où cette scène est décrite, et même s'il est peu probable que cette scène soit véridique (Jean-Yves Tadié ne la mentionne pas, en tout cas), l'attention qu'y porte l'officier polonais est ici pertinente pour notre propos.[39] Czapski savait que la mort pouvait venir pour lui et ses camarades à tout moment, et 'with a confidence in the perpetuity of great art, Czapski addressed this atmosphere of hovering mortality by ending his series of lectures by a description of the death of Bergotte, followed by Proust's own demise'.[40]

On imagine avec peine les paroles de Proust résonner en polonais dans un camp de prisonniers, où des hommes à bout de leurs forces les écoutaient dans le noir sans savoir s'ils survivraient la nuit. Ils les écoutaient, ou plutôt ils buvaient des paroles qui traduisaient la mort (la mort de Bergotte, celle de Proust, celle qui viendrait peut-être les chercher) 'en des mots humains'.[41]

Conclusions

À l'encontre du 'purisme populiste' de Gourmont, qui croit en une langue 'originaire' fermée sur elle-même, Proust pétrit son roman en une matière linguistique impure, 'a lumberfilled rhapsody' pleine de déchets et de restes, qui, dans leur 'étrangeté' radicale, n'en sont que plus féconds.[42] La pensée de la langue qui se développe dans l'écriture de Proust s'oppose en effet terme à terme à l'idéologie nationaliste qui, dès la fin du dix-neuvième siècle, pénètre la réflexion linguistique et littéraire en France. Au cratylisme de Ramuz, de Gourmont, et finalement de Céline (dans la langue du peuple les mots sont le réel, et ce réel est 'essentiellement' français), Proust oppose 'l'Âge des choses', que son héros comprend avec tant de peine, où l'impureté du vivant se fait style.

Notes to Chapter 16

1. Albert Cohen [Jean Mahan], 'Salut à la Russie (I)', *La France libre*, 4 (15 juin 1942), 97–104 (p. 104).
2. Cohen, toutefois, admirait Proust profondément. Sur l'ambiguïté de son attitude envers l'auteur de la *Recherche*, cf. Anne Simon, 'Cohen et Proust', in *La Rumeur des distances traversées : Proust, une esthétique de la surimpression* (Paris : Classiques Garnier, 2018), pp. 286–302.
3. Józep Czapski, *Lost Time: Lectures on Proust in a Soviet Camp*, trans. by Eric Karpeles (New York: New York Review of Books, 2018), p. 7.
4. Cf. Marisa Verna, 'Avoir le temps de vivre: Joseph Czapski et Proust', in *Marcel Proust e la significazione*, éd. Par Emanuela Piga Bruni, Ruggero Ragonese et Marion Schmid (= edition spéciale d'*E|C: rivista dell'Associazione Italiana di Studi Semiotici*, 15.3 (2021), 180–87 <https://mimesisjournals.com/ojs/index.php/ec/article/view/1734/1376> [consulté juin 2022].
5. Marcel Proust, lettre à Robert de Flers, début juillet 1919, in *Correspondance*, éd. par Philip Kolb, 21 vols (Paris: Plon, 1970–93), XVIII, 301.
6. Anne Simon, 'Maintenant, regardez', in *La Rumeur des distances traversées*, p. 237.
7. Marcel Proust, *Sodome et Gomorrhe*, in *A la recherche du temps perdu*, éd. par Jean-Yves Tadié et autres, 4 vols, Bibliothèque de la Pléiade (Paris: Gallimard, 1987–89), III, 28. Dorénavant les volumes de l'œuvre de Proust seront abrégiés comme suit: *Du côté de chez Swann*, CS; *À l'ombre des jeunes filles en fleurs*, JF; *Le Côté de Guermantes*, CG; *Sodome et Gomorrhe*, SG; *La Prisonnière*, P; *Le Temps retrouvé*, TR. Toutes les citations seront indiquées entre parenthèse dans le corps du texte.
8. Simon Porzak, 'Inverts and Invertebrates: Darwin, Proust, and Nature's Queer Heterosexuality', *Diacritics*, 41.4 (2013), 6–34 (pp. 7 et 11). Nous soulignons. Sauf différente indication, tous les italiques dans cet essai sont de notre fait.
9. Ibid., p. 12. Pour les études de Darwin sur le bernacle voir Charles Darwin, *Notebook E: Transmutation of Species*, CULDAR$_{124}$, transcribed by Kees Rookmaaker. Darwin Online: <http://darwin-online.org.uk/> [consulté octobre 2021].

10. Daniel Karlin, *Proust's English* (Oxford: Oxford University Press, 2007), p. 165.
11. Isabelle Serça, 'Langage', in *Dictionnaire Marcel Proust*, éd. par Annick Bouillaguet et Brian G. Rogers (Paris: Champion, 2014), pp. 549–53. Dorénavant *DIMP*.
12. Marcel Proust, lettre à Madame Straus, 6 novembre 1908, *Lettres*, éd. par Françoise Leriche (Paris: Plon, 2004), pp. 461–63 (pp. 461–62).
13. Gérald Antoine, *Histoire de la langue française 1880–1914* (Paris: CNRS Éditions via OpenEdition, 2016), p. 554.
14. Maurice Barrès, *Les Amitiés françaises* [1903], in *Romans et voyages*, 2 vols (Paris: Laffont, 1994), II, 124–26.
15. Philippe Roussin, *Misère de la littérature, terreur de l'histoire: Céline et la littérature contemporaine* (Paris: Gallimard, 2005), p. 340.
16. Lettre-dédicace de Marcel Proust à Jacques de Lacretelle sur un exemplaire de *Du côté de chez Swann*, avril 1918, in Proust, *Lettres*, p. 858.
17. Roussin, *Misère de la littérature, terreur de l'histoire*, p. 330.
18. Gérard Genette, 'L'Âge des noms', in *Mimologiques: voyage en Cratylie* (Paris: Seuil, 1976), pp. 315–28.
19. Roussin, *Misère de la littérature, terreur de l'histoire*, p. 334.
20. Remy de Gourmont, *Esthétique de la langue française* (Paris: Mercure de France, 1905), p. 90.
21. Édouard Drumont, *La France juive* (Paris: Victor Palmé, 1888), pp. 19–20.
22. Roussin, *Misère de la littérature, terreur de l'histoire*, p. 344.
23. Marcel Proust, lettre à Daniel Halévy, 19 juillet 1919, in Proust, *Lettres*, pp. 911–12 (p. 911).
24. Edward Hughes, *Proust, Class, and Nation* (Oxford: Oxford University Press, 2011), p. 23.
25. Stéphane Chaudier, 'Proust impolitique', in *Proust politique: de l'Europe du Goncourt 1919 à l'Europe de 2019*, éd. par Anne Simon et al. (= édition spéciale de *Quaderni Proustiani*, 14.1 (2020)), 47–61 (p. 60).
26. Marcel Proust, *Contre Sainte-Beuve précédé de Pastiches et Mélanges et suivi de Essais et Articles*, éd. par Pierre Clarac et Yves Sandre (Paris: Gallimard, 1971), p. 305. Dorénavant *CSB*, dans le corps du texte.
27. Gilles Philippe, *French Style* (Paris: Impressions Nouvelles, 2016), p. 182.
28. André Benhaïm, *Panim: visages de Proust* (Villeneuve d'Ascq: Presses universitaires du Septentrion, 2006), p. 316.
29. Paul Souday, *Marcel Proust* (Paris: Simon Kra, 1927); livre électronique de Project Gutenberg Canada: 339, 2009: <http://gutenberg.ca/ebooks/souday-proust/souday-proust-00-h-dir/souday-proust-00-h.html#c1> [consulté novembre 2021]. Le compte-rendu de Souday était le premier à être publié en France. Le premier en date à rendre compte de *Du côté de chez Swann*, avec une remarquable lucidité, avait été un italien, Lucio D'Ambra, en décembre 1913 dans la revue *Rassegna contemporanea*.
30. Nathalie Mauriac Dyer, '"Minor tongues" in Proust's Drafts and the Problem of Editing', in *Texts without Borders: Multilingualism and Textual Scholarship* (= édition spéciale de *Variants: The Journal of European Society for Textual Scholarship*, 9 (2012)), 149–62 (p. 154 n.).
31. Nathalie Azoulay, 'Proust apeuré', in *Proust politique*, éd. par Simon et al., pp. 19–31 (p. 28).
32. Marcel Proust, *Jean Santeuil précédé de Les plaisirs et les jours*, éd. par Pierre Clarac, Bibliothèque de la Pléiade (Paris: Gallimard, 1971), p. 988. Edward Hughes analyse cette page dans *Marcel Proust: A Study in the Quality of Awareness* (Cambridge: Cambridge University Press, 1983), p. 12.
33. Roussin, *Misère de la littérature, terreur de l'histoire*, p. 299.
34. Hughes analyse cette page dans *Marcel Proust*, p. 51.
35. Marcel Proust, lettre à Lionel Hauser, 28 avril 1918, in *Lettres*, p. 860.
36. Anne Simon, 'De l'histoire naturelle aux histoires surnaturelles: hybridités proustiennes', in *La Rumeur des distances traversées*, p. 347.
37. Porzak, 'Inverts and Invertebrates', p. 15. Porzak cite ici Darwin.
38. Ibid., p. 21.
39. François Mauriac, 'Sur la tombe de Marcel Proust', *La Revue Hebdomadaire*, 2 décembre 1922, aujourd'hui dans *Contreligne* <http://www.contreligne.eu/2016/07/mauriac-proust-litterature-france-tombe/> [consulté novembre 2021]. Karpeles, éditeur et traducteur des conférences de

Czapski, mentionne l'interprétation de George Painter, selon lequel le nom 'Forcheville' ne serait pas celui du comte de Forcheville, mais celui de Mademoiselle de Saint-Loup, la fille de Gilberte Swann et de Robert de Saint-Loup, 'the flesh and blood reconciliation of two previously incompatible "ways"': voir Eric Karpeles, 'Translator's Introduction', in Czapski, *Lost Time*, p. xxxi.
40. Karpeles, 'Translator's Introduction'.
41. Marcel Proust, lettre à Lucien Daudet, 27 novembre 1913, in *Correspondance*, XII, 324.
42. Malcolm Bowie, *Proust Among the Stars* [1998] (New York: Columbia University Press, 1999), p. 86.

CHAPTER 17

Proust, an Inevitable *engagé*?

Cynthia Gamble

In a letter to historian and journalist Jacques Boulenger in late November 1921, Proust states: 'I've not and never have been involved in politics, unless you count my having signed a petition for the revision of the Dreyfus case twenty-five years ago a political act'.[1] In keeping with this, Edward J. Hughes recognises Proust's 'independent-mindedness' and the 'unavailability of tidy labels' to attach to him.[2]

As early as 1936, John J. Spagnoli recognised the complexity of this subject: 'It is true that Proust was not a crusader, but we must not overlook the fact that, in spite of his predominant esthetic interests, he considered his social views important enough to himself to express them forcefully and dogmatically'.[3] Jean-Yves Tadié acknowledges Proust's struggle against sectarianism, 'be it anti-Semitic, militarist, sexist, bellicose or chauvinist. He would then step outside his middle-class comfort and arise from his sick bed, in support not of a social class, but of men and minorities, not those who were victorious'.[4]

In *The Chambers Dictionary* (2020), *engagé* is defined as a person 'committed to a point of view or to social or political action'. I am using *engagé* in the sense of 'committed to a point of view'. My essay explores Proust's diverse cultural and political universe that contributes to the visibility of his engagement.

1880

As I strolled in the square Darcy, in Dijon, one afternoon in late October 2013, a particular tree caught my attention. It was labelled 'Arbre de la laïcité, planté le 20 novembre 2012' [Tree of secularity, planted on 20 November 2012], and accompanied by the declaration:

> La France est une République indivisible, laïque, démocratique et sociale. Elle assure l'égalité devant la loi de tous les citoyens sans distinction d'origine, de race ou de religion. Elle respecte toutes les croyances (article 1er de la Constitution Française).
>
> [France shall be an indivisible, secular, democratic and social Republic. It shall ensure the equality of all citizens before the law, without distinction of origin, race or religion. It shall respect all beliefs (Article 1 of the French Constitution)].

This reminded me of the cleavage between secularity and religion as a backcloth to Proust's life.

An outward display of religious tolerance was, however, apparent on 13 February 1880, at the state funeral of Proust's Jewish great-great-uncle Adolphe Crémieux (born in 1796). Crémieux was one of the first Jewish *députés* in France, a minister of justice, senator, lawyer, freemason, generous benefactor and committed Republican. His name lives on today in the Crémieux decree of 1870, for which he was largely responsible, granting French citizenship to the Jews, but not to the Muslims, of French colonial Algeria. At his burial in the Jewish section of Montparnasse cemetery, politicians mingled with aristocrats, writers, friends, family members, Jews, Christians, anticlericals and those of no faith. Among the mourners were Léon Gambetta, famous for his oft-quoted declaration, 'Le cléricalisme, voilà l'ennemi!' [Clericalism, that's the enemy!], Jules Ferry, who pioneered free, secular and compulsory education, Alphonse de Rothschild, Ernest Renan and the comte Henry Greffulhe. The Chief Rabbi of Paris, Zadoc Kahn, officiated. Cavalry Commander Lichtenstein represented President Grévy.[5] Little eight-year-old Marcel Proust did not attend the funeral, but would have been made aware of its significance and grandeur from reports given by his parents and grandparents.

Provincial Anticlericalism

The year 1880 was nevertheless symptomatic of the increasingly divisive issue of the disestablishment of the Catholic church or *anticléricalisme* [anticlericalism] that would continue crescendo-like over the following decades.

From 11 October to 4 November, John Ruskin was in Amiens, preparing his homage to and defence of Christianity and the great Gothic Picardy cathedral. Rampant anticlericalism, promoted by Frédéric Petit, the Republican Mayor, had already infiltrated the cultural landscape as Ruskin witnessed:

> On the 19th of October, 1880, I saw the *Tartuffe* played at Amiens, in the little theatre which abuts in its back yard against a remnant of the king's palace, now decorated by an enormous gas lamp, lettered 'Billard'.
>
> The play was preceded by a lecture on Molière, admirably and pleasantly given by a well-to-do Amiens citizen — presumably one of their leading wool-manufacturers, who had interested himself in matters of taste.[6] He told the audience that in the honours of literature, with the *Tartuffe* alone, the French could challenge the world, 'et même Shakspire' [...]; but the *Tartuffe* was immortal, representing human nature in its entirety, and, above all, the horrors of religion; on which text he enlarged, with accusations of the existing priesthood, which I will not record, but which the audience heard with an under-murmur of eager satisfaction.
>
> The sight of that pit, full of unanimous blasphemy, foaming out its own shame within a few hundred yards of the altar of the cathedral which records the first Christianity of France, was a sign to me of many things.[7]

Petit's edict forbidding the traditional Catholic procession to the Madeleine cemetery on All Souls' Day, 2 November, was not universally respected.[8] Ruskin depicted considerable disobeyance in his sketch *Amiens. Jour des Trépassés. 1880*.[9] Claudia E. Gale, one of Ruskin's young protégés, recalled a:

> Long procession of people coming out of the town to carry wreaths to the cemetery for the *Jour des morts*. [...] group after group, some in rusty black put on for the day, others in long veils of coarse new crape, with garlands of yellow immortelles, or terrible wreaths of black and beads, with glass tears in them.[10]

Although Ruskin makes no mention of this sketch in his writings, Proust incorporated it into his preface to his translation of Ruskin's *Bible of Amiens*, and imagined Ruskin as an artist-Evangelist, on the bank of the Somme, with his disciples, depicting the cathedral as integral to the accompanying surroundings.[11]

Backdrop

Born in 1871, Proust is surrounded by living history, by people who have experienced life in both pre-and post-1870, of the Second Empire and the Third Republic. Many of his acquaintances endured the humiliation and defeat of France: the loss of Alsace-Lorraine and of their language; the Franco-Prussian War; the shortages of food and fuel; the fear of another German invasion, not forgetting for some the trauma of the Great War. These vivid personal memories remain as painful open wounds that frame many of the attitudes and policies of public figures such as Maurice Barrès, Raymond Poincaré and Jules Ferry, all born in Lorraine. Alphonse Daudet had been a participant in the Franco-Prussian War: 'La Dernière Classe' (1873), his short story depicting loss, was a prominent and haunting point of reference for many. In a letter to Julia Daudet in 1921, Proust recalled its impact: 'Je sais par cœur ces admirables *Contes du lundi*, auxquels la guerre a donné un nouvel accent, plus poignant encore' [I know by heart these fine *Contes du lundi*, which have been given a new, even more poignant meaning].[12] The views of Daudet's elder son Léon were informed very much by this historical backdrop.

The emotion felt by Proust's art dealer friend, René Gimpel, at the return of Alsace to France, and his homage to his father at his Jewish grave in Montparnasse cemetery — 'La joie enclose en mon cœur, j'ai dit à mon père que l'Alsace lui était rendue' [With a joyful heart, I told my father that Alsace had been returned to him] — are movingly expressed in his diary.[13] The 'Janus-faced' metaphor that Adam Watt applies to the position of Proust's novel also encapsulates Proust the man.[14]

Family Circle of Political Friends and Acquaintances

From an early age, Proust was accustomed to meeting politicians and diplomats. Maurice Bariéty, a medical doctor born in Illiers, identifies some who were regularly invited to the Proust family home: 'Nisard, G. Hanotaux, F. Faure, Camille Barrère, Thompson [*sic*], Charles Dupuy, Cruppi, Méline, Fallières, Barthou'.[15] Jean Cruppi and Gaston Thomson became Proust family members through marriage to Adolphe Crémieux's grand-daughters. Others were particularly close to Adrien Proust for professional or political reasons, such as Camille Barrère. Marcel Proust had a more distant, but courteous relationship with this older man, with whom he needed to be circumspect for the sake of his father's career. Barrère believed that he was the model for M. de Norpois, the pompous, opiniated ambassador in his novel, something the author denies in a letter to Benjamin Crémieux: 'M. Barrère, who thinks that simply because he dined once a week at home when I was a child, I meant to portray him in M. de Norpois. Now, M. de Norpois, though just as detestable, is exactly the opposite type of diplomat' (SL, IV, 419). We know little about the relationship between the Prousts and Armand Fallières, but the closeness and respect are confirmed by the fact that the future President of the French Republic attended Adrien Proust's funeral in 1903.

Politicians socialised at fashionable spa towns with the Prousts: in 1889 at Salies-de-Béarn in the Pyrenees, with Louis Tirman, Governor-General of Algeria, and his aristocratic Belgian wife Marie, née Donckier de Donceel Tirman (C, I, 128); in 1892, at Vichy with the comte de Montholon, French Ambassador to Switzerland. Proust's observations are immortalised in *A la recherche du temps perdu*, as he explains to Lucien Daudet:

> I admit [...] that I took into account (infinitesimally) the identical stupid remark made to me by Montholon and Félix Faure, the first about the Duc d'Orléans, the second about the Prince of Wales. Neither, in their opinion, being suitably solemn or majestic. (SL, IV, 153).

In 1900, at Évian-les-Bains, Mme Proust caricatures politician Charles Dupuy, 'un homme gros à nez rouge' [a fat man with a red nose] (C. II, 402), and Armand Nisard: 'L'Ambassadeur près du St. Siège Nisard est aussi très aimable mais très sourd. Il n'entend rien de ce qu'on lui dit et comme il parle tout bas on n'entend rien non plus de ce qu'il dit' [Nisard, the Ambassador to the Holy See, is also very nice but very deaf. He hears nothing anyone says to him and as he speaks in a very low voice nobody hears anything he says either] (C, II, 402–03). Proust's insights into politicians in these social settings provided him with a healthy scepticism as to the sincerity of their engagement, a boost to his own politicial independence and critical material for his writings.

Proust's University Teachers

The École libre des sciences politiques, a prestigious private institution and Republican stronghold, founded in 1872, was a training ground for future diplomats and politicians, providing a thorough comprehension of treaties and politics.[16] Between 1890 and 1892, Proust studied in the École's diplomatic section where he thrived in the stimulating atmosphere in which international crises, history and politics were examined and debated openly. Luc Fraisse demonstrates that Proust's hostility to the law of the Separation of Church and State emanated from the philosophy of the School.[17] Among its high-calibre teachers, Anatole Leroy-Beaulieu was noteworthy. This professor of contemporary history and eastern affairs, and a 'catholique engagé' [socially committed Catholic],[18] promoted social justice and tolerance, condemned all kinds of oppression, and denounced 'anti-Semitism, anti-clericalism and anti-Protestantism'.[19] Gérard Desanges affirms that Leroy-Beaulieu exerted the greatest enduring influence on Proust's social and political engagement, and goes as far as to suggest that the ideas in his letter of 29 July 1903 to Georges de Lauris about Church and State were inspired by those of this professor.[20] Writing to Fernand Gregh in early July 1905, expressing divergent political views, Proust states his own preference for those of Leroy-Beaulieu (C, v, 284).

At the Sorbonne, two philosophy teachers stand out in particular. Émile Boutroux, a strong Dreyfusard who comdemned anti-Semitism as 'abominable', was named as one of Proust's real-life heros, in a response in the famous questionnaire.[21] Gabriel Séailles was, in the words of Fraisse, 'engagé' in his defence of secularity and of Alfred Dreyfus.[22] Séailles was committed to mass education and became president of the *université populaire* where he also taught.

Proust's Social and Political Engagement

One of Proust's early statements about politics and religion is made in his article 'L'Irréligion d'État' [State Irreligion], published in the short-lived *Le Banquet* in May 1892 (*CSB*, 348–49). Although signed 'Laurence', the author was revealed by Robert Dreyfus to be Proust.[23] Fresh from the teaching of the École libre des sciences politiques, Proust stakes his position. He attacks the atheistic tenets of the 'écoles sans Dieu' [schools without God] (*CSB*, 348), the fanaticism, intolerance and persecution that have become a kind of state religion. These are references to Ferry's radical educational reforms in the 1880s. Various other decrees directed the dispersal and dismantling of religious orders, an integral part of the process of decoupling Church from State. Abbé Mugnier, with whom Proust became acquainted later, witnessed the forced expulsion of Jesuits, Dominicans and Marists, and compared the ferocity of these Government decrees to the horrors of the Commune.[24] In this article, Proust already propounds Ruskinian concepts of discipline and duty and the role of Christianity in producing in France 'ses plus purs chefs-d'œuvre' [its finest masterpieces] (*CSB*, 349).

The import of the École libre des sciences politiques is felt again in Proust's article 'Choses d'Orient' [Things from the East], published on 25 May 1892 in *Littérature et critique*, a serious monthly journal of which Anatole France was a founder member. The essay is ostensibly a critique of *Voyage en Turquie d'Asie: Arménie, Kurdistan et Mésopotamie* by the comte Armand-Pierre de Cholet, a lieutenant in Proust's regiment at Orléans in 1889. However, towards the end, Proust's own voice is heard loudly condemning the repressive, violent nature of the Turkish government and their treatment of the serfs who remain for ever victims of poverty. This strong, courageous political statement has overtones of the teaching, interests and philosophy of Leroy-Beaulieu.

Along with Anatole France, Jean Jaurès and Leroy-Beaulieu, Proust was a critic of the massacre of hundreds of thousands of Armenians by the Ottoman Muslims, in Constantinople and surrounding areas in 1894–96. On 9 June 1896, Leroy-Beaulieu delivered a stirring lecture entitled 'Les Arméniens et la question arménienne' [The Armenians and the Armenian Question] at the Hôtel des Sociétés savantes, in Paris. This political, well crafted, lyrical speech was warmly applauded throughout as he expressed his support for oppressed people whom he knew personally from his extensive travels. He gave a lesson on the geography, history, religions and great culture of the Armenians, and criticised the silence of the French government in the face of the crisis. Among the diaspora, Leroy-Beaulieu makes particular mention of the intellectual, moral and financial attributes of the Mekhitarists at the Armenian monastery on the Venetian island of San Lazzaro 'qui flotte poétiquement sur la lagune' [floating poetically on the lagoon].[25] We do not know if Proust was present, but he would surely have known about it, even if he was preoccupied with reading *Le Figaro* which published on that very day Anatole France's preface to *Les Plaisirs et les jours* and announced its publication date the following Saturday. Perhaps Proust's mysterious visit to the monastery on San Lazzaro in 1900 had its inception in Leroy-Beaulieu's invocation. In *Jean Santeuil*, the radical politician Couzon, identified by Georges Bataille as a fictional representation of Jean Jaurès, attempts in vain to protest at the French government's refusal to intervene.[26] Proust's sense of injustice is palpable.

Proust was immersed in live politics in the Chambre des députés. In 1896, he expressed his intention to attend the session in which Anatole Catusse, then director of indirect taxation, would be speaking. Kolb indentifies this as 26 November (*C*, II, 152, n. 2). Catusse was a politician and civil servant whose career culminated in his appointment as French Ambassador to Sweden from 1899 until his death. On another occasion, on 15 March 1897, Proust and his Romanian friend, Prince Constantin de Brancovan, seated in President Faure's private box at the Chambre des députés, follow the debate about France's position regarding the Turkish-dominated island of Crete, in danger of being invaded by Greece (*C*, II, 181–82), about which Gabriel Hanotaux, Minister of Foreign Affairs, is interrogated by the fiery socialist orator Jaurès.

A Literary-historico-political Dinner

A dinner party, with guests prominent in a range of fields, was hosted by Dr and Mme Proust at 9 boulevard Malesherbes in December 1895.[27] An important political guest was Hanotaux, historian, prolific writer and later Ambassador in Rome in 1920. Others included the two daughters of the President of the French Republic, the unmarried twenty-nine-year-old Lucie Faure, already her father's closest political adviser and confidante, and her twenty-four-year-old married sister Antoinette Berge. Robert de Billy, José-Maria de Heredia and his daughters were also present. Marcel issued an invitation to Robert de Montesquiou (*C*, I, 449) but we do not know if he accepted. The somewhat gauche seventeen-year-old art student Lucien Daudet arrived for the after-dinner reception.

This was a delicate moment in the lives of the Faures and Hanotaux, and of the nation, with the Dreyfus Affair in the headlines and Dreyfus in solitary confinement on Devil's Island. In early November 1895, an appeal to Félix Faure to review Dreyfus's case was rejected. Hanotaux, who had courageously questioned the evidence used to court-martial Dreyfus but who had been overruled, resigned his ministerial post though he was reinstated in April 1896 (*C*, I, 450, n. 3). Faure was suffering or was about to suffer the embarrassment of the revelations in the press about his wife's father, Antoine Martin Belluot, a lawyer who was sentenced to hard labour for embezzling clients' funds, but who fled to Spain, where he died at the age of thirty-nine, abandoning his pregnant wife who later gave birth to a daughter, Berthe, the future Mme Faure.[28] Philip Kolb regards the invitation to the Faure daughters as an act of support to the family at a difficult, politically dangerous and sensitive time (*C*, I, 449, n. 2).

Other scandals were swirling around, in particular that of the many malefactors who committed fraud on a huge scale relating to the failed project of building, among tropical swamps, an artifical interoceanic waterway in Panama. Among those involved were Gustave Eiffel, Ferdinand de Lesseps and Jacques de Reinach. André Maurois, in his preface to the first edition of *Jean Santeuil* (1952), (a preface written by Philip Kolb, according to his daughter Katherine)[29] maintains that part of the fifth section of the book is directly related to the Panama scandal and the Dreyfus Affair.[30] Tadié suggests that Maurice Rouvier, the Minister of Finance, compromised in the Panama scandal, was the model for *Jean Santeuil*'s M. Marie.[31] However, the wide-ranging political tensions and intrigues covered in the story, which also impinge on family loyalties, are more likely to be an amalgam of the web of corruption. In drafts of *A la recherche*, Françoise loses the inheritance received from Aunt Léonie after investing it in the Panama Canal Company.[32] Her misfortune mirrored that of hundreds of thousands of ordinary French citizens.

The closeness of Mme Proust to Eiffel's sister, Marie, the wife of Dr Albert Hénocque, and to Eiffel's daughter Claire and her mining engineer husband Adolphe Salles, would have inhibited Proust from publicly denouncing the fraudsters. Filial loyalty prevailed. Mme Proust was extremely sensitive to Eiffel's troubles (he was found guilty of misuse of funds, fined and sentenced to two years in prison, but acquitted on appeal) and protective of his family (*C*, II, 402–03).

Céleste Albaret reveals the degree to which Proust was well informed about Faure's personal life, his extramarital affairs, including his final hours in the arms of Marguerite Steinheil.[33] Discretion has prevailed, for so far no mention of this relationship has been revealed in Proust's extant correspondence. Albaret recalls the strong bond of mutual support and confidential exchanges between Mme Proust and Mme Faure, continuing until the former's death in 1905. Proust also related to his housekeeper, perhaps with a degree of hyperbole, the time in his youth when the Proust family had lunch regularly, once a week, at the Élysée Palace with the President.[34]

A Political Salon

Although Proust found common ground with Anatole France in relation to the Armenian massacres, their opinions diverged regarding the separation of Church and State, the latter advocated by France in *L'Église et la République* (1904). Jeanne Pouquet and Michelle Maurois have recorded valuable information about the salon of Mme Arman de Caillavet, Anatole France's muse, in the avenue Hoche, where Proust met some of the most powerful figures of the Third Republic.[35]

His encounter in 1898 with Georges Clemenceau, at the height of the Dreyfus Affair, with its heated discussions,[36] would also have been an opportunity for them to engage in literary, artistic discourse, for the politician, temporarily without a parliamentary seat, had written a laudatory article about Monet's series of paintings of Rouen Cathedral exhibited in May 1895 at the Durand-Ruel Gallery in Paris.[37] With patriotic zeal, Clemenceau defended the great Gothic cathedral, a symbol of the grandeur of France, and made a public appeal to President Faure to purchase quality, contemporary French art. Proust's visit to this Monet exhibition and his conversation with Clemenceau may have sown the seeds of his Ruskinian pilgrimage to Rouen in 1900. However, Proust's violent, uncontrolled pro-Dreyfus emotions caused embarrassment, as Jeanne de Caillavet noted in her diary:

> Poincaré dîne avenue Hoche avec Braga, Proust, Viefville et Vandérem. On parle de l'affaire Dreyfus en termes assez vifs. Marcel et Vandérem sont emportés et mettent à soutenir leur opinion une passion qui déconcerte Braga, embarrasse Viefville et désoblige singulièrement Poincaré qui est un homme prudent avant tout.[38]

> [Poincaré dines at avenue Hoche with Braga, Proust, Viefville and Vandérem. They have very heated discussions about the Dreyfus Affair. Marcel and Vandérem get carried away and express their opinions so passionately that Braga is disconcerted, Viefville embarrassed and Poincaré, a man not given to extremes, extremely offended.]

Louis Barthou, lawyer, politician and man of letters, also frequented this salon, along with such forceful figures as Jean Jaurès, Léon Blum, Aristide Briand, Joseph Reinach and Lucien Herr, the leading strategist seeking to overturn Dreyfus's conviction. To that list can be added the name of Paul Grunebaum-Ballin, Proust's contemporary at the Lycée Condorcet and the École libre des sciences politiques. In 1904, as head of Aristide Briand's cabinet, he was instrumental in formulating the law of the Separation of Church and State about which he wrote a comprehensive book, *La Séparation des églises et de l'état, étude juridique sur le projet Briand* (1905).[39]

The Catalytic Power of John Ruskin

Daniel Halévy, Proust's school friend, soon demonstrated a social conscience and a political temperament. For Halévy, as for Ruskin, writing publicly was an act of engagement, and in 1899 he wrote an open letter to the readers of the *Bulletin de l'Union pour l'action morale* (among whom was Proust) in which he proclaimed that it was insufficient and ineffectual to sit by the fireside reading passages of Ruskin in translation: action was necessary.[40] Later that year, Proust's discovery of a chapter of *The Seven Lamps of Architecture* in translation marked an epiphanic moment in his life and reinforced Halévy's message. Ruskin's death in 1900 accentuated Proust's immersion in his thought and role as a fearless social and cultural *engagé*. The loss of cultural heritage in the destruction of cathedrals, churches and historic buildings through inappropriate restoration, neglect, demolition or wars, was a leitmotif throughout Ruskin's pronouncements.

Proust's strongest public commitments, motivated by his British mentor, were his actions to save French churches and cathedrals from closure, a perceived likelihood of the consequences of the proposed law of the Separation of Church and State. His politico-cultural activism reached its zenith in 1904. In late February, his interpretation of Ruskin's *The Bible of Amiens*, translated as *La Bible d'Amiens*, was published. This was Proust's defence of the great Picardy cathedral, an act of engagement as well as a homage to the glorious Gothic edifice in danger of being a victim of the anticlerical laws.[41] On 11 July 1904, Albert Sorel's fine, lengthy, lyrical article in praise of *La Bible d'Amiens*, of Ruskin's philosophy and his religious views, was published in *Le Temps*.[42] This is one of the most important reviews and one greatly appreciated by the author's former student who described it as a 'magnificent essay' (*SL*, II, 57). As a non-religious person admiring church worship and architecture, Sorel aptly reinforces the argument for maintaining the Church-State status quo. In stark contrast, and immediately ajoining this remarkable article, is an official list of schools run by religious organisations that must close by 1 October, according to the new law of 7 July 1904.

Proust's increasing anger and anxiety are soon unleashed in a passionate, long polemic, 'La Mort des cathédrales: une conséquence du projet Briand sur la séparation' [Death of the Cathedrals: Consequences of the Briand Proposal for the Separation of Church and State], published in *Le Figaro* on 16 August 1904. In it, he attacks politicians directly and very publicly. The entire tone is masterly with Ruskinian oratory at its best and most persuasive, combined with artistic sensitivity. Ruskin's soul has transmigrated to Proust the Christian orator. Dramatic outbursts and attacks unfurl, with biblical quotations and material from *The Bible of Amiens* to support the argument. Proust invokes cathedral statues, the symbolism and beauty of the liturgy and age-old rituals. He pleads for state funding for French cathedrals 'qui sont probablement la plus haute mais indiscutablement la plus originale expression du génie de France' [which are probably the most original expression of the intellectual power and spirit of France].[43] As well as making a direct appeal to André Hallays, a journalist with a regular column in the *Journal des débats*, Proust criticises politicians for their hypocrisy in enjoying visiting cathedrals and churches, returning with religious fragments and relics for their own use, yet formulating anticlerical laws. Proust was conscious of his dual heritage, Jewish on his mother's side, versus the tolerant Christian of that of his father. As his friend René Peter observed, to ban religious organisations was to Proust as odious as the persecution of an innocent Jew a few years before.[44]

Ruskin's philosophy mirrored in many respects that of Jules Siegfried, born in Mulhouse, of a strict Protestant family. He was a pioneer of girls' education and social housing, a promoter of public health and a philanthropist with an acute social conscience. Siegfried is listed in Jeanne Proust's notebook as a friend of her husband.[45] His son André, who became an eminent political scientist and prolific writer, was also a student of Sorel and shared Proust's interest in international relations.[46]

Political Precariousness

Proust had a circle of friends and acquaintances with connections to many foreign countries, so his geo-political antennae were sensitively attuned. Robert de Billy spent most of his adult life as a diplomat, in embassies in Berlin, London, Sofia, Tangiers, Athens and Tokyo, and was a mine of information for Proust. It is via such means, as Philip Kolb remarks, that 'Proust se tient au courant de tout' [Proust keeps up to date with everything] (*C*, XXI, iii).

Alongside Proust's focus on the construction of his novel, there was no shortage of political crises on which to comment. The revolution in Portugal in October 1910 marked the overthrow of the centuries-old monarchy and the establishment of a republic. Proust followed these events in *Le Figaro* and *Le Journal des débats* and, in a letter to Robert Dreyfus, condemned the political anarchy that had contributed to the situation (*C*, X, 182–83).

Billy confirms Proust's close monitoring of the numerous international crises concerning Morocco and the conflictual teritorial claims.[47] Proust wrote to Billy, who was a representative at the International Conference at Algeciras in 1906:

> Je suis avec une émotion confuse vos travaux sur lesquels l'univers a les yeux fixés et où on ne distingue rien faute de renseignements. Mais moi qui sais votre intelligence et votre patriotisme je pense à ce que doit être ce combat où vous devez unir les ruses d'Ulysse à la vaillance d'Achille et dont j'aimerais être l'Homère. Je suis ému de penser que le drapeau et l'honneur de la France sont en des mains qui me sont si chères et que j'ai tant de plaisir à serrer. (*C*, VI, 31)

> [I am following in a very confused state your work which the whole world is watching and about which we have no information. But I know how intelligent and patriotic you are and I think about your challenge which requires a combination of the cunning of Ulysses and the valour of Achilles, and of which I'd like to be the Homer. I am moved at the thought of the flag and the honour of France being in hands that are so dear to me and that I have so much pleasure in shaking.]

From the security of the Normandy coastal resort of Cabourg in 1911, Proust is not a casual bystander, but one acutely aware of the tensions and dangers inherent in the arrival of a German warship in Agadir and the positioning of the European powers in relation to Morocco. He interrogates Billy, then in Tangiers: 'Est-ce qu'il n'y a pas refroidissement avec l'Angleterre, est-elle froissée d'être écartée des conversations de Cambon, et que l'Allemagne a-t-elle répondu à sa demande d'explication sur Agadir?' [Is there not some cooling off with England, is the country upset at being sidelined during discussions with Cambon, and has Germany responded to its request for an explanation about Agadir?] (*C*, X, 318).

Conclusion

Proust's epistolary engagement continued unabated. Other subjects in 1920–22 include President Woodrow Wilson's criticism of France's imperialism and his efforts to ratify the post-war Treaty of Versailles (*C*, XIX, 190); the Genoa

Conference concerning central and eastern Europe and relations with Russia (*C*, XXI, 147), and, only a few days before Proust's death, deep anxiety about the Turkish-Greek conflict (*C*, XXI, 531).

Throughout his life Proust remained politically and socially aware of the intricacies of structures and nuances, to such an extent that Desanges describes him as 'un vrai connaisseur de la politique' [a real connoisseur of politics].[48] However, his long familiarity with politicians generated scepticism, as he revealed to Antoine Bibesco: 'J'ai trop connu les séjours à l'Elysée, Rambouillet etc. dans ma jeunesse pour que recevoir un homme politique [...] me paraisse quelque chose' [I've stayed too often at the Elysée palace, or at Rambouillet etc. in my youth so that meeting politicians [...] doesn't mean anything to me] (*C*, XIX, 599).

Robert Dreyfus defines Proust's position:

> Proust ne fut assurément ni 'bolcheviste', ni 'nationaliste', — ni clérical, ni anticlérical. En politique, il s'est tenu toute sa vie, dans toutes les circonstances, au-dessus des passions et n'épousa aucune doctrine. Son âme étant la plus tolérante peut-être de notre temps, aucun signe d'intolérance ne lui paraissait tolérable.[49]
>
> [Proust was certainly not a 'Bolshevist' or a 'nationalist' — neither clerical nor anticlerical. In politics, he remained all his life and in all circumstances above passions and espoused no doctrine. His soul was perhaps the most tolerant of our time, he did not tolerate any sign of intolerance.]

Proust could have become publicly *engagé*, but instead chose to prioritise his energies for his great novel.

Notes to Chapter 17

1. Marcel Proust, *Selected Letters*, ed. by Philip Kolb, trans. by Ralph Manheim and others, 4 vols (London: HarperCollins, 1983–2000), IV, 260 (hereafter referenced as *SL* in main text).
2. Edward J. Hughes, *Proust, Class, and Nation* (Oxford: Oxford University Press, 2011), p. 4.
3. John J. Spagnoli, 'The Social Attitude of Marcel Proust', in *Marcel Proust Reviews & Estimates in English*, ed. by Gladys Dudley Lindner (Stanford, CA: Stanford University Press, 1942), pp. 213–27 (p. 215).
4. Jean-Yves Tadié, *Marcel Proust*, trans. by Euan Cameron (London: Viking, 2000), p. 704.
5. See Évelyne Bloch-Dano, *Madame Proust* (Paris: Grasset, 2004), pp. 153–57; *Le Figaro*, 14 February 1880, p. 2, col. 1–2.
6. The speaker was Francisque Sarcey (1827–1899), an influential theatre critic and anticlerical: see *Le Journal d'Amiens*, 23 October 1880.
7. *The Works of John Ruskin*, ed. by E. T. Cook and Alexander Wedderburn, 39 vols (London: George Allen, 1903–12), XXXII (1907), 117–18.
8. *Le Journal d'Amiens*, 3 November 1880.
9. *The Works of John Ruskin*, XXXIII, facing p. 25.
10. Claudia E. Gale, 'At Canterbury and Amiens with John Ruskin', *The Cornhill Magazine*, February 1913, pp. 266–67.
11. John Ruskin, *La Bible d'Amiens*, trans. by Marcel Proust, ed. by Yves-Michel Ergal (Paris: Bartillat, 2007), pp. 58–60.
12. *Correspondance de Marcel Proust*, ed. by Philip Kolb, 21 vols (Paris: Plon, 1970–93), XX, 39 (hereafter referenced as *C* in the main text).
13. René Gimpel, *Journal d'un collectionneur: marchand de tableaux* [1963], rev. edn (Paris: Hermann, 2011), p. 107.

14. Adam Watt, 'Marcel Proust's *A la recherche du temps perdu*', in *The Cambridge History of the Novel in French*, ed. by Adam Watt (Cambridge: Cambridge University Press, 2021), pp. 456–72 (p. 457).
15. Maurice Bariéty, 'Éloge d'Adrien Proust (1834–1903)', *Bulletin de l'Académie nationale de médecine*, 3rd ser., 153.32–33 (9 December 1969), 574–82, cited in Christian Péchenard, *Proust et son père* (Paris: Quai Voltaire, 1993), p. 258.
16. See Luc Fraisse, *L'Éclectisme philosophique de Marcel Proust* (Paris: Presses de l'Université Paris-Sorbonne, 2013), pp. 170–74.
17. Ibid., p. 172.
18. Michel Erman, 'Marcel Proust et la politique', in *Marcel Proust*, ed. by Jean-Yves Tadié (Paris: Cahiers de l'Herne, 2021), pp. 141–47 (p. 143).
19. Tadié, *Marcel Proust*, trans. by Cameron, p. 108.
20. Gérard Desanges, *Marcel Proust et la politique: une conscience française* (Paris: Classiques Garnier, 2019), p. 83. See *SL*, I, 342–46.
21. Boutroux's characterisation of anti-Semitism is noted in *Jean Santeuil précédé de Les Plaisirs et les jours*, ed. by Pierre Clarac with the collaboration of Yves Sandre, Bibliothèque de la Pléiade (Paris: Gallimard, 1971), p. 651. The questionnaire is reproduced in *Contre Sainte-Beuve précédé de Pastiches et mélanges et suivi de Essais et articles*, ed. by Pierre Clarac with Yves Sandre, Bibliothèque de la Pléiade (Paris: Gallimard, 1971), p. 336–37 (hereafter referenced as *CSB* in the main text).
22. Fraisse, *L'Eclectisme philosophique de Marcel Proust*, p. 886.
23. Robert Dreyfus, *Souvenirs sur Marcel Proust* (Paris: Grasset, 1926), p. 95.
24. *Journal de l'Abbé Mugnier (1879–1939)*, ed. by Marcel Billot (Paris: Mercure de France, 1985), pp. 33–34.
25. See <https://gallica.bnf.fr/ark:/12148/bpt6k870103r/f39.item> [accessed November 2021].
26. Proust, *Jean Santeuil*, ed. by Clarac, pp. 600–04. Georges Bataille, *La Littérature et le mal* (Paris: Gallimard, 1957), p. 99; quoted in Hughes, *Proust, Class, and Nation*, p. 8, n. 27.
27. Philip Kolb gives the tentative date of 14 December (*C*, I, 91).
28. See *Le Gaulois*, 10 and 14 December 1895.
29. Katherine Kolb, 'Postface. Du côté de chez Kolb: aperçus d'un chantier proustien', in Marcel Proust, *Lettres*, ed. by Françoise Leriche (Paris: Plon, 2004), p. 1167.
30. Marcel Proust, *Jean Santeuil*, 3 vols (Paris: Gallimard, 1952), I, 16.
31. Jean-Yves Tadié, *Marcel Proust* (Paris: Gallimard, 1996), p. 342, n. 2.
32. Marcel Proust, *A la recherche du temps perdu*, ed. by Jean-Yves Tadié and others, 4 vols, Bibliothèque de la Pléiade (Paris: Gallimard, 1987–89), I, 1273; II, 889, 1036.
33. Céleste Albaret, *Monsieur Proust* (Paris: Robert Laffont, 1973), p. 168.
34. Ibid.
35. Jeanne Maurice Pouquet, *Le Salon de Madame Arman de Caillavet* (Paris: Hachette, 1926); Michelle Maurois, *Les Cendres brûlantes* (Paris: Flammarion, 1986).
36. Maurois, *Les Cendres brûlantes*, pp. 126–28.
37. Georges Clemenceau, 'Révolution de cathédrales', *La Justice*, 20 May 1895.
38. Maurois, *Les Cendres brûlantes*, p. 127.
39. See John Ruskin, *'La Bible d'Amiens', 'Sésame et les lys' et autres textes*, trans. by Marcel Proust, ed. by Jérôme Bastianelli (Paris: Robert Laffont, 2015), pp. 703–06.
40. *Bulletin de l'Union pour l'action morale*, 6.1 (January 1899), 234–38, quoted in Sébastien Laurent, *Daniel Halévy: du libéralisme au traditionalisme* (Paris: Grasset, 2001), p. 105.
41. See Cynthia Gamble, *Voix entrelacées de Proust et de Ruskin* (Paris: Classiques Garnier, 2021), pp. 211, 278–79.
42. Reproduced in Jérôme Bastianelli, *Dictionnaire Proust-Ruskin* (Paris: Classiques Garnier, 2017), pp. 653–58.
43. See <https://gallica.bnf.fr/ark:/12148/bpt6k286706d/f3.item> [accessed November 2021].
44. René Peter, *Une saison avec Marcel Proust: souvenirs*, preface by Jean-Yves Tadié, foreword by Dominique Brachet (Paris: Gallimard, 2005), pp. 65–68.
45. Bloch-Dano, *Madame Proust*, p. 311.
46. Tadié, *Marcel Proust*, trans. by Cameron, p. 107.
47. Robert de Billy, *Marcel Proust: lettres et conversations* (Paris: Éditions des Portiques, 1930), p. 158.

See also Mireille Naturel, *Proust et le fait littéraire: réception et création* (Paris: Honoré Champion, 2010), pp. 95–110.
48. Desanges, *Marcel Proust et la politique*, p. 119.
49. Dreyfus, *Souvenirs sur Marcel Proust*, p. 338.

PART V

Marcel Proust:
Labours of Love

CHAPTER 18

Community in Solitude: Inter-art Epistolarity through Late-modern Critical Thought

Susan Harrow

In the celebrated iconography of the (male) group portrait, the French inter-art community of the later nineteenth century is visualised in its disrupted cohesiveness. Henri Fantin-Latour's studies of gatherings of artists and writers capture a certain loose or dispersed sense of community: *Un atelier aux Batignolles* (1870) is a homage to Manet and to innovators in his orbit (Zola, Monet, Bazille, Renoir, the sculptor and journalist Zacharie Astruc and the musician and arts patron Edmond Maître); his *Un coin de table* (1872) is an iconic portrait of Rimbaud and Verlaine and other participants at a dinner of the Vilains Bonshommes literary and artistic group. In both paintings, the multi-directional placing of the figures emphasises differences and distinctions, tensions even, between community and individuality, and gestures to the complexities of sociability, solitude, singularity and togetherness.

In this chapter I interrogate ideas of community and solitude that are in play, not in pictorial representations, but in the less prominent, critically underexamined, medium of inter-art letter-writing, angling the ethos and practice of togetherness and aloneness through the prism of late-modern critical thought. How might the contributions of Jacques Rancière, Maurice Blanchot, Giorgio Agamben, Jean-Luc Nancy and Jacques Derrida — themselves formative of a community of singular thinkers on community — help us explore letter-writing as a site of creative community and of sustaining solitude? And how, reciprocally, might inter-art letter-writing of the later nineteenth and earlier twentieth centuries help illuminate aspects of modern critical thought around ideas of community and solitude integral to the creativity of authors and artists. Finally, I will ask how the non-human solitude immanent in the literary or artistic work is reflected in modernist letter-writing.

My purpose is to explore the relationship of community and solitude, drawing on selections from the correspondence of Mallarmé, Cézanne, Zola, Van Gogh, Proust, and Edma and Berthe Morisot. The premises of this essay are intersectional: my choice of authors and artists, several who are world-leading and others who are lesser known, is synonymous with 'high' culture and boundary-breaking aesthetic innovation; my selection of letters reflects those artists' and authors' experience of the everyday in their lived experience — in this way, the 'prestige' values of modernism intersect with experiential questions of privacy, routine, health, nature, leisure, food and friendship, inter alia.

Epistolarity and Everyday Aesthetics

Epistolary communities are constituted by letter-writers and their correspondents, and their afterlife is sustained by new and coming communities, that is to say, readers present-day and future, drawn into the preoccupations, anxieties, desires and fantasies of correspondents.[1] I approach letter-writing as an exploratory site of subjectivity in the creative community, turning critical attention to the rhetoric of selected letters written by contributors to the inter-art aesthetic we call 'modernism'. Let's begin by reflecting more deeply, through the work of Jacques Rancière, on the relation of modernism and the everyday.

In his landmark study, *Aisthesis: scènes du régime esthétique de l'art* (2011), Rancière argues that the displacement of the 'representative regime' by the 'aesthetic regime', at the beginning of the long nineteenth century, creates an experimental space that is receptive to the everyday and the ordinary, a space where art and 'real world' co-exist and intermingle, disrupting falsely stabilised and separatist conceptions of 'elite' art and 'popular' culture.[2] Across fourteen sites of aesthetic modernity that include the Hanlon Lees Brothers' pantomime acrobatics, Loie Fuller's self-morphing performances of colour and light at the Folies-Bergère, Emile Gallé's glasswork and social art, and the filmic plasticity of Charlie Chaplin, Rancière demonstrates the political displacement and the reinvention of aesthetic values that emerge from the cultural privileging of the interrelation of perception, emotion, space and thought in the modern era. The touchstone of Rancière's thought is equality and the disruption of traditional partitions between 'high' aesthetic values and the assumed 'lowliness' (and, thus, marginality) of the everyday. The creative intersection of 'high' and 'low' in Rancière has implications for my reading of modernist letter-writing, which I approach as a critically under-explored space of everyday aesthetics, and one that, to my knowledge, remains unexplored by Rancière himself as a site of *aisthesis*. I argue that the integration of art and everyday life can be extended, beyond the remit of the performance art, popular culture and social art that Rancière investigates, to the letter-writing of modernist artists and authors. Here, everyday matters — concerns with habitat, with work habits, with the life of the senses, with sociability, with family and friends, with aloneness and togetherness — move *towards* aesthetics (through modes of analogy, metaphoricity, fantasy); and, reciprocally, modernist authors and artists probe, analyse, transform and resituate quotidian experience through the inventions and reflections of epistolary language.

At the core of Rancière's argument is the principle of critical redistribution ('redistribution of the sensible'). As the defining agency of everyday aesthetics, the principle of critical redistribution empowers relations of equality between things of widely differing scale and normatively assumed value, as Edward J. Hughes has explored through writers in French of the long twentieth century.³ Alertness to the redistributive capacity of a work introduces the possibility that *anything* has the potential to become art: this finds its epistolary resonance in Proust's repeated attempts to remediate his chronic experience of internal noise (in his boulevard Haussmann apartment block) across a series of letters to his upstairs neighbour; and in Mallarmé's concern that his acute suffering (from a boil on the posterior) may become the subject of local gossip.⁴ Such 'everyday' experiences are incorporated into letter-writing without hierarchy and thus participate in a process of 'flattening' where the sublime creative project (the task of composing *A la recherche du temps perdu* or the work of innovating reason-defying modernist poetry) and the everyday (builders at work, the experience of frustrated creativity, physiological and social discomfort) come together in relations of contiguity, connectedness or active comparison. The levelling and democratising work of the modernist comes into sharp focus in the epistolary community where 'high' art, and elevated artists, connect with the everyday, sounding their preoccupation with what it is to be alone and what it is to be together, with what it is to work and to play, to sleep and to eat. Their preoccupation with quotidian lived experience produces critical redistributions — of bodies, things, voices and actions — within and between letters, and in ways that resonate with readers today as we negotiate accelerated communications, the pressures of connectedness and, often, a sense of atomisation and intersubjective separation in the wrought fabric of our everyday.

I take forward Rancière's notion of critical redistribution by treating letters on a par with a work of art or literature, according them equal importance with what is traditionally defined as 'aesthetic', as letter-writing too often escapes the critical and analytical attention of researchers and remains the object of routine scholarly fact-mining and corroboration.⁵ In privileging epistolarity as a site of the aesthetic, everyday coincidence, I take my lead from modernist writers themselves: thus, in the midst of researching the art of Cimabue in Assisi, John Ruskin, in a letter to Susie Beever, illustrates the inferior quality of local food by inserting his scale drawing of a stunted asparagus (17 June 1874); and James Joyce constructs a persona of fiscal prudence that is performed through his detailed iterations of household expenditure in his serial 'begging' letters to his brother Stanislaus.⁶

Modernists' letters are a place where art and life, aesthetics and the everyday, intersect and connect, and where the democratisation of ideas and subjects occurs, producing 'political' disruptions in what is assumed important or appropriate. Rancière figures the effect of such upheavals and incidents in the artwork or in the cultural event as a relief map of fruitfully uneven relations and sporadic interruptions, a figure that is salient for our understanding of modernist letter-writing:

> Aesthetic experience has a political effect [... as] a multiplication of connections and disconnections that reframe the relation between bodies, the world where they live and the way in which they are 'equipped' for fitting it. [Aesthetic experience] is a multiplicity of folds and gaps in the fabric of common experience that change the cartography of the perceptible, the thinkable and the feasible.⁷

An exceptional example of the creative disruption of commonplace mappings of the perceptible and the thinkable is be found in Mallarmé's 'Récréations postales' (in *Vers de circonstance*), performative enactments in epistolary poetry of the coincidence of the aesthetic and the everyday.[8] On 8 July 1890, on an envelope, Mallarmé replaces the conventional recipient's address with a quatrain addressed to the postman, exhorting him to rush the enclosed letter to 'Madame Berthe Manet' (the painter Berthe Morisot). Mallarmé's postal quatrain inscribes the notion and the lexis of 'distribution' — the distribution of voice, body, idea and material thing across space, time and social class:

> Sans te coucher dans l'herbe verte
> Naïf distributeur, mets-y
> Du tien; cours chez madame Berthe
> Manet, par Meulan, à Mézy.
>
> Don't fall asleep on this green earth
> Innocent distributor, get busy
> Skates on, and speed to Madame Berthe
> Manet, Meulan way, at Mézy.[9]

The postal-quatrain affirms the critical agency of others: their intention, their inventions, their commitment, their kinetic (and here, also, readerly) capacity, beyond the letter-writer (whose own performance depends on all subsequent performances in the epistolary chain). The very next day, a delighted Berthe Morisot ('Mme Manet') reported that the postman, the innocent or ingenuous 'distributeur', was stunned to read the poem on the envelope addressed to him.[10]

Rancière's *aisthesis*, posited on the transformative encounter of art and the everyday, is founded on the sense of belonging to the human community through fresh, invigorated relations between art and the perceptual and affective world of lived experience. Understandings of community have been an intense subject of critical thought and re-thinking across the later twentieth and early twenty-first centuries, to which I now turn in the context of modernist letter-writing.

What Kind of Community? What Kind of Solitude?

Modernist epistolary communities reflect and represent real-world (and notional) communities — groupings, alliances, affinities, rivalries, family and friendship circles, collaborative partnerships and social networks — that link individual artists and writers across an extended period of inter-art innovation. At first blush, 'community' can appear to be a notion in conflict with the solitude required, and nurtured, by the author or the artist, working singly (and singularly) and self-representing in ways individual and often solipsistic, which calls up those forms of equivocal community that Fantin-Latour's group portraits capture in the mode of a visual oxymoron.

'Solitude' is commonly perceived as a negation of 'community' and a countervailing agency, the terms forming a familiar dichotomy that encourages and legitimates over-determinist, and potentially reductive, interpretations of the solitude (or the community) of the artist or author. Cézanne, often characterised, reductively, as an 'artist-in-retreat', is a limit-case in this respect. Philippe Sollers reflects on the internal and external solitude of the painter in his 1991 lecture 'Solitude de Cézanne' to the École Nationale Supérieure des Beaux-Arts, framing Cézanne's affirmations of the need for solitude without 'souci de personne' [caring about anyone] as evidence of solipsistic aloneness and of the absolute refusal of community: in Sollers's figuration, the artist is absorbed in the intensity of self's encounter with sensation, and aversively anti-social.[11] Marcelin Pleynet argues, in his 2006 essay on Cézanne, that the painter was determinedly 'marginal' and singularly 'solitaire', even if it could also be claimed that the artist's early letters reveal a more engaged social self, and that the end of his life saw him welcome younger painters to Aix-en-Provence to dialogue with him in a late-flowering realisation of creative community.[12] Van Gogh is reputed to have been notoriously solitary and 'asocial' yet, as his letters testify, he believed that artists should work and live together in mutually supportive relations; and he would later articulate a sense of empathic community with fellow 'patients' in his asylum letters. In mainstream representations, Proust is routinely offered up as the very incarnation of the self-sequestered author, an image belied, inter alia, by the astonishing ninety thousand letters that he is believed to have written between 1891 and his death in 1922.

But inter-art letter-writing, read in dialogue with late-modern critical thought on community, challenges and disrupts that familiar dichotomy in terms of the complex relationship of community and solitude. The modernist letter-writers I am referencing here tend to frame 'solitude', in an affirmative and enabling sense, in the context of a creative culture that is primarily, though not exclusively, individualist, and that shapes critical, historiographic and popular representations of the artist. Van Gogh, writing to his brother Theo from his lodgings in London in the Spring of 1874, develops a paean to the pleasure and benefits of solitary urban walking immersed in nature. In the process, the artist proffers a botanical model of well-being, visual appreciation and democratic care for Theo to follow:

> I walk here as much as I can, but I'm very busy. It's absolutely beautiful here (even though it's in the city). There are lilacs and hawthorns and laburnums &c. blossoming in all the gardens, and the chestnut trees are magnificent. If one truly loves nature one finds beauty everywhere. (Letter 022, 30 April 1874)[13]

In canonical modernist historiography, as in artists' self-representations, the solipsism of modernist innovation is a concept at variance with the collectivist ethos of the multifarious avant-gardes of the early twentieth century (e.g. 'unanimism', 'futurism', 'simultanism', 'Dadaism', 'vorticism'). Thus, it is with wry humour that the novelist and poet Marie de Régnier (Marie de Hérédia) addresses Proust as 'cher Canaque', so inscribing his role as *secrétaire perpétuel* of the Canaqadémie, a group founded by Marie and frequented by Gide, Léon Blum, Léon Daudet, Proust, Paul Louÿs and Henri de Régnier (letter of 11 December 1919).[14] Marie's playful reminder to Proust of his group allegiance affirms that modernism's singular figures exist both with and beyond the *cénacle* and the *groupuscule*, identified and self-identifying as 'independent' artists. One thinks of the creatively 'networked' poet and inter-art intermediary Guillaume Apollinaire, in the cubist moment, who asserted 'je ne veux pas faire école' [I don't see myself as the leader of some aesthetic 'chapel'], a position complicated by his parallel sense of belonging to a small visionary group of creative 'hills' (in the major, late poem 'Les Collines', in *Calligrammes*), an image that extends the lineage of Baudelaire's vision of individual 'beacons' of visionary creativity ('Les Phares', in *Les Fleurs du mal*) — all are connected but each luminary is singular.[15] As the name 'Salon des (artistes) indépendants' (founded in 1884) in the world of modern painting reminds us, individual artists are related by creative reciprocity, inspiriting rivalry, vitalising camaraderie and sustaining cultures of mutual support. Bertrand Marchal highlights the remarkable insight into contemporaneous networks of sociability ('réseaux de sociabilité littéraire') offered by Mallarmé's letters, the activity of these networks contesting the myth of the solitary poet.[16] Marchal's reflections on Mallarmé's networked sociability remind us that, even in the solipsism of 'difficult' modern poetry and thought (and the poet of *Un coup de dés jamais n'abolira le hasard* is in many ways a 'pure' exemplar of a quester after solitude and singularity) there is a countervailing ethos and practice of cultural affinity, intellectual togetherness and creative community. Epistolary communication articulates the values of 'community' in their diversity and singularity, and in their ethos of shared or reciprocal individuality and empowering solitude.

Critical Thought and Community

Contemporary critical thought can deepen our understanding of the inter-art community where the dialogue between individual(-ist) ethos (solitude) and modes of togetherness defines relationality in letter-writing. Spurred both by the erosion of 'traditional' community formation and by the enduring transmission of shared values in an atomised society, the radical redefinition of community as deregulated, heterogenous, supple, intimate and chosen — a major axis of late-modern critical debates — uncovers perspectives that are salient for our understanding of inter-art letter-writing in the modernist moment.

Concepts of community have been integral to the thought of Jean-Luc Nancy, Maurice Blanchot and Giorgio Agamben, each responding in convergent yet distinctive ways to the work of Georges Bataille.[17] Nancy, in an early essay, 'La Communauté désœuvrée' (1983), explores community as an exhausted agency, an agency suspended in terms of its instrumentalising and totalising agency, and thus 'not working' (*désœuvré*) in the conventional sense, but also as a body of values that persists and resurges in more pliant encounters of self and others.[18] Responding to Nancy's essay and to his view of 'community' as existing *outside* the literary work or other forms of creativity, Blanchot actively relates community to literary work (through his reading of Marguerite Duras's *La Maladie de la mort* (1982)) in *La Communauté inavouable* (1983), and thus he extends Bataille's concern with literature as non-utilitarian, sovereign and heterogenous, an aspect to which I shall return. Blanchot takes forward the concept of 'negative community', formulated by

Bataille in the 1950s: that is, the idea of a community formed of those who have 'no community' in the traditional, prescriptive and ideology-driven sense of the term. Blanchot asks what vanishes and what endures when traditional (and traditionally restrictive) communities disappear, a core question for our study of forms of togetherness in modernist letter-writing.

Van Gogh's letters provide one possible response: each individual, as every letter demonstrates, is part of a network of relations founded on family and friendship ties, and these relations involve, inter alia, mutual support, (inter-)dependence, influence, advice, empathy, solidarity, mentoring, engagement, commitment, collaboration, loyalty and affinity. Van Gogh's correspondence reveals a sustained feeling for what I shall call 'elective community': his letters to his brother Theo explore a sense of community support and succour, and this fraternal correspondence connects Van Gogh to his parents and his other siblings, and to a wider circle of friends and associates. In the sustained intensity of the epistolary relationship between the brothers, with its familial ricochets and resonances, Van Gogh's letters outline a pragmatic response to the need for solidarity and describe a form of creative community founded on the sharing of material and psychological benefits. The painter places significant emphasis on the need for the community of artists to be mutually supporting and care-giving. Creative community, in this instance, includes the possibility of living together whilst preserving the values of individual retreat. Thus, in letters written in the early summer of 1888, Van Gogh suggests sharing his home with Theo and Gauguin, an arrangement that would enable the brothers to support a fellow artist in an intimate community of three:

> [Gauguin] says that when sailors have to move a heavy load or raise an anchor, in order to be able to lift a greater weight, to be able to make an enormous effort, they all sing together to support each other and to give each other energy. That is just what artists lack. So I'd be really surprised if he weren't glad to come [and join the van Gogh brothers in Arles]. (Letter 623, 12 June 1888)

> I thought of Gauguin and here we are — if Gauguin wants to come here there's Gauguin's fare, and then there are the two beds or the two mattresses we absolutely have to buy. But later on, as Gauguin's a sailor, there's a likelihood we'll manage to make our grub at home.
> And the two of us will live on the same money as I spend on myself alone.
> You know I've always thought it ridiculous for painters to live alone &c. You always lose when you're isolated. (Letter 616, 28 or 29 June 1888)

Where Van Gogh extols practical solidarity and (a degree of) co-living in the creative community, others practise 'looser' and more individualist modes of sociability and inter-art exchange. Thus, Mallarmé's famous Tuesday evening gatherings are a legendary site of creative community-making. Hosted at the poet's rue de Rome apartment over a span of thirteen years, *les Mardis* were fluid inter-disciplinary gatherings of writers, philosophers, composers and painters: the *mardistes* formed a protean cosmopolitan community that included W. B. Yeats, Édouard Manet, Stefan George, Oscar Wilde, Berthe Morisot, Paul Verlaine, André Gide, Paul Gauguin, James Whistler, Edouard Dujardin, Méry Laurent and

Paul Valéry.[19] By means of these 'at home' gatherings, the creative community defines itself through regular and more intermittent modes of communication and reciprocity that connect with other forms of interaction — from dinners, visits, lectures and salons, to epistolary exchanges between individuals. In his correspondence, Mallarmé reveals how he carefully regulates social connection and community participation, and how he balances interpersonal relations with the requirements of writerly retreat: thus, in a letter to Huysmans, he explains how his 'habitudes invétérées de solitaire' [ingrained habits of a solitary soul] (22 October 1882) mean that he expects Huysmans to visit *him*, but *he* won't go to Huysmans, the centripetal movement of the poet drawing others towards him (as befits his lionised position) is a strategy for avoiding his own physical and intellectual dispersal.[20] So, the individual's balancing of his self-determined needs for solitude and for connection, in unequal measure, specifically excludes reciprocal equity in this instance. The pursuit of solitude is integral to the poet's ethos and practices, thus social and community interruptions are fastidiously calibrated by the *solitaire*. Togetherness is founded on a strong individual(-ist) ethos that is equivocal and precarious and often manifestly community-resistant, anticipating theorisations of *negative community* in our own time.

Giorgio Agamben, in *Comunità che viene* (1990), reflects on the 'community that isn't one'.[21] Here, Agamben explores 'communities without presuppositions' that are composed of 'whatever singularities', concepts expressive of the individuality that is inherent in modernist ethos and aesthetic practice, and integral to expressions of togetherness, reciprocity and solitude in the letter-writing of Mallarmé, Proust, Cézanne and Van Gogh, and others.[22] In its rejection of essentialist constructions of community, Agamben's 'coming community' is, in some ways (if, admittedly, not in all ways), comparable with the 'looser' sense of community discernible in the letter-writing (and in the real-world relations) of painters and writers who write letters to other painters and writers, and also to significant others in their lives, in terms of forms of togetherness based on various, individual, singular, porous, scattered and interrupted instances, rather than on identarian essences or sustained physical encounters. Proust's correspondence speaks of the power and perennity of friendship experienced in its true and *singular* place, that is in a quality of friendship that lies outside the rituals of social life and is nourished by solitude: responding to Madame Albert Hecht, who shared his interest in Manet's art, the novelist writes (*c.* September 1918), 'dans la solitude les amitiés persistent, sans être renouvelées par la société' [in solitude, friendships are sustained, without requiring to be renewed by social contact].[23]

The dialogue of Blanchot, Nancy and Agamben reveals a complexified situation where the old dichotomies of community and solitude themselves are disrupted and invalidated (this partly answers the question of what vanishes when community vanishes). As concepts of community are revisioned as 'negative community', so, at its core, solitude (often constructed in commonplace understanding as deleterious and in need of remediation) is reappraised, as we saw in the preceding example from Proust's valuing of friendship-infused aloneness. In advance of late-modern critical thought, inter-art epistolarity of the modernist era reveals the ethos of community founded on a culture of solitude and other forms of individualism, such that solitude and community form a vitalising, synthesising oxymoron that empowers and sustains creative working.

The late-modern debate around community (and, more precisely the positive term that is 'negative community', a balance of being together and being oneself, and being one's 'own self' beyond prescriptions), from Bataille to Blanchot, Nancy and Agamben, maps strongly onto the loose and porous understanding of community that emerges in the letter-writing that I am exploring: that is, in significant ways, a notional community, a community that isn't one, a community that *need* not speak its name (or, if it does speak its name, speaks it in playful and self-subversive ways like the Canaqadémie). This is precisely Blanchot's sense of the 'unavowable': that is, a community that is constituted of singular artists in a dispersed and flexible grouping. Individual artists and authors form a community through mutual values and through the shared practice of letter-writing (and, also, they form that community, in part, as a consequence of my actively relating them one to the other in this study).

In *La Communauté affrontée* (2001), published in the aftermath of the 9/11 attacks, Jean-Luc Nancy explains the shift of his thought away from 'community' and towards ideas of 'being together', for the term 'community' always risks implying an entity that may be appropriated for utilitarian and operative ends. (Indeed, one might venture that the variety of lexical and semantic qualifiers added to the root concept-word — from 'negative community' (Bataille, Blanchot), via 'inoperable community' (Nancy) and 'unavowable community', to 'coming community' with its 'whatever singularities' (Agamben) — captures the resistance to unqualified (and unreconstructed) 'community'.) The importance of being together (as opposed to being absorbed by community) comes vividly into focus in an exchange between Zola and Cézanne. The novelist urges the painter to defer his visit to Médan (Zola's country retreat on the Seine downstream from Paris) due to an 'invasion' of guests and their servants. He wants to enjoy with Cézanne their shared freedom and a sense of complicity without the pressures of sociability: '[être] plus libres, plus *entre nous*' (2 July 1885) [[being] freer, just the two of us].[24] Connected retreat is based thus on the nurturing of privileged relations with the few (often the one), rather than with the many. So, to return to Blanchot's question as to what persists when traditional community is superseded or resisted, one might venture that affinity, flexibility, desire, individual preference, freedom and a sense of balance persist. What vanishes? The burden of obligation, rule-bound rigidity and adherence to social expectations.

As the telling example from Proust's letter to Mme Hecht quoted above reveals, solitude is not dissociated from, or distinct from, the presence of others; rather, there is togetherness-in-absence. An important meditation on togetherness-in-absence is to be found in an early letter of Zola to Cézanne (15 April 1860). Here Zola extols solitude as a space haunted with the presence of those absent: 'Le temps passe vite, même dans la solitude, lorsque vous peuplez cette solitude de fantômes chéris' [the time passes quickly, even when one is alone, when one fills one's solitude with the phantom presence of beloved friends].[25] Here the experience of solitude is enriched by the active remembering of the subject's affinity with community, an instance of self-care and of the ethical perpetuation of the cherished other. Here Zola deploys a high-altitude metaphor, invoking resilience and a tenacious commitment to the other and to their bond; figuring the importance of his friendship with Cézanne, he writes, '[je me] cramponne' [[I] hold fast].[26] The climbing metaphor then dissolves in an unexpected pantheistic vision where mist and clouds suddenly part to reveal Cézanne's face lit by a ray of sunshine: in this rhapsodic and performative letter-text, Zola tracks his search for consolation in the active remembering — and the protean visualisation — of the absent friend and the singular experience of friendship.

So, where does friendship, lived or remembered, relate to the discussion of conceptions of 'looser' forms of community and togetherness that we have been exploring? Friendship comes into play in what I have been calling 'elective community' (and what one might also call 'true community'): in letters, this is often the community of two. Community contains the capacity for friendship, and friendships (from deep bonds through enduring empathies to more fleeting or interrupted associations) create the thickness and the diversity of community. In the epistolary context, as in other contexts, friendships bring particularity to community, which is to acknowledge the subtleties, shifting intensity and variable evolution of friendships, and of friendship itself.

The long tradition of literary and philosophical meditations on friendship encompasses Aristotle's analysis of transactional and virtue-based forms of friendship, Montaigne's reflection on his affinity with La Boétie ('De l'amitié' [On Friendship], in *Essais*, 1580), Nietzsche's principle of actively critical friendship ('Vom Freunde' [Of the Friend], in *Also sprach Zarathustra*, 1883–92) and Blanchot's ethics of friendship as always preceding the individual human in the pre-existing relationship that each human has with another (*L'Amitié*, 1971).[27] In his reflection on community and solitude, Jacques Derrida, in *Politiques de l'amitié* (1994), figures the community of solitary friends, metaphorised as an 'anchoritic community', as a basis for future politics.[28] Derrida's thought on the equivocations of friendship and solitude, and his notion of 'singular community', are, I propose, salient for my reading of modernist authors' and artists' letter-writing.

Writers and painters are, for the most part, writing towards others in the creative community from a situation of intentional solitude, and from the distance integral to letter-writing: they are *together* in cherishing both their separation from each other and their mutual connection, thus upholding their 'singular community', which is the community of those who value solitude and practise 'solitary singularity'.[29] To this, as noted above, Derrida gives the definition 'anchoritic community' (a term that brings to mind Barthes's late work on real-world and fictional forms of community in *Comment vivre ensemble* (1977): that is, 'the community of solitary friends' and the '"community of those who have no community"' (Derrida is quoting Blanchot quoting Bataille, revealing the late-modern lineage of thinking around 'negative community').[30] Similar ideas are evoked with singular poignancy in a confidential letter written by Edma Morisot to her sister and fellow artist, Berthe. Recently married to naval officer Adolphe Pontillon, Edma writes of the disconsolation that she is experiencing within the exclusive confines of bourgeois matrimony, for which she has renounced her artistic vocation.[31] Edma recalls that creative solitude and occasional fifteen-minute exchanges with artists such as Degas, who had a serious and supportive opinion of her work, were more rewarding than 'des qualités solides', an allusion to the stolid companionship afforded by her new husband. In response, in a bid to assuage those feelings of constraint and loss of artistic belonging, Berthe encourages her sister to count her blessings and appreciate that *solitude* (slanted now in the social sense and freighted with ideas of emotional lack) is not what a woman wants. Edma's reflection on the loneliness of socially sanctioned togetherness in marriage speaks powerfully of the countervailing richness of self-chosen solitude and the value of sisterly and peer support experienced in the creative community.

Solitude and the Immanence of the Work of Literature

In this final phase, I return to the earlier thought of Blanchot for it has specific relevance for the modernist epistolary context founded, not only on the shared experience of creative 'solitude vécue en commun' [solitude experienced together] (Blanchot's definition of community in *La Communauté inavouable*), but also on the assumed internal 'integrity' of modernist art forms.[32]

In *L'Espace littéraire* (1955) Blanchot takes solitude in a particular philosophical, and specifically textual, direction where he defines 'la solitude essentielle' as the solitude immanent in the literary work, distinct from the existential, 'lived' solitude of the 'author in the world'.[33] For Blanchot, the essential solitude of the work is terrifying and unknowable and is glimpsed in the abolition of the author; it is instanced by the hermetic, self-reflexive and autotelic qualities of modernist art — one might cite Picasso's analytical cubism, Paul Valéry's *Le Cimetière marin* or Pierre Boulez's serialist abstraction as examples of modernist intermedial interiority in the French tradition.

Mallarmé's letters to his friend and fellow poet Henri Cazalis afford a remarkable insight into what Blanchot comes to theorise almost a century later (where, it should be noted, Blanchot invokes the author of *Igitur* as a practitioner of 'pure', non-utilitarian language). Immersed in the 'Introduction' to his poem *Hérodiade*, Mallarmé tells Cazalis on 5 December 1865, 'Je vis dans une solitude et un silence inviolés' [I live in inviolate solitude and silence] (or a solitude 'violated' only by the sharing of ideas in epistolary friendship).[34] He wills the 'jewel' that is *Hérodiade* to emerge from 'le sanctuaire de ma pensée' [the sanctuary of my thought]. Thus, Mallarmé synthesises the immanent solitude of the work and a sense of the rarefied creative, and psychic, solitude of the author.

Several months later, in late April 1866, in another letter to Cazalis, Mallarmé explores two (related) forms of solitude: in a figurative move that prefigures the critical thought of Blanchot on the immanent solitude of the work itself. Here the poet describes a double void in which the self is engulfed both in its somatic interiority (the physical abyss that is his wheezing chest) and in the void that is the unachievable 'Livre', the solitude that the 'pure' modernist literary work demands and perpetuates.[35] This epistolary expression of the idea of the literary work as an abyss in which the poet contemplates his own abolition in the work, his own death, makes of Mallarmé, *épistolier*, with his critical lucidity on the 'essential solitude' of the work of art, a precursor of Blanchot. Here, in post-Mallarméan echo, is Blanchot:

> L'œuvre demande [...] que l'homme qui l'écrit se sacrifie pour l'œuvre, devienne autre, devienne non pas un autre, non pas du vivant qu'il était, l'écrivain avec ses devoirs, ses satisfactions et ses intérêts, mais plutôt personne, le lieu vide et animé où retentit l'appel de l'œuvre.[36]

> [The work demands [...] that the writer sacrifice himself for the work, becomes other, becomes not another, not in the living form that he was — the writer with his duties, his satisfactions and his interests — but rather becomes no one, the vacant, energised place that resounds with the call of the work.]

★ ★ ★ ★ ★

At the beginning of this chapter, I invoked Rancière's vision of inter-art modernity founded on the radical redistribution between 'high' art and everyday culture. I have sought to show that Rancière's redistributive principle has exportable salience for our understanding of modernist inter-art epistolarity as a space of everyday aesthetics, where the 'pure' art associated with modernist thought and practice is complexified by an encounter with the ordinary and experiential. Letter-writing is thus revealed as a singular space where traditional, dichotomous understandings of solitude and community are actively contested, in ways that anticipate — and may be explored through — some of the key concerns of late-modern critical thought. Examples of the letter-writing of some of the iconic artists and authors of the modernist moment reveal how values of creative community and their cognates, togetherness and friendship, are defined, understood and shared through the clarifying reflection of letter writers on the complementary and integral value that is solitude.

Just as modern critical thought, that of Blanchot, Agamben, Nancy and Derrida, can help us configure letter-writing as a site of community-in-solitude, so, reciprocally, letters of the later nineteenth and earlier twentieth centuries can help us illuminate and instantiate aspects of modern critical thought around the concept and practice of 'negative community' and lived forms of togetherness and intimacy in our own time, particularly in relation to bodies, affect, perceptions and the senses, which is to loop back, *in fine*, to Rancière's vision of the aesthetic redistribution of the sensible. Late-modern critical thought, in turn, can benefit from this expansion of its remit beyond notions of political community and of the community that is represented by the immanence of the work of art, just as epistolarity studies can benefit from critical frames that complexify understandings of the creative community of individual authors and artists.

Notes to Chapter 18

1. Epistolary communities may involve the few or the many: usually in the letters examined here, we gain a sense of two interlocutors, and an intimation of networks beyond, the wider 'connected community', however porous, dispersed and notional that community might be.
2. Jacques Rancière, *Aisthesis: Scenes from the Aesthetic Regime of Art*, trans. by Zakir Paul (London & New York: Verso, 2013). The original publication is *Aisthesis: scènes du régime esthétique de l'art* (Paris: Galilée, 2011).
3. Edward J. Hughes, *Egalitarian Strangeness: On Class Disturbance and Levelling in Modern and Contemporary French Narrative* (Liverpool: Liverpool University Press, 2021), examines, inter alia, novels by Proust, Simone Weil, Claude Simon, Marie Ndiaye, and Didier Éribon, alert to the redistributive agency of modern and contemporary fiction in its interrogation of the social order.
4. Marcel Proust, *Letters to the Lady Upstairs*, ed. by Estelle Gaudry and Jean-Yves Tadié, trans. by Lydia Davis (London: 4th Estate, 2017): the phenomenology, psychology and sociality of acoustic experience are a constant subject of these letters between neighbours. Stéphane Mallarmé, *Correspondance 1854–1898*, ed. by Bertrand Marchal (Paris: Gallimard, 2019), p. 145, letter of 23 December 1865.
5. There are however fresh signs of letter-writing being discussed on equal terms with modernist works of literature. Abbie Garrington explores epistolary ties, the belay metaphor and connective affect in Virginia Woolf's writing and in the correspondence of the mountaineer George Mallory, in 'The Line that Binds: Climbing Narratives, Ropework and Epistolary Practice', in *Modernism and Affect*, ed. by Julie Taylor (Edinburgh: Edinburgh University Press, 2015), Chapter 4.
6. For Ruskin's letter from Assisi, see <https://www.gutenberg.org/files/22230/22230-h/22230-h.htm> [accessed November 2021]. Xander Ryan, 'Modernist Letters: The Epistolary Selves of Flaubert, Joyce and Beckett' (unpublished PhD thesis, University of Reading, 2021), pp. 128–30, explores the financial and sartorial metonymics of material self-formation in Joyce's letters to Stanislaus.
7. The quotation is from Rancière's lecture, 'Aesthetic Separation, Aesthetic Community: Scenes from the Aesthetic Regime of Art' (2006) <http://www.artandresearch.org.uk/v2n1/ranciere.html> [accessed November 2021].
8. That the 'pure' aesthetics of Mallarmé is complexified by the encounter with the everyday has long been recognised by critics, notably Roger Pearson, Rosemary Lloyd, Damian Catani and Hélène Stafford, alert to the poet's concern across his *œuvre*, literary and journalistic, with the everyday, whether fashion, fog, infirmary walls, candied fruits or the ladies' fan. Indeed, *Un coup de dés jamais n'abolira le hasard* is a remarkable instance of the modernist scattering of everyday debris (feather, bone, sea foam) through the exploded structures of the experimentalist poem of catastrophe and revelation.
9. All translations are my own unless stated otherwise.
10. Stéphane Mallarmé, *Œuvres complètes*, ed. by Bertrand Marchal, 2 vols, Bibliothèque de la Pléiade (Paris: Gallimard, 1998–2003), I, 1250.
11. Sollers's lecture is reproduced at <http://www.pileface.com/sollers/spip.php?article333#section1> [accessed June 2022].
12. Marcelin Pleynet, *Cézanne marginal: Cézanne, sa vie et son enseignement* (Paris: Les Mauvais Jours, 2006), pp. 51–62.
13. The superbly annotated and full searchable on-line edition of Van Gogh's correspondence is at <http://vangoghletters.org/vg/> [accessed November 2021]. Quotations from the painter's letters are sourced there, via letter number and date.
14. This letter from Marie de Régnier is among the first to appear in *Correspondance Proust*, digital edition <http://proust.elan-numerique.fr/letter/03978> [accessed November 2021].
15. Apollinaire's letter to Toussaint-Luca is to be found in *Œuvres complètes*, ed. by Michel Décaudin, 4 vols (Paris: Baland & Lecat, 1965–66), IV, 697.
16. Bertrand Marchal, 'Introduction', in Mallarmé, *Correspondance 1854–1898*, p. 9.

17. See Patrick ffrench, *After Bataille: Sacrifice, Exposure, Community* (Oxford: Legenda. 2017), for a discussion of community and friendship in Bataille and after Bataille.
18. Jean-Luc Nancy, *La Communauté désœuvrée* (Paris: Galilée, 2001) (first published in *Aléa*, 4 (1983), 11–49).
19. Gordon Millan, *Les 'Mardis' de Stéphane Mallarmé: mythes et réalités* (Paris: Nizet, 2008), documents the thirteen-year period during which the poet held his *salon*.
20. Mallarmé, *Correspondance 1854–1898*, p. 495.
21. Giorgio Agamben, *The Coming Community*, trans. by Michael Hardt (Minneapolis: University of Minnesota Press, 1993), p. 85.
22. Ibid., pp. 1–2.
23. See the *Correspondance Proust* <https://proust.elan-numerique.fr/letter/03584>.
24. Paul Cézanne and Émile Zola, *Lettres croisées: 1858–1887*, ed. by Henri Mitterand (Paris: Gallimard, 2016), p. 410 (my emphasis).
25. Ibid., p. 139.
26. Ibid. See Garrington's study of climbing metaphors in modernist fiction and in letter-writing, 'The Line that Binds'.
27. See Leslie Hill's elegant translation of Maurice Blanchot, 'For Friendship', *Oxford Literary Review*, 22 (2000), 25–38.
28. Jacques Derrida, *Politiques de l'amitié* (Paris: Galilée, 1994), explores the equivocation between individual friendship and community in 'Replis'. Subsequent quotations are taken from *The Politics of Friendship*, trans. by George Collins (London: Verso, 1997).
29. Derrida, *The Politics of Friendship*, p. 35.
30. Ibid., p. 37.
31. Intimating the sensitivity and the confessional nature of her communication, Edma asks her sister to destroy the letter, aware that Berthe habitually leaves correspondence scattered around her home. *Berthe Morisot: Correspondence*, ed. by Denis Rouart (London: Moyer Bell, 1987), p. 24.
32. Maurice Blanchot, *La Communauté inavouable* (Paris: Minuit, 1983), p. 39.
33. Maurice Blanchot, *L'Espace littéraire* (Paris: Gallimard, 1955), pp. 11–25.
34. Mallarmé, *Correspondance 1854–1898*, p. 140.
35. Ibid., p. 161.
36. Maurice Blanchot, *Le Livre à venir* [1959] (Paris: Gallimard, 1986), p. 293.

CHAPTER 19

'Les noms magiques':
Names, Places and Persian-ness in
Noailles, Bibesco and Proust

Julia Caterina Hartley

The desire for unvisited places, the aura it confers upon their names and the disappointment experienced upon finally travelling to them are central themes in Marcel Proust's *A la recherche du temps perdu*.[1] In the diptych of chapters 'Noms de pays: le nom' and 'Noms de pays: le pays', Proust meditates on these themes in general terms, while also illustrating them through the young protagonist's desire for journeys to Normandy and Italy. His most prominent fantasy is that of the Norman town of Balbec, a name he associates with the image of a Persian church sprayed by ocean waves (*RTP*, I, 377–79; *SLT*, I, 462–64); an image that is irrevocably destroyed when he finally visits the real church (*RTP*, II, 19–21; *SLT*, II, 272–75). What has remained undiscussed until now is that this relationship between imaginary travel and physical travel, as manifested through the intertwined themes of names, places and Persian-ness, had in fact been previously explored by two authors whom Proust was reading at the time he began writing the 'Noms de pays' chapters: the Romanian cousins Anna de Noailles (née de Brancovan) and Marthe Bibesco (née Lahovary).[2] Noailles's collection of poems *Les Éblouissements* [Bedazzlements] (1907) and Bibesco's travelogue *Les Huit Paradis* [The Eight Paradises] (1908) both describe (though with very different conclusions) the relationship between the imaginary travel inspired by reading Persian poetry and their experiences of physical travel to the Middle East (Istanbul in Noailles's case, Persia in Bibesco's case).[3] In this chapter, I argue that it was these shared themes that drew Proust to their works, leading him to call *Les Éblouissements* 'un livre unique' [a unique book] and the author of *Les Huit Paradis* 'un écrivain parfait' [a perfect writer].[4] In doing so, I intend to shed new light on two celebrated yet forgotten writers of the belle époque, while also adding to our understanding of the role of women in the milieu that saw the genesis of *A la recherche*, not only as Proust's friends and hostesses, but as authors whose writing had an influence on his.

The poems of Anna de Noailles's *Les Éblouissements* (1907) explore a female lyric I's dazzlement by various forms of beauty, from the spectacle of nature to the pleasures of reading. For the purposes of this chapter, I shall be focusing on the collection's treatment of two themes: the expectations and disappointments of travel, which is the subject of the eighty-four-line poem 'L'Occident', and the unadulterated fantasy of Persia, to which four poems are devoted. 'L'Occident' (pp. 69–72) is a poem full of twists, surprises and reversals of perspective. It will therefore require the most attention.

> Le ciel est un flottant azur, jour sans pareil!
> L'air d'or semble la tiède haleine du soleil,
> On respire, sur tout l'éclatant paysage,
> Une odeur de plaisir, de départ: ô voyage,
> O divine aventure, appel des cieux lointains!
> Presser des soirs plus beaux, baiser d'autres matins,
> Se jeter, les yeux pleins d'espoirs, l'âme enflammée,
> Dans le train bouillonnant de vapeur, de fumée,
> Et qui, dans un parfum de goudron, d'huile et d'eau,
> Rampe, et pourtant s'élève aux cieux comme un oiseau!
> ('L'Occident', ll. 1–10)

[The sky is a floating azure, incomparable day! | The golden air seems the warm breath of the sun, | One breathes, over the entire brilliant landscape, | A scent of pleasure, of departure: O journey, | O divine adventure, calling from the distant skies! | To press more beautiful evenings, to kiss other hands, | To throw oneself, eyes full of hope, soul ablaze, | Into the train boiling with steam, with smoke, | And which, in a perfume of tar, oil and water, | Crawls, and yet flies, into the heavens like a bird!][5]

The poem's opening conjures the sense of anticipation that surrounds new journeys through the anaphoric repetition of verbs in the infinitive, a trope introduced in l. 6. The infinitive serves to convey that the actions are potential rather than enacted, in other words, that they belong to the realm of desire. The lure of the unvisited place is further emphasised in l. 6 through the use of verbs pertaining to romantic intimacy. As the first step in the journey, the train is metaphorised as having a magical quality, much like in Proust's 'Noms de pays: le nom', where the train is 'la chambre magique qui se chargeait d'opérer la transmutation' [the magical chamber which took care of performing the transmutation] (*RTP*, I, 385; *SLT*, I, 471, translation adapted). The poem then describes, through the continued anaphoric repetition of verbs in the infinitive, the pleasures to be found in Istanbul, combining references to sight, touch, taste and smell with proper names: 'Eyoub', 'Koran', 'Yildiz', 'Buyukdéré' (ll. 19, 33, 41). This pairing of names and the senses is also characteristic of 'Nom de pays: le nom' (see in particular *RTP*, I, 381–82; *SLT*, I, 467–68). Indeed, Proust himself was conscious of his stylistic proximity to Noailles: in a letter to Marthe Bibesco, he admits to cutting the original draft's use of vocative addresses to Quimperlé and Pont-Aven (towns on the imaginary train route between Paris and Balbec) because he feared that these might read like a pastiche of Noailles.[6] The continued use of infinitive verbs in Noailles's description of the pleasures to be found in Istanbul collapses the distinction between anticipation and realisation, since on the one hand, it reads as a continuation of the yearning expressed by the lyric 'I' for the destination, but on the other hand, its specific references to places, activities and foods suggests that she has now arrived in Istanbul. The ambiguity is resolved through a dramatic transition in l. 42:

> — Et puis, soudain, brûlant, fougueux, désespéré,
> N'ayant jamais trouvé l'ivresse qui pénètre,
> Le bonheur dont on meurt et dont on va renaître,
> [...]
> La volupté sans fin, sans bord, qui nous étouffe
> Sous ses roses tombant par grappes et par touffe,
> Partir, fuir, s'évader de ce lourd paradis,
> [...]
> Et rentrer dans sa ville, un soir tiède et charmant
> Où l'azur vit, reluit, respire au firmament;
> Voir la Seine couler contre sa noble rive,
> Dire à Paris: 'Je viens, je te reprends, j'arrive!'
> ('L'Occident', ll. 42–44, 47–49, 53–56)

[— And then, suddenly, burning, wild, desperate, | Having never found the drunkenness that penetrates, | The happiness that makes one die and come back to life, | [...] | Pleasure [*volupté*] without end, without limit, smothering | Under the roses falling in bunches and clumps, | To leave, to flee, to escape this heavy paradise, | [...] | And to return to your city, on a warm and charming evening, | Where the azure lives, shines and breathes in the heavens; | To see the Seine flowing against its noble bank, | To say to Paris: 'I'm coming, I'm taking you back, I'm here!']

The lyric 'I' had left home with her soul 'ablaze' (l. 7) and yet finds that her 'burning' desire (l. 42) remains unsatisfied, even after reaching her desired destination. As a result, the urgency of desire with which the poem had opened is now redirected in ll. 49–50 towards the opposite dream: escaping the exotic destination and returning home. The hemistich 'Et rentrer dans sa ville' provides a powerful sense of resolution. Its opening conjunction interrupts the seemingly endless concatenation of anaphoric verbs, the prefix *re-* emphasises the reversal of direction, and the possessive article denotes a familiarity and affection that had been absent in Istanbul. The *re-* prefix is then repeated in l. 56, in which the lyric 'I' addresses the city of Paris, further establishing their intimacy, its exclamation mark presenting home as just as exciting a destination as Istanbul. Proust depicts a similarly sudden redirection of desire towards an 'opposite dream' (*RTP*, I, 379; *SLT*, I, 465) in 'Nom de pays: le nom', when the child protagonist goes from dreaming of the cold misty shores of Balbec to craving Italy in the spring sun. But while for Proust's protagonist, who daydreams in Paris, this redirection remains in pursuit of unvisited places, Noailles turns against the very premise of her poem, and indeed the wider canon of French poems about travel, which had been the pursuit of that which is 'other' and 'more beautiful', by desiring instead her home — or does she?[7]

The description of Paris on which the poem ends relies on exactly the same tropes as the description of Istanbul had done, suggesting that home is in fact somewhere new and beautiful. We find, again, verbs in the infinitive referring to the senses of sight, taste, smell and touch, in combination with references to places: the Seine, the Pont Alexandre II, the Place Vendôme, and the Louvre (ll. 55, 57, 60, 64).

References to the 'azure' sky, in turn, echo the description of the departure, as does the metaphor of physical intimacy: the line 'Attirer dans ses bras, sur le cœur qui s'entr'ouvre' (l. 63) in particular reads as an expansion on the opening's 'Presser' (l. 6). Crucially, the repetition of lexical items serves to express a contrast, rather than a similarity: whereas in Istanbul the lyric 'I' bemoaned the absence of 'la volupté sans fin, sans bord' [pleasure without end, without limit] (l. 47), in Paris she finds 'la volupté | Montant à tout instant de toute la cité' [the pleasure | Rising at every moment from the entire city] (ll. 77–78). This leads to the emphatic hemistich 'Repousser l'Orient' [to reject the Orient] (l. 79), which inverts the poem's central trope: the verb in the infinitive no longer expresses desire, but repulsion. Instead of dreaming of the Orient, the lyric 'I' tells her readers, one should celebrate the West and enjoy summers spent 'sur les routes françaises' [on French roads] (l. 84). This conclusion can be read in light of Edward Said's analysis of the loaded opposition between Occident and Orient in nineteenth- and early twentieth-century French and British thought and literature; and the combination of desire and repulsion that often characterises the Western gaze on the Islamic Middle East.[8] But I would argue that the poem's tripartite structure, taking us from the excitement of departure, to the disappointment of arrival and, finally, the joy of returning to a home that has become somewhere new, goes beyond the France/Orient dichotomy to point to something more universal. The poem tells us that exoticism lies not in places, but in one's imagination; and that a defamiliarised gaze on one's own city can offer far more than distant journeys.

In *La Prisonnière*, Proust writes, 'le seul véritable voyage […] ne serait pas d'aller vers de nouveaux paysages, mais d'avoir d'autres yeux' [the only true journey […] would be not to visit strange lands but to possess other eyes] (*RTP*, III, 762; *SLT*, V, 291). He adds that artists such as the fictional painter Elstir take us on such journeys because they allow us to see the world through another person's eyes. This observation is foreshadowed in 'Noms de pays: le pays' when the protagonist, after having been disappointed by Balbec's church, rediscovers its aesthetic value through the guidance of Elstir, who calls it 'la plus belle Bible historiée que le peuple ait jamais pu lire' [the finest illustrated Bible that the people have ever had] (*RTP*, II, 196; *SLT*, II, 485). Although this change in perspective is framed by art rather than by travel, it does nonetheless mirror Noailles's progression: we go from a movement outwards towards the exoticism of the Orient — Istanbul in Noailles's case, the Persian-ness of Gothic art in Proust's case — to a new-found appreciation of what one has already seen and a celebration of local French culture. Moreover, this celebration of the local does not entail a complete rejection of the Orient; rather, the Orient is incorporated within the French whole. Indeed, Noailles's description of Paris gives a special pride of place to Asian flora: both the 'vernis du Japon' [Japanese lacquer tree] and 'arbre de Judée' [tree of Judea] are in rhyming positions (ll. 70, 72). Elstir, for all his admiration of Christian art, admits that there are details of Balbec's church façade that imitate Persian art, positing that these must have been copied from a casket brought back 'from the East' by sailors (*RTP*, II, 198; *SLT*, II, 487). Moreover, as I shall now show, Persian literary and visual culture holds a special significance for both authors.

Les Éblouissements contains four poems centred on Persian miniature art, poetry and architecture. Beyond their themes, these four poems also make a formal allusion to Persian versification through their exclusive use of quatrains.[9] The first two poems are inspired by Persian miniature art: in 'Danseuse persane' (pp. 11–15), the lyric 'I' describes and addresses a female figure whose enjoyment of sensual pleasures stands in opposition to the views of censorious male figures, a theme that one also encounters in the works of the Persian poet Hāfez; the second, 'Paysage persan' (pp. 46–47) offers a series of ekphrases of landscapes and characters typical of Persian miniature art. In 'Le Jardin-qui-séduit-le-cœur' (pp. 122–24), Noailles's lyric 'I' fantasises about travelling through space and time to medieval Shiraz, where she intends to spy on the poets Hāfez, Sa'di and Khayyām. The poem's opening stanzas explicitly refer to two kinds of journey: the journey of the soul that takes place through the act of reading and the journey of the body. The fantasy of the lyric 'I' is for these two journeys to become one:

> Je l'ai lu dans un livre odorant, tendre et triste,
>   Dont je sors pleine de langueur,
> Et maintenant je sais qu'on le voit, qu'il existe,
>   Le Jardin-qui-séduit-le-cœur!
>   [...]
> Mon âme, se peut-il que mon corps t'accompagne
>   Et vole vers ce paradis?
>
> ('Le-Jardin-qui-seduit-le-cœur', ll. 1–4, 7–8)[10]

[I read it in a fragrant, tender, melancholy book, | Which leaves me full of languor, | And now I know one can see it, it exists, | The Garden-that-seduces-the-heart! | [...] | My soul, might my body accompany you | And fly to this paradise?]

Noailles's final Persian poem 'Rêverie persane' (pp. 137–39) adopts a similar tone to 'Le Jardin'. This Persian fantasy, however, is not framed by the act of reading, but through the conceit of life after death. Whereas Istanbul was the 'heavy paradise' the lyric 'I' sought to escape, Esfahan and Shiraz are her true paradise.

> O Mort, s'il faut qu'un jour ta flèche me transperce,
>   Si je dois m'endormir entre tes bras pesants,
> Laisse-moi m'éveiller dans l'empire de Perse,
>   Radieuse, éblouie, et n'ayant que quinze ans.
>
> Alors, je connaîtrai, moi qui rêvais tant d'elle,
> Ispahan, feu d'azur, fruit d'or, charme des yeux!
> Les jardins de Chirâz et la tombe immortelle
>   Où Sâdi refleurit en pétales joyeux.
>
> ('Rêverie persane', ll. 1–8)

[O Death, if your arrow must one day pierce me, | If I must fall asleep in your heavy arms, | Let me awake in the empire of Persia, | Radiant, dazzled and only fifteen years old. | Then, I shall know, I who dreamed of her so long, | Esfahan, fire of blue, fruit of gold, charm of the eyes! | The gardens of Shiraz and the immortal tomb | Of Sa'di, who flowers again in joyous petals.]

'Rêverie persane' overlays the fantasies of two lost pasts or, to use Proust's phrase, two 'lost paradises' (*SLT*, IV, 449; *SLT*, VI, 222): the personal paradise of the poet's youth and the historic paradise of the Islamic Golden Age, during which Shiraz became a centre of power, and the Persian Renaissance under the Safavids, during which Esfahan became the capital of Persia and its city centre was rebuilt. The poem places a special emphasis on architectural landmarks: Esfahan is famous for the rich tile work (mostly in tones of blue and gold) adorning the city centre's façades and domes (see in particular Naqsh-e Jahan Square); Shiraz is celebrated for its gardens and is home to the mausoleums of the poets Sa'di and Hāfez. The poem also makes intertextual allusions to Persian poetry, for instance through its use of the conceit that roses rise from the dust of the dead.[11] Noailles's Persia is therefore constructed from Persian verse, Persian architecture and Persian miniature art. Unlike Istanbul, Persia cannot disappoint, because the fantasy is never enacted: Noailles never travelled there 'with her body', and indeed she could not have done in so far as this Persia is a fabrication.[12] As Proust writes in 'Nom de pays', there is an inherent contradiction 'à vouloir regarder et toucher avec les organes des sens ce qui avait été élaboré par la rêverie' [in wishing to look at and to touch with the organs of my senses what had been elaborated by the spell of my dreams] (*RTP*, I, 384; *SLT*, I, 470). But why was it Persia that inspired Noailles and Proust's reveries? What did Proust have in mind when he wrote of Balbec's 'Persian style'?

The belle époque was a turning-point for French research into the history of Persian art and architecture. Between 1884 and 1886, the married collaborators Jane and Marcel Dieulafoy excavated the Palace of Darius the Great at Susa. The finds, which are referred to in *Le Côté de Guermantes* (*RTP*, II, 488; *SLT*, III, 215), revealed the polychromy of ancient Persian art and significantly enhanced the Louvre's collections.[13] Yet Marcel Dieulafoy did not originally set out to become a famous archaeologist: he was primarily interested in demonstrating the influence of pre-Islamic Persian architecture on the European Gothic.[14] Émile Mâle in his survey of French Gothic architecture (1898), which Proust studied assiduously, equally argued that the stylised plants and animals on Romanesque cathedrals were copied from Persian fabrics and Arab carpets.[15] Thus, far from being outlandish, the idea that the imaginary façade of Balbec's Gothic church could have elements of Persian design would have seemed perfectly plausible to art historians. Proust would have formed his notions of Persian art from three further sources: French translations and pastiches of Persian literature (he wrote an enthusiastic letter to Henri Cazalis after reading his *Quatrains d'Al-Ghazali*),[16] the written descriptions and illustrations of French travelogues (these have a long history, but Pierre Loti's *Vers Ispahan* [The Way to Isfahan] (1904) and Bibesco's *Les Huit Paradis* are the most relevant) and the Persian decorative objects that circulated in belle époque Paris. These included the Persian carpets that Proust's father Dr Adrien Proust brought home from a trip to Tehran,[17] as well as the Persian artefacts exhibited and sold at the 1878 and 1889 Exposition universelle, and the French imitations that these inspired.[18] Persian miniature art, which plays such a prominent role in both Noailles's and Bibesco's visions of Persia, would also have been among the artefacts with which Proust was familiar, as made clear in 'Combray' when the narrator describes a garden as having 'les tons vifs et purs des miniatures de la Perse' [the pure and vivid colouring of a Persian miniature] (*RTP*, I, 134; *SLT*, I, 162). But which of these art forms is Swann referring to when he tells the child protagonist 'on dirait de l'art persan' [one is tempted to describe it as Persian in its inspiration] (*RTP*, I, 378; *SLT*, I, 463)? Is he speaking of architecture, book illustrations or arts and crafts? Islamic or pre-Islamic Persia? Elstir's subsequent reference to a casket acquired by sailors (*RTP*, II, 198; *SLT*, II, 487) would suggest Islamic Persian arts and crafts, but I would argue that Proust's vagueness is in fact intentional. The words 'église de style persan' [church in the Persian style] (*RTP*, I, 379; *SLT*, I, 464) stay with the protagonist not because they point to a single aesthetic (e.g. Sassanian architecture), but because of the plurality of meanings that 'Persian art' held at the time Proust was writing, from carpets to calligraphy, ancient palaces to renaissance mosques. This plurality is what 'Noms de pays' gained when Proust removed the reference to Mâle's book from his draft and replaced it instead with the words 'on dirait de l'art persan' (see *Esquisse* LXXVII, in *RTP*, I, 955).

That being said, there are however two threads that run through the variety of Persian art. First, Persian art from across the ages is characterised by an emphasis on the decorative arts, to which it brings a mastery of line and colour, and a sophisticated understanding of how diverse details can form one coherent whole, characteristics that would certainly have resonated with the author of *A la recherche*.[19] Secondly, Persian art is associated with a civilisation which developed independently from the Greco-Roman and Christian heritage that was considered the bedrock of French civilisation. This afforded it an inalienable patina of exoticism. Indeed, it is no accident that Swann's reference to Persian art follows Legrandin's observation that Balbec is geographically situated at the very edge of France: 'on y sent la véritable fin de la Terre française, européenne' [you feel there that you are actually at the end of French territory, of Europe] (*RTP*, I, 377; *SLT*, I, 463, translation modified). Plurality, refinement of detail and exoticism: therein lies the incantatory power of the Proustian adjective *persan(e)*. Margaret Topping has argued that Persia in *A la recherche* is 'a marker of fantasy and false impressions' and that it ultimately symbolises the illusions of youth, which are cast aside in *Le Temps retrouvé* when the narrator reaches maturity and envisions his future novel not as a Persian church, but as a church *tout court*.[20] Topping's interpretation speaks both to my argument that the adjective is left open to the imagination through its potential reference to multiple artforms and also to Persia's association with adolescence not only in Proust's novel, but also in Noailles's poem 'Rêverie persane'. Yet it bears noting that if this fantasy was so powerful, it was because it did not exist solely in the imagination, but had a basis in the cultural milieu of belle époque Paris. For both Proust and Noailles, Persia was an untravelled place whose name had rich evocative powers by virtue of the cultural products that had travelled from there to France both physically and metaphorically, leaving their mark on the façades of cathedrals, fashionable interiors and French poetry. But what happens when the name becomes a place?

Les Huit Paradis (1908) is a book based on the diary that Marthe Bibesco kept during her 1905 journey to Esfahan in the company of her husband Georges-Valentin and his two cousins, Proust's close friends Antoine and Emmanuel

Bibesco. The names of places are at the heart of this travelogue, informing both its structure and titles. The book has eight chapters, each named after one of the cities that Bibesco visited: Rasht, Tehran, Qom, Kashān and Esfahan in Persia; Lankaran in Azerbaijan; Trabzon and Istanbul in Turkey. These cities are the eight paradises referred to by the book's title, which, as Bibesco explains in her brief preface, was inspired by the eight-part structure of the Islamic Heaven and the etymology of the word 'paradise', from the Avestan *pairidaēza*, which referred to the parks of the ancient kings of Persia, upon which the Abrahamic faiths' image of paradise would later be based (*HP*, i). From the outset, then, Bibesco presents her journey as being both geographic and etymological; a journey to the origins of paradise. Whereas Noailles knew paradise existed because she had 'read it in a book',[21] Bibesco informs us that she personally witnessed it: 'Des villes d'Islam que j'ai visitées, trois me parurent incomparables, et les autres humbles ou jolies; mais toutes possédaient les "jardins traversés de courants d'eau" que Mahomet décrit aux paragraphes des promesses' [Of all the cities of Islam I have visited, I thought three beyond compare, the others humble and merely pretty; but all possessed the 'gardens watered by living streams' described by Mahomet in the paragraphs of the promises] (*HP*, i; *EP*, i]. The preface thus announces what I argue is the major theme of Bibesco's travelogue: the notion that imaginary travel, whether inspired by the names of places or the pages of Persian poetry, can be fulfilled through physical travel. This is in sharp contrast to Noailles's and Proust's treatment of imaginary and physical travel as two distinct and incompatible experiences.

The opening of Bibesco's travelogue conveys the same burning anticipation that had animated the writing of Noailles and Proust and highlights the important role played by the name of the untravelled place, in this instance, the continent of Asia.

> 'Le charme de ton nom s'étend comme l'huile épandue.'
> (*Cantique des Cantiques*)
> Le 9 mai
> Comment l'Asie m'apparaîtra-t-elle? j'attends; je la laisse venir à moi en fermant un peu les yeux, pour ne pas m'exténuer à l'apercevoir, lorsqu'elle n'est encore qu'une bande étroite sur le ciel du matin. Je pense pourtant avec ferveur: c'est l'Asie, l'Asie! (*HP*, 4)
>
> ['The charm of your name spreads as ointment poured forth.'
> — THE SONG OF SOLOMON
> May 9th.
> How will Asia appear to me? I wait and let her come to me, closing my eyes a little, unwilling to strain them in the effort: for as yet she is but a narrow band against the morning sky. And yet I think to myself passionately: this is Asia, Asia!] (*EP*, 2, translation modified)

A name's ability to reach far beyond the place it refers to is succinctly captured by the biblical quotation, which also continues the preface's association of Persia with the origin of religions.[22] Excitement is expressed through deixis and repetition, offering a striking contrast to Proust's use of the very same trope to express desperation at the rapidly vanishing charm of Balbec's church: 'c'est l'église elle-même, c'est la statue elle-même, ce sont elles' [it is the church itself, the statue itself, they, the only ones] (*RTP*, II, 20; *SLT*, II, 273). The evocative power of place names later returns through a reference to the *Contes des mille et une nuits*, the collection of tales in Arabic translated and adapted (1704–17) by Antoine Galland, which rapidly became a popular reference for imagining the Middle East:[23]

> À travers les quartiers actifs où s'exercent, selon d'immuables règles, toutes les professions d'autrefois, devant le spectacle de cette Asie trafiquante, je me souviens à tout instant des contes orientaux que j'écoutais dans mon enfance, et dont le merveilleux, bien différent de celui des légendes du nord, présente un curieux mélange de réalisme et d'ironie.
> On y parle du fils 'd'un riche marchand de Bassorah' et non d'un prince enchanté. [...] Et les noms magiques de Damas et de Bagdhad [*sic*] traversaient ces récits, oppressant de désirs nos cœurs d'enfants prédestinés aux voyages. (*HP*, 56–57)
>
> [In the busy quarters where, in accordance with immutable laws, all the professions of the past are practised; before the spectacle of this trafficking Asia, I am reminded at every moment of those Eastern tales I used to hear in my childhood, in which the element of the marvellous, very different from that of the legends of the North, affords a curious mixture of realism and irony.
> One hears in them of the son 'of a rich merchant of Basra' not of an enchanted prince. [...] And over all these stories hover the magical names of Damascus and Bagdad, loading with desire our hearts of children predestined to travel.] (*EP*, 47–48, translation modified)

Bibesco describes a desire long predating her journey, through a vocabulary that resonates with Proust's exploration of the desires animating children's hearts (*RTP*, I, 378; *SLT*, I, 464). But whereas in Proust the childhood dream ends in bathos when it makes the protagonist so excited that he is too ill to travel (*RTP*, I, 386; *SLT*, I, 473), Bibesco is able to witness the professions imagined in childhood. There is a textual reason for Bibesco's emphasis on the magic associated with the names of middle-eastern cities. Galland's approach to translating the *Mille et une nuits* involved the removal of most material details and, as a result of this stylistic choice, the names of cities and professions often became the only remaining clues to the tales' non-European origins; hence their evocative charge.[24] Bibesco did not travel to Basra, Damascus or Baghdad, but she felt closer to them by association when she witnessed professions from the names of stories in the Persian bazaar (most likely arts and crafts, such as carpet weaving and copper beating). As well as the names of Asia, its cities, and its professions, Bibesco also dwells on the charm of the names of people. Having admired the shrine of Fatima in Qom, she writes that whereas the names of Christian martyrs evoke suffering (*HP*, 87), 'de Sainte Fatméh au nom de sultane se dégage je ne sais quel imaginaire effluve d'ambre et de rose, odeur de sainteté ou parfum de sérail?' [from Saint Fatmeh with her sultana's name there arises, as it were, the scent of roses and amber iris. Is it the odour of sanctity or the perfume of the seraglio?] (*HP*, 88; *EP*, 71). The Shia martyr is imagined as alluring because of her Islamic first name, which Bibesco associates with the eroticism of the *Mille et une nuits*. This association has little to do with Fatima and all to do with Bibesco's own cultural biases. Bibesco acknowledges this indirectly through the adjective 'imaginaire', which is the closest she comes to admitting, as Proust does, that her fantasies are based on false premises (cf. *RTP*, I, 382; *SLT*, I, 468).

Bibesco's fantasy of Persia is in fact very similar to that of Noailles, since it is also based on Persian poetry and miniature art. Although Bibesco's intertextual references have a wider scope,[25] they centre on the same three poets: Khayyām and Hāfez, who are subject to vocative addresses,[26] and Sa'di, whose *Golestān* is a key point of reference.[27] The poets are central to the fulfilment of Bibesco's fantasies. Indeed, she claims to 'recognise' the plants and gardens described by Sa'di (*HP*, 98, 103), Khayyām (181) and Hāfez (199–200), and that the pottery shop that she visits is similar to the one that inspired Khayyām's poems (179). Bibesco not only identifies her physical surroundings with the landscapes of Persian poetry, but also with those of book illustrations. After describing the beautiful miniatures in a copy of the *Golestān*, she writes:

> J'ai fermé le livre. [...] Mais pour retrouver le décor d'une idylle persane, je n'ai qu'à repousser les rideaux de ces fenêtres. La voilà, l'herbe plus verte qu'un dos de perroquet! L'arbre en fuseau, la rose grimpante, les voici!
>
> Et derrière le mur qui sépare cet Eden d'un Eden pareil, se dérobent des mondes de jardins! Tous ombreux, tous beaux...
>
> Des amants littéraires s'y promènent; de vieux hommes s'y désolent encore auprès d'enfants boudeuses. (*HP*, 131)
>
> [I closed the book. [...] But to recover instantly the scenery of a Persian idyll, I have only to throw up the blinds. There it is again, grass greener than a parrot's back! The spindled tree, the climbing rose, lo! They are there! And behind the wall that separates this Eden from another Eden, hide worlds of gardens! All shady, all beautiful...
>
> Lovers out of books are walking there; old men still pine after sulking girls.] (*EP*, 106–07, translation modified)

The passage dissolves the boundaries between representation and reality, claiming that the imaginary landscape of a book illustration and the real city of Esfahan are interchangeable. Of course, in discarding the book to look out of her window, Bibesco seems to suggest that reality is more desirable than its representations. And yet, a closer look reveals that Bibesco not only describes what she can see out of her window, but also what she imagines lies 'behind the wall'. This leads her to conclude: 'Ah! secrète Ispahan! | Nous l'habiterions vingt ans sans la connaître, si notre imagination ne s'élevait au-dessus des vergers clos" [Ah! Mysterious Esfahan! | We could live there for twenty years without knowing her, if our imagination did not soar above the closed orchards] (*HP*, 131–32; *EP*, 107, translation modified). Bibesco imagines Esfahan while *in* Esfahan, and claims to know the city better through this act of imagination. In doing so, she demonstrates that if her physical journey conforms so closely to her fantasies, it is because her experience of the place continues to be mediated by literature and flights of fancy.

In 'Nom de pays: le nom', Proust writes, 'les pays que nous désirons tiennent à chaque moment beaucoup plus de place dans notre vie véritable, que le pays où nous nous trouvons effectivement' [The countries which we long for occupy, at any given moment, a far larger place in our actual life than the country in which we happen to be] (*RTP*, I, 383; *SLT*, I, 469). This is certainly true of *Les Huit Paradis*, a book in which the author's desired Persia is afforded greater weight than actual Persia. Bibesco's perspective on reality is so tainted by fantasy that this creates a confirmation bias: everything she witnesses becomes evidence that Persia is the beautiful land of Persian poetry. So much so, that Bibesco writes — in a complete reversal of reality and fantasy — that should she be allowed to stay in Esfahan, the memory of Europe would soon seem no more than a bad dream (*HP*, 213–14). And so, while 'Noms de nom: le pays' mourns the fantasy destroyed by the place (*RTP*, II, 21; *SLT*, II, 274–75), *Les Huit Paradis* mourns the place where fantasy came true. 'Si cette nuit m'attriste ainsi, c'est qu'elle ferme à tout jamais pour moi leurs portes basses, c'est que je viens brusquement de comprendre qu'ils [les jardins d'Ispahan] sont des paradis perdus' [If this night saddens me thus, it is because it slams in my face forever the gates of all the gardens, because I am suddenly aware that they are Paradises Lost] (*HP*, 217; *EP*, 164).

'Perse', 'désir', 'paradis', 'noms magiques': throughout this chapter, it has been clear that Anna de Noailles's and Marthe Bibesco's explorations of the relationship between real and imaginary travel share a common vocabulary with Proust. *Les Éblouissements* foreshadows the opposition between fantasy and physical experience described in 'Noms de pays', yet it also integrates this dichotomy with the revelation that beauty and exoticism can be found within the familiar, a revelation that only comes later in *A la recherche*. Bibesco shares Proust's fascination with the evocative power of names, but with the crucial difference that in *Les Huit Paradis* the charm of the name is unbreakable. If Persia came to mean so many things to Proust, it was in great part through reading and talking with these women. And, while it would be foolhardy to claim that it was Noailles and Bibesco alone who caused him to meditate on the relationship between names and places, it is fair to say that they enriched these meditations and influenced how they came to be formulated. The parallels and resonances between *Les Éblouissements*, *Les Huit Paradis* and 'Noms de pays' therefore show us a different side to Proust: not the solitary genius in the cork-lined room, but a member of an active community of men and women of letters.

Notes to Chapter 19

1. Marcel Proust, *A la recherche du temps perdu*, ed. by Jean-Yves Tadié, 4 vols (Paris: Gallimard, 1987–89) (hereafter referenced as *RTP* in the main text); *In Search of Lost Time*, trans. by C. K. Scott-Moncrieff and Terence Kilmartin, rev.by D. J. Enright, 6 vols (London: Vintage, 2000–02) (hereafter referenced as *SLT* in the main text).
2. Jo Yoshida indicates in the 'Notice' for 'Noms de pays: le nom' that Proust first explored these questions in his 1907 *Figaro* article 'Journée de lecture' and began to draft the chapter in either late 1908 or early 1909, working on it in earnest over the course of 1909 (*RTP*, I, 1250–51).
3. Anna de Noailles, *Les Éblouissements* (Paris: Calmann-Lévy, 1907). Marthe Bibesco, *Les Huit Paradis* (Paris: Hachette, 1908) (hereafter referenced as *HP* in the main text); *The Eight Paradises: Travel Pictures in Persia, Asia Minor, and Constantinople* (New York: Dutton, 1923) (hereafter referenced as *EP* in the main text).
4. Marcel Proust, 'Les Éblouissements', *Le Figaro*, 15 June 1907, p. 1. Marcel Proust, letter to Marthe Bibesco, 29 March 1908. The letter is quoted in its entirety in Marthe Bibesco, *Au bal avec Marcel Proust* (Paris: Gallimard, 1928), pp. 41–44 (p. 42).
5. Unless stated otherwise, all translations are my own.

6. Bibesco, *Au bal avec Marcel Proust*, p. 43. Proust is also likely to have noted Noailles's stylistic proximity to Baudelaire. Her emphasis on the materiality of travel echoes references to steam, sails and tar in 'Le Voyage' and 'La Chevelure'; her poem also pastiches 'L'Invitation au voyage', in which the desire to travel includes a vision of 'splendeur orientale'. Charles Baudelaire, *Œuvres complètes*, ed. by Claude Pichois, 2 vols, Bibliothèque de la Pléiade (Paris: Gallimard, 1975–76), I, 53.
7. Noailles's pairing of the verbs *fuir* and *partir* resonates in particular with Mallarmé's 'Brise marine', which emphasises the infinitive, 'Fuir! Là-bas fuir!', followed up a little later with the leading 'Je partirai!' (Stéphane Mallarmé, *Œuvres complètes*, ed. by Bertrand Marchal, 2 vols, Bibliothèque de la Pléiade (Paris: Gallimard, 1998–2003), I, 15), as well as Baudelaire's emphatic 'Ceux-là seuls qui partent | Pour partir' in 'Le Voyage' (Baudelaire, *Œuvres complètes*, I, 130).
8. Edward Said, *Orientalism* [1978] (London: Penguin, 2003).
9. The Persian quatrain had become fashionable in *fin-de-siècle* France following the popularity of Edward Fitzgerald's *Rubaiyat of Omar Khayyam* (London: Quaritch, 1859) (second edition 1861, third 1872, and then reissued throughout the 1880s, 1890s and 1900s). The French translation of reference was Jean-Baptiste Nicolas's *Les Quatrains de Khéyam* (Paris: Imprimerie impériale, 1867).
10. The 'livre odorant' of l. 1 is Sa'di's *Golestān* (the Persian title means 'the Rose Garden'), the single most translated work of Persian literature. On this see *S'adi Abroad* (= special issue of *Iranian Studies*, 52.5–6 (2019)).
11. Noailles would have discovered this in the quatrains of Khayyām and Sa'di's *Golestān*.
12. Noailles, *Les Éblouissements*, p. 122.
13. Julia Caterina Hartley, 'Gender, Decadence, and Orientalism in Jane Dieulafoy's Journal de fouilles (1888) and Parysatis (1890)', in *French Decadence in a Global Context: Colonialism and Exoticism*, ed. by Julia Caterina Hartley, Wanrug Suwanwattana and Jennifer Yee (Liverpool: Liverpool University Press, 2022), pp. 73–95.
14. Jane Dieulafoy, *La Perse, la Chaldée et la Susiane* (Paris: Hachette, 1886), p. 1.
15. Émile Mâle, *L'Art religieux du treizième siècle en France: étude sur l'iconographie du Moyen Âge et sur ses sources d'inspiration* [1898] (Paris: Armand Collin, 1910), p. 66. On Mâle's influence on Proust see Richard Bales, *Proust and the Middle Ages* (Geneva: Droz, 1975), esp. pp. 117–38.
16. Jean Lahor (Henri Cazalis), *Les Quatrains d'Al-Ghazali* (Paris: Lemerre, 1896). The letter is quoted in Lawrence A. Joseph, *Henri Cazalis: sa vie, son œuvre, son amitié avec Mallarmé* (Paris: Nizet, 1972), p. 271. For the full letter (dated towards the end of June 1896), see *Correspondance de Marcel Proust*, ed. by Philip Kolb, 21 volumes (Paris: Plon, 1970–93), II, 81–82. Cazalis is believed to have inspired the character of Legrandin, who contributes to the protagonist's desire to visit Balbec (*RTP*, I, 377; *SLT*, I, 462–63).
17. The purpose of the journey was to provide expert advice on cholera outbreaks. See Daniel Panzac, *Le Docteur Adrien Proust: père méconnu, précurseur oublié* (Paris: L'Harmattan, 2003).
18. Moya Carey and Mercedes Volait, 'Framing "Islamic Art" for Aesthetic Interiors: Revisiting the 1878 Paris Exhibition', *International Journal of Islamic Architecture*, 9.1 (2020), 31–59.
19. In this regard, Pierre Loti's descriptions of Esfahan's architecture certainly accord with Proust's definition of his novel as a cathedral (*RTP*, IV, 610–11; *SLT*, VI, 431–32). Pierre Loti, *Vers Ispahan* (Paris: Calmann-Lévy, 1904), p. 209. As has been shown by Edward Hughes, Loti also had an important influence on the association of sexual desire with exoticism in *A la recherche*. See *Writing Marginality in French Literature: From Loti to Genet* (Cambridge: Cambridge University Press, 2001), pp. 41–55.
20. See Margaret Topping, 'Proust and Persia', in *Eastern Voyages, Western Visions: French Writing and Painting of the Orient*, ed. by Margaret Topping (Oxford: Peter Lang, 2004), pp. 265–88 (p. 282).
21. Noailles, *Les Éblouissements*, p. 122.
22. Bibesco is paraphrasing Solomon 1:3, which reads 'Votre nom est *comme* une huile *qu'on a* répandue' in French (Bible Sacy) and 'thy name *is as* ointment poured forth' in English (King James Version).
23. The *Contes des mille et une nuits* are cited at the beginning of *A la recherche* as a literary reference accessible to women of little erudition, because they formed part of French popular culture (*RTP*, I, 18; *SLT*, I, 19).

24. Paulo Lemos Horta, *Marvellous Thieves: Secret Authors of the Arabian Nights* (Cambridge, MA: Harvard University Press, 2019).
25. Bibesco cites Attar, Ferdowsi, Rumi and Jami (*HP*, i, 112, 204, 207).
26. 'Écoute, vieux Khàyyàm' [Listen, old Khayyam] and 'N'ayez crainte, Hafîz!' [Fear not, Hāfez!] (*HP*, 181, 200).
27. Sa'di's *Golestān* is discussed twice (*HP*, 127–36, 207–08) and provides the epigraph on the book's cover.

CHAPTER 20

❖

L'Érotique d'
A la recherche du temps perdu

Jacques Dubois

'Tant le désir est parfois contagieux'.
Sodome et Gomorrhe

Parmi les nombreux commentaires du roman de Marcel Proust, rares sont ceux qui ont mis en évidence son caractère érotique dans ce qu'il a de soutenu et de prémédité. Il est pourtant deux volumes de la *Recherche* qui s'indexent dès le titre sur une thématique sexuelle, soit *Sodome et Gomorrhe* et, plus indirectement, *La Prisonnière*. Ceux-ci se consacrent d'entrée de jeu à l'évocation des homosexualités que le romancier a choisi de prendre en charge pour des raisons personnelles comme pour des raisons littéraires.

Par la suite et jusqu'à aujourd'hui, des essais critiques consacrés à la *Recherche* relanceront ce débat délicat sur l'homosexualité dans le roman proustien. Ainsi, pour l'époque récente, on retiendra le *Proust lesbien* d'Élisabeth Ladenson ou encore *Théories de la littérature* que Didier Éribon sous-titre en *système du genre et verdicts sexuels*.[1] Mais tout cela ne concerne pas encore le roman érotisé tel que nous l'entendons.

Notre propos dans la présente analyse sera bien autre et aura moins trait à la seule sexualité et aux affiliations qu'elle suscite qu'à une représentation diffuse et multiple des usages et pratiques des corps sexués comme autant de corps de désir. Et là, il est permis d'observer que le narrateur proustien est, à travers ses personnages, particulièrement en éveil ou, mieux encore, en alerte. Il y va chez lui d'une conviction selon laquelle l'homme social passe largement par un Eros diversifié, ce qu'un romancier appartenant à notre modernité se doit de faire ressortir. Et c'est bien un motif d'intérêt récurrent chez Proust auteur et narrateur, intérêt porté à l'activité physique dans ses appétits divers, le désir sexuel étant bien souvent celui qui fédère les autres. Tout cela veut que la catégorie la plus pertinente pour désigner un tel aspect du texte soit donc celle de l'érotique, d'une érotique à distinguer de l'érotisme au sens courant du terme. Notre référence à ce propos sera le bel ouvrage que publia en 1957 le philosophe et anthropologue Georges Bataille sous le titre de *L'Érotisme* mais tel que ce label dégage précisément la notion de son sens trop restreint pour en faire un concept multiforme.² Et si bien qu'il est permis de tenir Proust romancier pour un précurseur du théoricien que sera Bataille par la suite.

Pour Bataille, Eros n'est donc pas d'un seul tenant mais se démultiplie selon ses domaines d'exercice ou d'apparition. S'il est lié aux corps mais tout autant aux cœurs chez l'homme comme chez la femme, l'érotique se parle selon différents discours et différentes pratiques, qui vont de la guerre à la religion, du corps dans sa nudité à l'art, de la beauté à la souillure, sans que l'on puisse toujours distinguer entre ces discours-là. En tout cas, on ne le confondra pas avec l'amour comme sujet privilégié des romans de toute époque et c'est bien ce qu'évite de faire l'écrivain Proust tel que nous l'abordons. Car s'il est bien un roman d'amour typique à l'intérieur de son grand œuvre, il n'apparaît que dans une sorte de case réservée de la *Recherche*. Nous pensons évidemment ici à *Un amour de Swann* qui se déploie curieusement en appendice de *Combray* dans *Du côté de chez Swann* avec, à la clé, un effet rétrospectif réservé à la passion de jeunesse qui unit le prestigieux Charles Swann à la demi-mondaine qu'est Odette de Crécy. Soit une liaison toute sensuelle au cours de laquelle les amants 'font catleya' et entonnent volontiers 'l'hymne national de leur amour', un hymne signé Vinteuil. Cette passion ne se termine pourtant pas trop bien puisque, au moment d'élire durablement Odette par le mariage, Charles s'avise de ce qu'il prend pour femme quelqu'un qui n'est pas son genre. Les deux époux n'en donneront pas moins vie à la charmante Gilberte dont Marcel comme personnage s'éprendra au temps de l'adolescence. Bref, c'est bien d'un roman d'amour qu'il s'agit, un de ces romans dont la Belle Époque était friande. 'Réduit à sa plus simple expression,' écrit Alain Vaillant dans *L'Amour-fiction*, 'un roman d'amour est un type de texte où des gens se disent "je t'aime", et tirent ou subissent toutes les conséquences, souvent dramatiques, de cette parole qu'ils ont dite'.³

Certes, la *Recherche* aborde la problématique amoureuse en plusieurs de ses épisodes mais le propos érotique est loin de se limiter à cela, comme on le verra. Retenons donc qu'il est bien une constante érotique qui traverse le puissant roman mais qu'elle peut se prévaloir de bien d'autres apparences que celle du seul registre sensuel et sentimental. On traduira au mieux les choses en disant qu'*A la recherche du temps perdu* n'appartient pas à la littérature de genre, même si *Un amour de Swann* penche quelque peu de ce côté-là et que le roman de Proust a bien peu à voir avec des romans fortement licencieux parus par la suite dans une lignée toute sadienne comme l'*Emmanuelle* d'Emmanuelle Arsan (1959) ou encore *La Révocation de l'Edit de Nantes* de Pierre Klossowski (1959). Il nous arrive d'ailleurs d'étonner d'excellents lecteurs de Proust quand nous évoquons une érotique active et diffuse colorant l'ensemble du roman comme nous en étonnons d'autres — qui sont parfois les mêmes — quand nous attribuons au narrateur proustien un sens de l'humour sur lequel l'écrivain surfe volontiers à l'aide de paradoxes et d'inversions moqueuses. A se demander si, entre les deux, n'existerait pas un lien étroit. D'ailleurs, nous rencontrerons l'une ou l'autre scène du roman qui, tout érotisantes qu'elles soient, versent dans le comique.

Selon la conception de l'érotique qu'affiche ainsi le roman, il entre différentes valeurs et ce sont facilement des valeurs contradictoires. Partons à titre d'exemple de l'opposition vie/mort. S'adonner au plaisir des corps et à tout ce qui fait leur sexualité en particulier relève d'une exubérance vitale en même temps que celle-ci, qui est excès, trouve sa limite dans la 'petite mort' si ce n'est pas dans la grande. Soit une contradiction que Bataille résout avec élégance dans la formule: 'L'érotisme est l'approbation de la vie jusque dans la mort'.[4]

Partant de quoi, on conçoit l'activité érotique comme dirigée par deux forces structurantes, elles aussi antagonistes. D'un côté, il est au départ un désir qui peut se perpétuer en bienveillance mais qui conduit aussi bien à une violence frisant la violation. Dans tous les cas, il y aura transgression, une transgression qui se désigne diversement mais est toujours sa propre fin. Transgresser suppose en fait la contestation d'un ordre, quelle qu'en soit l'intention et fût-ce même par jeu. La transgression peut dès lors conduire à la lutte et au viol comme à la possession et à la tyrannie. Vu sous cet angle, le répertoire des possibles est considérable.

Qui sont donc les partenaires du commerce érotique chez Proust? Risquons ici et à la suite de Georges Bataille une sociologie impromptue de l'espace du roman, sachant qu'elle peut varier selon les époques. Chez le Proust des duchesses, le monde du travail n'est pas censé entrer en ligne de compte. Mais ce n'est pas aussi simple. Ainsi Marcel s'émerveille de la beauté des yeux chez telles employées ou telles ouvrières mais il ne le fait qu'avec l'intention quelque peu cynique de les séduire à l'occasion. Ainsi, de temps à autre, il attire à lui des gamines du peuple dont il apprécie la compagnie. De son côté, Charles Swann dit préférer telle bourgeoise provinciale à une aristocrate de haut rang et il s'éprend avec Odette de Crécy d'une semi-prostituée comme le fait aussi Robert de Saint-Loup avec sa Rachel. Quant à un Morel, issu lui-même du peuple, il aime à entraîner à la faute des filles de sa classe d'origine jusqu'à se plaire à les violer. Ainsi la *Recherche* en vient à empiéter sur l'univers d'en bas quand ce n'est pas celui de la pègre.

Mais l'espace social dans lequel se déploient plus normalement les jeux de l'amour est celui de la noblesse et de la grande bourgeoisie. C'est qu'il faut du loisir pour s'adonner aux plaisirs et aux caresses. Ce que l'on sait de toujours dans le milieu Guermantes. Pour ces gens-là, la 'bagatelle' est ludique par nécessité. Vers 1900, elle réclame donc du temps et des ressources financières. À cet égard, le duc et mari d'Oriane n'est jamais désœuvré, passant d'une maîtresse à l'autre. La récompense toute sociale des dames qu'il met ainsi à l'épreuve trouve son aboutissement dans l'accès au prestigieux salon de sa femme, le plus huppé de Paris. Cette alliance de l'adultère masculin et du salon féminin est comme l'emblème du roman. Et Robert de Saint-Loup s'émerveille même d'avoir vu une Mlle d'Orgeville, héritière de la meilleure noblesse, fréquenter une maison de passe rien que pour se désennuyer (*Sodome et Gomorrhe*, RTP, III, 92).[5]

Dans cet espace à l'intérieur duquel transgressions et violences se conjuguent, les femmes sont donc les premiers objets du désir masculin. Ce qui ne manque pas de charmer plusieurs d'entre elles qui trouvent avantage à la domination des hommes. Par ailleurs, il est des maîtresses qui sont des partenaires actives dans la copulation. Rencontrée lors du 'bal de têtes', une princesse de Nassau qui a collectionné les amants titrés au long de sa vie est de celles-là: '[Elle] portait légèrement sous sa robe, mauve comme ses yeux admirables et ronds et comme sa figure fardée, les souvenirs un peu embrouillés de ce passé innombrable' (*Le Temps retrouvé*, *RTP*, IV, 557). Elle et ses pareilles y engagent leur beauté que révèle ou avoue la nudité de leurs corps. Et cette beauté peut éventuellement atteindre à quelque sacralité jusqu'à gagner les membres de la grande bourgeoisie. Dans le coït peut ainsi se manifester une dimension sacrificielle qu'assume volontiers telle forme de galanterie partagée entre les sexes. Ainsi, dans un 'Post-scriptum' à *La Domination masculine*, Pierre Bourdieu évoque la relation amoureuse comme possible suspension de cette domination même, qui voit la violence virile s'apaiser comme la fin des stratégies visant à asservir.[6]

Les Fiancées de Marcel

Marcel aime successivement Gilberte Swann et Albertine Simonet. De la première, il obtient peu sexuellement parlant, timidité et inexpérience le paralysant. Mais il est tout de même quelques menus épisodes significatifs partagés avec cette délurée qu'est la fille Swann. C'est d'abord qu'à leur première rencontre, Gilberte accueille Marcel d'un geste indécent — mais lequel exactement? — que le garçon estime de rejet. Il faudra que les deux enfants se retrouvent à l'âge adulte pour que Gilberte affranchisse Marcel: le geste indécent était de désir amoureux. Mais avant cela, quand Marcel adolescent retrouvera la jeune Swann pour partager ses jeux aux Champs-Élysées, il luttera avec elle et, dans le combat, éjaculera par mégarde et en toute innocence. Et Gilberte d'enchaîner mais en vain à son grand regret: 'Vous savez,' dira-t-elle, 'nous pouvons lutter encore un peu' (*A l'ombre des jeunes filles en fleurs*, *RTP*, I, 485). Plus tard, voici le jeune héros accueilli chez les Swann où il est reçu comme un prétendant. Assis aux côtés de son amie, il ose à peine effleurer ses nattes, les célébrant par ailleurs en 'ouvrage unique pour lequel on avait utilisé le gazon même du Paradis' (*RTP*, I, 494). Touche de sacralité qui gagne l'érotique, comme elle le fera encore en d'autres endroits. On verra également le même héros timide partager un goûter tout mythologique où Gilberte sert à ses amies un gâteau select qui mime un palais de Darius en forme de 'pâtisserie ninivite' (*RTP*, I, 494). Et c'est là un autre moment érotique cette fois tout de gourmandise, une gourmandise que croit honorer en se gavant le héros. Érotique du chocolat et pourquoi pas?

Tout cela finira mal cependant: le jour où le héros vend à un antiquaire un vase de Chine dont il compte tirer maints cadeaux pour son élue, il aperçoit celle-ci cheminant avec un jeune homme et ce sera la rupture.

Vient alors Albertine Simonet rencontrée sur la digue de Balbec, un Balbec où Marcel passait des vacances. Albertine autant que ses amies proviennent visiblement d'un vaste atelier de la classe bourgeoise, classe qui, au cours du temps, a façonné les beaux corps de ses filles qui sont aujourd'hui d'une audace provocante. Ainsi au Casino de Balbec, Albertine danse avec son amie Andrée 'seins contre seins', conduite dont le docteur Cottard dénonce l'indécence, y voyant l'origine de leur jouissance (*Sodome et Gomorrhe*, *RTP*, III, 191). Plus tard à Paris, la jeune fille accordera facilement un baiser à Marcel et sans doute plus, pendant que le garçon connaît à cette occasion un nouvel orgasme imprévu.

Les deux jeunes gens se lient si bien que Marcel en vient à retenir son amoureuse dans l'appartement qu'il occupe. Elle est sa prisonnière, avec l'espoir qu'entretient le jeune homme d'éloigner la jeune fille de son goût pour les femmes. Chaque soir de son 'emprisonnement', la jeune femme gratifiera son amant d'un baiser nourrissant. Dans le même mouvement, Marcel aimera à déshabiller son amie pour l'admirer dans sa nudité, et ceci en contraste avec le ventre de l'homme où se loge, selon le narrateur, un 'crampon resté fiché dans une statue descellée' (*La Prisonnière*, RTP, III, 587). Albertine est sensuellement gourmande, tout autant que Gilberte, et raffole des crèmes glacées du Ritz sur lesquelles elle exerce une violence rageuse et toute de jouissance. Et c'est bien une réplique de la passion libidinale de Gilberte pour les gâteaux au chocolat. Et ceci encore: plutôt que d'assister à une soirée Verdurin, l'héroïne s'exclame en toute transgression qu'elle préférerait aller 'se faire casser le pot' (RTP, III, 840). Mais ce n'est sans doute guère plus qu'une façon de dire.

Mais la tentative de mettre la jeune femme dans le droit chemin n'est pas suivie d'effet. C'est alors qu'Albertine quitte Marcel et s'en va pour se tuer dans une chute de cheval. Après quoi, notre héros n'en finira pas de regretter la 'disparue' et, fort curieusement, il chargera son homme de confiance, cet Aimé qu'il connaît depuis le Grand Hôtel de Balbec, d'enquêter sur la conduite d'Albertine après son départ. Cette fois, le lesbianisme est patent. Couchant avec une blanchisseuse dont il exige qu'elle rejoue point par point la partie de plaisir qu'elle eut avec la défunte, Aimé aura droit à un lubrique 'Tu me mets aux anges' (*Albertine disparue*, RTP, IV, 106) comme en écho de l'obscène '[se] faire casser le pot'. Dans une autre circonstance, Marcel lit joliment à même le visage d'Andrée le désir qu'éprouvait Albertine pour son amie. Cette même Andrée raconte de plus qu'Albertine fréquentait naguère une maison de femmes, où le sadique Morel lui 'livrait' des jeunes filles prêtes à être violées (RTP, IV, 179).

Les séquences Marcel-Gilberte et Marcel-Albertine qu'on vient de survoler participent de deux érotiques différentes. Dans le premier cas, une adolescente hétérosexuelle donne le ton. Dans le second, une jeune fille à tendance lesbienne impose sa marque au moins insidieusement. C'est que, en chaque cas, des connotations viennent s'ajouter, qui font pencher la balance érotique d'un côté ou de l'autre. Toutefois, une tendance à la sensualité obscène est finalement commune aux deux séquences même si, avec Gilberte, la bienséance bourgeoise l'emporte quand, avec Albertine, un style plus débridé fait entendre ses accents. Mais nous avons trouvé plaisant que les deux amantes partagent une commune avidité destructrice envers d'élégantes sucreries.

Marcel et ses deux amies sont loin cependant d'être les seuls à entonner en roman la chanson d'Éros. Et, par exemple, étant acquis à l'idée que la *Recherche* est toute de raffinement et de distinction, on peut s'étonner qu'elle s'ouvre volontiers à telle ou telle évocation malséante au sens du scatologique. Et c'est ce qui se produit à quelques reprises et avec différents acteurs à l'intérieur d'un discours romanesque qu'on s'attendrait à être tout de distinction. En ces moments peu rares, on croirait entendre le romancier nous dire que prendre en charge le corps humain en texte, c'est s'aviser de sa présence et de son activité jusqu'en ses parties honteuses. Ainsi il est un 'sale' qui, de diverses origines, confirme l'érotique proustienne dans un réalisme du bas qu'identifiera Georges Bataille. Dans son essai majeur comme dans ses romans, Bataille manifestera un goût de la profanation en matière d'érotisme. Mais celle-ci apparaît très tôt dans la *Recherche* avec, dès Combray, la scène de Montjouvain à laquelle assiste le jeune Marcel qui surprend deux jeunes lesbiennes se livrant au plaisir tout en injuriant le portrait du défunt père de l'une d'elles.

Un snobisme de la scatologie

Certes, l'adepte de la scatologie sait aussi revêtir de pudeur son évocation. Ainsi, à nouveau dans la séquence des jeux aux Champs-Élysées, Marcel accompagne la brave Françoise qui joue les duègnes dans un refuge où des cabinets se proposent aux passants. Et voici que la tenancière des lieux invite le jeune héros à faire usage de l'un de ces lieux:

> Si la 'marquise' avait du goût pour les jeunes garçons en leur ouvrant la porte hypogéenne de ces cubes de pierre où les hommes sont accroupis comme des sphinx, elle devait chercher dans ses générosités moins l'espérance de les corrompre que le plaisir qu'on éprouve à se montrer vainement prodigue envers ce qu'on aime. (*A l'ombre des jeunes filles en fleurs*, RTP, I, 484)

Et l'adolescent Marcel de se hausser dans le style à l'élégance de la 'marquise' sans pour autant accepter la proposition de celle-ci.

On aura rencontré précédemment une notation moins digne avec la mention insistante du postérieur de Legrandin alors qu'à la sortie de la messe il met en œuvre son zèle mondain auprès d'une dame:

> Ce redressement rapide fit refluer en une sorte d'onde fougueuse et musclée la croupe de Legrandin que je ne supposais pas si charnue; et je ne sais pourquoi cette ondulation de pure matière, ce flot tout charnel, sans expression de spiritualité et qu'un empressement plein de bassesse fouettait en tempête, éveillèrent tout d'un coup dans mon esprit la possibilité d'un Legrandin tout différent de celui que nous connaissions. (*Du côté de chez Swann*, RTP, I, 123)

Évocation ironiquement méchante mais qui prélude au 'Il était snob' survenant implacablement deux pages plus loin à propos du personnage en cause. De fait, l'ingénieur voudrait devenir le familier d'une noblesse qui lui fait cruellement défaut comme le fera aussi sa sœur Cambremer plus avant dans le roman. L'objectif du ou de la snob est de pouvoir fréquenter à l'envi femmes chics et duchesses. Car là réside le principe même du snobisme qui s'ancre dans une condition jugée insuffisante ou indigne ('sans noblesse') et que l'on voudrait améliorer.

Mais apparaîtra dans *Sodome et Gomorrhe* un postérieur plus illustre et qui, lui, n'a pas besoin de faire le snob. C'est celui du baron de Charlus qui éveille l'admiration triviale de Jupien découvrant dans la personne du baron un éventuel partenaire sexuel susceptible d'améliorer le statut social du tailleur qu'il est et le poussant à passer à l'acte aux cris de 'Vous en avez un gros pétard!', et de 'Oui, va, grand gosse!' (*Sodome et Gomorrhe*, RTP, III,12).

Mais voici à présent qui verse dans une radicale obscénité. Et s'il y va cette fois encore d'un snobisme comme on nous l'assure, celui-ci plonge cette fois aux abîmes.

Nous sommes au moment où le héros fait l'expérience d'un petit monde populaire, celui des liftiers du Grand Hôtel. Il se trouve que, empruntant l'ascenseur comme cela lui arrive alors régulièrement, Marcel est piloté un beau jour par un portier intérimaire qui se répand inopinément en louanges à propos de sa sœur dont il estime qu'elle a superbement réussi. Lors des nombreux voyages que celle-ci fait avec son compagnon, elle se livre en toute occasion à un curieux passe-temps: 'Elle ne quitte jamais un hôtel,' explique son frère, 'sans se soulager dans une armoire, une commode, pour laisser un petit souvenir à la femme de chambre qui aura à nettoyer' (*Sodome et Gomorrhe*, *RTP*, III, 369). Bête, méchante et sale en somme que cette sœurette et ce au gré d'une grande médiocrité. Mais le liftier remplaçant ne s'en esbaudit pas moins pour autant. Il en vient tout juste à déplorer que sa réussite à lui se fasse attendre, envisageant même de se retrouver un jour président de la République. C'est là que l'humour proustien atteint sa limite.

Dans le même volume cependant mais cette fois avec un acteur situé au sommet de l'échelle sociale, une scatologie du même tonneau se répand (si l'on ose dire), encore qu'elle ne soit que verbale. L'esprit y est plus vif que chez le petit groom et l'on y entend le baron de Charlus y déclarer alors que l'invite à une réception chez elle Mme de Saint-Euverte: '"cet impertinent jeune homme", dit-il en me désignant à Mme de Surgis, "vient de me demander, sans le moindre souci qu'on doit avoir de cacher ces sortes de besoins, si j'allais chez Mme de Saint-Euverte, c'est-à-dire, je pense, si j'avais la colique"' (*Sodome et Gomorrhe*, *RTP*, III, 99).

Ainsi, du portier stupide au grand seigneur paillard, la boucle se boucle. Et l'on sent que le bourgeois Marcel savoure au passage ce mauvais goût de la mise en valeur d'un corps ignoble en deux versions.

Éros collectif et utopique

Mais c'est autrement encore que l'érotique proustienne donne toute sa mesure. Elle se fait plurielle en ce cas à travers plus d'un acteur du roman. Mérite ici de venir en tête Charles Swann, un Swann qui aima infiniment les femmes, y compris les plus humbles ou les plus timides. Et le voici qui, lors d'une réception et alors qu'il est âgé, se soulève difficilement de son siège pour saluer la belle Mme de Surgis, plongeant sans l'avoir voulu son visage dans le corsage de la personne. Vient alors ce commentaire avec la belle formule finale, déjà citée par nous en épigraphe: 'Brusquement il s'arracha au vertige qui l'avait saisi, et Mme de Surgis elle-même, quoique gênée, étouffa une respiration profonde, tant le désir est parfois contagieux' (*Sodome et Gomorrhe*, *RTP*, III, 106). Dans la même tonalité, nous avons mentionné déjà la princesse de Nassau qui collectionnerait sous sa robe les souvenirs de ses nombreux amants. Autre collectionneuse, d'après ce que rapporte Aimé, encore lui, selon les dires d'une doucheuse, la belle Albertine auprès de laquelle défilaient maintes personnes dans la cabine de bain.

Dans la même série, on comptera le couple fugace formé de Morel et d'Albertine engagés dans une manière de traite des blanches, l'un livrant des jeunes filles à l'autre après les avoir possédées lui-même.[7] Mais, en partenaire de Jupien cette fois, Charlus se multiplie autrement encore mais à rôles inversés. C'est au bordel tenu par son ami que le baron se fait fouetter au sang par différents jeunes 'apaches' dont il considère qu'ils n'en font jamais assez (*Le Temps retrouvé*, RTP, IV, 394–97). Illustration d'un masochisme pluralisé en même temps qu'encanaillé.

Mais, toujours dans *Le Temps retrouvé*, voici Marcel acteur, en intention tout au moins, et tirant un profit quelque peu scandaleux d'une attaque aérienne avec bombardement de Paris par l'aviation allemande. C'est que, là où déambule le héros, les passants n'ont d'autre ressource que de descendre dans les couloirs du métropolitain alors que la panne d'électricité plonge ceux-ci dans l'obscurité. Et cela donne ce morceau de bravoure quelque peu délirant et qui mérite d'être cité en sa totalité ou presque:

> Quelques-uns même de ces Pompéiens sur qui pleuvait déjà le feu du ciel descendirent dans les couloirs du métro, noirs comme des catacombes.[8] Ils savaient en effet n'y être pas seuls. Or l'obscurité qui baigne toute chose comme un élément nouveau a pour effet, irrésistiblement tentateur pour certaines personnes, de supprimer le premier stade du plaisir et de nous faire entrer de plain-pied dans un domaine de caresses où l'on n'accède d'habitude qu'après quelque temps. [...] Dans l'obscurité, tout ce vieux jeu se trouve aboli, les mains, les lèvres, les corps peuvent entrer en jeu les premiers. Il reste l'excuse de l'obscurité même et des erreurs qu'elle engendre si l'on est mal reçu. Si on l'est bien, cette réponse immédiate du corps qui ne se retire pas, qui se rapproche, nous donne de celle (ou celui) à qui nous nous adressons silencieusement, une idée qu'elle est sans préjugés, pleine de vice, idée qui ajoute un surcroît au bonheur d'avoir pu mordre à même le fruit sans le convoiter des yeux et sans demander de permission. (*Le Temps retrouvé*, RTP, IV, 413)

Le passage est d'une étonnante audace alors même qu'il embraye sur un retour de barbarie comme la Grande Guerre en connut d'autres. L'idée est donc que les Parisiens — dont certains clients de Jupien descendus dans les couloirs du métro en pleine alerte aérienne — se retrouvent plongés dans une totale obscurité, permettant que certains d'entre eux puissent en profiter pour se livrer à des audaces sexuelles diverses, ce que le terme de 'vice' suggère au passage.

Or, c'est bien de ce vice qu'il s'agit mais qui se voit considéré de façon complètement inverse par notre héros-narrateur. Car ce dernier se réjouit pleinement de cette étonnante libération des mœurs qu'il partagerait volontiers avec d'autres. Une manière d'allégresse traverse, en effet, le passage qui peut éventuellement être attribué à quelque humour suscité par la comparaison avec la catastrophe antique de Pompéi. Mais il n'en reste pas moins que le narrateur, et donc Marcel, perçoit la situation comme synonyme d'une avancée toute moderne. C'est qu'elle dispenserait les bénéficiaires des préambules et travaux d'approche qui sont ménagés dans des situations de pleine clarté et en particulier dans les salons du meilleur monde.

Or, le texte détaille les choses à cet égard. C'est que la vue étant mise hors-jeu, le restant du corps peut se manifester en plusieurs de ses parties et entrer en relation avec quelque partenaire pris au hasard et dûment accosté avec le risque d'être refoulé par la personne qui se trouve ainsi sollicitée. Ce viol plus ou moins bien reçu ouvre en somme à une utopie toute sociale. Dans un Paris des salons proustiens où les mondanités et autres conduites distinguées guindent les relations sociales, la scène imaginaire du métro — si elle est imaginaire — ouvre sans conteste à un espace de liberté. Pourquoi, s'agissant de sexe, perdre son temps à des manœuvres, désignées ici comme étant le vieux jeu? Pourquoi passer assez vainement par le regard du sujet désirant et par la permission au moins tacite du sujet désiré? Pourquoi ne pas faire en sorte que mains, lèvres et corps entrent d'emblée dans l'échange, dans la caresse et la jouissance?

On remarquera que, dans cette utopie rondement troussée, l'appartenance sexuelle et générique n'est pas évoquée comme si elle n'était plus pertinente à l'intérieur d'un métropolitain nocturne. Et, dans l'esprit de Proust, elle ne mérite sans doute pas à cet instant de l'être. C'est ce dont l'univers d'Albertine — et mieux encore celui de son complice Morel — donnait l'idée ailleurs et d'une autre façon. Les sujets désirants y passaient facilement d'un individu à un autre comme si l'appartenance générique était sans importance. Et c'est bien là une perspective qui, à plus d'un égard, effleure le texte de la *Recherche* à plus d'un moment.

D'une érotique de la *Recherche* pour conclure

Le dernier exemple évoqué nous procurera une manière de leçon valant pour l'ensemble du roman. Et ce sera comme l'ouverture à une lecture inédite inspirée par ce qui a semblé être son utopie conclusive comparable à un programme ou à une profession de foi.

Rassemblons ici quelques-unes des observations que l'on a pu faire au long de l'œuvre. Et plaçons au centre du faisceau pour la valeur emblématique qu'il acquiert en cours de route le personnage d'Albertine Simonet. L'enquête qui a suivi son décès établit qu'elle eut une activité lesbienne avérée. Mais le volume *La Prisonnière* qui la voit encore vivante atteste de ce qu'il ne lui déplaît pas de faire l'amour avec un homme, Marcel en l'occurrence. Comme si la distinction des sexes ou des genres n'était pas sexuellement opérante auprès de la jeune femme. Vouée à une sorte de binarisme, elle partage ce dernier avec son amie Andrée, une Andrée qui à l'occasion évoque tel épisode amoureux de Gilberte avec d'autres femmes. Ainsi les jeunes filles proustiennes venues de la Belle Époque seraient toutes plus ou moins doubles sexuellement à l'intérieur d'un certain milieu. Du côté masculin, Charlie Morel est visiblement 'à voile et à vapeur', lui qui doit se donner à l'occasion au baron de Charlus, son mécène. Robert de Saint-Loup, qui passe de Rachel à Gilberte, finit en homosexuel résolu tout en s'exhibant avec des maîtresses. Au temps de Combray et de son enfance, Marcel assiste subjugué à une séance de lesbianisme toute revancharde et profanatrice ainsi qu'on l'a vu. Et puis il y a le cas un peu extraordinaire du baron de Charlus doté d'un corps viril dans une robe mentale.

Mais arrêtons ici la liste et n'y introduisons pas Marcel lui-même, ce que le texte n'autoriserait pas. Bref, si on confronte la scène pompéienne du métropolitain à la *Recherche* dans son ensemble, c'est tout un symbolisme qui se déploie. En gros, il est de confusion des pratiques génériques et de mélange des sexes. S'agit-il d'un programme, voire d'une revendication? L'utopie métropolitaine ne nous autorise pas à le dire mais la tendance rapidement esquissée fleure bon une époque de libération qui éclot en mettant à profit la guerre telle que vécue à Paris tout au moins. Nous n'irons pas plus loin. Mais nous accepterons ce signe que nous fait le grand texte proustien en dernier recours et s'agissant d'érotique.

Notes to Chapter 20

1. Elisabeth Ladenson, *Proust's Lesbianism* (Ithaca, NY, & London: Cornell University Press, 1999); *Proust lesbien*, traduit par G. le Gaufey (Paris: EPEL, 2004). Didier Éribon, *Théories de la littérature: système du genre et verdicts sexuels* (Paris: PUF, 2015).
2. Georges Bataille, *L'Érotisme* (Paris: Minuit, 1957). Réédition en 2011.
3. Alain Vaillant, *L'Amour-fiction: discours amoureux et poétique du roman à l'époque moderne* (Vincennes: Presses universitaires de Vincennes, 2002), p. 11.
4. Bataille, *L'Érotisme*, p. 13.
5. Marcel Proust, *A la recherche du temps perdu*, éd. par Jean-Yves Tadié et al, 4 vols, Bibliothèque de la Pléiade (Paris: Gallimard, 1987–89). Toute référence sera incorporée dans le texte sous cette forme abrégée.
6. Pierre Bourdieu, *La Domination masculine* (Paris: Seuil, 1998), p. 117.
7. Cf. *Albertine disparue* (RTP, IV, 179–80).
8. Le narrateur fait des Parisiens en 1914–18 de nouveaux Pompéiens accablés par des bombardements de l'aviation allemande.

CHAPTER 21

Echoes of Sodom in Gomorrah: The Chastisement of Albertine in Proust's *La Prisonnière*

Margaret E. Gray

For all the comfortable, bourgeois sequestration of his cork-lined room on the boulevard Haussmann, Proust had a keen interest in the tensions and complexities of what Edward J. Hughes calls 'cross-class encounters'.[1] Stretching and contesting social strata, such episodes in *A la recherche du temps perdu* are invested with social dynamism and instability, inflected by circulating nuances, traces, assertions, denials, revelations and transgressions of class belonging. Erotic encounters and relationships provide particularly rich moments of class mobility, for, as Proust's Narrator puts it, 'dans cette vie romanesque, anachronique, l'ambassadeur est ami du forçat; le prince [...] en sortant de chez la duchesse s'en va conférer avec l'apache' [in this life of anachronistic fiction the ambassador is a bosom friend of the felon, the prince [...] on leaving the duchess's party goes off to confer in private with the ruffian].[2] We recall the bourgeois Swann's social agility as, son of a stockbroker, he frequents the Jockey Club when not lunching with the Prince of Wales, yet ultimately marries the demi-mondaine Odette; the Faubourg St-Germain aristocrat Saint-Loup's relationship with the prostitute Rachel; the bourgeois Narrator's own obsessive sequestering of the 'pauvre, obscure' [penniless, obscure] (*RTP*, IV, 88; *SLT*, V, 579), yet hauntingly enigmatic and elusive Albertine; Saint-Loup's uncle, the baron de Charlus, who — in one of the most extreme and detailed of such class-crossing encounters — initiates an erotic relationship with the tailor Jupien before taking up with the young violinist, Morel, son of the Narrator's uncle's valet (*RTP*, III, 255; *SLT*, IV, 300). This encounter, staged in the Guermantes courtyard and witnessed by Marcel, provoking the Narrator's sustained meditation on what he calls 'la ville maudite' [the cursed city], was to change the lives of baron and tailor, for Charlus renders Jupien's situation increasingly lucrative before taking him on as secretary, followed by setting him up in business as manager of a male brothel.

Neglected by literary critics, however, is the Guermantes-courtyard episode's Gomorrhan echo: the encounter of Albertine (now mistress of the bourgeois Marcel) and a working-class pastry-cook at the end of *La Prisonnière*. The episode implicitly reprises the Charlus–Jupien scene in many ways as it inscribes the biblical cities' destruction by divine fire and brimstone, while replaying other elements from the Sodom topos as rendered by the Proustian Narrator. We recall that *Sodome et Gomorrhe* opens with the epigraph from Alfred de Vigny's *Les Destinées*, 'La femme aura Gomorrhe et l'homme aura Sodome' [Woman shall have Gomorrah and man shall have Sodom], in syntax that reverses the cities' traditional, biblical order to place Gomorrah before Sodom in implicit anticipation and foregrounding, I would suggest, of *La Prisonnière's* Gomorrhan closing scene.[3] Furthermore, Proust was convinced that Vigny's line was inspired by the poet's jealousy over the friendship of his mistress, Marie Dorval, with another woman (George Sand, as rumour had it).[4] In placing an epigraph that, in Proust's reading, is particularly marked by Gomorrah as we enter the Guermantes courtyard to observe the encounter of Charlus and Jupien, the text implicitly proclaims Gomorrah's equal counterweight to the scene we are about to witness. In what follows, I aim to develop such implicit privileging of Gomorrah, bringing to *La Prisonnière's* closing episode — an excursion with Albertine that includes a stop for tea in a pastry-shop — the visibility it deserves as the Gomorrhan answer, through its re-inscription, echoes and variations, to the courtyard encounter that opens *Sodome et Gomorrhe*. In these ways, I hope to honour Edward Hughes's work by drawing on his insights into Proust's manipulation of the semiotics of homoeroticism; Proust's exploration of mobility and tensions across class boundaries; and *A la recherche's* engagement with industrialised modernity.

We might begin by noticing that each episode — that which opens *Sodome et Gomorrhe* and that which closes *La Prisonnière* — is set in a liminal, transient space. Inviting transformation via their function as passageway, such spaces invite us to reflect further on the dynamism by which they are inhabited as characters move through them. What previous habits, identities, selves are destabilised in these liminal sites, allowing for what disruptively new and unforeseen possibilities for recasting lives, as we see in the encounter of Charlus and Jupien? Separating the public from the private, the street from the boudoir, or, as it happens, Jupien's shop where the door will close upon the embraces of baron and tailor, the Guermantes courtyard becomes charged with transformative energy. Similarly, the pastry-shop episode at the end of *La Prisonnière* is staged in a site of passage yet further marginalised by its location 'almost' beyond the city of Paris: 'une grande pâtisserie située presque en dehors de la ville' [a big pastry-shop, situated almost beyond the town] (*RTP*, III, 907; *SLT*, V, 464, translation modified), where Marcel and Albertine stop for tea during their return to Paris from an outing to Versailles. Liminality, opening up vertiginous possibilities of transformation, is further evoked in Marcel's role as witness to each scene: a curious voyeur during the encounter of Charlus and Jupien in the Guermantes courtyard, he finds himself a helpless observer in the pastry-shop as the seated Albertine's insistent and imploring glances go ignored by the standing and aloof 'pâtissière' [pastry-cook], 'cette grande belle femme' [this large and handsome woman] (*RTP*, III, 908; *SLT*, V, 465). In each case, Marcel is bystander (in the first scene, by choice; in the second, involuntarily) to the heavily eroticised, potentially transformative encounter between two others.

Such transformative impact is realised in the case of Charlus and Jupien's subsequent extensive partnership, both erotic and commercial, as we see later in the male brothel managed by Jupien and financed by the baron. In the case of Albertine and the pastry-cook, the transformative power of such liminal, transitional sites is sensed and feared by Marcel, who resolves to return to the pastry-shop the following week to instruct the pastry-cook not to divulge his name and address to a woman customer he saw just leaving as he and Albertine arrived, for fear that the woman might establish contact with Albertine, and confirm Marcel's intuition that transitional spaces are heavily invested with erotic risk. What Marcel doesn't yet know during the pastry-shop scene is that, in a further demonstration of the scene's impact, the memory of this outing will return during his visit to Venice after Albertine's departure and death. In these ways, both liminal episodes realise their transformative potential by developing resonant afterlives.

Beyond their shared staging in spaces of transience, the two passages are lexically yoked through the sound of the 'bourdon' [bumblebee], governing metaphor of the *Sodome et Gomorrhe* encounter and morphing into a mechanical 'bourdonnement' [buzzing] in *La Prisonnière*. During the outing to Versailles, Marcel, hearing a sound he doesn't immediately recognise, compares it to 'le bourdonnement d'une guêpe' [the buzz of a wasp]; it is Albertine who recognises the sound as that of an aeroplane, directing Marcel's gaze skyward as she exclaims, 'il est très haut, très haut!' [[it's] high up there, very very high!] (*RTP*, III, 907; *SLT*, v, 463). However, rather than dropping the now-disproved possibility of an insect as source of the sound, the Narrator clings to it as metaphor, referring to the plane's 'minuscules ailes brunes' [a pair of tiny wings, dark and flashing] and describing it as 'ce petit insecte qui trépidait là-haut' [that little insect throbbing up there in the sky] (*RTP*, III, 907; *SLT*, v, 463–64); we are cued to remember the lengthy *Sodome et Gomorrhe* comparison of Charlus and Jupien's encounter to that of the fertilisation of an orchid by a bee. Just as the elaborate choreography of seduction unfolds laterally across the Guermantes courtyard, so the aeroplane's 'bourdonnement' in *La Prisonnière* now lures our gaze skyward to the mechanised 'petit insecte' in an upward sweep detailed by the Narrator. We are not surprised that it should be Albertine who first identifies the sound as that of an aeroplane, for we find the mention 'Albertine veut faire de l'aéroplane' [Albertine wants to go up in airplanes] in an early draft; furthermore, watching a plane rise into 'l'extase raidie' [static ecstasy] during excursions to the hangars that have sprung up around Paris, 'Albertine ne pouvait contenir sa joie' [Albertine could not contain her joy] (*RTP*, III, 613; *SLT*, v, 112, 113).[5] Marcel himself, perhaps in unconscious and ominous foreshadowing of Albertine's own 'flight' from her sequestration, views planes 'comme une image de la liberté' [like a symbol of liberty] (*RTP*, III, 612; *SLT*, v, 112).[6]

Seized by the beauty of 'le bourdonnement d'un aéroplane à deux mille mètres' during this excursion to Versailles, Marcel reminds us that 'les distances parcourues dans ce voyage vertical sont les mêmes que sur le sol' [the distances traversed in this vertical journey are the same as those on the ground], preparing us implicitly to recognise *Sodome*'s lateral, courtyard seduction scene in *La Prisonnière*'s vertical choreography of the seated Albertine's beseeching glances at the standing pastry-cook, herself 'extrêmement grande' [extremely tall] (*RTP*, III, 907, 908; *SLT*, V, 464). As the woman busily puts away spoons, cups, plates and teacakes, Albertine 'était obligée, sans trop lever la tête, de faire monter ses regards jusqu'à cette hauteur démesurée où étaient les yeux de la pâtissière' [was obliged, without raising her head unduly, to make her eyes ascend to that disproportionate height at which the woman's eyes were situated] (*RTP*, III, 908; *SLT*, V, 464). As the Narrator observes, 'Cela faisait une série de vaines élévations implorantes vers une divinité inaccessible' [This led to a series of vain imploring elevations before an inaccessible deity] as the pastry-cook improbably refuses to acknowledge Albertine's glances; for, 'plongée dans ses rangements, elle était presque impolie pour Albertine à force de n'avoir pas un regard pour les regards de mon amie' [engrossed in her task, she carried her disregard for Albertine's glances (which incidentally were in no way improper) almost to the point of rudeness] (*RTP*, III, 908; *SLT*, V, 465). Seemingly utterly indifferent to Albertine's gaze, the pastry-cook's dogged commitment to her work through 'la remise en place des petites cuillers, des couteaux à fruits' [the putting away of the coffee spoons, the fruit knives] (*RTP*, III, 908; *SLT*, V, 465) is compared by the Narrator to that of a machine in an 'isolement' [isolation] which, he claims, would not have been more indifferent to Albertine's glances. Yet, in this passage, methodical, mechanical labour appears to function as alibi, a pretext to ignore Albertine while nonetheless serving as covert means to display the pastry-cook's charms as she 'laissait briller ses yeux, ses charmes, en une attention à son seul travail' [allowed her eyes, her charms to shine in an undivided attention to her work] (*RTP*, III, 908; *SLT*, V, 465). Indeed, the pastry-cook's assiduous refusal takes on, for the observing Marcel, 'un tour invraisemblable d'impolitesse!' [improbable lengths of impoliteness] (*RTP*, III, 909; *SLT*, V, 465). The Narrator insists that if the pastry-cook had not been 'particulièrement sotte' [particularly stupid], such 'attention à son seul travail' [undivided attention to her work], such 'détachement' [detachment] from Albertine's wordless but insistent attentions, could have been 'un comble d'habileté' [a supreme proof of guile] (*RTP*, III, 909; *SLT*, V, 465) — thus acknowledging the potential ruse of her labour while immediately excluding the pastry-cook from such cunning. The Narrator then proceeds to assure the reader that he's well aware ('je sais bien' [I know very well]) that even the most dull-witted creature, 'si son désir ou son intérêt est en jeu, peut dans ce cas unique, au milieu de la nullité de sa vie stupide, s'adapter immédiatement aux rouages de l'engrenage le plus compliqué' [if his desire or his pocket is involved, can, in that sole instance, emerging from the nullity of his stupid life, adapt himself immediately to the workings of the most complicated machinery]: an admission followed by the Narrator's now hollow, unconvincing and shrilly repeated claim that this is 'une supposition trop subtile pour une femme aussi niaise que la pâtissière' [too subtle a supposition in the case of a woman as brainless as this] (*RTP*, III, 909; *SLT*, V, 465). And yet, he has also informed us that this dull-witted woman, though married, takes lovers, which she conceals masterfully (*RTP*, III, 908; *SLT*, V, 465); we are thus virtually invited to understand as ruse (well-rehearsed, perhaps, as her secret lovers might suggest) the imbecilic pastry-cook's studied indifference even while displaying her charms through her assiduous labour over spoons, cups and teacakes. The pastry-cook's labour, we suspect, has morphed into its own simulacrum as seduction strategy.

Indeed, it seems a strategy that, given the insistent, beseeching cast of Albertine's glances, appears successful in this eroticised construction of what Hughes — arguing that in *A la recherche*, 'proletarian bodies are recycled, serving bourgeois needs' — calls 'the social subaltern'. For Marcel, writes Hughes, 'a day's manual toil performed by a gendered subaltern mutates into an evening's pleasure delivered, across a social-class boundary, to a "nous" that designates, unproblematically, a male bourgeoisie'.[7] Hughes explores, in particular, the 'fetishization of the working-class woman's forearm', drawing on Marcel's voluptuous delight at imagining the nocturnal caresses delivered by the young milkmaid he has contrived to have Françoise escort to his room: a prospect intensified by contrasting the thought of these caresses with their arms' daytime labour through the 'gestes habituels de la profession' [habitual gestures of her profession] (*RTP*, III, 649; *SLT*, V,155).[8] In a gender-crossing version of Marcel's voluptuous fantasising over the proletarian body, Albertine appears as erotically susceptible to the pastry-cook's busy arms stowing tea things as the Narrator to the milkmaid's forearm, glimpsed as she hands him *Le Figaro*. And yet, further 'crossings', to which I shall return, circulate in this class-crossing, gender-crossing pastry-shop encounter.

The pastry-shop episode was to be Marcel's's last excursion with Albertine, for a mere few hours later she asks Françoise for her trunks and departs, bringing *La Prisonnière* to an end. In what the Narrator points to as an ominous 'présage', just days earlier, she opens her window so violently as to prompt his anguish at 'un bruit en apparence insignifiant mais qui me remplit de terreur' [a noise which, though, apparently insignifiant, filled me with terror] (*RTP*, III, 903; *SLT*, V, 459), followed by a night of pacing and soul-searching study as to why that noise, in particular, was so upsetting for him. The Narrator imagines two possibilities; since she had been strictly admonished never to open windows at night, didn't such a gesture mean that she no longer needed to take care not to offend him? In another explanation, the Narrator thinks that such an explosive act might suggest that her life with him is stifling her, and continues to think of her gesture 'comme à un présage plus mystérieux et plus funèbre qu'un cri de chouette' [as of an omen more mysterious and more funereal than the hoot of an owl] (*RTP*, III, 903; *SLT*, V, 459). It is with this violent window-opening, index of Albertine's frustration at her imprisonment and expression of her desire to escape, that filmmaker Chantal Akerman introduces what I propose as a variation of the pastry-shop encounter, structured around the duet 'Prenderò quel brunettino' [I'll Take the Dark-Haired One] from Mozart's *Cosi fan Tutte* (often translated into English as 'Thus Do They All'). Akerman's scene in her film *La Captive* — staged above a courtyard, in an echo of the *Sodome et Gomorrhe* courtyard seduction encounter of Charlus and Jupien — opens as Albertine, at first languidly, then with a frustrated, decisive yank, opens a window and emerges onto the balcony of what we understand to be her room in the

Parisian apartment of her sequestration with Akerman's protagonist, Simon.[9] As she emerges, she appears to be breathing with difficulty, evoking the Narrator's supposition in *La Prisonnière* that throwing open her window may be motivated by thinking, 'Cette vie m'étouffe, tant pis, il me faut de l'air!' [This life is stifling me. I don't care, I must have air!] (*RTP*, III, 903; *SLT*, V, 459). Limp and virtually lifeless, Akerman's Albertine seems on the point of collapse, supporting herself on the balcony railing, when a singer from a nearby open window begins the mezzo (Dorabella) part of the *Così* duet. Looking up from her slumped position over the balcony, Albertine straightens and joins in with Fiordiligi's responding soprano part while the camera, focused on Albertine's upward gaze, delays showing us its object. Like Proust's Marcel in the pastry-shop scene, and like the observing Simon, stopped in his tracks in the courtyard by the music, Akerman's spectator is made to focus on Albertine's own focus, which is insistently upward, elsewhere, away from ours, reinscribing the *A la recherche* Albertine's 'série de vaines élévations implorantes vers une divinité inaccessible' [series of vain imploring elevations before an inaccessible divinity] (*RTP*, III, 908; *SLT*, V, 464).

In the Mozart duet chosen by Akerman for this scene, sisters Dorabella and Fiordiligi agree to amuse themselves by toying with the affections of two swooning admirers, not knowing that these admirers are their own suitors in disguise, and testing the women's fidelity. The duet, then, announces a strategy of simulation, as the sisters revel in the entertaining prospect of pretending to return their new admirers' affections: simulation that ultimately backfires to become truth, as the sisters, still unaware of their true identities, succumb to their new admirers' unrelenting ardour. In detailing a plot of simulated flirtation in response to what the sisters are unaware is itself simulated flirtation disguising authentic attraction, the duet thus constructs layers of simulation and truth, itself flirting with, even as it scrambles, the boundary separating real desire from its imitation. While everything resolves happily in Mozart's opera once the visiting admirers are revealed to be none other than the sisters' own suitors, Akerman chooses to stage the duet scene in a context of unresolved boundaries separating truth and simulation, for we never discover the relationship of Albertine to the mysterious mezzo at her own higher window — although possible intimacy is implied not only in their duet performance, but in the mezzo's minimal dress, appearing to be no more than a slip. As Simon does as he enters the courtyard in the middle of the duet and, like the Proustian Narrator in the pastry-shop scene, reduced to the role of helpless witness, while Albertine and the other singer exchange lines about simulated desire for simulating (though again, beneath their disguises, authentic) admirers, we wonder what truth may lie underneath these layers of simulation.

During Akerman's scene, in what appears to allude to the upswept dynamic of the text's pastry-shop encounter, Albertine sings Fiordiligi's part skyward to the mezzo on a much higher floor, who, like the pastry-cook, never so much as lowers her glance to acknowledge Albertine's responding musical lines; in contrast, however, Albertine herself never takes her eyes off the other singer, despite Simon's entry into the courtyard. As Simon stops in his tracks to gaze first at Albertine, then at the other singer, the camera trained on his expressionless face implies his proximity through the music's immediacy — further emphasising, implicitly, Albertine's obsessive gaze with its refusal to leave the mezzo to acknowledge the listening Simon. In their analysis of this scene, Marion Schmid and Martine Beugnet, observing that the opera revolves around male suspicion of female infidelity, point to the window bars that implicitly cage the mezzo within her higher floor, and argue for 'the confined figure of the mysterious woman as a metaphor for the imprisonment of a dangerous female desire that needs to be kept in check'.[10] Similarly, we might add, the pastry-cook, with her charmingly busy proletarian arms and well-concealed lovers, embodies a dangerous eroticism behind the ruse of her mechanised aloofness.

In an interesting confirmation of the connection heavily thematised in *A la recherche* between desire and the exotic, we notice that Mozart's libretto exoticises the two sisters' 'mysterious' admirers through their disguises. Tested on the maid to be sure of their efficacy as camouflage, these disguises prompt her to wonder whether these curious gentleman are Wallachians (Romanians) or Turks (I.11); and of course, as the opera evolves, the exotic proves to be irresistible when the sisters' original plan merely to toy with the affections of their alluring admirers yields to real attraction. Returning now to the exotic inscribed by Vigny's epigraph on the biblical cities of Sodom and Gomorrah, we are reminded of Hughes's observation that Proust gets 'homosexuality onto the map' via 'a set of complex and mobile sexual identities, variously mediated through a number of textual antecedents' (p. 44). Through such mediation, argues Hughes, Proust 'indirectly proposes a mapping of homosexuality, to the extent that his text brings into play a symbolic cartography in which sexual mores are located often in spaces beyond Europe'.[11] The courtyard encounter opening *Sodome et Gomorrhe* is heavily marked, of course, by such exoticism, and not only that inscribed by the Vigny epigraph; the episode is introduced by the Narrator as a glimpse into 'quelque cité orientale dont je n'avais pas encore deviné le nom' [some oriental city, the name of which I had not yet divined], a city peopled by 'les invertis, qui se rattachent volontiers à l'antique Orient' [the race of inverts, who readily link themselves with the ancient East] (*RTP*, III, 7–8, 31; *SLT*, IV, 6, 34).

Picking up the exoticism of Charlus and Jupien's encounter in the Guermantes courtyard, the pastry-shop episode in *La Prisonnière* will ultimately begin and end with an exotic Venice. Inspired by the blossoms and scents of springtime bringing alluring memories of erotically charged lunches and boating parties in the country — the outdoors now seeming 'le pays des femmes aussi bien qu'il était celui des arbres' [the land of women just as much as it was the land of trees] (*RTP*, III, 905; *SLT*, V, 461) — Marcel feels a surge of desire for the beyond, far away from his own and Albertine's Parisian sequestration. Despite announcing 'Je voulais aller à Venise' [I wanted to go to Venice], he resigns himself instead to a dull local outing with Albertine who, reading in her room in a Fortuny peignoir, chooses between two Fortuny cloaks to throw over it for their excursion to Versailles: 'elle hésita une seconde entre deux manteaux de Fortuny pour cacher sa robe de chambre' [she hesitated for a moment between two Fortuny coats beneath which to conceal her dressing-gown] (*RTP*, III, 905, 906; *SLT*, V, 462–63). During the pastry-shop scene, Albertine — the bourgeois Marcel's mistress raising imploring glances to the working-class pastry-cook — is thus doubly swathed in the work of a designer profoundly influenced by Venice, and favoured by elegant *Parisiennes*.

And it is via these exotic yet bourgeois vestments that the memory of this outing returns painfully for the Narrator in *Albertine disparue* during the visit to Venice with his mother after Albertine's departure and death. As Proust indicates (borrowing his Narrator's use of the first-person pronoun) in a letter to Maria de Madrazo — a sister of his lover Reynaldo Hahn and Fortuny's aunt by marriage — his gifts of Fortuny dresses to Albertine 'm'évoquent surtout Venise, le désir d'y aller, ce à quoi elle est un obstacle' [evoke for me Venice, particularly, the desire to go there, a desire to which she is an obstacle].[12] In this request to Mme Madrazo for information about Fortuny's designs, Proust refers to the Venice episode he plans for his manuscript, where 'les tableaux de xxx (disons Carpaccio)' [the paintings of xxx (let's say, Carpaccio)] prompt the Narrator to remember the gift to Albertine of a Fortuny dress that came to punctuate his relationship with her: 'Autrefois cette robe m'évoquait Venise et me donnait envie de quitter Albertine, maintenant le Carpaccio où je la vois m'évoque Albertine et me rend Venise douloureux' [Previously, this dress aroused in me thoughts of Venice and made me want to leave Albertine; now, the Carpaccio painting in which I see it evokes Albertine for me, and renders Venice sorrowful].[13] In what ultimately became the Venice episode in *Albertine disparue*, admiring for the first time Carpaccio's *Patriarch Exorcising a Madman*, Marcel feels the sting of recognition for he recognises, on a young Venetian nobleman (a 'Compagnon de la Calza') the Fortuny cloak worn by Albertine during the excursion that included the tea-time stop in the pastry-shop, 'le soir où j'étais loin de me douter qu'une quinzaine d'heures me séparaient à peine du moment où elle partirait de chez moi' [the evening when I so little suspected that scarcely fifteen hours separated me from the moment of her departure from my house] (*RTP*, IV, 226; *SLT*, V, 743). Fortuny, as Malcolm Bowie observes, 'was a migrant from Spain to Venice to Paris' and 'like so many brilliant couturiers, [...] a plagiarist. He has plundered Carpaccio for his designs, and in removing a cape from fashionable fifteenth-century Venetian men has made it available to fashionable modern Parisian women'.[14] As Bowie points out, this exotic reminder of Albertine is heavily charged with her 'most threatening and most alluring' qualities: the enigma of her sexual preferences. 'This male figure in female-seeming garb in the painting is wearing the cape of one who was, as the remembering Narrator puts it [...], "toujours prête à tout" [always ready for anything]' (*RTP*, IV, 226; *SLT*, V, 743).[15] For Bowie, this reminder of Albertine's inscrutable sexuality is yet another exercise in *A la recherche*'s exploration of mobile desiring fantasy, whose dynamism he explores in the Narrator's description of Carpaccio's painting of a teeming Venice. As Bowie demonstrates, 'throughout this remarkable page, an unstoppable transformational machinery is in operation. There are no identities, only trajectories'.[16] Just as the pastry-shop encounter stages a gender-crossing fetishisation in Albertine's attraction to the pastry-cook's proletarian working arms, so the masculinity of the young 'Compagnon de la Calza' crosses genders and centuries to inflect Albertine in her bourgeois double layers (peignoir and cloak) of Carpaccio-inspired Fortuny. Perhaps such implicit gender-crossing is also at work in Albertine's performance of the soprano part of Mozart's duet in Akerman's *La Captive*, for, as it happens, Albertine sings the part an octave lower than written.

Just as the biblical city of Gomorrah is chastised for its transgressive eroticism by a rain of divine fire and brimstone (Genesis 19:24), Albertine is chastised by the 'petite leçon' [little lesson] of the aloof pastry-cook's rain of cold indifference. 'C'était peu aimable pour mon amie' [It was not very flattering for my mistress], summarises the Narrator, 'mais dans le fond je fus enchanté qu'Albertine reçût cette petite leçon et vît que souvent les femmes ne faisaient pas attention à elle' [when all was said, I was delighted that Albertine should receive this little lesson and should see that frequently women paid no attention to her] (*RTP*, III, 909; *SLT*, V, 465–66). A far more pleasant lesson for us all, however, is to be found in the inspiring work of Edward J. Hughes, whether enjoyed in pastry-shops or beyond, and to which both women and men would do well, as always, to pay attention.

Notes to Chapter 21

1. Edward J. Hughes, *Proust, Class, and Nation* (Oxford: Oxford University Press, 2011), p. 166. Following Hughes's lead, I will refer to the younger Narrator engaged in the action as 'Marcel', reserving the term 'Narrator' for the older, recounting voice.
2. Marcel Proust, *A la recherche du temps perdu*, ed. by Jean-Yves Tadié, 4 vols, Bibliothèque de la Pléiade (Paris: Gallimard, 1987–89), III, 19 (hereafter referenced as *RTP* in the main text); *In Search of Lost Time*, trans. by C. K. Scott-Moncrieff and Terence Kilmartin, rev. by D. J. Enright, 6 vols (London: Vintage, 2000–02), IV, 20 (hereafter referenced as *SLT* in the main text).
3. In the King James Bible's version of Genesis, every mention of the two 'cities of the plain' in Chapters 18 and 19 places Sodom before Gomorrah. In his discussion of the Vigny epigraph to *Sodome et Gomorrhe*, Hughes reminds us that 'the calamity occasioned by desire in Proust summons up a remote, biblical past' (*Proust, Class, and Nation*, p. 43).
4. As Antoine Compagnon points out in his 'Notes et variantes' to *Sodome et Gomorrhe* (*RTP*, III, 1265), Proust quotes Vigny's line twice in his piece 'A propos de Baudelaire', in *Essais et articles*, evoking his conviction that it was motivated by Vigny's jealous suspicions over Marie Dorval's feelings for another woman. For the full text of the Baudelaire essay, see Marcel Proust, *Contre Sainte-Beuve, précédés de Pastiches et mélanges, suivi de Essais et articles*, ed. by Pierre Clarac and André Ferré, Bibliothèque de la Pléiade (Paris: Gallimard, 1971), pp. 618–39.
5. Marcel Proust, Folio 34, quoted by Pierre-Edmond Robert, 'Notice' to *La Prisonnière* (*RTP*, III, 1676).
6. The association of Albertine with aeroplanes is, of course, biographically inspired by Proust's chauffeur, Alfred Agostinelli, who fled Proust's employ to take flying lessons on the Riviera under the name 'Marcel Swann', before drowning when the plane he was piloting crashed in Nice's Baie des Anges. See, among other discussions of this association, Pierre-Edmond Robert's historical analysis of Albertine's interest in 'Un air du temps: aéroplanes, automobiles' ('Notice', in *RTP*, III, 1675).
7. Hughes, *Proust, Class, and Nation*, p. 159.
8. Ibid, p. 161. For Hughes's discussion of this passage, see pp. 159–60.
9. *La Captive*, dir. by Chantal Akerman (Paulo Branco, 2000).
10. Marion Schmid and Martine Beugnet, *Proust at the Movies* (Aldershot, & Burlington, VT: Ashgate Press, 2004), p. 197.

11. Hughes, *Proust, Class, and Nation*, p. 44.
12. Pierre-Edmond Robert discusses what he calls 'le fil Fortuny' [the Fortuny thread], with a perhaps deliberate allusion to the designer's dressmaking craft in the word 'fil' ('Notice', *RTP*, III, 1670–75). See also Christie McDonald's analysis of Proust's interest in the designer Fortuny in *The Proustian Fabric: Associations of Memory* (Lincoln & London: University of Nebraska Press, 1991), pp. 132–53. The translation from Proust's letter is my own.
13. Marcel Proust, letter to Madame de Madrazo, 17 February 1916, in Marcel Proust, *Correspondance*, ed. by Philip Kolb, 21 volumes (Paris: Plon, 1970–93), xv, 57, quoted in McDonald, *The Proustian Fabric*, pp. 218–19, n. 3. The translation from Proust's letter is my own.
14. Malcolm Bowie, *Freud, Proust and Lacan: Theory as Fiction* (Cambridge: Cambridge University Press, 1987), pp. 89–90.
15. Ibid., p. 90.
16. Ibid.

CHAPTER 22

Edward Hughes and the Quality of Awareness

Alison Finch

Edward Hughes's first book, *Marcel Proust: A Study in the Quality of Awareness*, was a landmark in Proust studies.[1] It arose from the doctoral thesis whose topic he had formulated entirely independently in the mid-1970s as a student at Queen's University Belfast. (He had chosen not to do a PhD at Oxford or Cambridge.)[2] The book was hailed on publication for its quite new perspective on Proust, in particular on *A la recherche du temps perdu*. Hughes focused on the dialectic between the narrator's fine artistic and intellectual sensitivities and the sensibility of ostensibly 'simple' or 'primitive' characters. Hitherto the narrator's attraction to such characters had been cited largely as a symptom of his desire for love-objects who by definition could not fully respond to or appreciate him; he thereby exemplified the triangular desire for which René Girard had argued in the early 1960s.[3] Occasionally critics would mention other 'natural' figures as a less oppositional (albeit rather quirky) complement to the narrator's own temperament, for instance the sisters Céleste and Marie, those embodiments of landscape who appear in *Sodome et Gomorrhe*. But at the time Hughes conceived his subject no one had thought it worthwhile to enlist these characters themselves into a major structural analysis, let alone exfoliate their perceptions.

The picture changed once Hughes's book appeared. As a review said, it was

> one of those rare critical works that articulate a major and previously unrecognised pattern of meaning in *A la recherche*. [...] The new pattern described by Hughes is so obvious once it has been seen that one wonders what repressive mechanisms within our literary culture can have been keeping it invisible until now.[4]

The same review described the book as a 'compellingly original study'. (The present writer can claim a modest part in the recognition of Hughes's gifts, having read his thesis for Cambridge University Press and strongly recommended its publication.)

What aspects of Proust criticism did Hughes reset? During the first half-century, say 1920–70, Proust had attracted renowned commentators, among them Ernst Robert Curtius (1928), Walter Benjamin (1929), Samuel Beckett (1931), John M. Cocking (1956), Girard (1961), Leo Spitzer (1961) and Georges Poulet (1963).[5] But as a whole Proust criticism could find itself mired in two trends that underestimated the multifariousness of *A la recherche du temps perdu*: the simplistically biographical, and a focus on safer sides of the novel — or what were perceived as safe. Among these were Proust's similes, often corralled into a dispiriting categorisation by 'theme'; theories of involuntary versus voluntary memory; the artists in the novel; and the 'spiritual odyssey' that led the narrator to his vocation. Bergson was almost the sole acknowledged philosophical influence on Proust. Passed over rapidly, or ignored, were such disturbing subjects as homosexuality and the obsessiveness that shapes much of *La Prisonnière* and *La Fugitive*, frequently viewed as unfortunate. And even excellent critics saw it as their role to explicate the narrator's capacity for discrimination rather than his attraction to the uncomplicated.

In the 1970s fear of this troubling Proust began to lessen, perhaps corresponding to a gradual relaxation of repressive social attitudes. General readers, no longer coy about his depictions of gay sexuality and of racism, were concluding in growing numbers that he was the greatest twentieth-century European novelist. Scholars increasingly understood the importance of a conspectus of the whole novel; ever more outstanding critics, such as Jean-Pierre Richard, were turning to Proust.[6] However, the biographical approach clung on (an egregious case being the readable biography by George Painter, which barely acknowledged a gap between life and novel).[7] Among philosophical influences, Bergson still ruled the roost. Elstir and Impressionism, Vinteuil and César Franck: such topics continued to provide mainly comfortable insights.

Hughes was one of the Proustians of the 1970s who discarded these uncontroversial approaches and at the same time created tools for later criticism to work with. Apart from anything else, his discussion of Schopenhauer loosened the grip of Bergson on Proust criticism. However, beyond that, his book had startling implications, which will be obvious to those who have followed his trajectory, and that of international literary criticism, but were by no means predestined. Hughes's revolutionary concentration on relatively uneducated, even inarticulate, characters predated the surge of French cultural studies but can retrospectively be read through that lens. For example, linguistic dexterity and wit have long been a source of national pride for France, and at the *fin de siècle* aestheticism was prized; that period too gave birth to the self-styled 'intellectual' — Hughes incidentally points out that the 'intellectual' was not always left-wing: the designation was also adopted by the right.[8] But here was one of France's greatest prose stylists proposing a counterbalance, promoting something quite different and thereby (as elsewhere) undermining a chauvinistic literary and linguistic self-image. Hughes was therefore already quietly raising questions about nation; about class also, since Françoise and Jupien play their part. In Hughes's reading, the snobbish younger narrator is present, but so too is a wise and even egalitarian older one.[9]

At the time Hughes published his first book, the notion of an eco-Proust would probably have been laughed out of court. Yet remarkably he too is presaged in Hughes's study. Hughes demonstrates that in *A la recherche* all types of sentience are objects of curiosity and that there may be only a sliding-scale difference between human and animal consciousness. A kind of solidarity also links people with plant-life. Proust's metaphors suggest as much, the extended ones in particular blurring distinctions between hotel-boys and bushes, gay lovers and orchids and, yes, between servants and dogs. Writers' figures of speech have always entwined human, botanical and zoological, and Proust, an admirer of Nerval for instance, was attuned to animism. But Hughes was already in 1983 allowing us to radicalise this, beginning his career-long exploration of ways in which hierarchies and their dissolution interweave with metaphorical and sensory, as well as narrative, structures.

Proust was, needless to say, no eco-warrior or animal rights activist. But his description of the killing of the chicken in *Du côté de chez Swann* is couched in language that suggests he was aware of vegetarian debates and might even have read, among others, the polemic of the Communard Louise Michel on the subject.[10] Proustians will be familiar with this sequence and its embarrassing directness: the child would like Françoise to be dismissed for her brutality, but then who would cook him those self-same delicious chickens? 'Et en réalité, ce lâche calcul, tout le monde avait eu à le faire comme moi' [And, as it happened, everyone else had already had to make the same cowardly reckoning].[11] This statement echoes the description a hundred pages earlier of the child's cowardice when his great-aunt bullies his grandmother; there too he is 'déjà homme par la lâcheté' [in [his] cowardice [he] became at once a man] (*RTP*, I, 12; *SLT*, I,12), would like to hit the great-aunt but instead (as in the later passage) retreats upstairs in distress. The kindred dilemmas and reactions, the 'moraliste' phrasing, the lexical repetition ('lâcheté/lâche'), raise questions about speciesism and about bystander passivity, questions visible in the proto-ecological and political thrust of Hughes's arguments.[12]

The early book paved the way not only for Hughes's subsequent focus on major themes of social standing in Proust but also for numerous observations of significant detail: Hughes has continued to read with an unerring eye. In his book of 2001, for instance, he cites the cameo in *A l'ombre des jeunes filles en fleurs* of Mme Blatin's insulting '"Bonjour, négro!"', addressed to a Singhalese man 'on display' in 1883 in the Jardin d'Acclimatation. The man angrily replies: '"Moi négro, mais toi, chameau!"' ['Me negro, but you, old cow!'] (*RTP*, I, 526; *SLT*, II, 126, translation adapted). This laconic punch at white elitism, a jokey but highly charged mix of human and animal, had been 'under the radar' in Proust studies until Hughes's telling remarks on it.[13] And eight years later, in an essay of 2009, Hughes cites an again oddly neglected aside in *Le Temps retrouvé* that is apposite to any revisiting of his first book. Proust suggests (in the context of anti-German hysteria) that ethical awareness may be long in development: 'Notre époque sans doute, pour celui qui en lira l'histoire dans deux mille ans, ne semblera pas moins baigner certaines consciences tendres et pures dans un milieu vital qui apparaîtra alors comme monstrueusement pernicieux et dont elles s'accommodaient' [And our own age no doubt, when its history is read two thousand years hence, will seem to an equal degree to have bathed men of pure and tender conscience in a vital element which will strike the future reader as monstrously pernicious, but to which at the time these men adapted themselves without difficulty] (*RTP*, IV, 416; *SLT*, VI, 181).[14]

Fortunately we have not had to wait two millennia for Hughes's early analyses to bear fruit. With hindsight we can see that his pioneering book was not only a powerful conceptual breakthrough but that it bequeathed an equally powerful legacy; it was a brilliant start to a brilliant career.

Notes to Chapter 22

1. Edward J. Hughes, *Marcel Proust: A Study in the Quality of Awareness* (Cambridge: Cambridge University Press, 1983).
2. Personal testimony, supplied in conversation, from Hughes's supervisor Richard Bales (1946–2007). Hughes was a doctoral student from 1976 to 1979.
3. René Girard, *Mensonge romantique et vérité romanesque* (Paris: Grasset, 1961).
4. Malcolm Bowie, 'Minds, Great and Small', *Times Literary Supplement*, 17 February 1984, pp. 155–56; reproduced in *Selected Essays of Malcolm Bowie*, ed. by Alison Finch, 2 vols (Oxford: Legenda, 2013), II, 213–18.
5. Ernst Robert Curtius, *Marcel Proust* [1928] (Frankfurt am Main: Schöffling & Co., 2021); Walter Benjamin, 'The Image of Proust' [1929], in *Illuminations*, trans. by Harry Zohn (London: Fontana, 1973); Samuel Beckett, *Proust* (London: Chatto & Windus, 1931); J. M. Cocking, *Proust* (London: Bowes & Bowes, 1956); Leo Spitzer, 'Le Style de Marcel Proust' [1961], in *Études de style*, trans. by Alain Coulon (Paris: Gallimard, 1970), pp. 397–473; Georges Poulet, *L'Espace proustien* (Paris: Gallimard, 1963).
6. Jean-Pierre Richard, *Proust et le monde sensible* (Paris: Seuil, 1974).
7. George D. Painter, *Marcel Proust*, 2 vols (London: Penguin, 1977).
8. Hughes, *Marcel Proust*, pp. 174–76.
9. These areas of enquiry and analysis would be developed and brought together with outstanding acuity in Hughes's later study *Proust, Class, and Nation* (Oxford: Oxford University Press, 2011), as well as in his recent *Egalitarian Strangeness: On Class Disturbance and Levelling in Modern and Contemporary French Narrative* (Liverpool: Liverpool University Press, 2021).
10. See the passionate discussion of cruelty to animals in Louise Michel, *Mémoires de Louise Michel, écrits par elle-même* [1886] (Paris: Maspero, 1976), for example pp. 91–92, 97–98, 266; and Ceri Crossley, *Consumable Metaphors: Attitudes towards Animals and Vegetarianism in Nineteenth-Century France* (Bern: Peter Lang, 2005).
11. Marcel Proust, *A la recherche du temps perdu*, ed. by Jean-Yves Tadié and others, 4 vols, Bibliothèque de la Pléiade (Paris: Gallimard, 1987–89), I, 120 (hereafter referenced as *RTP* in the main text); *In Search of Lost Time*, trans. by C. K. Scott-Moncrieff and Terence Kilmartin, rev. by D. J. Enright, 6 vols (London: Vintage, 2000–02), I, 145 (hereafter referenced as *SLT* in the main text).
12. Hughes refers to the chicken episode in another context in his book: *Marcel Proust*, p. 150, n. 11. See also his discussion of a young Mme de Guermantes's cruelty to animals, here inextricable from her social status: 'une cruelle petite fille de l'aristocratie' [a cruel little girl from the aristocracy] (*RTP*, II, 793; *SLT*, III, 581, translation adapted); *Marcel Proust*, p. 117.
13. Edward J. Hughes, *Writing Marginality in Modern French Culture from Loti to Genet* (Cambridge: Cambridge University Press, 2001), pp. 167–68. This set the stage for, inter alia, André Benhaïm's later deconstruction of the same passage: see André Benhaïm, 'Proust's Singhalese Song (A Strange Little Story)', in *The Strange M. Proust*, ed. by André Benhaïm (Oxford: Legenda, 2009), pp. 57–70.
14. Edward J. Hughes, 'Hierarchies', in *Le Temps retrouvé Eighty Years After/80 ans après*, ed. by Adam Watt (Bern: Peter Lang, 2009), pp. 117–31 (p. 123); this chapter was subsequently incorporated into *Proust, Class, and Nation*, pp. 223–38.

EDWARD J. HUGHES

A Select Bibliography 1983–2021

Books and Edited Volumes

Marcel Proust: A Study in the Quality of Awareness (Cambridge: Cambridge University Press, 1983) (paperback repr., 2010)
Albert Camus, 'Le Premier Homme'/ 'La Peste' (Glasgow: University of Glasgow French and German Publications, 1995)
with Peter Dunwoodie (eds), *Constructing Memories: Camus, Algeria and 'Le Premier Homme'* (Stirling: Stirling French Publications, 1998)
Writing Marginality in Modern French Literature: From Loti to Genet (Cambridge: Cambridge University Press, 2001) (2nd edn, 2006)
(ed.), *The Cambridge Companion to Camus* (Cambridge: Cambridge University Press, 2007)
Proust, Class, and Nation (Oxford: Oxford University Press, 2011)
Albert Camus, Critical Lives (London: Reaktion Books, 2015) (repr. 2016; Chinese translation, Peking University Press, 2018). Awarded the Franco-British Society Literary Prize in April 2016
Egalitarian Strangeness: On Class Disturbance and Levelling in Modern and Contemporary French Narrative (Liverpool: Liverpool University Press, 2021)

Articles and Book Chapters

'"La vérité est carrée": Reflections on Camus's *Le Renégat ou un esprit confus*', *La Chouette*, 10 (1983), 76–86
'Proust's "petits personnages barométriques"', in *Humanitas: Studies in Honour of Henri Godin*, ed. by Robert McBride (Belfast: Modern Languages Association of Northern Ireland, 1984), pp. 125–35
'Space and Place in Duras's *L'Amant*', *La Chouette*, 15 (1986), 35–45
'Parisian Pastoral in *A la recherche du temps perdu*', *Romance Studies*, 22 (1993), 17–25
'Meaning, Money and Knowledge: A Reading of Balzac's *La Recherche de l'absolu*', *Romance Studies*, 23 (1994), 31–42
'Prisons and Pleasures of the Mind: A Comparative Reading of Cervantes and Proust', in *Cervantes and the Modernists: The Question of Influence*, ed. by Edwin Williamson (London: Tamesis, 1994), pp. 55–72
'Sexual Topographies in Proust's *Recherche*', *Journal of the Institute of Romance Studies*, 3 (1994–95), 205–14
'The Mapping of Homosexuality in Proust's *Recherche*', *Paragraph: A Journal of Modern Critical Theory*, 18.2 (1995), 148–62
'Introduction' and '"Tranquillement monstrueux": Violence and Kinship in *Le Premier Homme*', in *Constructing Memories: Camus, Algeria and 'Le Premier Homme'*, ed. by Peter Dunwoodie and E. J. Hughes (Stirling: Stirling French Publications, 1998), pp. v–viii, 21–32

'Proustian Metamorphosis: The Art of Distortion in *A la recherche du temps perdu*', *Modern Language Review*, 94.3 (1999), 660–72
'Building the Colonial Archive: The Case of Camus's *Le Premier Homme*', *Dissident Algeria* (= special issue of *Research in African Literatures*, 30.3 (1999)), 176–93
'Entre la banalité et la marginalité: refus et quête du sens dans *La Vie matérielle* de Marguerite Duras', in *Lectures de Duras*, ed. by Brian Stimpson (= special issue of *Dalhousie French Studies*, 50 (2000), 117–27
'Cultural Stereotyping: Segalen against Loti', in *Segalen: Reading Diversity/ Lectures du Divers*, ed. by Charles Forsdick and Susan Marson (Glasgow: University of Glasgow French and German Publications, 2000), pp. 25–38
'Proust and Social Spaces', in *The Cambridge Companion to Proust*, ed. by Richard Bales (Cambridge: Cambridge University Press, 2001), pp. 151–67
'Marcel Proust', in *Encyclopaedia of Life Writing*, ed. by Margaretta Jolly (London: Fitzroy Dearborn, 2001), pp. 730–33
'Cataclysm at One Remove: The War in *Le Temps retrouvé*', in *Approaches to Teaching Proust's Fiction and Criticism*, ed. by Elyane Dezon Jones (New York: Modern Language Association of America, 2003), pp. 38–43
'The Good Cause', *Francophone Postcolonial Studies*, 2.1 (2003), 79–82
'Textual and Tribal Assimilation: Representing Jewishness in *A la recherche du temps perdu*', *Jewish Culture and History*, 6.1 (2003), 152–73
'Textual and Tribal Assimilation: Representing Jewishness in *A la recherche du temps perdu*', in *The Image of the Jew in European Liberal Culture*, ed. by Bryan Cheyette and Nadia Valman (London: Frank Cass/ Vallentine Mitchell, 2004), pp. 152–73
c. 30,000-word contribution (7 main articles, 20 short articles, 12 notes), in *Dictionnaire Marcel Proust*, ed. by Annick Bouillaguet and Brian Rogers (Paris: Champion, 2005). Awarded the 2005 Prix Emile Faguet of the Académie Française
'Exotic Drift: Pierre Loti Between Contemporaneity and Anteriority', in *Eastern Voyages, Western Visions: French Writing and Painting of the Orient*, ed. by Margaret Topping (Bern: Peter Lang, 2004), pp. 241–64
'Haunted and Haemorrhaging: The Representation of Violence in Mohammed Dib's *La Nuit sauvage*', *French Studies*, 59.1 (2005), 63–69
'L'Ordre social dans Combray', *Marcel Proust Aujourd'hui*, 3 (2005), 63–80
'"Sous un signe double": Language and Identity in Assia Djebar's *L'Amour, la fantasia*', in *Challenges of Translation in French Literature*, ed. by Richard Bales (Bern: Peter Lang, 2005), pp. 221–35
'"Le prélude d'une sorte de mort historique": Underpinning Assimilation in Camus's *Chroniques Algériennes*', *L'Esprit Créateur*, 47.1 (2007), 7–18
'A Witness on the Edge: Jean Genet and the Shatila Massacres', in *Aesthetics of Dislocation in French and Francophone Literature and Art: Strategies of Representation*, ed. by Daisy Connon and others (Lampeter: Edwin Mellen Press, 2009), pp. 53–68
'Hierarchies', in *Le Temps retrouvé: Eighty Years After/ 80 ans après. Critical Essays/ Essais critiques*, ed. by Adam Watt (Berlin: Peter Lang, 2009), pp. 117–31
'"Sur un point solitaire du globe": Camus, Algeria, Conflict and Art', *Expressions maghrébines*, 9.2 (2010), 135–50
'Perspectives sur la culture populaire dans l'œuvre de Proust', in *Morales de Proust*, ed. by Mariolina Bertini and Antoine Compagnon (= special issue of *Cahiers de littérature française*, 9–10 (Bergamo: Bergamo University Press; Paris: L'Harmattan, 2010)), 69–82
'On the Nation and its Culture: Proust, Barrès and Daniel Halévy', in *Au seuil de la modernité: Proust, la littérature et les arts. Essays in Memory of Richard Bales*, ed. by Nigel Harkness and Marion Schmid (Oxford: Peter Lang, 2011), pp. 129–48

'Pierre Michon, "Small Lives", and the Terrain of Art', *Romance Studies*, 29.2 (2011), 67–79

'Albert Camus', in *Encyclopaedia of the Bible and its Reception*, ed. by Constance M. Furey and others, vol 4. (Berlin & Boston: Walter de Gruyter, 2012), pp. 852–53

'Expérience et connaissance du quotidien dans l'œuvre de Camus', in *Albert Camus au quotidien*, ed. by André Benhaïm and Aymeric Glacet (Lille: Presses universitaires du Septentrion, 2013), pp. 159–75

'Politics and Class', in *Marcel Proust in Context*, ed. by Adam Watt (Cambridge: Cambridge University Press, 2013), pp. 160–66

'The Dreyfus Affair' in *Marcel Proust in Context*, ed. Adam Watt (Cambridge: Cambridge University Press, 2013), pp. 167–73

'Lacunary Knowledge in Sebald and Proust', *Modern Language Review*, 109.1 (2014), 15–34

'"Les lignes vaines et solitaires de mon écriture": "Word" and "World" in Proust's *Recherche*', *Romanic Review*, 105.3–4 (2014), 201–13

'Proust, Benda et "la passion nationale"', in *Proust écrivain de la Première Guerre mondiale*, ed. by Philippe Chardin and Nathalie Mauriac–Dyer (Dijon: Éditions universitaires de Dijon, 2014), pp. 101–09

'"Cette ignorance si envahissante": Oblivion, Posterity, Art', in *Swann at 100/ Swann à 100 ans*, ed. by Adam Watt (= special issue of *Marcel Proust Aujourd'hui*, 12 (2015)), 18–34

'The Renewal of Narrative in the Wake of Proust', in *The Cambridge Companion to French Literature*, ed. by John D. Lyons (Cambridge: Cambridge University Press, 2016), pp. 187–203

'"Et la raison vacilla"': Sociality as Burden in Tahar Djaout and Mohammed Dib', in *Lucidity: Essays in Honour of Alison Finch*, ed. by Ian James and Emma Wilson (Oxford: Legenda, 2016), pp. 157–68

'Nation et Narration dans *Du côté de chez Swann*', in *'Du côté de chez Swann' ou le cosmopolitisme d'un roman français*, ed. by Antoine Compagnon and Nathalie Mauriac–Dyer (Paris: Honoré Champion, 2016), pp. 189–201

'"Cette fermeture du sens sur quoi, migrant, je bute": Crossing Cultures in Mohammed Dib', *Contemporary French and Francophone Studies*, 21.3 (2017), 298–305

'"Comme on aimait en Dieu, je vois dans la guerre": Identität und Identifikation in Marcel Prousts Briefwechsel während der Kriegsjahre', in *Marcel Proust*, ed. by Wolfram Nitsch and Jürgen Ritte (Berlin: Insel Verlag, 2017), pp. 181–200

'Circuits of Reappropriation: Accessing the Real in the Work of Didier Éribon', in *What Forms Can Do: The Work of Form in 20th- and 21st-century French Literature and Thought*, ed. by Patrick Crowley and Shirley Jordan (Liverpool: Liverpool University Press, 2020), pp. 179–94

'Le Commun et le quelconque : Proust en 1919', in *Proust politique: de l'Europe du Goncourt 1919 à l'Europe de 2019*, ed. by Anne Simon and others (= special issue of *Quaderni proustiani*, 14 (2020)), 63–72

INDEX

Agamben, Giorgio 9, 229, 234, 236, 237, 240, 242 n. 21
Ageron, Charles-Robert 77, 81, 87 n. 18
Ahrne, Marianne 150
Akerman, Chantal 8, 144, 145, 151–54, 270–72, 274 n. 9
Akkouche, Mouloud 63–65, 72–75
Albaret, Céleste 219, 224 n. 33
Ali, Mustapha Hadj 71, 76 n. 26
Amiri, Linda 71, 72, 76 n. 25, n. 28
Apollinaire, Guillaume 234, 241 n. 15
Arsan, Emmanuelle 257
Astruc, Zacharie 229
Austin, Guy 110, 112 n. 20

Badinter, Robert 69, 76 n. 21
Balah, Yacine 8, 101–13
Bales, Richard 3, 4, 5, 11 n. 12, 99 n. 4, 168 n. 9, 201 n. 2 & 20, 254 n. 15, 279 n. 2, 281
Baraitser, Lisa 144, 151, 154 n. 2, 155 n. 21
Bariéty, Maurice 215, 224 n. 15
Barrère, Camille 215–16
Barrès, Maurice 5, 211 n. 14, 215, 281
Barthes, Roland 4, 39, 57, 59 n. 37, 150, 200, 202 n. 50, 203 n. 51, 54 & 55, 238
Bataille, Georges 24 n. 13, 218, 224 n. 26, 234–35, 237, 238, 242 n. 17, 256–57, 258, 261, 265 n. 2 & 4
Baudelaire, Charles 100 n. 22, 201 n. 10, 208, 234, 254 n. 6 & 7, 274 n. 4
Bazille, Frédéric 229
Beauvoir, Simone de 28, 29, 34 n. 11, 145, 147–50, 154 n. 4, 155 n. 17–20
Beckett, Samuel 194, 199, 201 n. 5 & 12, 276, 279 n. 5
Bégaud, Caroline 52, 54, 58, nn. 18 & 21, 59 n. 28 & 34
Belbenoît, René 69
Bellour, Raymond 199, 202 n. 44 & 49
Benda, Julien 5, 282
Benhaïm, André 11 n. 21, 96, 100 n. 22, 211 n. 28, 279 n. 13, 282
Benjamin, Walter 1, 10 n. 1, 92, 99 n. 10, 124, 130 n. 33 & 46, 197, 198, 202 n. 28 & 32, 276, 279 n. 5
Bennett, Jill 109, 112 n. 18
Bergounioux, Pierre 78–79, 87 n. 6 & 8
Bergson, Henri 124, 277
Berlusconi, Silvio 156, 159, 168 n. 14

Beugnet, Martine 272, 274 n. 10
Bibesco, Antoine 223
Bibesco, Marthe 9, 243, 244, 248, 249–53, 254 n. 6 & 22, 255 n. 25
Blanchot, Maurice 24 n. 13, 229, 234–35, 236, 237, 238, 239, 240, 242 n. 27, 32, 33 & 36
Boccioni, Umberto 2
Bolsonaro, Jair 40, 47 n. 12
Bon, François 2, 7
Bouchareb, Rachid 101, 111 n. 3
Bouillaguet, Annick 5, 11 n. 16, 211 n. 11, 281
Boulenger, Jacques 213
Bourdieu, Pierre 2, 10, 11 n. 31, 259, 265 n. 6
Bourget, Paul 5
Bowie, Malcolm 171, 179 n. 1, 191 n. 27 & 29, 201 n. 14 & 22, 203 n. 53, 212 n. 42, 273, 275 n. 14, 279 n. 4
Braque, Georges 119
Breton, André 157
Brewster, David 91–92
Brozgal, Lia 110, 112 n. 19
Brugère, Fabienne 147, 154 n. 8, 155 n. 16
Brun, Bernard 3
Bunting, Madeleine 144, 154 n. 1 & 3
Burns, Robert 162
Butler, Judith 108, 112 n. 16

Caillavet, Jeanne de 219, 220, 224 n. 35
Caillois, Roger 28
Caldwell, Erskine 28
Camus, Albert 1, 2, 4, 5, 6, 7, 10 n. 5 & 11, 11 n. 18, 19, 24, 26, 15–24, 25–35, 36–47, 48–59, 63–76, 280, 281, 282
 Carnets 25, 26, 27, 32, 33, 35 n. 25, 42, 65, 75 n. 11
 La Chute 20, 21, 24 n. 14
 L'Envers et l'endroit 5, 11 n. 19, 15, 24 n. 6, 25, 26, 35 n. 17, 58 n. 16
 L'Été 25, 26, 33
 L'Étranger 16, 28, 36, 49, 65
 L'Exil et le royaume 15, 16, 21, 22, 25, 31, 56, 57, 59 n. 35
 'La Femme adultère' 23, 31, 56, 59 n. 35
 L'Homme révolté 36, 65, 75 n. 13
 'L'Hôte' 16, 17, 18, 19, 20, 22, 23, 24 n. 6, 57
 Journaux de voyage 25, 27, 29
 Les Justes 65, 75 n. 8 & 13
 'Le Minotaure ou halte à Oran' 4, 52

'La Mort dans l'âme' 27, 32
La Mort heureuse 25
Le Mythe de Sisyphe 26
Ni victimes ni bourreaux 37, 39, 42, 65
Noces 4, 25, 26, 31
La Peste 4, 7, 8, 10 n. 11, 21, 35 n. 26, 36–47, 48–59, 280
'La pierre qui pousse' 21–22, 31
Carpaccio, Vittore 273, 274
Casarès, Maria 33, 34 n. 8 & 9, 35 n. 18 & 30
Cazalis, Henri 239, 248, 254 n. 16
Céline, Louis-Ferdinand 25, 30, 34 n. 1, 35 n. 19, 157, 206, 207, 210, 211 n. 15
Cendrars, Blaise [Frédéric-Louis Sauser] 8, 117–31
Cézanne, Paul 9, 229, 233, 236, 237–38, 241 n. 12, 242 n. 24
Chamoiseau, Patrick 64, 70–71, 74, 75, 75 n. 6, 76 n. 23
Chaplin, Charlie 126, 230
Char, René 15, 33
Chardin, Jean-Baptiste-Siméon 208
Charrière, Henri 63, 64, 69
Charton, Édouard 82
Châtelet, Noëlle 154, 155 n. 22
Chaudier, Stéphane 191 n. 19, 207, 211 n. 25
Chekov, Anton 1
Cherubini, Bernard 69, 76 n. 22
Cixous, Hélène 59 n. 28, 142 n. 11, 154, 155 n. 22
Clemenceau, Georges 220, 224 n. 37
Cocking, John 276, 279 n. 5
Cohen, Albert 204, 210 n. 1 & 2
Cohn-Bendit, Daniel 36, 46 n. 1
Compagnon, Antoine 2, 201 n. 10, 274 n. 4, 281, 282
Conrad, Joseph 80, 83, 84
Coquet, Marine 72, 76 n. 32
Crémieux, Adolphe 51, 53, 57, 214, 215
Crémieux, Benjamin 216
Culler, Jonathan 194, 201 n. 13
Curtius, Robert 276, 279 n. 5
Czapski, Józep 204, 209, 210 n. 3 & 4, 212 n. 39

Damas, Léon-Gontran 64, 75 n. 7
Daoud, Kamel 23 n. 1, 39, 46 n. 8, 47 n. 30
Darwin, Charles 205, 209, 210 n. 8 & 9, 211 n. 37
Daudet, Alphonse 215
Daudet, Julia 215
Daudet, Léon 215, 233
Daudet, Lucien 212 n. 41, 216, 218
Debord, Guy 156, 159, 167 n. 2, 168 n. 10
Degas, Edgar 239
Delaunay, Robert 2
Delaunay, Sonia 119, 129 n. 10
Deleuze, Gilles 2
Derrida, Jacques 4, 19–20, 21, 24 n. 9 & 12, 143 n. 21, 146, 208, 229, 238, 240, 242 n. 28 & 29
Desanges, Gérard 216, 223, 224 n. 20, 225 n. 48

Descartes, René 171
Detambel, Régine 145, 154 n. 10
Dib, Mohammed 2, 5, 281, 282
Dickens, Charles 195, 207
Didi-Huberman, Georges 92–93, 99 n. 10
Dieulafoy, Jane 248, 254 n. 13 & 14
Dieulafoy, Marcel 248
Djebar, Assia 2, 5, 281
Dollimore, Jonathan 4
Dos Passos, John 28, 34 n. 13
Dreyfus, Alfred 11 n. 16, 52, 69, 98, 213, 217, 218, 219, 220, 282
Dreyfus, Robert 217, 222, 223, 224 n. 23, 225 n. 49
Drumont, Édouard 11 n. 16, 206, 211 n. 21
Dubois, Jacques 2
Duclos, Jacques 104, 112 n. 12
Dufourmantelle, Anne 19, 24 n. 12, 145–46, 149, 150, 152, 154, 155 n. 12
Duhamel, Marcel 28, 35 n. 14
Dunwoodie, Peter 4, 10 n. 11, 280
Duras, Marguerite 2, 58 n. 9, 234, 280, 281

Eiffel, Gustave 219
Elsner, Anna 110
Engels, Friedrich 204
Éribon, Didier 241 n. 3, 256, 265 n. 1, 282
Ernaux, Annie 8, 145, 154 n. 5

Fantin-Latour, Henri 229, 232
Farès, Tewfik 110
Faulkner, William 28, 34 n. 13
Faure, Félix 215, 216, 218, 219, 220
Faure, Francine 49
Fellini, Federico 8, 156, 158, 160, 161, 163, 165, 167, 168 n. 18 & 23
Felten, Uta 172, 179 n. 6
Ferry, Jules 214, 215, 217
Fontanier, Pierre 182, 183
Fortuny y Madrazo, Mariano 272–73, 274, 275 n. 12
Foucault, Michel 2
Flaubert, Gustave 79, 157, 198, 208
Fleuri, Cynthia 145, 154 n. 7
Fraisse, Geneviève 146, 155 n. 14
Fraisse, Luc 172, 179 n. 7 & 8, 192, 201 n. 3 & 7, 202 n. 34, 216, 217, 224 n. 16 & 22
France, Anatole 217, 218, 219
Franck, César 277
Frazer, James 2
Frechtman, Bernard 133, 142 n. 2, 3 & 7
Fumaroli, Marc 86, 88 n. 27, 180 n. 20

Gale, Claudia E. 214, 223 n. 10
Galland, Antoine 251
Gambetta, Léon 214
Gance, Abel 123
Gauguin, Paul 4, 235

Gaulle, Charles de 103–04, 110, 112 n. 11 & 12
Gauny, Louis-Gabriel 7
Gefen, Alexandre 145, 154 n. 9
Genet, Jean 1, 2, 4, 5, 8, 10 n. 5, 132–43, 254 n. 19, 279 n. 13, 280, 281
Genette, Gérard 182, 206, 211 n. 18
Gérin, René 65
Giacometti, Alberto 134, 135, 137, 142 n. 16
Gide, André 84, 233, 235
Gilroy, Paul 53, 59 n. 25
Gimpel, René 215, 223 n. 13
Girard, René 276, 279 n. 3
Glissant, Édouard 4
Godin, Henri 3, 10 n. 8, 280
Goncourt, Edmond de 193
Gourmont, Remy de 206, 207, 210, 211 n. 20
Goya, Francisco de 78
Green, Christopher 122, 129 n. 2, 130 n. 18, 23 & 27
Greffulhe, Henry 214
Gregh, Fernand 217
Grévy, Jules 214

Hâfez 247, 248, 252, 255 n. 26
Hahn, Reynaldo 273
Halévy, Daniel 5, 206, 211 n. 23, 220, 224 n. 40, 281
Hamington, Maurice 146, 155 n. 13
Hammadi, Rodolphe 70, 75 n. 6
Haneke, Michael 110
Hanotaux, Gabriel 215, 218
Hauser, Lionel 208, 211 n. 35
Haydn, Joseph 118
Heaney, Seamus 11 n. 26
Hemingway, Ernest 28
Homer 17–18, 19, 24 n. 5, 7 & 9, 87 n. 6, 154, 155 n. 22, 222
Hughes, Edward 1–11, 16, 17, 23 n. 3 & 4, 58 n. 7 & 16, 76 n. 34, 79, 80, 87 n. 11 & 13, 88 n. 25, 90, 96, 98, 99 n. 4, 100 n. 21 & 25, 117, 128, 129 n. 1 & 4, 131 n. 57, 168 n. 9, 171, 190 n. 1, 195, 198–99, 201 n. 6, 19 & 20, 202 n. 38 & 42, 203 n. 54, 207, 208, 211 n. 24, 32 & 34, 213, 223 n. 2, 224 n. 26, 231, 241 n. 3, 254 n. 19, 266, 267, 270, 272, 274, 274 n. 1, 3, 7 & 8, 275 n. 11, 276–79
Hugo, Victor 79
Huhtamo, Erkki 92, 93, 99 n. 6 & 13
Huxley, Aldous 138, 143 n. 20

James, Henry 193, 194, 196, 197, 199, 201 n. 8, 202 n. 27
Jauffret, Régis 80
Jaurès, Jean 217, 218, 220
Jeanson, Francis 41, 47 n. 16
Jennings, Jeremy 11 n. 20
Joyce, James 231, 241 n. 6

Kafka, Franz 199

Kahn, Zadoc 214
Kant, Immanuel 19
Keefe, Terry 149, 155 n. 18
Khayyām, Omar 247, 252, 254 n. 9 & 11, 255 n. 26
Klossowski, Pierre 19, 20–21, 24 n. 10, 257
Kolb, Philip 201 n. 2, 210 n. 5, 218, 219, 222, 223 n. 1 & 12, 224 n. 27 & 29, 254 n. 16, 275 n. 13
Kornbluh, Anna 193, 194, 195, 201 n. 9, 15–18 & 22, 202 n. 27
Kristeva, Julia 26, 34 n. 6, 59 n. 31

La Boétie, Étienne de 238
La Bruyère, Jean de 171, 172, 180 n. 19
Ladenson, Elisabeth 256, 265 n. 1
La Fayette, Mme de [Marie-Madeleine Pioche de la Vergne] 181
La Fontaine, Jean de 9, 79, 171–80
Laing, R.D. 4
Lallaoui, Mehdi 71, 76 n. 24
La Rochefoucauld, François de 171, 172, 179 n. 4 & 7
Laugier, Sandra 145, 154 n. 6
Lauris, Georges de 217
Le Cuziat, Albert 11
Léger, Fernand 8, 117–31
Leiris, Michel 4
Lenin, Vladimir Il'ich 39, 204
Leroy, Claude 120, 128, 129 n. 7, 8, 11 & 16, 130 n. 20 & 44, 131 n. 59
Leroy-Beaulieu, Anatole 216–17, 217–18
Lespès, René 47 n. 21, 51, 58 n. 13, 59 n. 27
Levi, Primo 2, 7, 10 n. 6, 11 n. 26 & 28
Levinas, Emmanuel 108
Lévi-Valensi, Jacqueline 23 n. 2, 34 n. 3, 46 n. 2, 48, 57 n. 2, 58 n. 3, 75 n. 1
Levy, Bernard-Henri 15
Li, Wenliang 56
Loosley, David 11
Loti, Pierre 1, 2, 3, 4, 10 n. 5, 248, 254 n. 19, 279 n. 13, 280, 281
Lucey, Michael 141, 143 n. 26
Luckhurst, Nicola 172, 179 n. 5

Macron, Emmanuel 102, 112 n. 9
Madrazo, Maria de 273, 275 n. 13
Maître, Edmond 229
Malabou, Catherine 146
Mâle, Émile 248, 249, 254 n. 15
Mallarmé, Stéphane 9, 133, 198, 229, 231, 232, 234, 235, 236, 239–40, 241 n. 4, 8, 10 & 16, 242 n. 19, 20, 34, 254 n. 7 & 16
Man, Paul de 183, 190, 191 n. 14
Manet, Édouard 229, 232, 235, 236
Marchal, Bertrand 234, 241 n. 4, 10 & 16, 254 n. 7
Mariani, Annachiara 160, 168 n. 13
Marsh, Kate 80, 87 n. 17
Marshall, Bill 74, 76 n. 33

Marx, Karl 36, 39, 204
Mauriac, François 209, 211 n. 39
Mauriac-Dyer, Nathalie 202 n. 29 & 41, 207, 211 n. 30, 282
Maurois, André 35 n. 14, 219, 224 n. 35, 36 & 38
Maurras, Charles 206
Mauss, Marcel 19
Mauvignier, Laurent 110
Mavor, Carol 95, 100 n. 16
McMahon, Laura 89, 99 n. 2 & 15
Mehlman, Jeffrey 183, 191 n. 14
Melion, Walter 183, 191 n. 17 & 18
Memmi, Albert 4
Michaux, Henri 199
Michel, Louise 69, 278, 279 n. 10
Michelet, Jules 3
Michon, Pierre 2, 7, 8, 11 n. 29, 77–88, 282
Miller, J. Hillis 183
Milly, Jean 3
Mitterrand, François 104
Molière [Jean-Baptiste Poquelin] 36, 49, 177, 214
Monet, Claude 220, 229
Montaigne, Michel de 24 n. 13, 171, 191 n. 9, 238
Montherlant, Henry de 2, 4
Morand, Paul 3
Moravia, Alberto 157
Morisot, Berthe 229, 232, 235, 239, 242 n. 31
Morisot, Edma 229, 239, 242 n. 31
Mourgues, Odette de 172, 179 n. 3
Mozart, Wolfgang Amadeus 270, 271, 272, 274
Mugnier, Abbé 217, 224 n. 24
Mussolini, Benito 52

Nancy, Jean-Luc 229, 234, 236, 237, 240, 242 n. 18
Ndiaye, Marie 7, 241 n. 3
Nerval, Gérard de 278
Nietzsche, Friedrich 41, 238
Nitsch, Hermann 165
Nizan, Paul 7
Noailles, Anna de 9, 243–55
Nora, Pierre 1, 8, 10 n. 1, 70, 77, 78, 81, 86, 86 n. 1, 87 n. 18, 88 n. 27

Orwell, George 36, 40, 42, 47 n. 18
Oulmi, Saïd 72

Painter, George 180 n. 15, 212 n. 39, 277, 279 n. 7
Panaïté, Oana 80, 85–86, 87 n. 14, 88 n. 26
Pascal, Blaise 171, 172, 199
Paxson, James J. 183, 190 n. 2 & 3, 191 n. 10, 14 & 15
Péguy, Charles 2, 7
Perec, Georges xv, 200, 202 n. 45–49
Petit, Frédéric 214
Picasso, Pablo 119, 239
Pierre, Michel 71, 72, 76 n. 29
Pirandello, Luigi 157

Pisanello [Antonio du Puccio Pisano] 157
Pleynet, Marcelin 233, 241 n. 12
Poincaré, Raymond 215, 220
Poirot-Delpech, Bertrand 141
Porter, Dennis 26, 34 n. 4
Poulet, Georges 276, 279 n. 5
Pratt, Marie-Louise 34 n. 2, 56, 59 n. 23 & 36
Prendergast, Christopher 11 n. 22
Proust, Adrien 215, 216, 224 n. 15, 248, 254 n. 17
Proust, Marcel 1–11, 90, 91, 95–100, 142 n. 18, 156–68, 171–80, 181–91, 192–203, 204–12, 213–25, 229, 231, 233, 236, 237, 241 n. 3, 4 & 14, 242 n. 23, 243–55, 256–65, 266–75, 276–79, 280–82
  A la recherche du temps perdu 2, 5, 9, 10 n. 4, 90, 95, 96, 97, 100 n. 17 & 19, 156, 157, 158, 163, 164, 166, 168 n. 11, 171, 172, 179 n. 5 & 8, 183, 185, 187, 190, 190 n. 1, 191 n. 27 & 28, 193, 196, 197, 198–99, 199, 200, 201 n. 1, 4 & 25, 202 n. 46, 203 n. 54, 210 n. 7, 216, 219, 224 n. 14 & 32, 231, 243, 249, 253, 253 n. 1, 254 n. 19 & 23, 256, 257, 264, 265 n. 5, 266, 267, 270, 271, 272, 273, 274 n. 2, 276, 277, 279 n. 11, 280, 281
  Albertine disparue [*La Fugitive*] 187, 189, 191 n. 26, 192, 202 n. 41, 260, 265 n. 7, 273, 277
  A l'ombre des jeunes filles en fleurs 98, 181, 185, 208, 209, 210 n. 7, 259, 261, 278
  Du côté de chez Swann 2, 100 n. 19, 207, 209, 210 n. 7, 211 n. 16 & 29, 257, 261, 278, 282
  Jean Santeuil 183, 191 n. 21, 208, 211 n. 32, 218, 219, 224 n. 21, 26 & 30
  La Prisonnière 9, 205, 210 n. 7, 246, 256, 260, 264, 266–75, 277
  Le Côté de Guermantes 183, 184, 196, 199, 205, 210 n. 7, 248
  Le Temps retrouvé 160, 177, 180 n. 14, 186, 208, 209, 210 n. 7, 249, 259, 263, 278, 279 n. 14, 281
  Les Plaisirs et les jours 158, 191 n. 21, 211 n. 32, 218, 224 n. 21
  Sodome et Gomorrhe 9, 196, 199, 205, 208, 210 n. 7, 256, 258, 259, 261–62, 267, 268, 270, 272, 274 n. 3 & 4, 276
  Un amour de Swann 195, 257

Quilliot, Roger 25, 48, 57 n. 2, 75 n. 8 & 10
Quinan, C. L. [Christine] 90, 93, 99 n. 5, 110–11, 112 n. 22
Quintilian 181, 182, 190 n. 3 & 4, 191 n. 8 & 23

Racine, Jean 172, 177
Ramakers, Bart 183, 191 n. 17 & 18
Ramuz, Charles-Ferdinand 206, 207, 210
Rancière, Jacques 1, 2, 9, 10 n. 2 & 3, 193, 197, 198, 201 n. 6, 202 n. 30, 35, 38, 39, 41, 203 n. 54, 229, 230, 231, 241 n. 2 & 7
Régnier, Marie de [Marie de Hérédia] 233, 241 n. 14

Rembrandt [Rembrandt Harmenszoon van Rijn] 132, 134–35, 140, 141, 142 n. 1, 163, 208
Renan, Ernest 214
Renoir, Pierre-Auguste 229
Resnais, Alain 8, 58 n. 9, 89–100, 110
Richard, Jean-Pierre 202, 277, 279 n. 6
Riffaterre, Michael 182, 183, 191 n. 13, 20 & 24
Rimbaud, Arthur 78, 83, 84, 87 n. 23, 208, 229
Rochefort, Henri 69
Rogers, Brian 5, 11 n. 16, 211 n. 11, 281
Rothberg, Michael 67, 76 n. 17
Rothschild, Alphonse de 214
Roussin, Philippe 206, 211 n. 15, 17, 19, 22 & 33
Ruskin, John 207, 214–15, 217, 220–21, 223 n. 7, 9, 10 & 11, 224 n. 39, 41 & 42, 231, 241 n. 6

Sa'di [Saadi Shirazi] 247, 248, 252, 254 n. 10 & 11, 255 n. 27
Said, Edward 35 n. 15, 246, 254 n. 8
Saint-Simon, Henri de 172
Salinas, Alfred 49, 58 n. 4
Sand, George 267
Sartre, Jean-Paul 4, 15, 28, 30, 34 n. 12 & 13, 35 n. 19, 133, 134, 136, 142 n. 7 & 8, 149
Sbragia, Albert 158, 166, 167, 167 n. 2, 168 n. 3, 8, 12, 16, 17, 20, 22 & 23
Schmid, Marion 210 n. 4, 272, 274 n. 10, 281
Schubert, Franz 93, 94
Séailles, Gabriel 217
Segalen, Victor 4, 281
Sénac, Jean 111, 112 n. 23
Sévigné, Mme de [Marie de Rabutin-Chantal] 172, 175, 176, 177, 181
Sheringham, Michael 5, 202 n. 50
Simmel, Georg 124, 130 n. 32
Simon, Anne 10 n. 9, 209, 210 n. 2 & 6, 211 n. 25 & 36, 282
Simon, Claude 2, 80, 241 n. 3
Slater, Maya 171
Smith, Ali 9, 11 n. 30
Sontag, Susan 89, 93, 99 n. 1 & 11
Sophocles 138, 181
Sorel, Albert 221
Sorrentino, Paolo 8, 156–68
Souday, Paul 207, 211 n. 29
Soustelle, Jacques 103

Spagnoli, John J. 213, 223 n. 3
Spitzer, Leo 276, 279 n. 5
Steinbeck, John 28
Steiner, George 1, 10 n. 1
Stendhal [Henri Beyle] 77
Stephens, Sonya 5
Stora, Benjamin 102, 111, 112 n. 4 & 8, 113 n. 24

Tadié, Jean-Yves 100 n. 19, 168 n. 11, 179 n. 8, 190 n. 1, 201 n. 1 & 4, 209, 210 n. 7, 213, 219, 223 n. 4, 224 n. 18, 19, 31, 32, 41 & 46, 241 n. 4, 253 n. 1, 265 n. 5, 274 n. 2, 279 n. 11
Thompson, Carl 26, 34 n. 5
Todorov, Tzvetan 182
Topping, Margaret 249, 254 n. 20, 281
Trump, Donald 40, 47 n. 12

Vaillant, Alain 257, 265 n. 3
Valéry, Paul 236, 239
Vallye, Anna 121, 130 n. 19, 42 & 45, 131 n. 47
Van Eyck, Jan 20
Van Gogh, Vincent 9, 229, 233, 235, 236, 241 n. 13
Verlaine, Paul 208, 229, 235
Vermeer, Jan 163, 177
Vigny, Alfred de 267, 272, 274 n. 3 & 4
Virilio, Paul 123, 130 n. 26 & 36

Wagner, Richard 163, 208
Warning, Rainer 172, 179 n. 6
Watt, Adam 129 n. 8, 168 n. 21, 191 n. 27, 202 n. 46, 215, 224 n. 14, 279 n. 14, 281, 282
Watteau, Jean-Antoine 78
Weil, Simone 7, 241 n. 3
White, Edmund 133, 136, 137, 139, 142 n. 4 & 12, 143 n. 22
Wild, Jennifer 126, 130 n. 45
Wilde, Oscar 26, 235
Wilson, Emma 97, 98, 99 n. 3, 100 n. 23, 282
Wittgenstein, Ludwig 28
Wood, James 1, 10 n. 1

Yoshikawa, Kazuyoshi 3

Zola, Émile 15, 229, 237–38, 242 n. 24
Zuili, Ludovic 105

www.ingramcontent.com/pod-product-compliance
Lightning Source LLC
Chambersburg PA
CBHW080439170426
43195CB00017B/2821